Flash Professional CS6

KATHERINE ULRICH

 Peachpit Press

Visual QuickStart Guide
Flash Professional CS6
Katherine Ulrich

Peachpit Press
1249 Eighth Street
Berkeley, CA 94710
510/524-2178
510/524-2221 (fax)

Find us on the Web at www.peachpit.com
To report errors, please send a note to errata@peachpit.com
Peachpit Press is a division of Pearson Education

Project Editor: Nancy Peterson
Production Editor: Katerina Malone
Development Editor: Bob Lindstrom
Copyeditor: Jacqueline Aaron
Compositor: David Van Ness
Technical Editor: Andreas Heim
Indexer: Emily Glossbrenner
Interior Design: Peachpit Press
Cover Design: RHDG / Riezebos Holzbaur Design Group, Peachpit
Logo Design: MINE™ www.minesf.com

ISBN 13: 978-0-321-83219-1
ISBN 10:   0-321-83219-1

9 8 7 6 5 4 3 2 1

Printed and bound in the United States of America

Dedication

To Perry Whittle, whose support, both moral and technical, helps me keep it all in perspective, and who downplays my failings and promotes my successes shamelessly.

Special Thanks to:

I'd like to thank the entire editorial team for bringing all the pieces of this edition of the *Flash Visual QuickStart Guide* together. Here's a rousing cheer for Bob Lindstrom, development editor. His deft edits bring a wonderful real-world perspective. And one cheer more for Nancy Peterson, the project editor of this edition, for overseeing the various pieces of the project. Her editorial direction and words of encouragement throughout the revision process helped keep me going. I continue to be grateful to Andreas Heim, associate technical director, Smashing Ideas Inc., for writing Chapter 15 (originally for the CS3 edition of this book) and for once again taking on the role of technical editor/technical resource for this edition. A round of applause for Jacqueline Aaron, copy editor; it's a gift to have this eagle-eyed guardian of the style guide watching my back for errors of style, grammar, and logic. Special thanks to compositor David Van Ness for laying out the pages expertly and quickly, and for engaging with the text to fit in as much material as possible. Kudos to Production Editor Katerina Malone for making these pages clean and clear, and to Liz Merfield for her proofing of those pages. Thanks also to Emily Glossbrenner of FireCrystal Communications for excellent indexing on a tight time line.

A tip of the hat to those whose various forms of assistance in past editions still echo in this one: Jay Armstrong, Brad Bechtel, Marisa Bozza, Lisa Brazieal, Erika Burback, Pat Christenson, Jeremy Clark, Cliff Colby, Peter Alan Davy, Jen deHaan, Jane DeKoven, Jonathan Duran, David Durkee, Lupe Edgar, Victor Gavenda, Suki Gear, Connie Jeung-Mills, Mark R. Jonkman, Becky Morgan, Erica Norton, Christi Payne, Janice Pearce, Nancy Reinhardt, Sharon Selden, Wendy Sharp, Craig Simmons, Kathy Simpson, Alan Stearns, James Talbot, Tiffany Taylor, Kenneth June Toley III, Michael J. Ulrich, Valerio Virgillito, Bentley Wolfe, and Lisa Young.

And finally, a special note of thanks in memory to Marjorie Baer, who brought me to this project in the first place and is in my thoughts whenever I delve into it again.

Contents at a Glance

Table of Contents

Introduction

Adobe Flash Professional CS6 is the latest version of this enormously popular animation and content creation tool. Early versions of Flash gave web designers an efficient way to send artwork and animation over limited-bandwidth connections. With time, Flash became an important tool for creating animated web content, and Flash Player became the dominant plug-in for viewing it. Flash's use of progressive downloading and streaming allowed some elements of a website to display immediately, making sites more responsive.

Although high-speed Internet connections have reduced the the need to create the tiniest files, the prevalence of smartphones and tablets—and their lower-powered processors—has kept Flash in the spotlight as an efficient means to optimize web-based content.

Flash continues to offer designers a robust set of tools for creating and animating artwork, displaying video, working with text, and creating interface elements. Flash's publishing features make it easy to prepare that content for viewing on various platforms. (This book will concentrate on using SWF files and HTML to display content in a web page via a browser.) Flash also provides a full-fledged object-oriented scripting language.

To address the adoption of HTML5 as a delivery system, Adobe provides an extension to Flash, called Toolkit for CreateJS. The toolkit translates Flash's animation and artwork to JavaScript code; exports sound, bitmap, and video assets; and provides access to a set of JavaScript libraries to make Flash-created media run in an HTML5-compatible browser.

Flash Animation

Flash CS6 offers five techniques for creating animation in the authoring environment. Here's a quick, general overview.

In *frame-by-frame animation,* you create a series of still images in keyframes. At runtime, Flash creates the illusion of movement by playing the keyframes in succession. In *classic tweening* and *shape tweening,* you create only the first and last image in the series (an initial keyframe and an ending keyframe). Flash interpolates the differences between the keyframes' content to create the images for playback at runtime. With *motion tweening,* you start with a single graphic object in a single keyframe and define changes to the object over time. Flash creates a series of images that animate the object's changes. With *inverse kinematics,* you pose a skeleton-like structure at different points in time. Flash animates the structure from one pose to the next.

Flash Interactivity

Over the years, Flash's tools for creating interactivity have become more robust. Flash CS6 contains a full-fledged object-oriented scripting language, ActionScript 3.0, that is compliant with the ECMA-262 specification. This spec is also the foundation for JavaScript, so ActionScript should feel familiar to anyone who already knows JavaScript.

Flash File Formats

Flash Professional CS6 provides both an authoring environment for creating content (the Flash application) and a runtime environment (the Flash Player application) for displaying that content. When you start working in Flash, you choose a type of document to open. In this book, we'll work exclusively with ActionScript 3.0 Flash files. A Flash file has the extension .fla and is often referred to as a FLA (pronounced *flah*).

Starting with version CS5, Flash began storing the assets, data, and code of a Flash movie as separate subfiles in XFL format, a version of XML (extensible markup language). By default, when you save an

ActionScript 3.0 Flash file, the artwork, animation, and interactivity you've created are compressed in an XFL format that hides the subfile structure from you. The XFL file has the .fla extension and looks and acts like a traditional FLA.

The tasks in this book assume you will continue to work with the compressed XML file. If you want to access the sub-files of your movie—so that, for example, you can use them in other applications that understand XML (such as Adobe Photoshop, Illustrator, or After Effects)—choose File > Save As, then save your Flash content in Flash CS6 Uncompressed Document (.xfl) format.

Eventually, you must prepare your movie for playback. To make your Flash creation viewable on the web, you can publish (or export) the FLA, converting it to Flash Player, AIR (Adobe Integrated Runtime), or Flash Lite format. In this book, we'll concentrate on publishing to Flash Player. A Flash Player file has the extension .swf and is often referred to as a SWF (pronounced *swif*).

How Flash Delivers Content

Flash's publishing feature creates the HTML code necessary to display your Flash content in a web browser. You can also choose to deliver Flash content in other file formats—such as animated GIF images—by creating those alternate files during the publishing process. Flash can create AIR applications for Google Android and Apple iOS; generate PNG sprite sheets for use in game development; and—using the Toolkit for CreateJS—translate Flash animation and symbols to JavaScript for use in HTML5 projects.

Flash's Movie Metaphor

Flash started life as an animation tool (named FutureSplash), so concepts from the world of film remain in the names of some key Flash concepts. The content you're creating is referred to as a *movie*. An open Flash document contains a *Stage*, a rectangular area where you create the graphic elements that populate each *scene* of your movie. The Timeline panel organizes the movie as a series of *frames* and layers. Crucial frames, called *keyframes,* are containers for graphic elements, sounds, and video. The frames line up in playback order. The layers act like pieces of film in a stack; at each frame, graphic elements on higher layers obscure elements on lower layers.

How to Use This Book

Like all of the *Visual QuickStart Guide* series, this book seeks to take you out of passive reading mode and help you get started working in the program. The book is task oriented, as opposed to project based. Each chapter presents a series of short tasks on related themes. Each task focuses on a particular tool, feature, or operation. You can work through the chapters in order or use the book for reference, reviewing specific items as you need them. The book is suitable for beginners who are just starting to use Flash and for intermediate-level Flash designers.

The initial chapters cover the basics of creating graphic elements by using Flash's unique set of drawing tools. Next, you learn how to turn graphic elements into animations. After that, you will create basic user-interface elements, such as rollover buttons. To make your content interactive, you'll write ActionScript. You'll also learn about importing and working with sounds and video. Finally, you'll use Flash's publishing and exporting features—including the new Toolkit for CreateJS extension—to prepare your Flash creations for delivery.

What You Should Already Know

To get started quickly, you should make sure that:

- Adobe Flash CS6 is already installed on your computer.

- You're familiar with the workings of your operating system.

- You can carry out basic tasks, such as opening, closing, and saving documents; opening, closing, resizing, collapsing, and expanding document windows and dialogs; using hierarchical menus, pop-up menus, radio buttons, and checkboxes; and carrying out standard application commands such as copy, cut, paste, delete, and undo.

Cross-Platform Issues

The Flash authoring environment has a similar interface on the Macintosh and Windows platforms. Still, at some points the user interfaces of these platforms diverge. When these differences are substantial, I describe the procedures for both platforms.

Originally, Macintosh computers required Macintosh keyboards, and some key names were unique to that keyboard: for example, Return (instead of Enter) and Delete (instead of Backspace). I generally use Enter and Delete for these two key names.

Contextual Menus

Both the Macintosh and Windows platforms offer contextual menus. To access them when using OS X, Control-click an element (or right-click if you have a two-button mouse); when using Windows, right-click an element. You'll open a menu of commands that are appropriate for working with that element. For the most part, these commands duplicate commands in the main menu; therefore, I don't generally note them as alternatives for the commands described in the book. I do point out when using the contextual menu is particularly handy or when a contextual menu contains a command that is unavailable in the main menu bar.

Artwork, Scripts, and More

The Flash graphics in this book are easy to draw. Most of the examples are based on simple geometric shapes, so you can spend more time watching the Flash features in action instead of recreating fancy artwork. To make it even easier, Flash files containing the graphic elements that you need for each task are available on Peachpit Press's companion website for this book. In Chapter 15, you'll learn to create scripts for basic interactivity, and Flash files containing the completed scripts for these tasks are also available. In addition, the site offers additional content that I just couldn't squeeze into the pages of this book.

To access the website, you must register at www.peachpit.com. Click the Account Sign In button to create an account (or log in to your existing account). Click the "Register your products here" (or "Register another product") link and enter the book's ISBN (0321832191) in the text field that appears. A link to the supplemental content will appear on your account page. You should also be able to download the files by registering or logging into your account at www.peachpit.com/flashcs6vqs.

The Flash Authoring Tool

Before you start working in Adobe Flash Professional CS6, you should familiarize yourself with the authoring environment.

When you first open Flash, you'll see the default workspace in an *application frame*. This application frame contains pieces of the Flash application in a resizable window. At the top of the frame, the application bar includes Maximize, Minimize, and Quit buttons; a menu for choosing workspace layouts; and a text field for searching Flash's Help system. Various docked panels appear around the edges of the window.

By default, the center of the application frame displays any open Flash documents. When no documents are open, a Welcome screen is present with options for creating new documents or opening recent ones. You can drag documents and panels so that they float over the workspace rather than dock to the application frame.

In This Chapter

Working with Flash Documents

The basic document operations in Flash—opening, closing, and saving files—will be familiar to most computer users. Creating new Flash documents may be a little different compared with other programs because Flash can create a variety of document types. By default, Flash opens with a Welcome screen that helps you open and create documents, although you can set other launch options.

To set launch preferences:

1. From the Flash application menu (OS X) or Edit menu (Win), choose Preferences.

   The Preferences dialog appears. The General category is selected by default.

2. From the On Launch menu **A**, choose one of the following:

   No Document Flash's menu bar, application frame, and panels appear at launch, but no document opens.

   New Document Flash opens a new document at launch.

   Last Documents Open Flash opens the documents that were open when you ended the previous work session.

   Welcome Screen By default Flash displays the Welcome screen at launch and any time you have closed all the documents during a work session **B**.

3. Click OK.

A The On Launch options in the General category of the Preferences dialog determine which type of document, if any, opens when you launch Flash.

B The Welcome screen lets you perform common operations by clicking a link. This figure shows Welcome screen links for creating documents from templates, opening documents that you worked on recently, and creating new Flash documents.

About Preferences

To see, or not to see, the Welcome screen is just one of many preference settings in Flash. You can choose new settings in the Preferences dialog. From the Flash menu (OS X) or Edit menu (Win), choose Preferences, and select a category from the list in the left-hand pane. In the main window, choose settings for that category. Preferences fall into ten categories: General, Action-Script, Auto Format, Clipboard, Drawing, Text, Warnings, PSD File Importer, AI File Importer, and Publish Cache. You'll learn about specific Preferences settings throughout this book.

TIP To quickly set the No Document option, click the Don't Show Again button at the lower-left corner of the Welcome screen. A dialog reminds you that the launch settings must be changed in the General tab of the Preferences dialog to redisplay the Welcome screen.

TIP In General Preferences, check out the Auto-recovery option. When it's selected, Flash periodically creates a temporary backup of your document with *RECOVER* added to the file name. Auto-recovery is turned on by default and set to back up your work every 10 minutes. To change the backup frequency, enter a new value in the Minutes field (from 1 minute to 1440 minutes). Flash deletes all RECOVER files when you quit the program normally. If Flash crashes before quitting properly, however, you'll have the opportunity to open the RECOVER copy.

To create a new Flash document:

In the Welcome screen's Create New section, click the ActionScript 3.0 link.

Flash opens a new blank document.

or

1. Choose File > New, or press Command-N (OS X) or Ctrl-N (Win).

   Flash opens the New Document dialog , which has two views: General and Templates. General is selected by default.

2. In the General view, from the Type list on the left side of the dialog, select ActionScript 3.0.

3. To set basic document properties, on the right side of the dialog, do one or more of the following:

   ▸ To set the size of the Stage using the hot-text controls for Width and Height, enter values for the desired dimensions **D**.

   ▸ To set the units of measure, from the Ruler Units menu, choose the desired units **E**.

   ▸ To set the frame rate, use the Frame Rate hot-text control to enter the number of frames that Flash displays in 1 second **F**.

C To create a new document in Flash, choose File > New. The New Document dialog opens with the General view and ActionScript 3.0 selected by default.

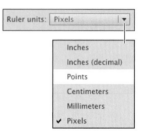

D To set the Stage size for your new document, enter values using the Width and Height hot-text control in the New Document dialog.

E The Ruler Units menu offers six options. Flash uses the specified units to calculate all measured items on the Stage: rulers, grid spacing, the dimensions of objects, and the dimensions of the Stage, itself.

F Frames are the lifeblood of your animation, and the frame rate is the heartbeat that keeps that blood flowing at a certain speed. Flash's default frame rate—24 frames per second (fps)—is the standard frame rate for film and a reasonable rate for animations viewed over the Web.

Which Flash File Type to Create?

The Create New section of the Welcome screen lists 11 file types. Which one is right for you? In this book, you'll work exclusively with Flash for ActionScript files, but you still have two choices: ActionScript 3.0 or ActionScript 2.0. This book uses ActionScript 3.0 for all scripting tasks. (You'll learn about scripting in Chapter 15.) When an exercise asks you to create a new file, choose ActionScript 3.0.

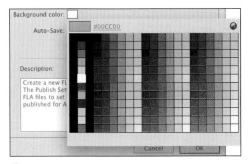

G To assign your Stage a new color, click the Background Color control to display a set of color swatches. Click a swatch to choose a color, or use the hot-text control to enter a color's hexadecimal value. You can also change the Alpha value to set a transparency percentage for the current color.

Auto-Save: ☑ 10 minutes

H The Auto-Save option in the New Document dialog instructs Flash to automatically save a document at user-specified intervals. Select Auto-Save to activate automatic saves, and use the hot-text control to enter the interval between saves, from 1 minute to 1440 minutes.

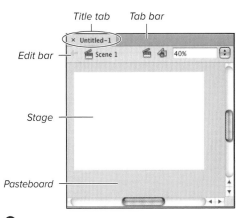

Title tab   Tab bar
Edit bar
Stage
Pasteboard

I Each Flash document consists of the Title tab; the Edit bar, which displays identifying text and menus for choosing symbols and scenes; the Stage, in which your movie appears; and the Pasteboard, the extra space around the Stage. By default, open documents are docked, filling the middle of the application frame. You can drag documents out of the dock and let them float over the workspace if you prefer. You can drag tabs within the Tab bar to change the document order. (See "Using Panels" in this chapter.)

▸ To set the underlying color of the document—the Stage's background— click the Background Color control, and choose a new color **G**.

4. To automatically save the document periodically, select Auto-Save, and use the hot-text control to enter the desired save frequency **H**.

5. Click OK.

   Flash opens a new blank document **I**.

TIP To use the current settings for all new documents, click the Make Default button.

TIP The Description field of the New Document dialog briefly outlines the basic purpose of the selected document type and identifies the target delivery system (such as Flash Player) that is selected by default for publishing the document. (To learn about settings for publishing, see Chapter 17.)

About the Pasteboard

Flash's Pasteboard, the area surrounding the Stage, has the capacity to grow as you drag items into it. Imagine dragging a huge graphic object from the Stage to the Pasteboard; drag the object so far that part of it disappears beyond the edge of the document window. As you drag the object, the window's scroll bar moves because the document is getting bigger. Though you can't see it yet, the Pasteboard is now larger than before you started dragging. Resize the document window, or use the scroll bars to view your graphic object and the enlarged Pasteboard.

To open an existing document:

From the Welcome screen, in the Open a Recent Item section ⓙ, click a file name.

Flash opens that file directly.

or

1. In the Welcome screen, in the Open a Recent Item section, click the Open link.

   or

   Choose File > Open.

   The Open dialog appears.

2. Navigate to the file you want to open.

3. Select the file.

4. Click Open.

TIP In Flash's default environment, multiple open documents appear as tabs within the application frame. Tabs for inactive documents are a dark gray. Click a tab to bring that document to the front ⓚ.

TIP You can change the tab order for open documents by dragging a tab horizontally to a new position.

Open a Recent Item
- TestSceneTryout.fla
- FbyFBall-frm1-cs6.fla
- Bounce-5frms-cs6.fla
- AboveHawkNest.fla
- Open...

ⓙ The Open a Recent Item section of the Welcome screen lets you view links to the last four documents you worked on. Clicking a filename opens the document.

Click to close document   *Click to view document*

ⓚ Viewing multiple open documents as tabs in a single window is the default setting for Flash CS6. Click an inactive title tab to bring that document to the front. To close the active document, click the Close button in the tab.

Modifying Document Properties

After you've created a document, you can modify all of the properties that you set when creating it—Stage dimensions, background color, units of measure, frame rate, and auto-save—in the Document Settings dialog. You'll also find additional settings, including an option for automatically resizing content when you change the Stage size.

To open the Document Settings dialog:

Choose Modify > Document, or press Command-J (OS X) or Ctrl-J (Win).

The Document Settings dialog appears Ⓐ.

TIP When the Stage has focus, the Document Property inspector's Properties section contains a shortcut to the Document Settings dialog. In the Size section, click the Edit button ✎.

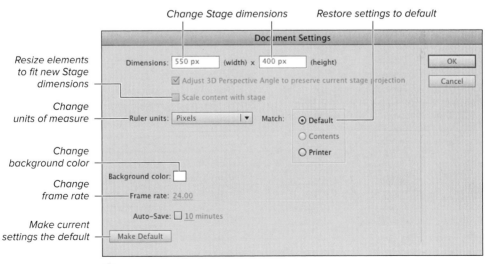

Change Stage dimensions   Restore settings to default

Resize elements to fit new Stage dimensions

Change units of measure

Change background color

Change frame rate

Make current settings the default

Ⓐ The Document Settings dialog lets you change all of the properties for the movie. When you change Stage dimensions, you can opt to have Flash resize all of your content to fit proportionally within the new space.

To change the size of the Stage:

1. Open the Document Settings dialog, and do one of the following:

   ▸ To set precise dimensions, enter new values in the Width and Height fields.

   ▸ To create a Stage just big enough to contain all the elements in your movie, select the Contents radio button in the Match section **B**.

   ▸ To set the Stage size to the maximum print area currently available, select the Printer radio button in the Match section.

   Whenever you change the Stage size, options appear for controlling how existing content adapts to the new dimensions.

2. To have Flash resize and relocate graphic elements to fit proportionally in the new Stage space, select "Scale content with Stage" **C**.

3. Click OK.

TIP Preferences settings govern which content scales and where it appears relative to the new Stage size. To access these settings, c hoose Flash > Preferences (OS X) or Edit > Preferences (Win). When you want to resize content from all layers—including hidden or locked layers (see Chapters 6 and 12)—in the General category's Scale Content section, select "Include locked and hidden layers." Deselect the option when you want such content to remain untouched. When you select Align Top Left, it's as if Flash selects all the content on the Stage with the free transform tool, then Shift-drags the lower-right resize handle to proportionally resize the set of elements. When you deselect Align Top Left, Flash centers the set of resized elements in the new Stage area.

B When you select Contents in the Match section of the Document Settings dialog, Flash resizes the Stage, making it just big enough to show all the objects currently on the Stage and Pasteboard.

C The "Scale content with Stage" checkbox becomes available when you modify the height or width of the Stage. When "Scale content with Stage" is selected, Flash resizes and relocates every graphic element in every frame of your movie to proportionally fit them within the new Stage area. When this option is not selected, your content remains exactly as it is, staying at its original coordinates on the virtual graph that underlies the Flash workspace. If you shrink the Stage, some objects may wind up on the Pasteboard. (To learn more about resizing individual elements and how Flash tracks and positions elements, see Chapter 4.)

Why Scale Content?

The ability to scale content when you change the Stage's dimensions is a real boon for anyone developing Flash applications for multiple devices. Once you've created an application using a Stage size appropriate for one device's screen, you can save a new version of your document, modify the size of the Stage to fit a different device, and select the "Scale content with Stage" option. Flash does the bulk of the resizing work. Obviously, when the aspect ratio (the ratio of width to height) of your Stage changes, you'll still need to adjust the layout, moving elements around to get the best arrangement for the new device; but the process takes much less time than scaling all of the elements individually.

A The Save As Template command lets you save Flash documents for reuse. You can create custom template categories and provide a brief description of the template file you're saving in the Save As Template dialog.

Closing the Master Template

After you save a document as a template (Step 7 in the task at right), it's easy to forge ahead with changes to customize it for a particular use. Until you actually close the file, however, you're working in the master template, and not in a new file based on that template. Any changes you make will continue to change the master file. When you're done creating the basic template, be sure to close the document.

Working with Template Documents

If you work repeatedly with one type of Flash document—for example, you create banner ads of a specific size with a consistent background or several consistent elements—you can save that basic document as a template.

To create a template document:

1. Open the document that you want to turn into a template.

2. Choose File > Save As Template.

   A dialog warns that you will lose SWF history data—a record of the file size of each SWF generated as you test and publish your movie.

3. Click Save As Template.

   The Save As Template dialog appears, showing a preview of your document **A**.

4. In the Name field, type a name for the template.

5. To specify a category, do one of the following:

   ▸ Choose an existing category from the Category pop-up menu.

   ▸ Type a name in the Category field to create a new category.

6. In the Description field, type a brief summary or reminder of the template's purpose or use.

7. Click Save.

   Flash saves the file as a master template document in a folder named Templates in the Configuration folder.

8. Close the document.

To open a new document from a template document:

1. In the Welcome screen, in the Create from Template section, click a template category link **B**.

   The New from Template dialog appears.

   or

   Choose File > New.

   The New Document/New from Template dialog appears **C**. The New Document dialog and the New from Template dialog are identical (except for their names) and display two views: General and Templates. The dialog's name changes to reflect the active view. When you click a template folder in the Welcome screen, the Templates view is selected by default.

2. From the Category list, choose the appropriate category.

   The category you click in Step 1 is selected by default, and its contents appear in the Templates list. To view other templates, select another category.

3. From the Templates list, choose the template you want to use.

   The dialog previews the selected template's first frame and provides a brief description of the template, if one is available.

4. Click OK.

   Flash opens a new document with all the contents of the template.

TIP When you choose File > New, Flash displays the document-creation dialog based on the type of file you created previously. The New Document dialog appears if the most recent file you created was a document. The New from Template dialog appears if you created the most recent file from a template.

Create from Template

- Advertising
- AIR for Android
- Animation
- Banners
- Media Playback
- Presentations
- More...

B Click a template category link in the Welcome screen's Create from Template section to access the New from Template dialog.

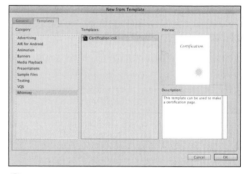

C The Templates view of the New from Template (or New Document) dialog displays a preview and a description (when available) for the item selected in the Category and Templates lists.

Finding the Configuration Folder

The operating systems that run Flash CS6 can be configured for multiple users, separately storing each user's files and special settings. To manage customized settings, Flash uses several types of Configuration folders. At the application level, Configuration folders govern settings for everyone who uses Flash on the computer. At this level, Flash has language-specific Configuration folders (that store settings for each language installation of Flash on a single system) and a Common configuration folder (that stores settings common to all Flash installations on a system). You must have administrative privileges to change folders at this level.

At the user level, the Configuration folder contains the files that the user has customized while working with Flash. (Each user has a separate user-level Configuration folder.) When you create a template document, for example, Flash stores it in a Templates folder inside your user-level Configuration folder. (The templates installed with Flash are stored in one of the application-level Configuration folders.)

To manually add, delete, or rename items in a Configuration folder, you must have the appropriate access privileges and navigate the hierarchy of nested folders on your hard drive to locate and open the folder. The folder that you need to access for this book is the user-level Configuration folder for your specific language version. The first part of this folder hierarchy is slightly different in each Flash-compatible operating system:

Windows 7 and Vista: **BootDrive\Users\userName\AppData\Local**

Windows XP/2000: **BootDrive\Documents and Settings\userName\Local Settings\ Application Data**

Mac OS X: **HardDriveName:Users:userName:Library:Application Support:**

Note: In Mac OS X version 10.7 (Lion), the Library folder within the userName folder is hidden by default. To navigate through the initial set of folders, in the Finder, choose Go > Go to Folder, and then in the search field, enter **~/Library/Application Support**.

After you navigate through the initial set of folders, the folder hierarchy is the same on every system. For those using the English version of Flash, it's **Adobe\Flash CS6\en_us\Configuration**. Users of localized versions will see their language code instead of **en_us** in the folder hierarchy.

About the Workspace

Flash CS6 appears on the desktop in an application frame that displays panels and documents in a resizable window **Ⓐ**. A menu bar containing the Flash commands appears above the application frame. The layout of elements within the application frame is called the *workspace*. Flash includes seven preset workspaces; each uses a different set of docked panels. The workspace is customizable. You can open and close documents and panels, docking them where you prefer within the frame. Or, you can drag panels and documents out of the dock, so they float above items on the desktop. You can save these configurations in new workspaces, and rely on Flash to remember the current workspace configuration from one work session to the next.

To save a custom workspace:

1. Arrange panels in the application frame and/or in floating windows, using the techniques you'll learn later in this chapter.

2. Choose Window > Workspace > New Workspace.

    The New Workspace dialog appears **Ⓑ**.

3. In the Name field, enter a title for this workspace.

4. Click OK.

    Flash saves that workspace configuration and adds the name to the Workspace menu.

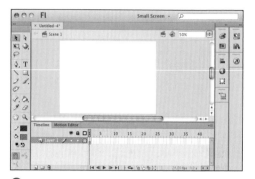

Ⓐ Flash includes seven preset workspaces, each with a different configuration of open panels and docking locations. The bare-bones setup shown here, Small Screen, is a good option when screen real estate is limited.

Ⓑ Choose Window > Workspace > New Workspace to open the New Workspace dialog. Enter a name for your current desktop configuration and click OK.

C The Workspace pop-up menu in the Application bar provides quick access to preset and custom workspaces as well as workspace-management commands.

To choose a workspace:

1. Choose Window > Workspace.

2. From the submenu, choose one of the available workspaces.

    The seven workspace presets in Flash are designed to serve a variety of uses:

    Animator opens a set of panels that are useful for creating Flash animation.

    Classic opens a small set of panels, with the Timeline at the top of the workspace and the Tools panel on the left (as they appeared in early versions of Flash).

    Debug opens just the panels needed to troubleshoot ActionScript.

    Designer opens panels commonly used in creating artwork.

    Developer opens panels commonly used in creating ActionScript.

    Essentials (the default setting) opens a small set of panels, with the Timeline at the bottom of the workspace and the Tools panel on the right.

    Small Screen opens an even more minimal set, with all of the panels set to work as panel icons, in their collapsed states.

    Custom workspaces also appear in the Workspace submenu.

TIP You can also save and choose workspaces from the Workspace pop-up menu at the right side of the Application bar **C**.

TIP To restore a workspace, choose it by name from the Window > Workspace submenu, or from the Workspace pop-up menu in the Application bar.

Using Panels

Flash organizes drawing and authoring tools in *panels*. You can dock panels within the application frame or have them float independently. Figure Ⓐ shows some general ways to manipulate panels.

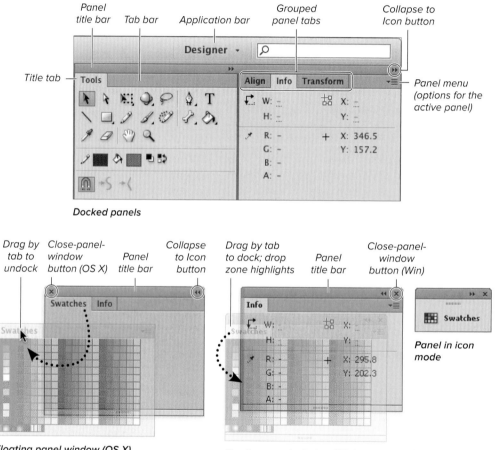

Panel title bar Tab bar Application bar Grouped panel tabs Collapse to Icon button

Title tab

Docked panels

Drag by tab to undock Close-panel-window button (OS X) Panel title bar Collapse to Icon button Drag by tab to dock; drop zone highlights Panel title bar Close-panel-window button (Win)

Panel menu (options for the active panel)

Panel in icon mode

Floating panel window (OS X)

Floating panel window (Win)

Ⓐ An open panel appears as a tab inside a panel frame; the frame may appear in a dock in Flash's application frame or in a floating window. You can group multiple panels within one panel frame; they appear as horizontal tabs. Clicking a tab in a group activates that panel, making it visible in the frame. Individual panels can be in floating windows or docked. Drag panels to reconfigure them: group them, stack them, or dock them. Blue drop zones highlight to indicate how panels combine. You can also collapse panels to icons to save space.

B You can close panels individually or as groups. In the Tab bar of the frame containing one or more panels you want to close, from the panel menu, choose Close or Close Group.

To open and close panels:

From the Window menu, select the desired panel.

One of the following actions takes place:

- When the panel is closed, a frame opens containing that panel.

- When the panel is minimized (to the Tab bar) or collapsed (to an icon), it expands.

- When the panel is behind other tabs in the same frame or behind other floating panel windows, the selected panel moves to the front.

- When the panel is already open, expanded, and in front in a floating window, the entire window closes.

- When the panel is the only tab or the front tab in a docked frame that is open and expanded, the frame containing that panel and all its tabs closes. Other frames stacked within the dock remain open.

TIP To remove one panel from a panel frame, from the panel menu at the right side of the Tab bar, choose Close. The active panel closes. To remove all the panels from that frame, choose Close Group. The panel frame (and all the panel tabs in it) closes. Any panel frames stacked above or below that frame remain open **B**.

TIP To quickly close all the panels in a floating window, click the window's Close button. The window closes, along with all the panel frames within it.

To minimize or maximize a panel frame:

Double-click a Title tab.

or

Control-click (OS X) or right-click (Win) the panel's Tab bar, and choose Minimize Group/Restore Group from the contextual menu.

The frame toggles between a minimized state (showing only panel tabs) and a maximized state (showing the full panel frame) **C**.

TIP To save even more space, use the panels in icon mode. In a full-sized panel, click the Collapse to Icon button (the double triangles at the right side of a panel's title bar) to collapse the panel to a small icon. When the panel is in icon form, click the Collapse to Icon button to restore the panel to its full size.

TIP To resize panels, position the pointer along the left, bottom, or right edge of the panel frame; or at one of the bottom corners. When the resize pointer (a double-headed arrow) appears, drag to change the panel's dimensions.

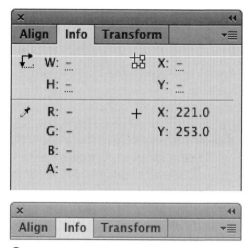

C Double-clicking an empty area of the Tab bar minimizes a panel frame to show only the tabs.

Tab Bar vs. Tab

The Flash documentation doesn't have a name for the area of a panel frame that holds a panel's tabs, but it is an important element. Dragging the gray area to the right of the tabs moves the frame with all its panels. Dragging a tab moves only that panel. For the purpose of this book, the gray area to the right of the tabs is called the *Tab bar*.

About Hot-Text and Color Controls

Computer-savvy users will find most of Flash's user-interface (UI) elements similar to those of other applications. However, two UI elements found throughout Flash—*hot-text* and *color controls*—might be less familiar.

Hot-Text Controls

Many Adobe products provide hot-text controls for entering numeric values. A hot-text value appears in blue (as if it were an active link) X: 10.00 . When you place the pointer over the hot-text control, a finger pointer with a double arrow appears X: 10. , indicating that you can enter new values. There are multiple ways to enter values:

- Click the hot-text control and drag the double-arrow pointer, as if using an invisible slider. To increase the value, drag upward or to the right 39.00 ↔ . To decrease the value, drag downward or to the left.

- When you finish dragging, a dark blue box highlights the text X: 51.00 . While this highlight is present, use the Up Arrow or Down Arrow key to change the value incrementally. Pressing Up Arrow increases the value by 1, while pressing Shift–Up Arrow increases it by 10. Pressing Down Arrow reduces the value by 1, and pressing Shift–Down Arrow reduces it by 10.

- You can also click the hot-text control to open a text entry field X: 51 . Clicking once selects the current value. Start typing to replace it with a new value, or click a second time to place the I-beam pointer inside the field for editing the current value. To confirm the new value, press Enter or click outside the text field.

Color Controls

Color controls let you select colors for different uses: set the background color for your movie; choose colors for strokes, fills, text; and so on. A Color control is a rectangular color chip—often located next to a pencil icon for stroke color, or a paint bucket for fill color. (See Chapter 2.) Clicking the chip opens a set of color swatches and other color-input options. The pointer changes to an eyedropper as you move it over swatches or items on the Stage. Click the pointer to select the color beneath the eyedropper's tip **D**. The swatch set closes and the new color appears in the color chip. (Sometimes, the eyedropper fails to appear. When the swatch set is open, however, the pointer still selects the color beneath the tip when you click.)

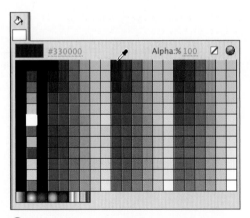

D Clicking the color chip below the paint bucket icon opens one of Flash's standard color controls.

Some swatch sets include other options for choosing a new color. The Hex Color hot-text control #262626 lets you enter a precise hex value. The Alpha hot-text control Alpha:% 100 lets you enter a transparency percentage. The No Color button ☑ lets you toggle fills or strokes on or off. (See Chapter 2.) The Color Picker button ◉ gives you access to the System Color Pickers.

The Property Inspector: A Special Panel

Think of the Property inspector as a context-sensitive super panel; it changes based on which item currently has focus (the document, the Timeline, an object on the Stage, or a tool). When you select a tool, for example, the panel displays properties associated with that tool. (Some tool functions appear as settings in the Property inspector instead of as options in the Tools panel.)

When you select the line tool, that tool has focus, and the Property inspector becomes the Line Tool Property inspector, where you set all the line tool's attributes: color, thickness, and style. When you click a blank area of the Stage, the document has focus, and the panel becomes the Document Property inspector, which gives you access to document settings. For some items, the Property inspector organizes properties into sections. You can hide or show a section's information by clicking the collapse/expand triangle to the left of the section name **E**.

To access the Property inspector, choose Window > Properties, or press Command-F3 (OS X) or Ctrl-F3 (Win).

E To display fewer properties in the Property inspector, collapse a section by clicking the downward-pointing triangle. To view more properties, expand a section by clicking the right-facing triangle.

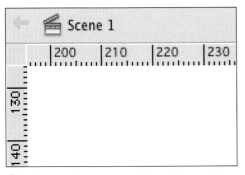

Ⓐ Choosing View > Rulers makes rulers visible on the Stage.

Ⓑ Grid lines work a bit like lines on graph paper. Use them to position elements on the Stage during authoring. Elements snap to these lines when you activate Snap to Grid.

Using Rulers, Grids, and Guides

In Flash's View menu, you can access rulers, grids, and guides that help place content on the Stage, but won't appear in your final movie.

To show/hide grids, guides, and rulers:

From the View menu, choose any of the following:

- Choose Rulers, or press Option-Shift-Command-R (OS X) or Ctrl-Alt-Shift-R (Win).

  Ruler bars appear on the left side and top of the Stage Ⓐ. You can set ruler units in the Document Settings dialog.

- Choose Grid > Show Grid, or press Command-' (apostrophe) (OS X) or Ctrl-' (apostrophe) (Win).

  Flash superimposes a grid of vertical and horizontal lines on the Stage Ⓑ. The grid acts as a guide for drawing and positioning elements.

- Choose Guides > Show Guides, or press Command-; (semicolon) (OS X) or Ctrl-; (semicolon) (Win).

  All guides you've placed become visible. To place guides, see "To work with guides" in this chapter.

To set grid parameters:

1. Choose View > Grid > Edit Grid, or press Option-Command-G (OS X) or Ctrl-Alt-G (Win).

   The Grid dialog appears **C**.

2. To set grid spacing, type values in the Width and Height fields **D**.

3. To select a grid color, click the Color control, and choose a color from the pop-up swatch set; or enter a value using the hex-color hot-text control **E**.

4. To set the distance at which an item snaps to the grid, choose a tolerance setting from the Snap Accuracy menu.

5. Click OK.

TIP Grids need not consist of squares.

TIP You can create new default settings for the grids in all new documents. After entering the desired settings in the Grid dialog, click the Save Default button, and then click OK.

C Choosing View > Grid > Edit Grid opens the Grid dialog, where you can change grid size, color, and other parameters.

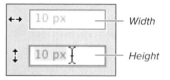

D Type values in the Width (top) and Height (bottom) fields to set grid spacing.

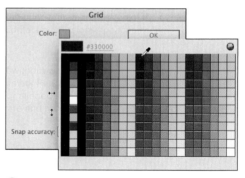

E To select a new grid color, click the Color control, and using the eyedropper pointer, click a color swatch. The swatch set displays the current color set. You can also use the hex-color hot-text control to enter a new color.

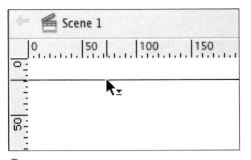

F As you drag a guide from the ruler bar, a direction indicator appears next to the selection tool.

Inches
Inches (decimal)
Points
Centimeters
Millimeters
✓ Pixels

| Scene 1 |
| 0   50   100   150   200   250   300 |

Move Guide

Position: 19   Pixels ▼

[OK]   [Cancel]

G Double-click a guide on the Stage to open a dialog for precisely positioning the guide. For horizontal guides, the Position value corresponds to the *y*-axis; for vertical guides, the value corresponds to the *x*-axis. (For more about element positioning, see Chapter 4.)

To work with guides:

1. With rulers visible, position the pointer over the vertical or horizontal ruler bar and click.

   On a Mac, when you use a tool other than the selection tool, the pointer changes to the selection arrow. In Windows, the pointer of the currently selected tool remains visible until you click the ruler bar.

2. Drag the pointer onto the Stage.

   When you click, a small directional arrow appears next to the pointer, indicating which direction to drag **F**.

3. Release the mouse button.

   Flash places a vertical or horizontal line on the Stage.

TIP To move a guide, position the selection tool over the guide. A direction arrow appears next to the pointer, indicating that the guide can be dragged. Drag the guide to a new location. To remove a guide, drag it completely out of the open document window.

TIP After you place a guide, you can assign it a precise location on the Stage. Using the selection tool, double-click the guide to open the Move Guide dialog. From the pop-up menu, choose a unit of measure. In the Position field, enter a value for the precise location you want **G**.

TIP To avoid repositioning guides accidentally, choose View > Guides > Lock Guides, or press Option-Command-; (semicolon) (OS X) or Ctrl-Alt-; (semicolon) (Win). To unlock the guides, choose View > Guides > Lock Guides, or press the keyboard shortcut again.

TIP To set parameters for guides, open the Guide dialog by choosing View > Guides > Edit Guides, or pressing Option-Shift-Command-G (OS X) or Ctrl-Alt-Shift-G (Win).

Working with Snapping

The snapping options help you position elements on the Stage. Snap Align displays guides when you drag one element near another element or the edge of the Stage. Snap to Grid helps align the edge or center of an element to a user-defined grid. Snap to Guides helps align elements with any guidelines you've set. Snap to Pixels helps move elements in whole-pixel steps. Snap to Objects helps align elements relative to one another.

To turn snapping options on and off:

1. Choose View > Snapping.

2. From the Snapping submenu, select an unchecked option to activate it (or select a checked item to deactivate it).

   ▸ *To snap elements to a grid,* choose Snap to Grid, or press Shift-Command-' (apostrophe) (OS X) or Ctrl-Shift-' (apostrophe) (Win). A circle called the *snap ring* appears near the selection tool. As you drag an element closer to a grid line, Flash highlights potential snap points by enlarging the snap ring 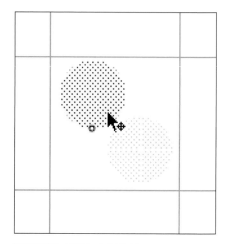.

   ▸ *To snap elements to guides,* choose Snap to Guides, or press Shift-Command-; (semicolon) (OS X) or Ctrl-Shift-; (semicolon) (Win).

   ▸ *To snap elements to elements,* choose Snap to Objects, or press Shift-Command-U (OS X) or Ctrl-Shift-U (Win).

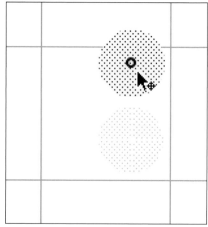

Ⓐ Snap to Grid helps align elements. As you drag an item, the snap ring (a small circle) appears near the pointer (top). The snap ring grows larger when it moves over another item that you've chosen to snap to. In this example, the enlarged snap ring (bottom) shows that the center of the circle being dragged will snap to the grid line above it.

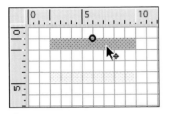

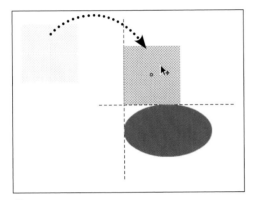

B Snap to Pixels displays a 1-pixel grid at magnifications of 400 percent or greater. Use this mode when you need to position graphic elements precisely.

C Snap Align displays a dotted alignment guide whenever the element you're dragging meets certain conditions. For example, you can set Snap Align to display a dotted line when the edge of the dragged object aligns with the edge of another object, or when the dragged object's edge is a specified distance from the edge of the Stage.

Snap accuracy:	Normal	▼
	Must be close	
	✔ Normal	
	Can be distant	
	Always Snap	

D Choose a Snap Accuracy setting to determine the distance at which an element will snap to the grid line. Choosing Always Snap forces the element's transformation point (located at an object's center by default) to lie directly on a grid line.

▸ *To snap elements to pixels,* choose Snap to Pixels. When you set the Stage's magnification to at least 400 percent, Flash displays a grid of 1-pixel-by-1-pixel squares **B**.

▸ *To view alignment guides* while positioning elements, deactivate Snap to Grid and choose Snap Align. Snap Align displays dotted lines whenever you drag one element's edge or center close to the edge or center of another element, when the dragged element comes within a user-specified distance from another element's edge or center, or near the edge of the Stage **C**.

TIP Although the Snap to Pixels feature uses a 1-pixel grid, the graphic elements you move won't snap to the grid's coordinates unless you set the element's *x* and *y* positions to a whole number in the Info panel or Property inspector. (You'll learn to set coordinates for graphic elements in Chapter 4.)

To set snapping parameters for the grid:

1. Choose View > Grid > Edit Grid, or press Option-Command-G (OS X) or Ctrl-Alt-G (Win).

2. In the Grid dialog, choose a setting from the Snap Accuracy pop-up menu **D**.

3. Click OK.

To set parameters for snapping to guides:

1. Choose View > Guides > Edit Guides, or press Option-Shift-Command-G (OS X) or Ctrl-Alt-Shift-G (Win).

2. In the Guides dialog, choose a setting from the Snap Accuracy pop-up menu **E**.

3. Click OK.

To set Snap Align options:

1. Choose View > Snapping > Edit Snapping, or press Command-/ (slash) (OS X) or Ctrl-/ (slash) (Win).

   The Edit Snapping dialog opens. If the Snap Align settings aren't visible, click the Advanced triangle to expand that section of the dialog **F**.

2. To display alignment guides as you drag objects on the Stage, do one of the following:

   ▸ Enter a value in the Stage Border field. Dotted lines appear when the edge of a dragged object reaches the specified distance from the edge of the Stage.

   ▸ In the Object Spacing section, enter values in the Horizontal and/or Vertical fields. Flash places virtual guides at the specified distance from stationary objects. Dotted lines appear when any side of a dragged object meets a virtual guide.

   ▸ In the Center Alignment section, select the Horizontal and/or Vertical checkboxes. Dotted lines appear when the center of a dragged object aligns horizontally and/or vertically with the center of another object.

3. Click OK.

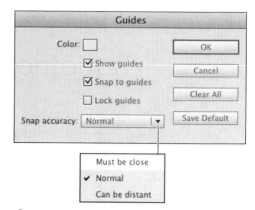

E In the Guides dialog, you can set the snapping distance for items. You can also set a guide color, the visibility of guides, and their status as locked or unlocked.

Click to hide Advanced options

F Set the tolerance levels for Snap Align in the Advanced section of the Edit Snapping dialog. The default settings are shown here.

Creating Simple Graphics

Adobe Flash Professional CS6 offers natural drawing tools that imitate the feel of working on paper with a pencil or brush, tools that create predefined geometric shapes, and a pen tool that lets you draw using Bézier curves.

You can create three types of shapes. Tools set to Merge Drawing mode create raw shapes that interact with other raw shapes on the same layer. (You'll learn about shape interactions in Chapter 5.) Tools set to Object Drawing mode create editable shapes that don't interact with other shapes. Flash's rectangle- and oval-primitive tools create *primitive-shapes*, non-interactive shapes with a set of defining parameters. You can edit a primitive's parameters (to change the roundness of a rectangle's corners, for example), but you can't freely edit a primitive's outline (say, to turn an oval into a free-form blob).

In This Chapter

Touring the Tools

The Tools panel **A** includes tools for creating graphic elements, for scrolling the Stage and zooming in and out, and for setting colors for the elements you create.

Click a tool to select it. Any settings or modifiers for the tool appear in the Options area at the bottom of the Tools panel and in the Property inspector. Click an option's icon to select it or display a menu of choices.

TIP Tool tips are active by default. When the pointer hovers over a tool, an identifying label appears. You can change the tool tip setting in the Preferences dialog. Select the General category, select (or deselect) the Show Tooltips checkbox, and click OK to close the dialog. (For details on opening the Preferences dialog, see Chapter 1.)

TIP In addition to displaying tool names, tool tips show keyboard shortcuts. As you get more familiar with the tools, selecting them using those shortcuts will speed your workflow.

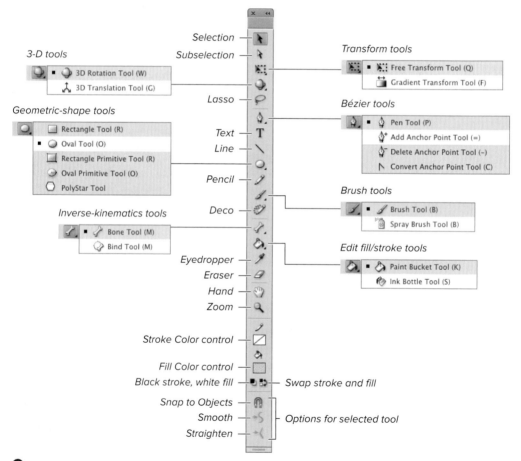

A The Tools panel contains tools for drawing, editing, and manipulating graphic elements in Flash. To save space, some tools are grouped. Click the current tool icon to open a submenu with all the tools in that group.

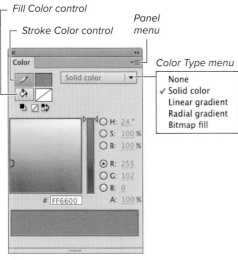

Fill Color control

Stroke Color control

Panel menu

Color Type menu

None
✓ Solid color
Linear gradient
Radial gradient
Bitmap fill

H: 24°
S: 100%
B: 100%
R: 255
G: 102
B: 0
FF6600
A: 100%

A The Color panel lets you define colors for use with Flash's drawing tools. Choose Solid Color from the Color Type menu to create solid colors. There are also options for creating gradients, using bitmaps, or using no color.

B When defining colors in the Color panel, it's important to choose whether the color applies to strokes or to fills. You can do so by activating the appropriate color control; the active color control's icon has a gray highlight. Click the pencil icon to apply the color to strokes, or click the paint bucket icon to apply the color to fills.

Creating Solid Colors and Gradients

Although most color controls let you specify new colors, the Color panel offers the widest variety of options, and greatest precision, for defining colors. Before you define a color or gradient, you must choose whether it applies to fills or strokes by activating the Fill Color control or the Stroke Color control.

To assign solid-color attributes in the Color panel:

1. Access the Color panel **A**. If it's not open, choose Window > Color, or press Shift-Command-F9 (OS X) or Alt-Shift-F9 (Win).

2. To determine where Flash applies the new color, do one of the following:

   ▸ To set a new stroke color, choose the Stroke Color control by clicking the pencil icon.

   ▸ To set a new fill color, choose the Fill Color control by clicking the paint bucket icon **B**.

3. From the Color Type menu, choose Solid Color.

Saving Color Swatches

You can save a newly defined color or gradient for reuse during your work session. From the panel menu in the Color panel's upper-right corner, choose Add Swatch. The currently displayed color in the Color panel becomes a new swatch in the Swatches panel (and in every color control's swatch set).

Here's a shortcut for adding swatches when the Swatches panel is open. Move the pointer to a blank area of the Swatches panel, and when the paint bucket pointer appears, click the mouse button. To access the Swatches panel, choose Window > Swatches, or press Command-F9 (OS X) or Ctrl-F9 (Win). To permanently save custom colors, in the Swatches panel menu, choose Save Colors. To access your custom swatch set again, choose the Add Colors command.

To define a new color visually in the Color panel:

1. Access the Color panel.

   In the color selection window, a set of hot-text controls let you set values for six color properties, from two color models. **HSB** controls let you set the hue, saturation, and brightness of a color. **RGB** controls let you set the amount of red, green, and blue in a color. The values shown define the currently selected color.

2. To "pin" one property, click the radio button for that property: H, S, B, R, G, or B.

   The color selection window displays all the colors you can create with the selected property set to its current value **C**.

3. Position the pointer over the color selection window.

   A circular color-selection pointer appears.

4. To preview new colors, drag the color selection pointer within the color selection window.

   As you drag, the value of the property you selected in Step 2 remains constant, while values for the remaining properties change, creating new colors. When the color you want appears, release the mouse button. Flash updates the RGB and HSB values to create that color.

TIP When you don't need to preview the new color, you can position the pointer over the color model, and click to select the color that appears inside the circle.

TIP The color you define in the Color panel appears in color controls of that type throughout Flash. If you define a shade of pink for fills, that pink also appears in the Fill Color control in the Tools panel and the Property inspector.

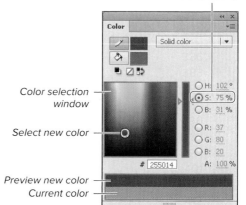

Pinned color property

Color selection window

Select new color

Preview new color

Current color

C Selecting a radio button in the Color panel keeps values for that color constant as you drag in the color selection window. A preview of the new color appears above the old color in the preview window. Selecting a radio button also determines the range of colors that appear in the color selection window. Click the Saturation (S) radio button when it has a value of 100 percent, for example, and the color selection window shows a full spectrum of colors with bright versions at the top, shading to black at the bottom. If the saturation value is less than 100 percent when you click the Saturation radio button, the color selection window shows the same spectrum of colors, but dimmer, because you can't create fully saturated colors with the current saturation value.

 Enter HSB values to specify a color by hue, saturation, and brightness. Enter RGB values to specify the amount of red, green, and blue that make up the color. The new color appears in the selected color control.

What Are Hex Colors?

The term *hex color* is short for *hexadecimal color*, which is a fancy way of saying a color defined by a number written in base 16.

Hex coding is the way to specify color in HTML. In Flash, entering a single hex code for your color may be easier than entering values for hue, saturation, and brightness (H, S, B); or for red, green, and blue (R, G, B).

If you remember studying bases in high-school math, you'll recall that the decimal system is base 10, represented by the numbers 0 through 9. In hex color, to get the extra six digits, you continue coding with letters A through F.

To define a new color numerically in the Color panel:

1. Use the Color panel's H, S, B, R, G, and/or B hot-text controls  to enter precise values for any of the following:

   ‣ To define the hue (H), enter values from 0 to 360 degrees.

   ‣ To define a percentage for saturation (S) and brightness (B), enter values from 0 to 100.

   ‣ To define the amount of red, green, or blue in a color, enter values from 0 to 255 for red (R), green (G), and/or blue (B).

TIP The selected color property's value remains constant when you change other values or drag in the color selection window. Use the hot-text control to the right of the radio button to change that property's value.

TIP You can use the slider between the color selection window and the radio buttons to change the value of the "pinned" property. Drag the slider's triangles up to increase values, and down to decrease values. The slider can also help you visualize the possibilities created by changing the value of the pinned property. The slider displays the range of colors you can make by changing the value of the pinned property.

TIP Flash CS6's Color panel provides two systems—or color models—for specifying colors: HSB and RGB. Each system uses three properties in defining a color. The Color panel simultaneously shows you the values for all of them. As you change the value of a property in one system, Flash automatically updates the values in both systems. If you create a new color by changing the value for hue (H), for example, the values for red (R), green (G), and blue (B) will update to reflect that color.

To define a color's transparency:

In the Color panel, use the Alpha hot-text control to enter a value between 0 percent and 100 percent . A value of 100 defines a completely solid color, while a value of 0 defines a completely transparent color.

E Enter an alpha value of less than 100 percent to define a transparent color.

To create a linear gradient:

1. From the Color panel's Color Type menu, choose Linear Gradient **F**.

   The tools and options for defining gradients appear **G**. The color preview window becomes a gradient definition window with pointers for defining colors in the gradient. The default gradient starts with two pointers, black on the left and white on the right.

2. Leave Flow at its default setting, Extend Color (the Black-to-White Gradient button).

   Flow determines how gradient colors fill a shape when you resize the gradient to be narrower than the shape it fills. (To learn about resizing gradients, see Chapter 4.)

3. To add a new color to the gradient, do the following:

   ▸ Position the pointer on or below the gradient definition window. Flash adds a plus sign to the pointer ▸₊, indicating that you can add a new gradient pointer in this area.

   ▸ Click anywhere along the gradient definition window. Flash adds a new gradient pointer.

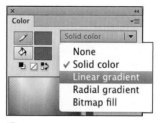

F Choose Linear Gradient from the Color Type menu to access the tools for defining linear gradients.

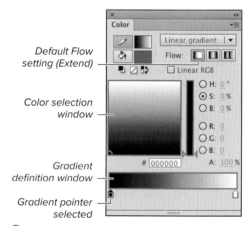

Default Flow setting (Extend)

Color selection window

Gradient definition window

Gradient pointer selected

G When you choose Linear Gradient or Radial Gradient as the Color Type, the Color panel's color preview window becomes the gradient definition window.

Gradient starts with white and blends first to gray and then to black

Move pointers in to increase the width of outside bands

Click to add pointers

Choose a color for each gradient pointer. The colors and positions of the pointers in the window define a gradient's color transitions. Place pointers closer together to make the transition between colors more abrupt; place pointers farther apart to spread the transition over more space.

About Gradients and File Size

Here's something to be aware of when you use gradient fills. They increase file size and slow the loading of published movies. Each area of gradient fill requires an extra 50 bytes of data not required by a solid fill. In addition, gradients use processor power. Too many gradients may result in slower frame rates, which can cause slower animations in your movie.

4. To change the color of a gradient pointer, select it, and define a new color using any of the methods described in the preceding section.

   or

   Double-click the gradient pointer to open a pop-up swatch set that works like a color control. Click a swatch or an item on the Stage to copy its color, or use the hex-color hot-text control to enter a new value, or click the Color Picker button to access the System Color Picker(s).

5. To remove a color from the gradient, drag its pointer downward, away from the gradient definition window. The pointer disappears as you drag. The gradient preview changes to blend the colors in the remaining gradient pointers.

6. Repeat Steps 4 and 5 to create the colors you want in your gradient. You can add up to 13 pointers to a gradient for a total of 15 colors.

7. Drag the pointers to position them in the gradient definition window .

   As you modify the gradient, your changes appear in all the color controls for strokes or fills, depending on whether you assigned the gradient to strokes or fills.

To create a radial gradient:

1. From the Color panel's Color Type menu, choose Radial Gradient.

   The tools for defining circular gradients appear. The gradient definition window looks the same as it does for linear gradients . The leftmost pointer defines the inner ring; the rightmost pointer defines the outer ring.

2. Follow Steps 2–7 of the preceding task, "To create a linear gradient," to define the color transitions in the radial gradient.

TIP To modify an existing gradient, choose it in the Swatches panel. Flash switches the Color panel to the Linear Gradient mode (or Radial Gradient mode) and displays the selected gradient's pointers. Now you can make any changes you need.

TIP Gradients can have transparency. You simply use a transparent color in one or more gradient pointers. (See the sidebar "To define a color's transparency" in this chapter.) If a gradient has transparency, a grid appears in the gradient pointer, in the Fill Color or Stroke Color control, and in the transparent part of the gradient in the gradient definition window 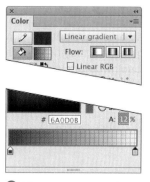.

TIP Each pointer in a gradient can have a different alpha setting. To create fade effects, try creating a gradient that blends from a fully opaque color to a transparent one.

I Choose Radial Gradient from the Color Type menu to create a circular gradient. The leftmost pointer translates to the center of the gradient circle.

J When transparent colors are placed in a gradient, grid lines appear in the gradient pointer, the Fill Color or Stroke Color control, and the gradient preview window.

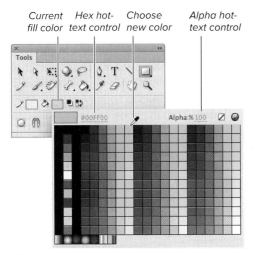

Fill Color control

Expand/Collapse section   Fill Color control

Ⓐ When you select a tool or graphic element that uses fills (top) the Property inspector includes a Fill and Stroke section, which contains a Fill Color control (bottom). If you don't see the control, click the expand/collapse triangle to display the contents of the section.

Current   Hex hot-   Choose   Alpha hot-
fill color text control new color   text control

Ⓑ Click the Fill Color control—the color chip identified by a paint bucket icon—to open a set of swatches. Click a swatch to choose a new color, or use the hot-text control to enter new hex or alpha values. The Fill Color control works similarly in the Tools panel and the Fill and Stroke portion of the Property inspector.

Setting Fill Attributes

To assign colors or gradients to selected tools or graphic elements, you can use a Fill Color control; one is always present in the Color panel and Tools panel. The Fill and Stroke section of the Property inspector displays a Fill Color control when a tool or graphic element that uses fills is selected.

To assign fill colors from the Property inspector:

1. With the Property inspector open, in the Tools panel, select a tool that creates fills. The rectangle, oval, rectangle-primitive, oval-primitive, polystar, brush, and paint bucket tools all create fills.

   The Property inspector's Fill and Stroke section appears displaying a Fill Color control (identified by a paint bucket icon) Ⓐ.

2. Click the Fill Color control to access its pop-up swatch set and other color settings Ⓑ.

   continues on next page

3. To assign a new color or gradient for fills, do one of the following:

- ► To assign a gradient, select one of the linear or radial gradient swatches.

- ► To assign a solid color, select a solid swatch or an item on the Stage.

- ► To specify a hex color, use the Hex hot-text control to enter a new value.

- ► To define transparency for the current fill color, use the Alpha hot-text control to enter a percentage less than 100. Note that an Alpha hot-text control is not present when a gradient is the current fill color because transparency is a part of the gradient definition.

The new color appears in all regular Fill Color controls (in the Tools panel, the Fill and Stroke section of the Property inspector, and the Color panel). Flash changes the fills of any shapes or drawing objects selected on the Stage; any tools that create fills are set to use the new color.

TIP To assign new fill colors, you can also use the Color panel. Its Fill Color control works just like the ones in the Tools panel and Property inspector.

TIP To access a System Color Picker for assigning fill colors, click the color chip in one of the Fill Color controls, then click the Color Picker button from the pop-up swatch window **C**.

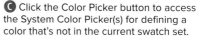

Color Picker button

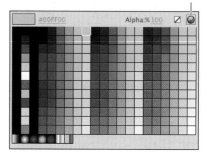

C Click the Color Picker button to access the System Color Picker(s) for defining a color that's not in the current swatch set.

About Fills and Strokes

What do the terms *fill* and *stroke* mean? A stroke is an outline, and a fill is a solid area of color. Think of a coloring book: the black lines creating the pictures are strokes, and the colorful area inside the lines is the fill. In a coloring book, you start with an outline and create the fill inside it. In Flash, you can also work the other way around—start with a solid shape and then create the outline as a separate element.

With Flash's rectangle, oval, rectangle-primitive, oval-primitive, and polystar tools, you can create an element that's just a fill or just a stroke; you can also create the fill and stroke elements simultaneously. The line and pen tools, as you might guess, create only strokes.

The concept of fills and strokes is a bit trickier to grasp in relation to the brush tool, which creates fills. These fills may look like lines or brushstrokes, but they are shapes you can outline with a stroke. Flash has special tools for adding, editing, and removing strokes and fills: the ink bottle, the paint bucket, and the faucet eraser. See Chapter 4 for more details.

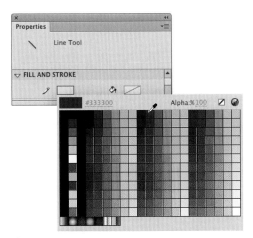

A Click the Stroke Color control (the color chip identified by a pencil icon) in the Fill and Stroke section of the Property inspector to open a set of color swatches and access an eyedropper pointer to select a new color.

Select value using slider   *Type new value*

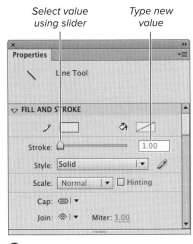

B When you select a tool that creates strokes, the Property inspector includes a Fill and Stroke section. Enter a new value in the Stroke field to prepare the selected tool to create strokes with the specified stroke height.

Setting Stroke Attributes

In Flash, lines and outlines (also known as strokes) have three main attributes: color, stroke height (thickness), and style. You can set all three in the Fill and Stroke section of an appropriate Property inspector. That section also lets you control the way the ends of lines (caps) look and the way lines connect (joins).

To set stroke properties:

1. With the Property inspector open, in the Tools panel, choose a tool that creates strokes. (The pen, line, rectangle, oval, rectangle-primitive, oval-primitive, polystar, pencil, and ink-bottle tools all create strokes.)

   When one of these tools is selected, the Property inspector's Fill and Stroke section appears, displaying a Stroke Color control (identified by a pencil icon) and other stroke settings for the selected tool. The Tools panel also displays a Stroke Color control.

2. Click any Stroke Color control to access its pop-up swatch set and other color settings **A**.

   To assign a new color or gradient for strokes, use any of the techniques described in Step 3 of the preceding task. (Because you're working with the Stroke Color control, however, your choices here apply to strokes.)

3. To set the stroke height, in the Stroke field, enter a number between 0.10 and 200, or drag the slider next to the field **B**.

continues on next page

4. To set the stroke style, choose one from the Style pop-up menu **C**.

There are seven styles: Hairline, Solid, Dashed, Dotted, Ragged, Stippled, and Hatched.

5. To determine how a solid or hairline stroke ends, from the Cap pop-up menu, choose one of the following styles:

None to end the stroke exactly where you stop drawing it

Round to extend the stroke by half the current stroke height, to create a rounded end

Square to extend the stroke by half the current stroke height, to create a square end **D**

6. To set the way solid or hairline strokes form corners, from the Join pop-up menu, choose one of the following styles:

Miter to create a sharp corner

Round to create a slightly curved corner

Bevel to create a slightly flattened corner **E**

TIP The Tools panel displays two buttons for setting basic stroke and fill colors. Clicking the overlapping black and white squares ◼ sets the Stroke Color control to black and the Fill Color control to white. Clicking the small squares with an arrow next to them ⬒ makes the current stroke and fill colors change places.

TIP In Flash, the hairline setting is considered a stroke style, not a stroke height. (Use the Style pop-up menu in the Fill and Stroke section of the Property inspector to locate the Hairline setting.) Hairlines in a symbol don't change thickness when the size of the symbol changes. If you want the strokes in your symbol to grow thicker or thinner as you scale the symbol up or down, be sure to use a style other than hairline. (To learn about symbols, see Chapter 7.)

Selected stroke style

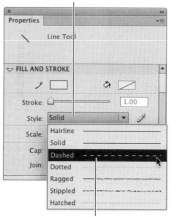

Preview of stroke settings

C Choose a stroke style from the pop-up menu in the Fill and Stroke section of the Property inspector.

D Set a Cap style to control the way lines end. The None option retains the line's original length and makes the ends flat; Round extends and rounds the ends; and Square extends and squares off the ends.

E Choose a Join style in the Fill and Stroke section of the Property inspector to control the way lines connect. Miter makes a pointed corner; Round makes a rounded corner; and Bevel slices a flat piece off of the corner. Choosing Miter activates the Miter hot-text control, which accepts values between 1 and 60. With Miter set to 1, Flash flattens the join slightly by slicing off the very tip of the point—the flat area is smaller than in a bevel join. Settings of 2 and above create a very sharp point.

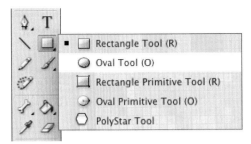

Making Geometric Shapes

Flash provides separate but similar tools for drawing ovals, rectangles, and polygons (or stars). All can draw a shape as an outline (a stroke), as a solid object (a fill), or as an object with an outline (a fill and a stroke created simultaneously). Rectangles and ovals have additional properties that you can set in the Property inspector.

A The Tools panel combines all the geometric-shape tools in a pop-up submenu. To view them, click the geometric-shape tool that's visible, then click a tool to select it and close the submenu.

To create geometric outlines:

1. In the Tools panel, click the active geometric-shape tool to open a submenu of tools, and choose the tool you want **A**.

2. To set the tool to create an outline with no fill, do the following:

   ▸ Open the Color Panel—or press Shift-Command-F9 (OS X) or Ctrl-Shift-F9 (Win)—and click the Fill Color control's paint bucket icon. Flash highlights Fill Color as the active control.

   ▸ Click the No Color button **B**.

Continues on next page

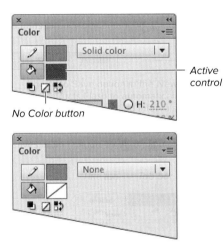

Active control

No Color button

B To set a geometric-shape tool to create an outline shape (without a fill), you need to set the fill to No Color. Here's one way to do that. In the Color panel, click the Fill Color control's paint bucket icon. Flash highlights the control in gray, indicating that it's the control to which the current panel settings apply. Then click the No Color button (top). Flash sets the fill type to None (bottom).

3. In the Fill and Stroke section of the Property inspector, enter values and choose settings for the stroke color, height, and style. (See "Setting Stroke Attributes" in this chapter.)

4. Move the pointer over the Stage. The pointer turns into a crosshair +.

5. Drag to preview the geometric shape **C**.

6. Release the mouse button to complete the outline shape.

TIP To make a perfect circle (or square), hold down the Shift key while you draw with the oval, oval-primitive, rectangle, or rectangle-primitive tool.

TIP To make an oval (or a rectangle) grow outward from the center point as you draw, position the pointer where you want the center of the shape, and hold down Option (OS X) or Alt (Win) as you drag. Shapes drawn with the polystar tool always grow from the center.

TIP To create an outline with no fill, you can click any Fill Color control and choose **No Color** from the pop-up swatch set.

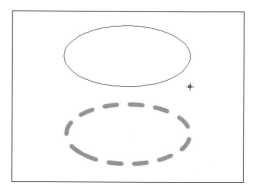

C With a geometric-shape tool selected, click the Stage and drag to create an outline preview of a shape (top). Release the mouse button to create the shape using the current settings for fills and strokes. In this case, the oval tool is set to use no fill and a green, dashed stroke, with a stroke height of 2 points (bottom).

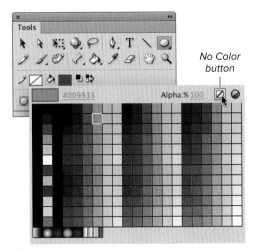

No Color button

D To create a geometric shape that's just a fill (without an outline stroke), you must set the stroke to No Color. Here's one way to do that. Click any Stroke Color control (in this example it's the control in the Tools panel). When the swatch set appears, click the No Color button.

E As you drag using the rectangle tool, Flash creates an outline preview of a rectangle (left). To complete the fill shape, release the mouse button (right).

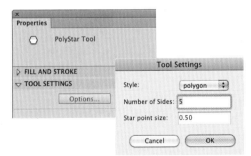

F Select the polystar tool to create polygons and stars, then click the Options button in the Tool Settings section of the Property inspector (top). In the Tool Settings dialog that appears, you can set the number of sides or points in your shape.

To create geometric fills:

1. In the Tools panel, click the active geometric-shape tool to open a submenu of tools, and choose the tool you want.

2. To set the tool to create just a fill with no outline, do the following:
   - Click any Stroke Color control (in the Tools panel, the Fill and Stroke section of the Property inspector, or the Color panel).
   - Click the No Color button from the pop-up swatch set **D**.

3. Use any Fill Color control to select a fill color. (See "Setting Fill Attributes" in this chapter.)

4. Follow Steps 4–6 in the preceding exercise, "To create geometric outlines." Flash draws a geometric fill, using the currently selected fill color **E**.

TIP You can create polygons and star shapes using the polystar tool. To set the number of sides in the polygon and switch from polygons to stars, make sure that nothing is selected on the Stage, and then choose PolyStar Tool from the geometric-shape tool's submenu in the Tools panel. The Tool Settings section appears in the Property inspector. Click the Options button in that section to open the Tool Settings dialog **F**. From the Style menu, choose Polygon or Star, then enter values to set the number of sides and the sharpness of the star points. Click OK to confirm the settings and close the dialog.

TIP To create a fill with no outline, you could use the Color panel to set the stroke to No Color. Click the pencil icon to apply settings to the Stroke Color control, then click the No Color button.

To set rectangle properties:

1. In the Tools panel, select the rectangle or rectangle-primitive tool.

   The Property inspector displays settings for the selected tool **G**. The properties are the same for both tools.

2. To create a rectangle with four identical corners, set the Lock Corner Radius button to the constrained state **H**.

   Clicking the chain-link icon toggles between the unconstrained (open link) and constrained (closed link) states.

3. To create a rectangle with rounded corners, in the Rectangle Corner Radius field, enter a positive number.

   or

   To create a rectangle with indented corners, in the Rectangle Corner Radius field, enter a negative number.

To set oval properties:

1. In the Tools panel, select the oval or oval-primitive tool.

   The Property inspector displays settings for the selected tool **I**. The properties are the same for both tools.

2. To create variations on the oval shape, in the Oval Options section of the Property inspector, do any of the following:

   ▸ To create a pie-wedge shape, in the Start Angle and/or End Angle field, enter a number from 0 to 360 **J**.

▽ RECTANGLE OPTIONS

0.00		0.00
0.00		0.00
		Reset

G When you select the rectangle or rectangle-primitive tool, the Property inspector's Rectangle Options section displays four Rectangle Corner Radius fields. Use them to define the angles or curves of a rectangle's corners.

Constrain corner radius →

0.00		0.00
0.00		0.00
		Reset

H By default, the rectangle and rectangle-primitive tools create shapes whose corners all have the same radius. When the closed-link icon appears (constrained state), only the first Rectangle Corner Radius field can be altered because the settings are linked.

▽ OVAL OPTIONS

Start angle: 0.00

End angle: 0.00

Inner radius: 0.00

☑ Close path   Reset

I Properties for defining ovals appear in the Property inspector's Oval Options section when you select the oval or oval primitive tool.

Drag slider to reposition control point

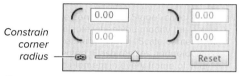

Start angle: 176.54

End angle: 90.00

J Entering values in the Start Angle and End Angle fields creates partial ovals such as those often used in pie charts. You can also drag the sliders to enter start- and end-angle values.

Shape with closed path

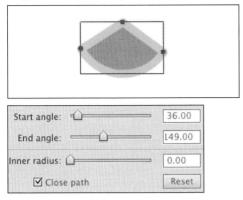

Shape with open path

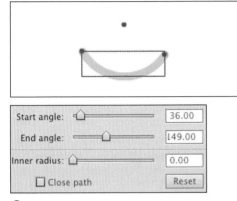

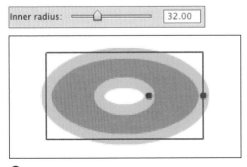

K Deselecting the Close Path checkbox lets you create arcs out of pie-wedge oval shapes. If the shape has an inner-radius setting greater than 0, its open-path form appears as two arcs.

L Entering a number greater than 0 in the Inner Radius field creates an oval with a hollow center.

‣ To create an open arc, deselect the Close Path checkbox. When you create a pie-wedge shape, this setting creates an open path. Flash removes the shape's fill (if one is present) and deletes the straight-line segments from the wedge shape **K**.

‣ To create an oval with a hollow center, in the Inner Radius field, enter a number from 0 to 99.

Flash draws a hollow oval inside the first oval **L**. The Inner Radius setting corresponds to the percentage of the outer oval's "fill" that is removed by the inside oval. (The outer oval may have a fill of No Color, in which case the inner oval appears as an outline.)

TIP You can interactively change an oval-primitive's start- or end-angle settings. Select the shape on the Stage. In the Oval Options section of the Property inspector, drag the Start Angle or End Angle slider to change the setting; you thereby modify the selected shape on the Stage.

TIP You can also interactively change start and end angles using the keyboard. Click the pointer of the slider for the value you want to change. The pointer highlights in blue, indicating that it has focus. Press the Right Arrow key (or Up Arrow key) to increase the value; press the Left Arrow key (or Down Arrow key) to decrease the value. Hold down Shift as you press the arrows to increase or decrease the value by larger increments.

Merge Drawing vs. Object Drawing vs. Primitive-Shapes

Flash CS6 creates three types of graphic objects: *merge-shapes* (also called *raw shapes*), *drawing-objects,* and *primitive-shapes.* You can use most of the drawing tools to create merge-shapes or drawing-objects simply by selecting the appropriate drawing mode. To create primitives, you must select either the rectangle-primitive or the oval-primitive tool.

Merge Drawing mode creates strokes and fills as raw shapes that you can edit directly on the Stage (see Chapter 4); raw shapes on a single layer interact with one another (see Chapter 5).

Object Drawing mode also creates strokes and fills that you can edit directly on the Stage, but these shapes don't interact with other shapes on the same layer.

Primitive-shapes do not interact with other shapes on the same layer. Behind the scenes, Flash creates these shapes in Object Drawing mode but locks and constrains them so that they always exhibit certain defining characteristics. Those characteristics are editable and appear as properties in the Property inspector when you select a primitive tool in the Tools panel or a primitive-shape on the Stage. You can edit these properties of a primitive anytime, but you can't freely edit a primitive the way you can edit a shape created in Merge/Object Drawing mode.

Flash's default mode for drawing tools is Merge Drawing. To turn on Object Drawing mode, select a tool that creates strokes and/or fills, then click the Object Drawing button in the Tools panel 🖸. Once you activate Object Drawing mode, it remains active until you click the Object Drawing button again to return to Merge Drawing mode (or press J on the keyboard to toggle between Merge Drawing and Object Drawing). Whichever Merge/Object Drawing setting is active when you end a work session will be active the next time you open Flash. The Merge/Object Drawing–mode button is absent from the Tools panel when you choose one of the primitive tools.

For many tasks, you'll see no difference between working with the three types of shapes; in some tasks, however, the difference is crucial. For the exercises in this book, unless otherwise noted, you can create shapes using either drawing mode or the primitive-shape tools.

About Drawing Assistance

Flash's pencil tool offers two assisted line-drawing modes: Straighten and Smooth. For total freedom in drawing, the pencil's Ink mode leaves shapes exactly as you create them.

Straighten mode refines the blips and tremors of a hand-drawn line into straight line segments and regular arcs. This mode also performs *shape recognition*. Flash evaluates each hand-drawn shape, and if it comes close enough to Flash's definition of an oval or a rectangle, Flash turns the drawing into a shape neat enough to please your high-school geometry teacher.

Smooth mode transforms a rough drawing into smooth, curved line segments. Note that Smooth mode doesn't recognize shapes, but simply smoothes out the curves you draw. Smoothing reduces the number of points in a shape, thus producing smaller file sizes and improving the performance of the published movie.

Tolerance settings are all-important, especially for Straighten mode. You can set Flash to change almost any ovoid shape into a circle and a slightly more oblong shape into a rectangle. You set the degree of drawing assistance in the Preferences dialog. Choose Flash > Preferences (OS X) or Edit > Preferences (Win). In the Preferences dialog that opens, choose Drawing from the Category list, then choose tolerance levels from the Connect Lines, Smooth Curves, Recognize Lines, and Recognize Shapes menus. Click OK to close the dialog.

Creating Free-form Shapes

Flash includes three tools for creating free-form shapes: the pencil, pen, and brush. The pencil and pen tools create outline shapes—strokes without fills. The brush tool creates solid shapes—fills without strokes. After you've created a shape, you can modify it at any time—for example, to fill an empty outline or add an outline to a filled shape.

Using the pen tool, you can create strokes by placing anchor points and adjusting Bézier curves. You can add or remove points from these curves using the pen tool, or using one of the three anchor-point tools (add anchor point, delete anchor point, and convert anchor point). The pencil tool lets you draw strokes freehand using the mouse or a graphics tablet and pen. Flash hides precise details about the anchor points and curves of a stroke drawn using the pencil tool.

You'll use the pencil, pen, and brush to create free-form shapes in this chapter; in Chapter 4, you'll learn to modify those shapes.

Set Drawing Preferences

For the following tasks, make sure the grid is visible (see Chapter 1) and set drawing preferences as follows: choose Flash > Preferences (OS X) or Edit > Preferences (Win) to open the Preferences dialog. From the Category list, choose Drawing, and select the Show Pen Preview and Show Solid Points checkboxes. Leave the other options at their default settings. Click OK to close the dialog.

To draw freeform strokes using the pencil tool:

1. In the Tools panel, select the pencil tool ✏️, or press Y.

2. From the Pencil Mode menu 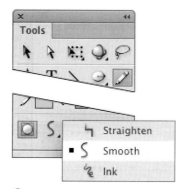, choose one of the following assistance modes:

   Straighten resolves minor variations into straight-line segments.

   Smooth resolves minor variations into smooth curves.

   Ink provides very little assistance, leaving minor variations.

3. Move the pointer over the Stage. The pointer changes to a pencil icon.

4. Drag to draw a squiggle on the Stage. Flash previews your rough line.

5. Release the mouse button.

   Flash recasts the line you've drawn according to the assistance mode you chose in Step 2, creating a set of straight-line segments and regular curves Ⓑ.

> **TIP** You can apply smoothing and straightening (and even shape recognition) to an existing outline or shape by selecting the shape on the Stage and then clicking the Straighten or Smooth modifier of the Selection tool. (You'll learn more about making and modifying selections in Chapter 4.)

> **TIP** To perform a more controlled type of smoothing and straightening, select an outline or shape, then choose Modify > Shape > Advanced Smooth or Advanced Straighten. In the dialog that appears, enter new values to refine your shape, and click OK. To preview various settings, select the Preview checkbox; Flash applies the current settings to the selected shape.

Ⓐ When the pencil tool is selected, the Tools panel displays a pop-up menu of pencil modes.

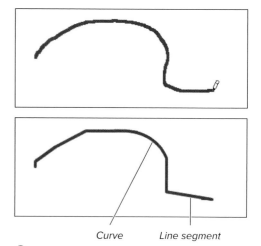

Curve   *Line segment*

Ⓑ With the pencil tool in Straighten mode, Flash creates a preview as you draw. When you release the mouse button, Flash applies straightening and turns your rough squiggle (top) into a set of straight-line segments and smooth curves (bottom).

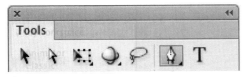

 Select the pen tool to create paths.

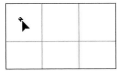 **D** The x next to the pen tool indicates that you're about to start a new path. Click to place the first anchor point.

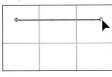

First point previewed   *Preview line segment*

Click to place second point   *Completed line segment*

E Flash previews points as you place them (top), and it adds a stroke to the path as soon as you complete a segment (bottom).

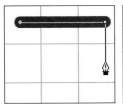

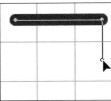

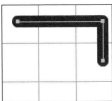

F Continue clicking to add segments to your free-form shape. A click (top) adds a straight-line segment (bottom).

To draw freeform strokes using the pen tool:

1. In the Tools panel, select the pen tool, or press P **C**.

2. In the Fill and Stroke section of the Property inspector, set the stroke attributes for your path.

3. Move the pointer over the Stage. A small x appears next to the pen pointer to indicate that you're ready to place the first point of a path **D**.

4. Click where you want your line segment to begin. The pointer changes to a solid arrowhead with a small hollow circle that indicates the location of the anchor point on the Stage.

5. Reposition the pen tool where you want to end your line segment. With Drawing Preferences set to Show Pen Preview, Flash extends a preview of the line segment from the first point to the tip of the pen as you move around the Stage.

6. Click to place the end of the line segment.

   Flash completes the segment using the selected stroke attributes. With Drawing Preferences set to Show Solid Points, the anchor points appear as solid squares **E**.

7. To add a straight segment to your line, click the Stage where you want the segment to end **F**.

Continues on next page

8. To add a curve segment, click the Stage, then drag where you want the curve segment to end. Flash places a preview point on the Stage, the pointer changes to a solid arrowhead, and Bézier handles (sometimes referred to as tangent handles) appear 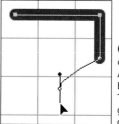.

9. Drag the pointer away from the direction in which you want your curve to bulge.

   The Bézier handles extend from the anchor point, growing in opposite directions as you drag. Flash previews the curve as you draw 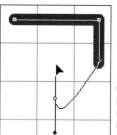.

10. While still holding down the mouse button, drag the pointer to reposition the Bézier handle.

   Dragging the handle clockwise or counterclockwise around its anchor point controls the direction of the bulge. Dragging the handle farther from the anchor point deepens the curve, while dragging closer makes the curve shallower .

11. When the curve preview looks the way you want, release the mouse button. Flash completes your curve segment with a stroke 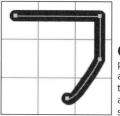.

G Click and drag to create a curve point. As you drag, the point's Bézier handles appear. The bulge of the curve grows away from the direction of your drag.

H To make the curve bulge downward, drag upward. Dragging the handles out farther deepens the curve.

I Drag the handles clockwise or counterclockwise around the anchor point to modify the curve shape (top). Drag the handles in or out to make the curve deeper or shallower (bottom).

J When you finish positioning handles for a segment and release the mouse button, Flash adds a stroke to the segment.

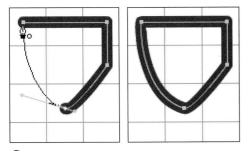

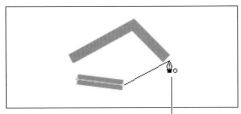

K To create a closed shape, position the pointer over the first anchor point you placed. When a hollow-circle icon appears, click that first point (left). Flash adds the finishing segment, thereby creating a closed path (right).

Extend Line

Join Line

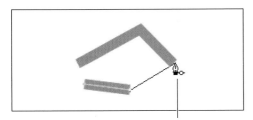

Modifier icon for merge-shape

Modifier icon for drawing-object

L You can use the pen tool to add to existing line segments. Click the end point of the existing line (top), then click again wherever you want to place more points. Or, you can first place new points, then position the pointer over the end point of the line you want to join (bottom). When the modifier icon appears, click to join the lines.

12. To create an open path, Command-click (OS X) or Ctrl-click (Win) the Stage.

or

To create a closed shape, do the following:

‣ Position the pointer over your first anchor point. Flash previews the closing segment of your shape. A small hollow circle appears next to the pen tool **K**.

‣ Click the first anchor point. Flash closes the shape, adding a stroke to the path.

When the path is complete, the pen tool pointer displays a small x, indicating that the tool is ready to place the first anchor point of a new path.

TIP You have several other options for ending open paths. Choose Edit > Deselect All, or press Shift-Command-A (OS X) or Ctrl-Shift-A (Win). In the Tools panel, you can click a different tool. You can also double-click the last point you placed.

TIP To extend a line created earlier **L**, position the pen pointer over the end of the line (the *terminal anchor point*). A small slash appears next to the pen icon. Click the terminal anchor point to link the pen to that point, as if you'd just placed it, then continue adding segments normally. You can also join to an existing line when creating a new line. To do so, the pen tool must be in the same drawing mode as the existing line. Click to place the anchor points of the new line, but don't double-click to end the line. Instead, position the pointer over a terminal anchor point in the line you want to join. A modifier icon appears next to the pen icon (a small circle for Merge Drawing mode, a chain-link for Object Drawing Mode). Click the existing terminal anchor point to join the two lines.

TIP The pen tool creates only strokes. To add a fill to a closed shape drawn with the pen, use the paint bucket tool.

To create free-form solid fills with the brush tool:

1. In the Tools panel, click the current brush tool 🖌. From the submenu that opens, select the brush tool. Brush options appear at the bottom of the panel **M**.

2. To optimize the brush for a particular painting task, select options from the following pop-up menus at the bottom of the Tools panel:

   Brush Mode controls how new brush-stroke fills interact with existing shapes. (You'll learn about shape interactions in Chapter 5.) For this exercise, choose Paint Normal **N**.

   Brush Size offers eight graduated brush sizes.

   Brush Shape offers nine brush tips that work a bit like the nibs of a calligraphy pen to create fluid shapes **O**.

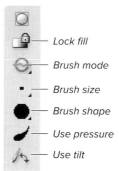

— Lock fill
— Brush mode
— Brush size
— Brush shape
— Use pressure
— Use tilt

M When you select the brush tool, its options appear at the bottom of the Tools panel. The pressure and tilt options appear only when a compatible pressure-sensitive tablet is connected to the computer.

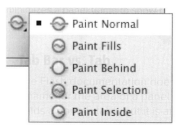

Paint Normal
Paint Fills
Paint Behind
Paint Selection
Paint Inside

N The options portion of the Tools panel has three pop-up menus of brush settings. Brush Mode options control how fills created with the brush tool interact with other shapes on the same layer. Choosing Paint Normal lets you paint merge-shape fills that act like any other fills when they overlap other shapes.

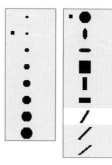

O The Brush Size (left) and Brush Shape (right) menus let you customize the brush tool. Slanted brush tips are great for creating thick and thin lines, allowing the brush to emulate a calligraphy pen.

P Selecting the brush tool's Use Pressure modifier ✎ activates the pressure-sensitive capabilities of a connected Wacom pen and graphics tablet. In this mode, the pointer appears as a circle with a crosshair ⊕. As you draw, the pointer changes to reflect brush-tip size and shape. To vary line thickness, apply more or less pressure as you draw. All the lines in this cat were created using a single brush size and shape.

3. To paint brushstroke fills that vary in thickness according to how hard you press, select the Use Pressure button. This option appears only when a graphics tablet is connected to your computer **P**.

4. Select or define a solid fill color using any of the techniques outlined earlier in this chapter.

5. Move the pointer over the Stage. The pointer icon reflects the current brush size and shape.

6. Drag to draw on the Stage. Flash previews your brushwork in the currently selected fill **Q**.

Continues on next page

Q Drawing with the brush creates a preview of your shape (left). Flash recasts the shape as a vector graphic with the currently selected fill color and smoothing settings (right).

About Path Math in Flash

A *path*—a series of points and connecting lines—is the skeleton of your graphic-object. With most Flash tools, the math that goes into creating a path takes place behind the scenes. You draw a complete line or a shape; Flash places points (without showing them), connects them, and adds a stroke. With the pen tool, you place the defining points—called *anchor points*—and adjust the curve segments that connect them, using controllers called *Bézier handles* (also known as *tangent handles)*. When you've finished placing points with the pen tool, Flash fleshes out the path by applying a stroke to it. You can use the selection and subselection tools to modify any path—even one whose points start out hidden (see Chapter 4).

7. When you complete your shape, release the mouse button. Flash creates the final shape, smoothing it according to settings in the Property inspector. (See the sidebar "About Brush Smoothing" below.)

TIP You can change the brushstroke size by changing the magnification at which you view the Stage. To create a fat stroke without changing your brush-tip settings, set the Stage view to a small percentage. To switch to a thin stroke, zoom out to a higher percentage **R**. However, be sure to check your work in 100% view.

TIP By default the Tools panel groups two brush tools (brush and spray brush) under one submenu. To select the brush tool currently showing in the panel, press **B**. When one of the brush tools is selected in the panel, you can switch to the other brush tool by pressing **B** again.

Created with 200% magnification

Created with 100% magnification

Created with 50% magnification

R Each of these three brushstrokes was created with exactly the same brush size. Only the magnification level of the Stage was changed.

About Brush Smoothing

Flash's Smoothing setting controls how brushstrokes translate into vector shapes. When the brush tool is active, the Property inspector contains a Smoothing section, with hot-text control for Smoothing. This control sets the brush tool's stroke-smoothness value (from 0 to 100, with a default of 50). Stroke smoothness determines how closely Flash re-creates each movement of the brush as a separate vector segment. The lower the setting, the more faithfully Flash reproduces the shapes you draw (by using more vectors, which has an impact on the size and animation performance of your final file). A higher setting re-creates your flourishes more roughly, using fewer vectors.

To see the difference clearly, select the brush tool, assign a Smoothing value of 1, and draw a curved line on the Stage. Change the Smoothing setting to 30 and draw a second curved line. Using the subselection tool (see Chapter 4), select each shape. The line drawn with Smoothing set to 1 displays many more points—that is, it contains many more vector segments.

Gradient Fills and Flash's Drawing Modes

For the tasks in this section, you create strokes and fills using solid colors, but you could also use gradients. Gradient strokes and fills work straightforwardly for the line, pen, ink-bottle, and geometric-shape tools: you choose the tool, set the Stroke and/or Fill Color control to the desired gradient, then create your graphic object. The full range of the gradient appears in each object you create with the tool. When you select the brush tool or paint bucket tool, however, you'll see a Lock Fill button ▣ in the Options section of the Tools panel. This option makes working with gradients a bit more complex.

When Lock Fill is deselected, the gradients you create come out the same whether you are working in Merge Drawing mode or Object Drawing mode. The gradient is centered in the shape's bounding box (an invisible rectangle that's just the right size to enclose the shape); the full gradient is visible in the shape.

When Lock Fill is selected, however, gradient fills created in the two drawing modes behave differently.

For locked fills, Flash creates a virtual gradient that underlies the Stage and Pasteboard. (By default, Flash aligns the center of the locked gradient with the left edge of the Stage.) Each shape you create with a locked fill reveals just the portion of the gradient that corresponds to that area of the Stage. If you paint multiple merge-shapes with a locked gradient, the same virtual gradient underlies each shape; you can use the gradient-transform tool to shift the gradient within all the shapes (see Chapter 4). Multiple drawing-objects each have their own virtual gradient. These virtual gradients start out being centered in the same way; initially it looks as though there's one underlying gradient, as with merge-shapes. But the gradient-transform tool shifts the gradient in each drawing-object separately.

To get a feel for the difference between locked and unlocked gradient fills, try painting a variety of brushstroke fills in Merge Drawing mode and in Object Drawing mode, with Lock Fill selected and deselected; use different areas of the Stage, and make the shapes different lengths. Notice the way each shape displays the gradient.

Adding Strokes and Fills

As you learned earlier in this chapter, you can create outline shapes (strokes without fills) and solid shapes (fills without strokes). But at any time you can use the paint bucket tool to add fills to outline shapes and the ink-bottle tool to add strokes to solid shapes. (You can also use these tools to modify existing strokes and fills, as you'll learn in Chapter 4.)

To add strokes to fills:

1. On the Stage, draw a solid shape that has no stroke, or use an existing solid shape.

   For a merge-shape, make sure the fill is deselected; for a drawing-object, the fill can be selected or deselected.

2. In the Tools panel, click the current fill/stroke tool; and from the submenu that opens, select the ink-bottle tool, or press S Ⓐ.

3. In the Fill and Stroke section of the Ink Bottle Tool Property inspector, set the desired stroke attributes. (See "Setting Stroke Attributes " in this chapter.)

4. Position the pointer over a fill shape that has no stroke. The pointer appears as an ink bottle spilling ink.

Ⓐ The ink-bottle tool applies all the stroke attributes currently set in the Fill and Stroke section of the Ink Bottle Tool Property inspector.

Hot spot

Outside edge
of fill shape

Before

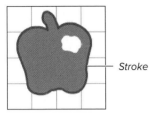

Stroke

After

B As you move the ink bottle over a filled shape, a hot spot appears at the end of the ink drip that's spilling out of the bottle. To add a stroke around the outside edge of your fill shape, position the hot spot along that edge (top), and click. Flash adds a stroke with the current attributes set in the Fill and Stroke section of the Ink Bottle Tool Property inspector (bottom).

Before

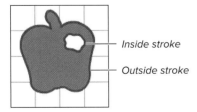

Inside stroke

Outside stroke

After

C Position the ink bottle's hot spot in the middle of your fill shape (top), and click. Flash uses the current stroke attributes to add a stroke around the outside and inside of your shape (bottom).

5. Using the hot spot at the tip of the ink, click a fill shape in one of the following ways:

   ▸ To add a stroke around the outside of the shape, click near the outside edge of the shape **B**.

   ▸ To add a stroke around the inside of a shape that has a hole cut out of it, click near the inside edge of the shape.

   ▸ To outline both the outside of a shape and the hole inside the shape, click in the middle of the shape **C**.

   Flash adds strokes to the outside edge, inside edge, or both; the ink bottle tool applies the color, thickness, and style currently specified in the Fill and Stroke section of the Property inspector.

TIP Flash lets you use gradients for strokes. In Step 3 of the preceding task, in the Fill and Stroke section of the Property inspector, choose a linear or radial gradient from the Stroke Color control's pop-up swatch set. Why might you want a gradient stroke? For an oval shape, adding a thick stroke with a radial gradient can help create the illusion of 3D depth or make the shape appear to glow.

TIP Another way to add strokes to drawing-objects and primitive-shapes is to modify them using the Property inspector. First, select the drawing-object or primitive on the Stage. Then in the Property inspector, change the stroke properties, including color. You can use this technique to add strokes to multiple drawing-objects and/or primitives. (This technique doesn't work for merge-shapes.) You'll learn more about modifying graphic objects in Chapter 4.

To fill an outline shape with solid color:

1. On the Stage, draw an outline shape that has no fill, or use an existing outline shape. The outline should not be selected.

2. In the Tools panel, click the current fill/stroke tool; and from the submenu that opens, select the paint bucket tool, or press K **D**.

3. In the Tools panel, from the Gap Size menu, choose the amount of assistance you want **E**.

   If you draw your shapes precisely, a medium or small gap closure serves you best. You don't want Flash to fill areas that aren't meant to be shapes. If your drawings are rougher, choose Close Large Gaps, which enables Flash to recognize less-complete shapes.

4. From any Fill Color control, select a solid fill color.

5. Place the paint bucket's hot spot inside the outline shape, and click. The shape fills with the currently selected fill color **F**.

> **TIP** You may be unaware that your shape has gaps. If nothing happens when you click inside a shape using the paint bucket, try changing the Gap Size setting, as in Step 3.

> **TIP** Gap-closure settings are relative to the level of magnification you're using to view the Stage. If the paint bucket's largest gap-closure setting fails at your current magnification, try again after reducing magnification **G**.

> **TIP** When you work with a selected drawing-object, you needn't click inside the shape; the fill color changes automatically when you select it, as in Step 4. You'll learn more about modifying selected shapes in Chapter 4.

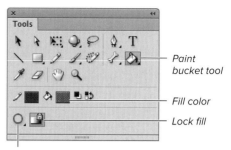

Gap size

— *Paint bucket tool*

— *Fill color*

— *Lock fill*

D When you select the paint bucket tool, its modifiers appear in the options section of the Tools panel.

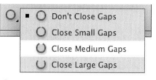

E The Gap Size menu controls Flash's capability to fill shapes that aren't fully closed.

F Clicking inside an outline shape with the paint bucket (left) fills the shape with the currently selected fill color (right).

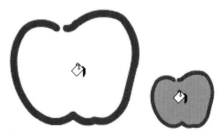

G The paint bucket can't fill this apple shape using Close Large Gaps and a magnification of 100 percent (left). But in a 50 percent view, the paint bucket with the same large gap closure setting recognizes this shape as complete and fills it.

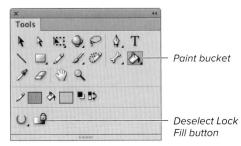

Paint bucket

Deselect Lock
Fill button

H Deselect the Lock Fill button to fill a shape with an unlocked gradient.

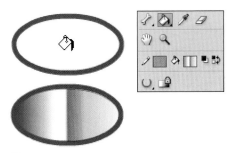

I You can use the paint bucket tool to apply a linear gradient fill. An unlocked gradient is centered within the outline shape's bounding box.

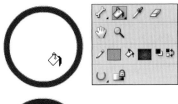

J The paint bucket tool can also apply a radial gradient fill. Click where you want to locate the center of the gradient.

To fill outline shapes with unlocked gradients:

1. In the Tools panel, click the current fill/stroke tool, and from the submenu that opens, select the paint bucket tool, or press K.

2. From any Fill Color control, select a gradient fill.

   You can use a linear or radial gradient. (To learn how to define a new gradient using the Color panel, see "Creating Solid Colors and Gradients," in this chapter. To select an existing gradient, see "Setting Fill Attributes," in this chapter.)

3. In the Options section of the Tools panel, make sure the Lock Fill button is deselected **H**.

4. Using the paint bucket's hot spot, click inside the outline shape.

   Each outline shape you click fills with the gradient currently displayed in the Fill Color control. If you chose a linear gradient in Step 2, Flash centers the unlocked gradient within the outline shape **I**. If you chose a radial gradient, the location you click with the paint bucket's hot spot sets the center of the unlocked gradient **J**.

To fill outline shapes with locked gradients:

Follow the steps in the preceding task, but in Step 3, select the Lock Fill button.

Each outline shape you click fills with a portion of the gradient currently set in the Fill Color control. (See the sidebar "Gradient Fills and Flash's Drawing Models" in this chapter.)

Creating Simple Patterns

Flash CS6 offers two tools that create patterns: the spray-brush tool and the deco tool 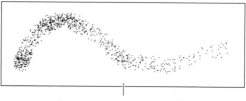. By default, the spray-brush tool creates a random dot pattern. You determine where the pattern goes by painting on the Stage. The deco tool uses predefined patterns. Some deco tool patterns, such as Vine Fill and Grid Fill, spread throughout a selected shape and fill it automatically. Other deco tool patterns, such as Building Brush or Flower Brush, require a bit of guidance from your mouse movements. As you paint with the deco tool's Flower Brush pattern, for example, you lay down a string of randomly repeating leaves, petals, and stems. The deco tool's brush patterns can quickly populate a scene with repetitive elements.

To make the finished spray brush and deco patterns easier to work with, Flash unites pattern elements in a special object called a *group*. (You'll learn about groups in Chapter 5.)

Some of the deco tool's patterns—such as Fire Animation Brush and Lightening Brush—let you automatically create animation using the frame-by-frame technique. (You'll learn about frame-by-frame animation in Chapter 8.)

Deco tool   Spray-brush tool

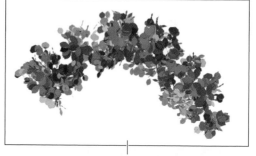

Floral spray created with one sweeping mouse movement using the deco tool's Flower Brush pattern

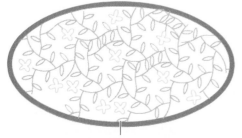

Shape filled with a vine pattern

Dots from one "brushstroke" using the Spray Brush tool

 The spray-brush tool works somewhat like an airbrush to create a pattern of dots or symbols as you move the mouse. The deco tool can fill a shape (or the Stage) with a predefined pattern, or it can paint with a series of randomly repeating graphic elements such as flowers, trees, and buildings.

Working with Text

Adobe Flash Professional CS6's text tool creates two types of text fields: Classic and TLF (Text Layout Framework). The exercises in this book cover using TLF text.

A TLF text field is not just a container full of graphic-objects in the shape of letters; the field holds live text that is fully editable in the authoring environment. As you create text elements, you must decide how they will be used in the published movie and assign them a Type property. When you want the end user to be able to copy information, set the text field's Type property to *Selectable*. When you want to do something with the text at runtime (for example, use ActionScript to process data entered in a form), set the Type property to *Editable*. If the text will just sit there looking pretty, set the Type property to *Read Only*.

In this chapter, you'll learn about working with English text using Read Only and Selectable TLF text fields. To process data from Editable TLF text fields at runtime requires a level of ActionScripting that is beyond the scope of this book.

In This Chapter

Creating TLF Text Fields

The text tool creates containers that hold text. You can set the text to read horizontally or vertically. You can also apply a variety of text attributes, including text and paragraph styles. For the tasks in this chapter, you'll use the text tool to create TLF text.

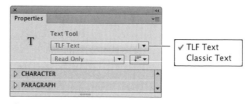

A To work with TLF text blocks, in the Text Tool Property inspector, choose TLF Text from the Text Engine menu.

To choose the TLF text tool:

1. In the Tools panel, select the text tool **T**, or press the T key. The Text Tool Property inspector appears.

2. From the Text Engine menu in the upper portion of the Property inspector, choose TLF Text **A**.

   The Text Tool Property inspector appears with options for setting text and container attributes. Use the current settings. You'll learn how to change these settings in upcoming tasks.

TLF Playback Requirements

To display TLF text correctly, Flash Player must access special instructions at runtime. These instructions are available only in Flash Player 10 and later. If you need to publish for earlier versions of the player, you must use Classic text. For more details about publishing, see Chapter 17.

Point Text vs. Area Text

A text field is basically a container that holds and displays text. The TLF text tool creates two types of text-field containers that Adobe refers to as *point-text* containers and *area-text* containers. If that terminology seems a little abstract, you can think of them as flexible- and fixed-size text fields.

Point-text Fields (Flexible Size)

A point-text container has flexible dimensions. A point-text field grows when you enter more text and shrinks when you delete text.

Area-text Fields (Fixed Size)

An area-text field doesn't change size as you enter or delete text. The container accepts all the text you type, but the field reveals only as much text as can fit inside the borders of the field at the current dimensions. You can resize an area-text text field to show more text, or use TLF's linking feature to allow the excess text to flow into another text field. There are also options for letting end users view "hidden" text by scrolling. When you set the text's Type property to *Selectable* or *Editable*, end users can scroll within text using the I-beam cursor and arrow keys. You can also add a UIScrollBar component to any type of TLF text field and then set the component to target the field's instance name. You'll learn about working with one type of component, a button, in Chapter 14.

B TLF text comes in three types. End users can interact with Selectable and Editable text at runtime, while Read Only text is just a graphic object to end users. You can choose the style you need from the Text Type menu in the Text (Tool) property inspector.

C Click the Stage with the TLF text tool to create a text field. The round resize handle in the lower-right corner of the field indicates a point-text field. The field grows as you enter text; there is no word wrap.

D As you type, the point-text field grows horizontally to accommodate your text. The text doesn't wrap.

TIP For a TLF text field with default container settings, the bounding box is invisible when the field is not selected. To view the bounding box, click anywhere in the text with the text tool or the selection tool.

TIP You can use the selection tool to move text fields just as you would any other graphic element.

To create non-wrapping point text:

1. With the TLF text tool selected, from the Text Type menu in the Text Tool Property inspector, choose one of the three types. For this task, choose Selectable or Read Only **B**.

   Read Only text is not accessible to end users; it acts purely as a graphic element in the published movie.

   Selectable text is partly accessible to end users; they can copy this text.

   Editable text is fully accessible to end users; they can select it, edit it, and delete it.

   Note that Flash developers can target all three types of TLF text fields for updating at runtime using ActionScript.

2. Using the text-tool pointer ⊣ᵣ, click the Stage to place the left side of the text field.

   Flash creates a resizable bounding box with a blinking insertion point, ready for you to enter text **C**. Each corner and side of the box has a resize handle. The round handle in the lower-right corner indicates that this field does not have word wrap.

3. Start typing your text.

   The bounding box grows to accommodate the text **D**. By default, the point-text field's Behavior property is set to Multiline No Wrap (see "Setting Container Attributes" in this chapter); as you enter characters, the box grows horizontally, creating a single line of text. The box grows vertically when you press Enter to add a new line.

4. When you finish typing, click elsewhere on the Stage (or choose a new tool in the Tools panel) to deselect the text.

To create area text with word wrap:

1. With the TLF text tool selected, click the Stage to place the text field.

2. Move the pointer over any of the resize handles at the corners or sides of the field's bounding box. The pointer changes to a double-headed arrow ↔.

3. Drag one of the handles until the dotted-line preview of the bounding box is the size you want 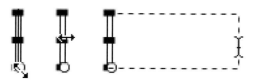 **E**.

4. Release the mouse button.

   An active text field appears **F**. The field is in *Text Edit mode*, ready to accept text, with a tab ruler and *text-flow ports* for creating text flow between TLF text fields. (See "Creating Linked Text Fields" in this chapter.) The normal square resize handle in the lower-right corner indicates that word wrap is set for this text field.

5. Enter your text.

   As you type, the text wraps to fit inside the text field's bounding box. If you type more text than the field can display, the text scrolls upward, and the field shows the last text you typed **G**. When you leave Text Edit mode, the text reflows and the first text you typed appears at the top of the field. For this task, enter enough text to force scrolling. A red plus sign that appears in the field's Out port indicates the presence of additional text—often referred to as *overflow text* or *overset text*.

E Drag any resize handle of a text field's bounding box to create a text field with a specific width.

In port   Tab ruler   Out port

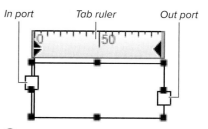

F When an area-text field is in Text Edit mode, a tab ruler and In and Out ports (indicating text flow for linked fields) appear. In addition, the lower-right handle is a square (not the round resize handle of a point-text field). Any text you enter will wrap to fit the column width of the text field.

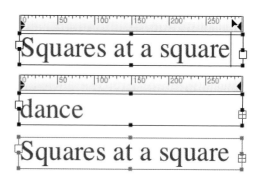

G When you enter text, the field displays what you type (top). When you reach the display limit of the field, the text you entered first seems to disappear (middle); but when you leave Text Edit mode, the text scrolls back to the beginning (bottom). The red plus sign in the TLF text field's Out port indicates that the field contains overflow text.

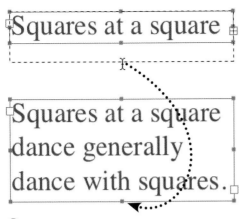

H Drag any resize handle to enlarge the TLF text field (top). When you make the field big enough to show all its contents, the red plus sign disappears from the Out port (bottom).

6. To resize the text field, drag any resize handle.

When you release the mouse button, the text reflows to fit the new field. When the text field is large enough to display all its contents, the red plus sign disappears from the Out port **H**.

TIP Drag on the Stage to quickly create an area-text field with word wrap. A dotted-line rectangle previews the text field's proportions. When you release the mouse button, the tab ruler and text-flow ports are already in place.

TIP To activate Text Edit mode for a deselected TLF text field, click in the field with the text tool, select some of the text with the text tool, or double-click the field with the selection tool. The Tools panel switches to the text tool, the tab ruler and text-flow ports activate, and the blinking I-beam cursor appears, ready to edit the field's text.

TIP To convert an area-text field (fixed-size) to a point-text field (flexible-size), activate Text Edit mode, then double-click one of the text-flow ports. The circular resize handle reappears in the TLF text field's lower-right corner, indicating that word wrap is not turned on; the text field grows horizontally as you type a line, and vertically when you press Enter.

TIP If you have no need to process your TLF text using ActionScript at runtime, and your application doesn't require users to enter text, you can reduce the size of your published movie (the SWF file) by setting all of your TLF text fields to Read Only or Selectable (you must also avoid assigning instance names to those text fields). Setting up TLF text this way allows Flash to use its Text Container Manager (TCM) and avoid embedding some extra code required for processing TLF text with Action-Script. Another way to avoid embedding this code is to use only Classic text, but doing so means giving up TLF's typographic and text-layout features.

TIP To create a TLF text field that limits user input (to create a password field, for example), choose Editable as the field's text style. Enter the text you want the field to display initially (it can be of any length), then use the Max Chars hot-text control to enter the number of characters you want the field to accept at runtime. (It's best to enter the field's display text before setting a limit. Once activated, the Max Chars value limits text entry during authoring as well as at runtime. If you forget, just increase the Max Chars value, enter your text, and then decrease the value.)

Classic Text vs. TLF Text

This book concentrates on TLF text because it offers rich text-layout and typographic capabilities. However, Classic is the default text engine for Flash CS6. To publish for Flash Player 9 and earlier versions, you must use Classic text.

Classic text is also useful, for example, when you need to minimize file sizes, or you want to translate your content to to JavaScript (for use with HTML5) using the CreateJS extension (see Chapter 17).

Creating Classic Text

The mechanics of creating text fields are similar for both types of text. To use Classic text, choose Classic Text from the Text Engine menu. Click the Stage to create a flexible-size Classic text field (the text doesn't wrap and the field grows horizontally as you enter more text), or drag on the Stage to create a fixed-width field. (The text wraps and the field grows vertically as you enter more text.)

In most cases, the techniques and UI elements for setting the properties of Classic text have changed very little since Flash CS4. If you'd like more help creating Classic text fields, you can review the text tasks from *Flash CS4 Professional Visual QuickStart Guide* on the companion website to this book (www.peachpit.com/flashcs6vqs).

Choosing a Text Engine

How do you decide which kind of text to use? Here are some crucial requirements that will influence your decision:

Player requirements—To use TLF text, you must work in an ActionScript 3.0 document and set your movie to publish in Flash Player 10.3 or later (see Chapter 17). When you want to use earlier ActionScript versions or publish for earlier player versions, you must use Classic text.

Font requirements—TLF text works only with Type 2 (OpenType) and TrueType fonts. If you plan to use PostScript fonts, you must use Classic text.

Masking requirements—If you place a TLF text field on a mask layer, you wind up seeing a rectangular mask (the size of your text's bounding box) when you choose Show Masking during authoring. In Flash Player, you see a knock-out version of your text against that rectangle in Flash Player. (You'll learn about masking in Chapter 6.) To create a text field with letterforms that act as individual masks, you must use Classic text.

Exporting to HTML5—If you plan to develop content for delivery on mobile devices that do not support Flash Player, you might want the ability to translate your content to JavaScript for use with HTML5. The Flash Professional Toolkit for CreateJS—a downloadable extension that works with Flash CS6—does just that. However, the toolkit exports only Classic text.

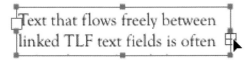

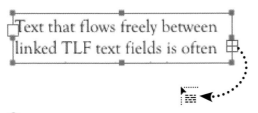

A When the pointer hovers over a text-flow port, the pointer changes to a solid arrowhead. Clicking with it begins the linking process.

B Once you've "loaded" the pointer with overflow text, the loaded-text icon appears. Clicking the Stage with that pointer creates a new, linked field.

Creating Linked Text Fields

An area-text field is like a window into a huge container of endless possible text. A red plus sign in the Out port is your clue that the window is showing only some of the text in the container. You have two options for revealing more of the text: resize the field to display all the text, or link the field to another TLF text field, thereby creating another window into that huge container of text.

To create linked text fields:

1. Create an area-text field (see the preceding task).

   Enter a moderate amount of text, at least 20 words. Make sure to enter some overflow text so that a red plus sign appears in the field's Out port. Let's call this Field 1.

2. Position the pointer over Field 1's Out port. The begin-link pointer ⊞▸ appears **A**.

3. Click the Out port and move the pointer away from the port. The loaded-text pointer appears ⌐☰ **B**.

About Threaded Text

Text that flows freely between linked TLF text fields is often referred to as *threaded text*. Linked fields may also be called *threaded fields*, and this book often refers to them as a chain of linked fields. Resizing one field in the chain causes the remaining text to reflow in response. Similarly, text reflows in response to changes you make to the threaded text's font family, type size, leading, and so on. Selecting one threaded text field (with the selection tool) activates the entire chain of linked fields with these results: the bounding box of each threaded field highlights (in light blue by default), triangular *text-flow indicators* appear in the In and Out ports, and a *link line* (or *thread*) connects each linked pair of In and Out ports. These graphic elements indicate the direction the text flows from one field to the next.

4. To create a new TLF text field that automatically links to Field 1, position the pointer outside Field 1 and do one of the following:

▸ To create a field that duplicates the dimensions and other properties of Field 1, click the Stage with the loaded-text pointer.

▸ To create a field with different dimensions, drag the loaded-text pointer on the Stage to create a new TLF text field of the dimensions you want.

When you release the mouse button, another TLF text field appears ⑥. Let's call it Field 2. A link line connects the Field 1 Out port to the Field 2 In port. Overflow text from Field 1 flows into Field 2.

TIP You can use this technique to automate creation of multiple linked TLF text fields before you enter any text. Create Field 1, click its Out port, and then click the Stage to create Field 2. Click the Field 2 Out port, and then click the Stage to create Field 3. Repeat as necessary.

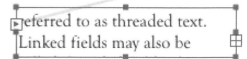

⑥ After you click the Stage with the loaded-text pointer, Flash creates a linked field. All fields in the chain activate. Text-flow direction triangles and link lines appear to indicate which fields link directly and which way the text flows. Here, the link line connects the Field 1 Out port to the Field 2 In port.

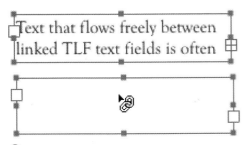

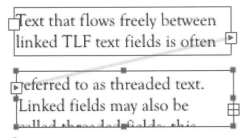

D Moving a loaded-text pointer over another TLF text field activates the end-link pointer. (The icon is a bit hard to decipher, but it's actually two links of a chain, and both are closed.)

E Clicking the end-link pointer in an unlinked TLF text field links the two fields—a link-line connects the Out port of the first field to the In port of the second field. Small triangles appear in the linked ports, indicating the direction of the text flow.

Long-Distance Linking

You can link TLF text fields on different layers. You can even link fields in different frames (somewhat like linking across a page break in a text-layout application). All linked fields must be on the same Timeline, however. You'll start working with layers in Chapter 6, and you'll learn about working with frames and the Timeline in Chapter 8.

To link text fields manually:

1. Create two area-text fields.

    To see the text flow in action, give Field 1 enough text for overflow text and leave Field 2 empty.

2. Using the selection tool, click Field 1 to activate it.

3. Click the Field 1 Out port.

4. Position the pointer over Field 2. The pointer becomes an end-link pointer 🔗 **D**.

5. Click Field 2. Flash creates a link and pours overflow text into Field 2 **E**.

TIP You don't have to link *from* the full field to the empty field. Clicking the Field 2 In port, then clicking Field 1 creates the same type of link. Text pours from Field 1 to Field 2.

TIP If your TLF text field is narrow from top to bottom, its Out port may be located on top of the resize handle on the right side of the field, which makes it hard to get the begin-link pointer instead of the resize pointer. Position the pointer at the right edge of the Out port and the arrowhead icon will appear.

To break links between text fields:

1. Create a pair of linked TLF text fields containing threaded text (Field 1 and Field 2).

2. Using the selection tool, click either of the two fields.

   Both fields activate, revealing their text-flow ports (with text-flow triangles) and a link line. The directly selected field also displays resize handles.

3. Position the pointer over the Field 2 In port. When the arrowhead icon appears, click the In port **F**.

4. Position the pointer anywhere inside the bounding box of Field 1. With the break-link pointer active, click the field **G**. Flash breaks the link between Fields 1 and 2 **H**.

> **TIP** The preceding task shows just one way to break links. You have several other options. Starting at either end of the link line, you can click the **Field 1 Out port** *or* click the **Field 2 In port**. Then, with the break-link pointer active, click the port on the other end of the link line, or click anywhere in the other field. You can also simply double-click an In port or an Out port to sever its link.

> **TIP** You can also use the text tool to activate the text fields in Step 2 of the task above. The directly selected field enters Text Edit mode; direction arrows appear in the linked text-flow ports, but there is no link line. Breaking links may be a challenge when you can't see what links to what.

Click to begin breaking link

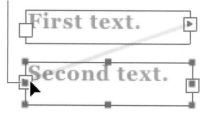

F The arrowhead pointer hovering over a port at one end of a link line indicates that you're ready to start breaking the link.

Click to finish breaking link

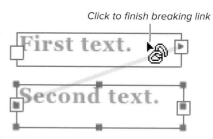

G Once you've begun the process of severing a link between TLF text fields, the break-link pointer—a broken-chain icon—appears as the pointer hovers over places where you might sever the link. The easiest way to see it is by positioning the pointer over a blank area of the text field at the opposite end of the link line from the port you clicked.

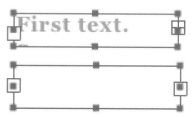

H After you break a link, the link line disappears and the text from Field 2 moves back into Field 1. The red plus sign in the Field 1 Out port indicates the presence of more text.

Images Amid Text

Flash CS6 cannot automatically flow text around images or objects, but it does streamline the process of creating text to surround objects. Create a chain of multiple linked TLF text fields and distribute them around the object. Resize the individual fields as needed to open space for the object. The threaded text inside the linked fields reflows automatically.

CS6 cannot *create* inline graphics (images embedded within a line of text), but when you import Adobe Illustrator text that contains inline graphics to a TLF text field, the inline graphics appear in Flash.

TIP When you have a chain with three or more linked TLF text fields, you can use the method described in the preceding task to sever the link between fields at any point in the chain. Upstream fields (those that come earlier in the chain than the broken link) retain their linkages, text remains threaded, and the red plus sign indicating overflow-text appears in the Out port of the last linked field. Downstream fields (those that come later in the chain than the broken link) retain their linkages but contain no text. If you enter enough text into one of these fields, you will see the threading.

TIP After you've clicked a port to start breaking a link, when you move the pointer over a blank area of the Stage, you'll see the loaded-text pointer. Clicking the Stage with this pointer adds a new linked TLF text field between the two original linked fields. (The new field duplicates the size of the field whose port you clicked to break the link.)

TIP If you delete a field in the middle of a chain of linked TLF text fields, the text in the remaining fields remains threaded.

The Many Modes of the TLF Text Tool

Choosing the text tool in the Tools panel puts you in Text Tool mode: a T icon (for text) and the words *Text Tool* appear at the top of the Property inspector, and Character and Paragraph sections appear in the body of the inspector. Clicking the text tool inside a TLF text field or using the text tool to select a chunk of TLF text puts you in Text Edit mode. In this mode, the name *Text Tool* disappears from the inspector, but the T icon and the Character and Paragraph sections remain, while two new sections appear—Advanced Character and Container and Flow. Using the selection tool to select one or more TLF text fields puts you in Text Object mode. In this mode, the Property inspector displays sections relating to properties of the text fields themselves including Position and Size, 3-D Position and View, Color Effect, Display, and Filters.

This book generally uses the name "Text (Tool) Property inspector," but will use the names "Text Tool Property inspector" and "Text Property inspector" when you need to distinguish between modes.

Setting Character Attributes

The Property inspector is the main tool for setting text attributes. This panel is context sensitive. (See the sidebar "The Many Modes of the TLF Text Tool" in this chapter.)

You can set attributes in advance so the text tool applies them automatically as you type, or you can apply attributes to existing text.

TIP For the following tasks, keep the Property inspector open (choose Window > Properties, if necessary), and expand the Character section.

To choose a font family:

1. On the Stage, select the TLF text you want to modify, and access the Character section of the Text Property inspector.

2. Click the Family pop-up menu. A menu opens, listing the font families installed on your system .

3. To view all the available font families, drag the scroll bar.

   This list doesn't autoscroll when you move the pointer to the top or bottom of the menu. As you move the pointer over a font family, its name highlights.

4. Click to select the currently highlighted font family and close the scrolling list.

   The selected font name appears in the Family field. Flash changes the selected text to the new font.

TIP Another way to select a font family is to choose Text > Font and choose the desired font family from the submenu.

TIP You can also enter a font-family name by typing it in the Family field in the Character section of the Text (Tool) Property inspector. As you type, Flash autocompletes the name from the list of installed fonts.

A Use the Family pop-up menu in the Character section of the Text (Tool) Property inspector to choose a font family. The scrolling list contains all the installed font families. The word *Sample* shows what text looks like in that font.

B The Style pop-up menu in the Character section of the Text (Tool) Property inspector lists any variants available for the currently active font (such as bold and italic).

C If the current, selected font has no bold or italic variants, the Style menu is disabled.

D Drag the Size hot-text control to change the point size of selected text interactively on the Stage.

To choose a character style:

1. Select the TLF text you want to modify, and access the Character section of the Text Property inspector.

2. From the Style pop-up menu, choose a style **B**.

   The Style menu displays the available variants of the font selected in the Family field. If the current font has no variants, the Style menu is disabled **C**.

   TIP If selected text is currently set in a font that has a boldface variant, you can toggle between the regular and bold variant by pressing Shift-Command-B (OS X) or Ctrl-Shift-B (Win). To toggle an italic variant, press Shift-Command-I (OS X) or Ctrl-Shift-I (Win). If the selected text's font lacks bold or italic variants, these commands have no effect.

To set the font size:

1. Select the TLF text you want to modify, and access the Character section of the Text Property inspector.

2. Use the Size hot-text control to enter a value between 1 and 720 points **D**.

   TIP You can also choose Text > Size to select from 13 common font sizes ranging from 8 points to 120 points.

To set leading:

1. Select the TLF text you want to modify, and access the Character section of the Text Property inspector.

2. To determine the method of measuring the space between lines, from the Leading Style pop-up menu , choose one of the following:

   ▸ To specify an exact amount of space, choose points (pt).

   ▸ To specify a percentage of the current font size, choose percent (%).

3. Use the Leading hot-text control to enter the amount of space you want between lines.

   ▸ With points as the method of measure, enter a value between 0 and 720.

   ▸ With percent as the method, enter a value between 0 and 1000.

   Leading governs the amount of vertical space between lines of text. A setting of 0 would have all lines of text sitting right on top of one another; positive values place lines farther apart.

TIP Leading is actually the space between baselines—the baseline is the imaginary line on which all the letters of a text line sit.

TIP You can apply leading to one line, many lines, or entire paragraphs. For English text, if you choose a new leading value while you have selected text in just one line, the new setting affects the space above the line containing the selected text.

TIP When a text paragraph combines characters of various point sizes, setting the paragraph's leading method to percent, and using a value greater than 100 percent, ensures that the spacing above each line accommodates the various sizes **F**.

E Choose a method for measuring leading (the space between lines of text) from the Leading Style pop-up menu. Choose points to use a precise measurement; choose percent to calculate leading as a percentage of the current font size.

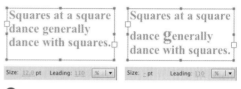

F The text on the left has a font size of 12-points and leading set to 110 percent (that is, 110 percent of 12 points). The text on the right has the same settings, except that one letter is set to 18-point. Flash increases the space above the line with the larger letter, making it 110 percent of 18 points, while the space below the line with the larger letter remains at 110 percent of 12 points.

TIP If you're not familiar with typographic conventions, you may find it easier to specify leading as a percentage—120 percent is a common leading value. A very rough rule of thumb when specifying leading in points is to make the leading 2 points bigger than the current point size of your text.

Tracking: 0

Tracking: -80

Tracking: 80

G Enter a negative tracking value to position characters (or words) closer together. Enter a positive value to space them out. Enter 0 to remove tracking.

TIP Another way to increase spacing for selected text is to choose Text > Letter Spacing > Increase, or press Option-Command–Right Arrow (OS X) or Ctrl-Alt–Right Arrow (Win). To decrease spacing, choose Text > Letter Spacing > Decrease, or use the same keyboard combination but with the Left Arrow.

TIP You can also interactively adjust the space between letters using the keyboard shortcuts described in the preceding tip. The space continues to expand or contract as long as you hold down the keys.

To adjust space between letters and/or words:

1. Select the TLF text whose spacing you want to change, and access the Character section of the Text Property inspector.

   To adjust only the space between letters, select the letters or select a single word. To adjust the space between letters and words, select an entire line, paragraph, or text field.

2. Use the Tracking hot-text control to enter a value between –1000 and 1000.

   Flash measures tracking in 1000ths of an em space. A negative value reduces the space between letters in the selection, while a positive value increases it **G**. When the selection contains multiple words, the setting also adjusts the space between words.

TIP Flash adjusts tracking by setting the space after a selected character. If you want to change tracking between a pair of letters, select just the first letter. For example, to adjust the space between the *e* and the *a* in the word *leaf*, select the *e* and set the desired tracking value. To adjust the spaces between the *e, a,* and *f,* select *e* and *a*.

TIP To reset the font's original letter spacing, choose Text > Letter Spacing > Reset, or press Option-Command–Up Arrow (OS X) or Ctrl-Alt–Up Arrow (Win).

TIP When TLF text is set to justify—so that it fills the column and the text aligns at both margins—changing the tracking between selected letters may affect spacing between other letters and words in the same line or paragraph. (You'll learn more about creating justified text in "Setting Paragraph Attributes" in this chapter.)

To set the font-rendering method:

1. Select one or more TLF text fields that you want to modify, and access the Character section of the Text Property inspector.

Font rendering applies to all the text in a thread, whether that text fits into one text field or flows through several linked fields.

2. In the Character section, from the Anti-alias pop-up menu **H**, choose one of the following:

Use Device Fonts Choose this setting when smaller file sizes are more important than re-creating the precise font outlines on the end user's system.

Readability Choose this setting for text fields that you don't plan to animate. (This is the default setting when

Anti–alias: | Readability | ▼ |

Use device fonts
✓ Readability
Animation

H To control the degree of anti-aliasing, in the Character section of the Text (Tool) Property inspector, choose an option from the Anti-alias pop-up menu.

Typography 101: Kerning

While *tracking* affects the space between characters and words in an entire chunk of selected text, *kerning* affects the space between a pair of letters. Because fonts are constructed with each letter as a separate element, some pairs of letters have odd spacing between them. The space between a capital *T* and a lowercase *o*, for example, may seem too large because of the white space below the crossbar of the *T*. To make the characters look better, you can reduce the space between them, or *kern in* the pair. Conversely, some letter pairs (such as a *t* and an *i*) may seem to be too close together. You can *kern out* the pair to make it look better.

Font designers often build in kerning information to address troublesome letter pairs. Flash takes advantage of that embedded information when you select the Auto Kern checkbox in the Character section of the Text (Tool) Property inspector. It's a good idea to turn on kerning to make your type look its best.

In addition, TLF text can take advantage of ligature information built into a typeface. Ligatures create special spacing (or special letterforms) for problem letter pairs. At some ligature settings, the pair acts more like a single character for tracking purposes, so selecting the pair and changing the tracking has no effect. You can set ligature usage in the Advanced Character section of the Text (Tool) Property inspector.

You can kern TLF text manually instead of, or in addition to, using embedded kerning. Select a character; then, to adjust the space following it, use the hot-text control to change the Tracking value. Larger values increase the space, and smaller values decrease the space.

About Anti-aliasing

Anti-aliasing is a method of *rendering*—drawing lines and curves to the screen—that smoothes edges. For text, this makes the letterforms appear slightly blurry. Anti-aliasing text at large point sizes makes it easier to read; but at smaller sizes, text may appear fuzzy and indistinct. In early versions of Flash, anti-aliased text in small font sizes was difficult to read. With Flash's current font-rendering engine, you can apply anti-aliasing to small font sizes and still have readable text, provided the text isn't animated.

publishing to Flash Player 8 and later. See Chapter 17.) The Flash Type font-rendering engine draws text with this setting on the Stage as you create your FLA file. The Flash Type engine renders this text for playback. This setting requires embedded font outlines. (See the sidebar "About Font Embedding" in this chapter.)

Animation Choose this setting for animated text fields. To help speed playback, at runtime Flash Player ignores some information about aligning and kerning. (See the sidebar "Typography 101: Kerning" in this chapter.) Flash Type doesn't do the rendering. This setting requires embedded font outlines.

TIP Although font-rendering methods apply to an entire block of threaded text, you don't actually have to select the whole thing to apply the method. If you make a selection within the threaded text, and then choose a new method for font rendering, Flash automatically applies the new style to all the threaded text in all the linked fields.

Multinational Multidirectional Text

English and Western European languages traditionally present text in horizontal lines to be read left to right. You may want to create vertical text for display, or create text in languages that don't read left to right. Because the possibilities for TLF text display are so numerous, Flash hides some of them by default. You can access these hidden options in the Text (Tool) Property inspector's panel menu. The ins and outs of dealing with text in other languages is beyond the scope of a *Visual QuickStart Guide,* but here's a brief rundown of where to find options for truly international typography:

- The Text Orientation menu is in the top section of the Text (Tool) Property inspector. The icon's arrow ▣▾ changes direction to indicate horizontal or vertical text.

- To choose a direction for horizontal text, choose Show Right-to-Left Options from the Text (Tool) Property inspector's panel menu. A new menu, Direction, appears in the Paragraph section of the inspector.

- To view text options for Asian languages, from the Text (Tool) Property inspector's panel menu, choose Show Asian Options. Additional settings and options appear in the panel when you select text on the Stage.

To apply additional properties:

1. Select the TLF text that you want to format with color, highlighting, strikethrough, underscore, or super-script/subscript positioning.

2. Access the Character section of the Text Property inspector ❶, and do any of the following:

   ▸ To set text color, click the Color control and choose a new color from the swatch set.

   ▸ To create highlighted text, click the Highlight color control and choose a new color from the swatch set.

   ▸ To create underlined text, click the Underline button.

   ▸ To create strikethrough text, click the Strikethrough button.

   ▸ To create predefined superscripts or subscripts, click the Superscript or Subscript button.

   The underscore, strikethrough, super-script, and subscript buttons are all toggles. To apply the effect to selected text, click the appropriate button. The button highlights to indicate when the effect is on. To remove an effect from selected text, click the highlighted button.

TIP Flash considers text to be a fill. When the text tool is active, or text is selected on the Stage, you can change the text color by using any of the methods described for setting fill attributes in Chapter 2.

TIP To remove highlighting from a selected TLF text field, click the Highlight color control and choose No Color from the swatch set.

❶ Color controls in the Character section of the Text (Tool) Property inspector let you change the color of the text or add a highlight color to identify selected text. Click a button to turn on (or off) underscore, strikethrough, superscript, or subscript.

About Font Embedding

Embedding makes specific fonts available in the published SWF file, so that your content looks the same, regardless of which fonts are installed on the end user's system. By default, Flash CS6 automatically embeds the specific characters that appear in any TLF text fields. For TLF text fields that will be processed with ActionScript at runtime—such as fields in which users enter contact information—you should embed a wider range of characters than what might first appear in the fields. If the look of your text is important for your Flash creations—and you aren't positive that your end user will have the necessary fonts—it's safest to embed fonts when you set TLF text's font-rendering method (anti-aliasing) to Readability or Animation.

You can choose embedding options in the Font Embedding dialog. To access the dialog, click the Embed button in the Character section of the Text (Tool) Property inspector, or choose Text > Font Embedding. (You can also work with fonts and embedding in the Library panel.)

The Options section of the Font Embedding dialog makes it easy to embed subsets of characters that users are likely to need. (Good choices for all-purpose text include Basic Latin, Latin I, and Punctuation. When you embed those subsets, you have enough characters to localize the text for most Western European languages, except Greek. You also get special characters—such as accents and umlauts—that often appear in people's names.) Embedding a font subset avoids adding the entire font, which can add significantly to file size. Embedded characters become a *font symbol,* an asset in the current document's library. (You learn about libraries in Chapter 7.) The font symbol also appears near the head of the Font/Family menus for the current document. Font-symbol names end with an asterisk (*), and they group together. All the text fields in the document that use the font symbol acquire embedding information from the symbol; you don't need to choose embed settings for each field.

The ActionScript section of the Font Embedding dialog provides settings for exporting font symbols for use with ActionScript. You must export if you plan to manipulate your text with ActionScript.

You can avoid the need for font embedding by using device fonts. Device fonts allow Flash Player to work with fonts found on the end user's system to create text during playback. Device fonts help keep your movie's file size down, but they may play havoc with the appearance of your text.

Setting Paragraph Attributes

In the Paragraph section of the Text (Tool) Property inspector, you can align and justify text as well as create margins, indents, and spacing between paragraphs. Tab rulers attached to TLF text fields govern tab stops for the text inside.

The following tasks show how to modify existing English text. To load paragraph attributes in advance, so that they apply to new text fields you create, follow the same steps, but select the Text tool in the Tools panel and deselect all text on the Stage.

For the tasks in this section, keep the Property inspector open. If necessary, choose Window > Properties, or press Command-F3 (OS X) or Ctrl-F3 (Win). Expand the Paragraph section.

To set paragraph alignment— ragged text:

1. Select the TLF paragraphs you want to modify, and access the Text Property inspector.

2. In the Align area of the Paragraph section, click one of the three alignment buttons **Ⓐ**.

   ▸ To align text at the starting edge of the column, click the first (far left) alignment button.

   ▸ To center text within the column, click the second alignment button.

   ▸ To align text at the ending edge of the column, click the third alignment button.

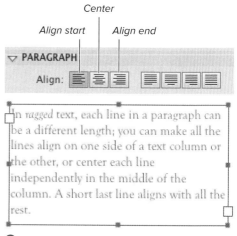

Center
Align start   Align end

Ⓐ The first set of buttons in the Align area of the Paragraph section controls alignment for paragraphs of ragged TLF text. All lines can align at the starting edge of the column (for English, the left edge), center within the column, or align at the ending edge of the column (for English, the right edge).

TIP Remember that the settings in the Paragraph section of the Text Property inspector apply at the paragraph level. When you are working with threaded text and you select a paragraph by clicking it once with the text tool, the settings you apply affect the entire paragraph, including the portions that flow to or from a linked field.

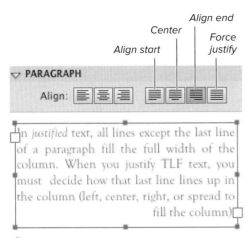

Align end
Center
Force justify
Align start

B The second set of buttons in the Align area of the Paragraph section controls alignment for the last line in a paragraph of justified TLF text. You can align the last line at the starting edge of the column, center the last line, align the last line at the ending edge of the column, or force the last line to justify (fill the column width).

To set last-line alignment— justified text:

1. Select the TLF paragraphs you want to modify, and access the Text Property inspector.

2. In the Align area of the Paragraph section, click one of the four justification buttons **B**.

   ▸ To align the last line at the starting edge of the column, click the first (far left) justification button.

   ▸ To center the last line within the column, click the second justification button.

   ▸ To align the last line at the ending edge of the column, click the third justification button.

   ▸ To justify the last line (force it to fill the full column width), click the fourth justification button (the far-right button).

TIP Flash includes two text spacing options to justify lines. In the Paragraph section of the Text (Tool) Property inspector, from the Text Justify Menu, choose Letter Spacing to adjust spacing between characters; choose Word Spacing to adjust spacing between words.

TLF Terminology: Start and End vs. Left and Right

When working with English language text, we tend to describe various paragraph attributes in terms of *left* and *right* text flow. TLF text fields, however, can manage text that reads in other directions. (See the sidebar "Multinational Multidirectional Text" earlier in this chapter.) To support this flexibility, Flash describes TLF paragraph attributes in terms of where you start and end each line of text relative to the edge of a column. That means text *aligns to start* or *aligns to end*, and a block of text has a *start margin* and an *end margin*.

To set paragraph-related spacing:

1. In the Text (Tool) Property inspector, access the Paragraph section.

2. To create space on either side of a selected paragraph (set to horizontal text), in the Margins area, uses the Start Margin and/or End Margin hot-text controls to enter a value between 0 and 720 pixels **C**.

3. To create a first-line indent, use the Indent hot-text control to enter a value between −999 and 999 pixels **D**. Flash calculates the indent from the start margin.

4. To create space between paragraphs, in the Spacing area, use the Space Before hot-text control (left) or Space After hot-text control (right) to enter a value between 0 and 999 pixels **E**.

TIP The Space Before value never applies to a paragraph in which the first line falls at the top of a column. To create space above a top-of-column paragraph, you must use the First Line Offset property in the Container and Flow section of the Text (Tool) Property inspector.

TIP Although you can apply separate values to the spacing before and after a paragraph, in fact, TLF text uses just one value—whichever is largest—for the spacing between paragraphs. If, for example, you set Space Before to 5 pixels and Space After to 10 pixels, the spacing between paragraphs will be 10 pixels, not 15.

TIP You can use Flash's Indent hot-text control to create paragraphs with hanging indents (the first line aligns farther left than the other lines), but there's a bit of a trick to it. You can't simply enter a negative Indent value; you must have a sufficiently large start margin, enough padding, or a combination of the two to encompass that "negative" first-line text. For example, to create a paragraph in English in which the first line starts 5 pixels to the left of the other lines, set Indent to −5 and set Start Margin to 5 or greater.

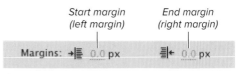

Start margin (left margin)   *End margin (right margin)*

C In the Paragraph section of the Text (Tool) Property inspector, use the hot-text controls in the Margins section to enter values for left and right margins (in horizontal English text). Flash uses those values to create margins from the left and right sides of the text field's bounding box. (The end user may not see the margins, which show up best when you add a visible border or background to the text field, or when you apply different margin settings to different paragraphs in one text field.)

Indent: 17.0 px

> "I really would advise something to go with the coffee my friend. I'm sure a nice poached egg—with maybe a fried tomato and a dash of Tabasco—would do wonders for a man in your, uh, condition, if you don't mind my saying . . ." Brett interrupted him.
> "And if I do mind you saying? You're not my nursemaid, or my valet, or even my friend—friend. So don't be so quick to 'advise' me. But come to think on it, an egg would do me fine."
> "Very good sir, right away." The waiter

D Use the Indent hot-text control to create an indent for the first line of a paragraph of TLF text.

Spacing: 5.0 px   0.0 px

E Use the Space Before (left) and/or Space After (right) hot-text controls to specify spacing between paragraphs.

TIP When a TLF text field is in Text Edit mode, you can also create a hanging indent by dragging the two triangles to the left side of the ruler. The top triangle sets the first-line indent; the bottom triangle sets the start margin.

Setting Container Attributes

You can transform a single TLF text field into a frame holding up to ten columns of text, turn the field's bounding box into a border, and fill the field with a background color. You set these properties in the Container and Flow section of the Text (Tool) Property inspector. Container and Flow properties apply to *all* of the text within the active text field, even if you selected just one word within that field.

To control text wrap:

1. Activate an area-text field containing several paragraphs of text.

   Use the selection tool to select the entire field, or use the text tool to click anywhere within the text field.

2. Access the Container and Flow section of the Text (Tool) Property inspector **A**.

Continues on next page

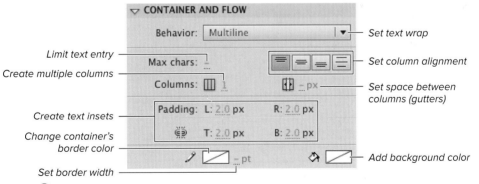

A The Container and Flow section of the Text (Tool) Property inspector lets you set the attributes of the text field itself.

3. From the Behavior menu **B**, choose one of the following:

Single Line The field displays one line of text, but you can change the field's width to show more or less text in that line. You have no option for overflow text, and the Out port of the text field does not show a red plus sign.

Multiline The field displays multiple lines of text, wrapping the text to fit within the current column width. If overflow text is present, a red plus sign appears in the Out port.

Multiline No Wrap The field appears to display multiple "lines," but it's really displaying multiple paragraphs, each of which is set to single-line.

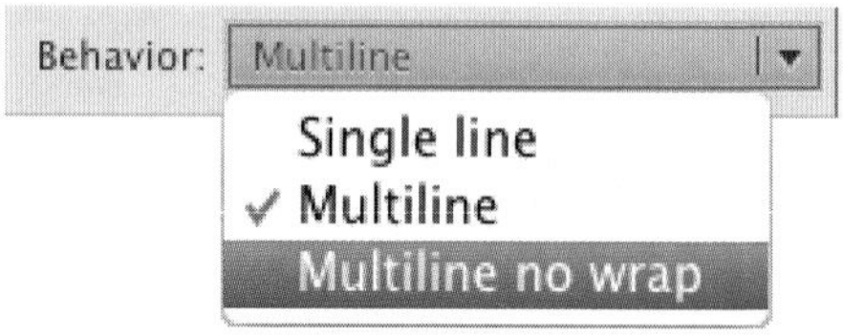

B Multiline is the only behavior that allows you to create multicolumn text. When you choose Single Line or Multiline No Wrap, Flash disables the Columns hot-text control.

TIP Only unlinked TLF text fields can have the single-line behavior. For example, if you link two fields that have Single Line as the behavior setting, Flash changes the behavior setting for both fields to Multiline No Wrap.

TIP Behavior settings apply to all the threaded text in a chain of linked TLF text fields. For example, you can't set the first field to Multiline and the second field to Multiline No Wrap.

TIP When you create a point-text field (flexible size), Flash automatically sets the behavior to Multiline No Wrap. When you create an area-text field (fixed size), Flash automatically sets the behavior to Multiline.

TIP When you have a point-text field into which you've typed multiple lines by pressing Enter, and you then change the behavior to Single Line, Flash deletes the paragraph returns and combines the text into one long line, resizing the field to display all the text. Returning the field's behavior to Multiline doesn't restore the original paragraphs.

Columns: ⊞ 1

Get a CCE calendar today. It's never too late to start saving your dates! There are still plenty of calendars available. These beautiful four-color calendars feature the work of CCE painters and descriptions of the studio and process painting. Great gifts for family and friends. Pick one up at the studio ($20 each) or request by mail ($20 plus $5 postage and handling). **Visit us at www.ccesf.org.**

Columns: ⊞ 2

Get a CCE calendar today. It's never too late to start saving your dates! There are still plenty of calendars available. These beautiful four-color calendars feature the work of CCE painters and descriptions of the studio and process painting. Great gifts for family and friends. Pick one up at the studio ($20 each) or request by mail ($20 plus $5 postage and handling). **Visit us at www.ccesf.org.**

⊙ Use the Columns hot-text control to set the number of columns that the selected TLF text field will display. A single field holds up to ten columns.

⊞ 10.0 px

Gutters that are too narrow hinder reading

Yep, that's right, Brett Malone was just a runaway, trying to pass himself off as someone he surely wasn't, but maybe thought he ought to grow into. The rumpled front of his shirt gave a clue to his partially intoxicated state. But he wasn't intoxicated with alcohol, no sir. Brett Malone was full of the heady feel of being off on his own, alone in the world as far as anyone around him knew. He was away from his aunts, and his manipulative stuffed shirt of a guardian. Who was he anyway to try to tell Brett what to do? Brett had no interest in playing the connection cards his guardian laid out for him. A hand dealt from the bottom of a greasy pack that had been parceled and shuffled to a fare thee well with scheming and planning and laying traps to snare his freedom-loving soul. Brett sat down at the linen covered table in the furthest corner of the saloon from the double front doors. A server appeared at his side with a steaming pot of coffee and a basket of rolls. "Can I interest you in an egg today, Mr. Malone?" the waiter hovered over the table rearranging the silver ware slightly, positioning the knife and fork, just so and moving the pots of butter and jam to a slightly different spot, so as to

⊞ 20

Adequate gutters aid reading

Yep, that's right, Brett Malone was just a runaway, trying to pass himself off as someone he surely wasn't, but maybe thought he ought to grow into. The rumpled front of his shirt gave a clue to his partially intoxicated state. But he wasn't intoxicated with alcohol, no sir. Brett Malone was full of the heady feel of being off on his own, alone in the world as far as anyone around him knew. He was away from his aunts, and his manipulative stuffed shirt of a guardian. Who was he anyway to try to tell Brett what to do? Brett had no interest in playing the connection cards his guardian laid out for him. A hand dealt from the bottom of a greasy pack that had been parceled and shuffled to a fare thee well with scheming and planning and laying traps to snare his freedom-loving soul. Brett sat down at the linen covered table in the furthest corner of the saloon from the double front doors. A server appeared at his side with a steaming pot of coffee and a basket of rolls. "Can I interest you in an egg today, Mr. Malone?" the waiter hovered over the table rearranging the silver ware slightly, positioning the knife and fork, just so and moving the

⊙ Use the Column Gutter hot-text control to create space between multiple columns in a single TLF text field. Be sure to balance the amount of space: too little space and the columns are hard to read; too much, and the columns start to lose the look of multiple related text columns.

To create multicolumn text fields:

1. Activate an area-text field on the Stage and access the Container and Flow section of the Text Property inspector.

2. From the Behavior menu, choose Multiline.

3. To set the number of columns, using the Columns hot-text control, enter a value between 1 and 10 **⊙**. Flash divides the text in the field into the specified number of columns.

4. To set the amount of space between columns, using the Column Gutters hot-text control **⊙**, enter a value between 0 and 200 pixels.

TIP With multicolumn TLF text, be careful when assigning paragraph alignment settings, especially for large text blocks. Using the paragraph-alignment settings for center or justify can introduce column creep into the final column of a multicolumn text field: the baselines of the last column no longer line up horizontally with the baselines of the preceding columns. This makes the text difficult to read and looks unprofessional.

To hide/show tab rulers:

Choose Text > TLF Tab Ruler, or press Shift-Command-T (OS X) or Ctrl-Shift-T (Win). Tab rulers display by default and appear along the top edge of any area-text field in Text Edit mode. (To put an existing area-text field into Text Edit mode, click the field with the text tool or double-click the field with the selection tool.) In fields with multicolumn text, the ruler matches the column width **E**. The default tab ruler has preset stops every 50 pixels.

To set additional tab stops:

1. Create a new area-text field

   or

   Activate Text Edit mode for an existing area-text field and select the text to which new tab settings should apply.

2. To add tabs, position the pointer over the tab ruler. The pointer changes to a solid arrow ▲.

3. Click the ruler at the desired location. A tab marker appears in the ruler **F**. Any selected text containing tab characters reflows.

4. Repeat Steps 2 and 3 for as many tabs as you want.

> **TIP** When no text is selected in the field, added tab stops apply only to the line of text where the I-beam cursor is currently located.

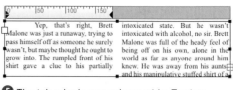

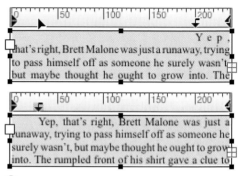

E The tab ruler is one column wide. To view the ruler for a different column, select text in the column or click with the I-beam cursor. The default preset tab stops (used here) have no visible markers.

F When the pointer changes to a solid arrow (top), click the tab ruler to add a new tab stop (bottom).

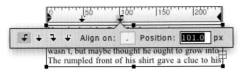

G Double-clicking a tab marker opens a menu for setting tab alignment style and location.

dog	cat	horse	10
elephant	dragon	fly	200.6
girl	boy	giraffe	0.37

H You can align columns of tab-delimited text using the four tab-alignment styles: align left, center, align right, and decimal align.

To set tab location interactively:

1. Position the pointer over a tab marker in an active tab ruler. The double-arrow pointer appears.

2. Drag the pointer along the ruler to the desired location. As you drag, any tabbed text in the field reflows to match the current tab position.

To set tab alignment style:

1. To open a menu of tab settings, double-click a tab marker G.

2. To choose tabbed text alignment for this tab, click one of the four tab-type icons:

   aligns tabbed text on the left.

   centers tabbed text.

   aligns tabbed text on the right.

   aligns tabbed text on a specified character. Use this setting to align columns of data separated by tabs— for example, a column of numbers that align on the decimal point.

3. To confirm the settings and close the menu, click away from the tab ruler.

   The selected text reflows to match the current tab settings H. Be sure to click outside the area of the tab ruler because clicking in the ruler adds another tab stop to the ruler.

> **TIP** You can set an alignment style for multiple tab stops. Shift-click to select the tab markers, then double-click one of the selected markers to access the tab-settings menu.

> **TIP** By default, clicking the style icon aligns on the period (.) character for decimal alignment. To choose another character, enter it in the **Align On** field.

To remove tabs:

Drag the tab marker down into the text area, or up above the tab ruler. You must drag quite a distance, but eventually the marker disappears from the ruler.

TIP The tab ruler displays triangular markers for setting paragraph margins and the first-line indent. These markers correspond to the Start Margin, End Margin, and Indent settings in the Paragraph section of the Text (Tool) Property inspector. Dragging a marker in the ruler changes its value in the Property inspector and vice versa. Drag the small top triangle at the left side of the tab ruler to set the paragraph's first-line indent; drag the bottom triangle to set the paragraph's start margin. Drag the large triangle at the right side of the ruler to set the paragraph's end margin.

About Advanced Character Properties

Flash CS6's Text Layout Framework supports many advanced typographic capabilities built into True Type and Type 2 (OpenType) fonts. For English text, TLF can work with ligatures, case (such as small caps), old-style numbers, lining numbers, proportional-width numbers, and tabular numbers. You set these properties in the Advanced Character section of the Text (Tool) Property inspector.

Setting advanced-character properties is just like setting character properties: select some text, and then choose specific settings from the Property inspector. However, not every font has all the Advanced Character properties, and unfortunately, the Property inspector won't tell you which properties are available. All the Advanced Character property menus appear whether or not the current font has those properties. Generally, if the font of the selected text lacks the property you choose, the selected text remains unchanged. (A notable exception is the Lower-Case to Small-Caps option in the Case menu. This command changes selected text to all caps if the font has no small-caps version.)

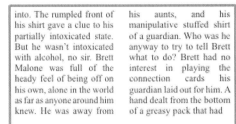

I Choosing a color with the Container Border Color control (identified by the pencil icon) creates a solid-color border around a block of TLF text.

J Choosing a color with the Container Background Color control (identified by the paint bucket icon) puts a solid-color background beneath the text in the field.

To create borders and backgrounds for text fields:

1. Activate an area-text field on the Stage and access the Container and Flow section of the Text Property inspector.

2. To give the field a visible border, do the following:

   ▸ Use the Container Border Color control (identified by a pencil icon) to choose a color. The Border Width property activates.

   ▸ Use the Border Width hot-text control to enter a value between 1 and 100 points.

   Flash creates a border for the text field, using the current Container Border Color, the specified number of points wide **I**. (The border is basically the text's bounding box made visible.)

3. To create a background color within the field, use the Container Background Color control (identified by a paint bucket icon) to choose a color. The background color fills the text field **J**.

Continues on next page

TLF Strokes and Fills: Not Like the Others

The color controls that appear in the Container and Flow section of the TLF Text (Tool) Property inspector look like Flash's regular Stroke Color and Fill Color controls, but they're different. The Container Border Color control, which has a pencil icon, lets you create solid outlines for TLF text fields. The Container Background Color control, which has a paint-bucket icon, allows you to fill a TLF text field with a solid color. Despite using the same icons, the container color controls do not link to the Stroke Color and Fill Color controls in other panels.

4. To determine how close the text can come to the border (or if no border is set, to the sides of the field's bounding box), use the hot-text controls in the Padding area to specify any of the following text insets 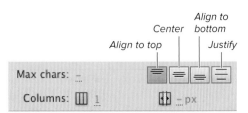:

L creates space between the left edge of the bounding box and any text. **R** creates space at the right edge. **T** creates space at the top edge. **B** creates space at the bottom edge.

You can create inset values from 0 to 200 pixels. To allow different padding values at each edge of a field, set the Constrain/Unconstrain modifier to the open-link icon ⚌.

TIP A TLF text field's borders always grow outward from the bounding box; you don't have to worry about the border covering the text inside the field.

TIP You can align text columns relative to the edges of the text-field's bounding box by clicking one of the Column Alignment buttons **L**.

Padding: L: 10.0 px   R: 35.0 px
⚌   T: 5.0 px   B: 30.0 px

into. The rumpled front of his shirt gave a clue to his partially intoxicated state. But he wasn't intoxicated with alcohol, no sir. Brett Malone was full of the heady feel of being off

on his own, alone in the world as far as anyone around him knew. He was away from his aunts, and his manipulative stuffed shirt of a guardian. Who was he anyway to try to

K Padding settings create a text inset—a buffer of space between the bounding box of the text field and the text inside. (It's easiest to see the effects of padding when the text field has a border.) When the Constrain/Unconstrain modifier is set to the open-link icon, you can use different padding values for each side of the text.

Align to top   Center   Align to bottom   Justify

Max chars: –

Columns: 1   – px

L The column-alignment buttons in the Container and Flow section of the Text (Tool) Property inspector govern how a block of text fits into its bounding box. The text's position is most noticeable when the text field has a border. **Align to Top** places the first line in each column as close as possible to top edge of the bounding box. **Center** centers each column vertically in the bounding box. **Align to Bottom** places the last line in each column as close as possible to the bottom edge of the bounding box. **Justify** adds space between the lines of text so that each column fills the available vertical space.

Modifying Simple Graphics

One way to modify graphics in Adobe Flash Professional CS6 is to select one or more shapes and edit their attributes (such as color, size, and location) in the Property inspector or in other appropriate panels.

You can also modify the path that creates the shape of an element. When you perform some operations—such as straightening lines, adjusting Bézier curves, and assigning new attributes—the element must be selected. When you perform others, such as reshaping a line segment or curve with the selection tool, the element must be deselected. A few operations let you edit the element whether it's selected or not, such as changing the fill color using the paint bucket tool.

In this chapter, you'll use the selection, lasso, and subselection tools to select and modify the elements you learned to make in Chapter 2. You'll modify elements' attributes using the Property inspector and other panels.

In This Chapter

Setting Selection Preferences

You have two basic ways to make a selection in Flash: click an element directly, or enclose all or part of an element with a selection outline. You can set preferences to gain more control over these methods.

To set selection methods:

1. From the Flash menu (OS X) or the Edit menu (Win), choose Preferences.

2. From the Category list, choose General .

3. In the Selection section, select one of the following checkboxes:

   Shift Select With Shift Select active (Flash's default setting), you must Shift-click with the selection or subselection tool to add items to a selection. With Shift Select inactive, you need only click additional items to add them to the current selection.

   Contact-Sensitive Selection and Lasso Tools With Contact-Sensitive Selection active (the default), Flash selects an entire element when a selection outline merely touches the element—such as a graphic-object or text field, a grouped shape, or a symbol instance. With Contact-Sensitive Selection inactive, the selection outline must fully enclose an item to select it. (Whether contact sensitivity is on or off, a selection outline always selects just the enclosed portion of a merge-shape.)

4. Click OK.

Ⓐ Choose General in the Category list of the Preferences dialog to choose a selection method.

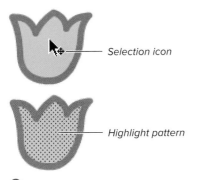

Selection icon

Highlight pattern

A When the pointer sits above a filled area, the icon changes into the selection arrow (a cross icon appears next to the regular pointer arrow, indicating that the tool is ready to move or select an item). Click a fill to select it. A dot pattern in a contrasting color highlights the selected fill.

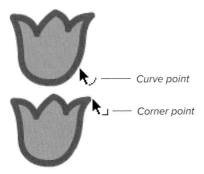

Curve point

Corner point

B As you prepare to select a line, additions to the pointer icon indicate the type of point located beneath the pointer.

Selected curve segment

Selection pointer in selection mode

C When you click a merge-shape line, Flash selects and highlights just one segment.

Making Selections

Merge-shapes, drawing-objects, and primitives all behave slightly differently as you select them because what you see as a single shape may contain several segments. An outline rectangle created as a merge-shape consists of four separate line segments. Clicking one side of the object selects just that segment of the outline. In an outline rectangle created as a drawing-object or primitive the segments are fused into a unit, so clicking any side of the object selects the entire outline.

To make selections by clicking:

1. In the Tools panel, select the selection tool, or press V.

2. To select elements created as merge-shapes, do one of the following:

   ▸ To select a merge-shape fill, position the pointer over the fill and click. The selection icon appears next to the pointer arrow when the pointer is over the fill. Flash highlights the selected fill with a dot pattern **A**.

   ▸ To select a merge-shape stroke, position the pointer over a line segment and click. Flash appends a little arc or a little right-angle icon to the selection tool **B**. These icons indicate that the tool is over a point in a line segment and show whether it is a curve point or a corner point. (For more information about points, see the sidebar "About Curve and Corner Points" in this chapter). Flash uses a dot pattern to highlight just the segment you clicked **C**.

Continues on next page

3. To select elements created as drawing-objects, position the pointer over any portion of the shape and click.

The arc or angle icon appears next to the selection pointer for merge-shape fills and strokes. Flash selects the entire shape and highlights it by displaying a bounding box that encloses the shape **D**.

4. To select elements created as primitives, position the pointer over any portion of the shape and click.

The selection icon appears next to the selection pointer whether it's over a fill or a stroke. Flash selects the entire shape and highlights its bounding box **E**.

5. To add elements to a selection, do one of the following:

▸ When Shift Select (Flash's default selection style) is active, Shift-click each item you want to add **F**.

▸ When Shift Select is inactive, click each item you want to include.

TIP To temporarily switch to the selection tool while using another tool, press Command (OS X) or Ctrl (Win). The selection tool remains in effect as long as you hold down the modifier key.

TIP The bounding box for a round or irregular drawing-object or primitive-shape is easy to see because the box sits outside the shape like a frame. The bounding box for a rectangle-primitive has control points that make it more visible, but the bounding box for a drawing-object rectangle sits on the edge of the rectangle. Therefore, depending on the color of your drawing-object rectangle, the highlighted bounding box can be difficult to see. When you have trouble seeing the highlight on selected drawing-object rectangles, choose a contrasting highlight color in the General category of the Preferences dialog.

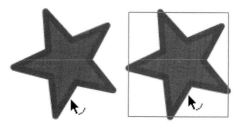

D When you position the selection tool over an unselected drawing-object (left), the pointer displays the same icons as for merge-shapes (move/select cross for fills, curve-point arc or corner-point angle for strokes). When you click anywhere on the drawing-object, Flash selects the entire drawing-object and highlights its bounding box (right).

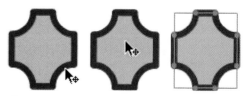

E Whether you position the selection pointer over the stroke (left) or fill (middle) of a primitive-shape, the cross icon appears in the pointer. Clicking anywhere on the shape selects the entire shape (right).

First selection   *First addition*   *Second addition*

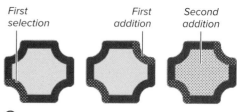

F With Flash's default Preferences setting for selections, Shift-click unhighlighted line segments or fill areas to add them to a selection.

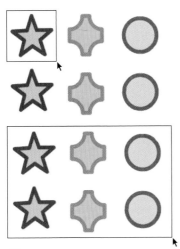

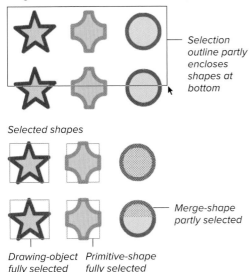

G Dragging with the selection tool creates a selection rectangle (top). Be sure to start from a point that allows you to enclose all the elements you want to select (bottom). When you release the mouse button, Flash selects those elements.

Drag contact-sensitive selection rectangle

— *Selection outline partly encloses shapes at bottom*

Selected shapes

— *Merge-shape partly selected*

Drawing-object   *Primitive-shape*
fully selected   *fully selected*

H In Flash's contact-sensitive selection style (the default), any drawing-objects or primitives that are touched or partially enclosed by the selection rectangle are fully selected; but only the parts of merge-shapes that fall within the selection rectangle are selected. (Here the star shapes are drawing-objects, the indented rectangles are primitives, and the circles are merge-shapes.)

To use a contact-sensitive selection rectangle:

1. Make sure the selection preferences are set for contact sensitivity.

2. In the Tools panel, select the selection tool.

3. On the Stage, use the tool to draw a rectangle that touches (or encloses) the objects you want to select **G**. This rectangle isn't a graphic element; it just defines the boundaries of your selection.

4. Continue dragging until the rectangle encloses all the merge-shapes you want to select and at least some part of each drawing-object.

5. Release the mouse button. Flash selects the shapes in the following ways:

   Merge-shapes Flash highlights any portions of fill or stroke that fall inside the selection rectangle; portions of merge-shape fills or strokes that lie outside the rectangle remain unselected **H**.

   Drawing-objects and primitive-shapes If the selection rectangle touches any part of a drawing-object or primitive, Flash selects the entire thing, highlighting its bounding box.

To use a non-contact-sensitive selection rectangle:

1. Make sure contact sensitivity is deselected.

2. Follow Steps 2–5 in the preceding exercise; but this time, fully enclose the merge-shapes and drawing-objects you want to select. Flash selects the shapes in the following ways:

   Merge-shapes Flash highlights any portions of fill or stroke that fall inside the selection rectangle; portions of merge-shape fills or strokes that lie outside the rectangle remain unselected ❶.

   Drawing-objects and primitive-shapes Flash selects only those drawing-objects or primitives that are completely enclosed within the selection rectangle. If the selection rectangle touches or includes just a part of a drawing-object or primitive, Flash leaves the entire object deselected.

   TIP To create an irregular selection outline, in the Tools panel, select the lasso tool 𝒫, or press L. Then draw a free-form line around the elements you want to select ❶. Keep drawing until the lasso pointer is back over your starting point, and then release the mouse button. Flash closes the selection outline and highlights everything inside the lasso shape.

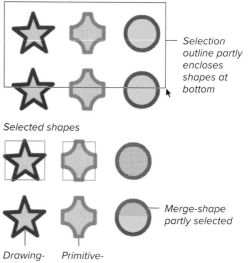

Drag non-contact-sensitive selection rectangle

— Selection outline partly encloses shapes at bottom

Selected shapes

— Merge-shape partly selected

Drawing-object not selected   Primitive-shape not selected

❶ When contact-sensitivity is not active, a selection includes only the parts of merge-shapes that fall within the selection rectangle. To select drawing-objects or primitives, you must enclose them fully in the selection rectangle. (Here the star shapes are drawing-objects, the indented rectangles are primitives, and the circles are merge-shapes.)

❶ The lasso tool lets you select elements that are oddly shaped or too near other elements to allow use of the selection rectangle. Any merge-shapes inside the selection outline are highlighted and selected when you release the mouse button. Whether or not you must fully enclose drawing-objects and primitives in a lasso selection outline to select them depends on the contact-sensitivity setting in the Preferences dialog.

K In Polygon mode, the lasso tool creates a series of connected line segments to outline the element you want to select. To finish the lasso shape, double-click. Flash draws a line from the double-click location to the starting point. (Note that you must double-click, even when you position the pointer over your starting point.)

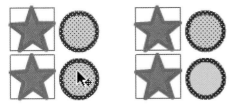

L Position the selection-tool pointer over the element you want to remove from the selection (left). Shift-click the item to deselect it (right). (In this image, the stars are drawing-objects, and the circles are merge-shapes.)

Double-Click to Select

Double-clicking any segment in a series of connected merge-shape strokes selects all the segments. Double-clicking the fill of a merge-shape that has a fill and a stroke selects both the fill and the stroke.

TIP The lasso tool's Polygon mode lets you define a selection area with a series of connected straight-line segments. With the lasso tool selected, click the Polygon Mode button in the Options section of the Tools panel. Now you can click your way around the elements you want to select **K**. Double-click to end the selection outline.

To deselect individual items:

1. In the Tools panel, select the selection tool, or press V.

2. Hold down the Shift key.

3. Click any highlighted drawing-objects, primitives, or merge-shape strokes or fills you want to remove from the current selection.

   Flash deselects the items you clicked **L**. No matter which selection method is active, you must Shift-click with the selection tool to remove items from a selection.

TIP To deselect everything, choose Edit > Deselect All, or press Shift-Command-A (OS X) or Ctrl-Shift-A (Win).

TIP To deselect all elements quickly, click the selection tool in an empty area of the Stage or Pasteboard.

How Flash Tracks Elements

To track an element's size and position on the Stage, Flash encloses each element in a *bounding box*—an invisible rectangle just big enough to hold the element. Flash then treats the Stage as a giant graph, with the top-left corner of the Stage as the center of the *x*- and *y*-axis 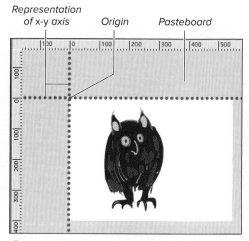. The graph uses the units of measure currently set in the Document Settings dialog. (To learn more about document properties, see Chapter 1.)

The Property inspector and the Info panel display the size of the element (the width and height of the bounding box) and the position of the element (the *x*- and *y*-coordinates for one important point in the element).

To change an element's size, you can enter new values for Height and Width in the Position and Size section of the Property inspector or in the Info panel. By entering new *x*- and *y*-coordinates in those panels, you can also change an element's position on the Stage.

Ⓜ The dotted line here represents the *x-y* axis of the Stage. The origin point—the 0 point both horizontally and vertically—is at the top-left corner of the Stage.

Depending on which panel you use to enter values, you can use either of two points to position an element: the *registration point* or the *transformation point*. For merge-shapes, drawing-objects, and primitives, the registration point is always located at the top-left corner of the bounding box. For symbols, you determine the location of registration point. For all types of objects, Flash initially places the transformation point at the center of the bounding box, but you can reposition it using the free-transform tool. You can position the transformation point differently for individual symbol instances (see Chapter 7).

The Property inspector always tracks elements by the registration point. The Info panel lets you track elements by either point. Choose which point is tracked by clicking the Registration/Transformation Point model to toggle between the two tracking styles. When a crosshair appears in the top-left corner of the model, the Info panel positions and sizes elements using the registration point. When a circle appears in the bottom-right corner of the model, the Info panel positions and sizes elements using the transformation point.

When you use ActionScript to dynamically move symbol instances at runtime, Flash always positions them using the registration point.

When you change the dimensions of the Stage, Flash can scale existing content to match the new Stage size. In the General section of the Preferences dialog, you'll find the Scale Content option Align Top Left. With that option selected, Flash relocates your content, approximating its original location on the Stage. One way to visualize this is to think of grouping the original Stage and its contents in a giant rectangle (with its top-left corner at the center of the *x*- and *y*-axis), selecting it with the free-transform tool, and dragging the bottom-right corner of the group's bounding box. The entire group—Stage and graphic elements—scales together.

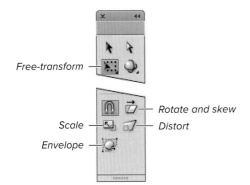

Free-transform

Rotate and skew

Scale

Distort

Envelope

(A) The free-transform tool lets you select and transform elements interactively. The tool's modifiers (in the Options section of the Tools panel) govern the types of changes you can make to a selected object. With no modifiers selected, you can scale, rotate, and skew; the pointer changes to an appropriate icon as it interacts with different areas of a selected object on the Stage.

Original

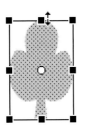

Drag top or bottom handle to change height

Drag left or right handle to change width

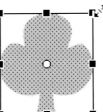

Drag corner to scale proportionally

(B) In Scale mode, the free-transform tool can only resize a selected object. Choosing Scale mode prevents you from accidentally rotating or skewing a selected object when dragging a transformation handle.

Resizing Graphic Elements

Flash gives you several ways to resize, or *scale,* selected graphic elements. You can interactively scale one or more selected items on the Stage. You can also set specific scale percentages or dimensions for a selected item in the Transform panel, the Position and Size section of the Property inspector, and the Info panel.

To resize a graphic element interactively:

1. In the Tools panel, from the transform-tools submenu, select the free-transform tool, or press Q **(A)**.

2. Select a graphic element on the Stage. The element highlights, and transformation handles appear at the sides and corners of the element's bounding box.

3. In the Tools panel, select the Scale modifier ⌐.

4. Position the pointer over a handle. The pointer changes to a double-headed arrow ↔.

5. To resize the element, do one of the following:

   ▸ To change the element's width and/ or height, drag a side handle, top handle, and/or bottom handle.

   ▸ To scale the element proportionally, drag a corner handle.

Dragging toward the center of the element reduces it, while dragging away enlarges it **(B)**.

To resize an element via the Transform panel:

1. With the Transform panel open, select an element on the Stage.

    Scale Width and Scale Height percentages appear in hot-text controls in the top section of the Transform panel. When you select an element that hasn't been resized, width and height are set to 100 percent.

2. To resize the element without changing its aspect ratio (the proportion of width to height), do the following:

    ▸ In the top section of the Transform panel, set the Constrain/Unconstrain modifier to Constrain mode ⊜. Clicking the icon toggles between Constrain and Unconstrain modes.

    ▸ Use the Scale Width or Scale Height hot-text control to enter a new percentage **C**.

    In Constrain mode, changing the Scale Width percentage also changes the Scale Height percentage (and vice versa).

    or

    To resize the element and allow the aspect ratio to change, do the following:

    ▸ Set the Constrain/Unconstrain modifier to Unconstrain mode ⊜.

    ▸ Use the Scale Width and/or Scale Height hot-text controls to enter new percentages.

    In Unconstrain mode, you can enter different values for Scale Width and Scale Height.

Constrain mode (preserve aspect ratio)

Unconstrain mode

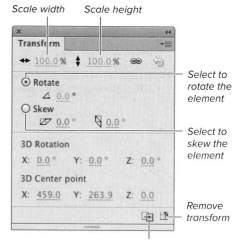

C To resize a selected element, use the Transform panel's Scale Width and Scale Height hot-text controls to enter new percentages. In Constrain mode (top), when you change the percentage of one dimension, Flash automatically updates the other. The Transform panel also lets you enter values for rotating and skewing selected elements.

Scale from the Center

In its default scaling mode, the free-transform tool scales a selected graphic element relative to the handle opposite the handle you're dragging. To scale relative to the center of a selection, Option-drag (OS X) or Alt-drag (Win). For symbols (see Chapter 7), the tool functions in the reverse: the default mode scales the symbol from its transformation point (the center by default), and holding down the Option key (OS X) or Alt key (Win) while dragging lets you scale from the opposite handle.

Properties

Drawing object

POSITION AND SIZE

X: 270.50   Y: 26.15

W: 67.65   H: 67.65

D When you select a drawing-object (top), the Position and Size section of the Property inspector displays the dimensions of that element's bounding box (bottom). To resize the element, use the Width and/or Height hot-text controls to enter new values. In Constrain mode ⊜, Flash preserves the ratio of width to height. In Unconstrain mode ⊞, you can enter independent width and height values.

To resize an element using the Property inspector:

1. With the Property inspector open, select an element on the Stage.

    The Position and Size section of the Property inspector contains Width and Height hot-text controls displaying the dimensions of the selected shape's bounding box.

2. To resize the element, do one of the following:

    ▸ To preserve the aspect ratio, set the Constrain/Unconstrain modifier to Constrain mode ⊜. Use the Width or Height hot-text control to enter a new value **D**. Changing the value for one dimension automatically changes the other.

    ▸ To allow the aspect ratio to change, set the Constrain/Unconstrain modifier to Unconstrain mode ⊞; use the Width and/or Height hot-text controls to enter new values.

TIP By default, a shape's transformation point lies at the center of its bounding box; a hollow circle represents the point. To change the transformation point, select the shape, then use the free-transform tool to drag the hollow circle to a new location.

Positioning Graphic Elements

You can position elements visually by dragging them around the Stage using the selection tool. You can also position a selected item numerically by entering its *x*- and *y*-coordinates in the Property inspector or the Info panel.

To position elements numerically:

1. Select an element on the Stage and open the Property inspector and Info panel.

   The Property inspector's Position and Size section displays coordinates for the element's registration point **A**. The Info panel can display coordinates for the element's registration point or transformation point **B**. (See the sidebar "How Flash Tracks Elements" in this chapter.)

2. To set the element's horizontal position, use the X hot-text control to enter a new *x*-coordinate in either panel.

3. To set the element's vertical position, use the Y hot-text control to enter a new *y*-coordinate in either panel.

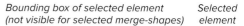

Bounding box of selected element *(not visible for selected merge-shapes)*   Selected element

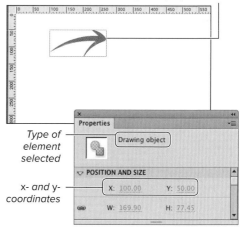

Type of element selected

x- and *y*-coordinates

A The Position and Size section of the Property inspector displays the *x*- and *y*-coordinates of the element's registration point. This drawing-object's registration point (its upper-left corner) is 100 pixels to the right along the horizontal axis and 50 pixels down the vertical axis.

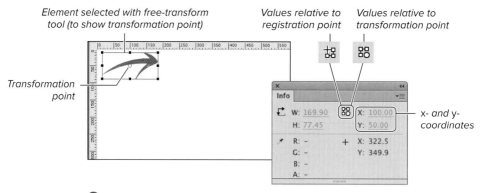

Element selected with free-transform tool (to show transformation point)

Values relative to registration point

Values relative to transformation point

Transformation point

x- and *y*-coordinates

B The Info panel lets you position a selected element by its registration point or transformation point. Click the Registration/Transformation Point model to toggle between modes.

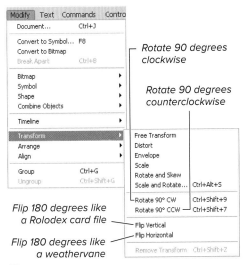

Rotate 90 degrees clockwise

Rotate 90 degrees counterclockwise

Flip 180 degrees like a Rolodex card file

Flip 180 degrees like a weathervane

A The Modify > Transform submenu includes commands for flipping graphic elements vertically and horizontally. It also has commands for rotating an element in 90-degree increments, clockwise and counterclockwise.

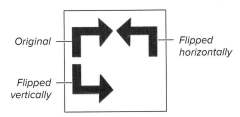

Original

Flipped horizontally

Flipped vertically

B These are the results of flipping an element by using the Flip commands in the Modify > Transform submenu.

Flipping, Rotating, and Skewing

Flash lets you flip, rotate, and skew selected elements. You can either manipulate elements freely with the free-transform tool's Rotate and Skew modifier or use a variety of commands to do the job with more precision.

To flip a graphic element:

1. Select the element you want to flip.

2. Choose Modify > Transform.

3. From the submenu **A**, do one of the following:

   ▸ To reorient the element so that it spins 180 degrees around its horizontal central axis (like a Rolodex card file), choose Flip Vertical.

   ▸ To reorient the element so that it spins 180 degrees around its vertical central axis (like a weathervane), choose Flip Horizontal.

   The accompanying figure **B** shows the results of the two types of flipping.

TIP You can rotate an element in 90-degree increments using menu commands. Select the element you want to rotate, then choose Modify > Transform to choose commands for rotating the item clockwise (Rotate 90° CW) or counterclockwise (Rotate 90° CCW).

To rotate an element by a user-specified amount:

1. Select the element and access the Transform panel **C**. If the panel isn't open, choose Window > Transform.

2. Select the Rotate radio button.

3. To specify the direction and amount of rotation, do one of the following:

   ▸ To rotate the element counterclockwise, use the Rotate hot-text control to enter a negative value (–0.1 to –360).

   ▸ To rotate the element clockwise, use the Rotate hot-text control to enter a positive value (0.1 to 360).

TIP When you work with drawing-objects and primitive-shapes, you can undo changes in width, height, rotation, and skewing at any time, even after you've deselected the item and made changes to other items. To restore the original Width, Height, Rotate, and Skew settings, select the item and click the Remove Transform button ⊞ in the lower-right corner of the Transform panel.

TIP When you work with merge-shapes, the Reset and Remove Transform buttons work only as long as the shape remains selected.

To skew an element by a user-specified amount:

1. Select the element you want to skew and access the Transform panel.

2. Select the Skew radio button.

3. Use the Skew Horizontal and Skew Vertical hot-text controls to enter the desired skew values **D**.

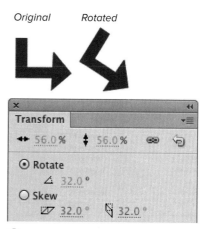

Original   *Rotated*

C You can use the Transform panel to rotate graphic elements in precise increments. Select the Rotate radio button and use the hot-text control to enter a value for the degrees of rotation. Positive values rotate the element clockwise; negative values rotate it counterclockwise.

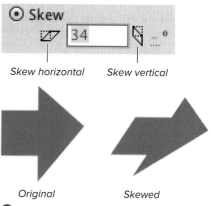

Original   *Skewed*

D Use the Transform panel to skew selected elements. You can set separate values for horizontal and vertical skewing.

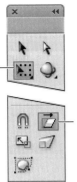

Free-transform tool

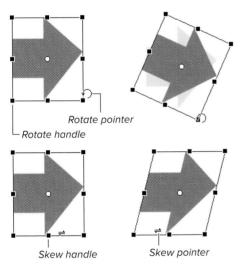

E Select the free-transform tool's Rotate and Skew modifier to access handles for rotating or skewing a selected element interactively.

Rotate and Skew modifier

Rotate pointer

Rotate handle

Skew handle

Skew pointer

F With the free-transform tool's Rotate and Skew modifier selected, you can drag one of the corner handles of a selected element's transform box to rotate that element (top), or drag one of the side handles to skew the element (bottom).

To rotate or skew an element interactively:

1. Select an element to rotate or skew.

2. In the Tools panel, select the free-transform tool. Then select the Rotate and Skew modifier **E**.

   A transform box (similar to the element's bounding box but with square handles) encloses the element.

3. To modify the selected element, do one or both of the following:

   ▸ To rotate the element, position the pointer over one of the corner handles. The pointer changes to a circular arrow. Drag to rotate the element around its transformation point **F**.

   ▸ To skew the element, position the pointer over one of the side handles of the transform box. The pointer changes to a two-way arrowhead. Drag the side handle to skew the element.

4. Release the mouse button.

TIP To rotate an element around one of its corners instead of its transformation point, Option-drag (OS X) or Alt-drag (Win).

TIP To constrain rotation by 45-degree increments, hold down the Shift key while dragging.

TIP Use the free-transform tool's Distort modifier ▱ to change the shape of the transform box by individually dragging each corner handle **G**. The Distort modifier works only on merge-shapes and single, selected drawing-objects; Distort doesn't work on primitive-shapes, text fields, groups, symbols, or selections with multiple drawing-objects.

TIP The free-transform tool's Envelope modifier ▱ turns each handle of the transform box into a Bézier-style anchor point with handles for adjusting curves. You can edit the shape the of the bounding box as you would a Bézier path **H**.

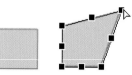

G The free-transform tool's Distort modifier lets you move individual transform handles to modify shapes.

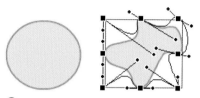

H The free-transform tool's Envelope modifier displays a set of Bézier-like handles for modifying a shape. By changing the path of the bounding box you change the shape(s) inside it.

Adding Perspective

As beginning art students discover, it's not difficult to add depth to two-dimensional objects made up of rectangular shapes. You adjust the appropriate edges to align with imaginary parallel lines that converge at a distant point on the horizon—the *vanishing point*. Doing so creates the illusion that the objects recede into the distance. The free-transform tool's Distort modifier ▱ can help you create the same illusion for nonrectangular shapes because it encloses your selected shape— circle, oval, or squiggle—within a rectangular transform box. You can drag each handle of the box so that the sides of the box angle inward like converging perspective lines. The shapes within adjust accordingly.

Flash CS6 also provides more sophisticated tools for putting two-dimensional objects into three-dimensional space. The 3D-rotation and 3D-translation tools work only on movie-clip symbols (which you'll learn to create in Chapter 7). With Flash's 3D tools you can rotate and position movie clips not only along the *x*-axis and *y*-axis (for horizontal and vertical positions, respectively) but also along the *z*-axis (for depth), redrawing the object to make it appear to recede into space. (Using 3D tools to create artwork that simulates three-dimensional environments is a complex technique and is beyond the scope of this book.)

After you learn to create symbols, try applying the 3D tools to a movie-clip symbol containing a simple shape, such as a square. Experimenting at this basic level gives you a feel for how the tools distort the movie clip's "plane" to create the 3D illusion.

Note that the 3D-rotation and 3D-translation tools available in the authoring environment do not create objects that take advantage of the new Stage 3D architecture in Flash Player 11.

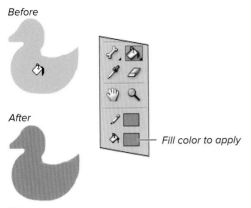

Before

After

Fill color to apply

Ⓐ Click a fill with the paint bucket tool to apply the color currently selected in the Fill Color control. Use this technique to change existing fills.

Modifying Fills and Strokes

Flash provides two methods for modifying existing fills and strokes: you can apply new attributes with a tool (the paint bucket tool for fills, the ink bottle tool for strokes), or you can select the fill or stroke on the Stage and choose new attributes in an appropriate panel. For fills or strokes that contain a gradient, you can also modify the way the gradient fits in the shape by using the gradient-transform tool.

To change fill color with the paint bucket tool:

1. In the Tools panel, click the active edit-fill/stroke tool, and select the paint bucket tool from the submenu, or press K.

2. Select new fill attributes (see Chapter 2).

3. Click the paint bucket's hot spot (the tip of the drip of paint) somewhere inside the fill you want to change. The fill can be selected or deselected. The fill changes to the new color Ⓐ.

To change stroke color with the ink bottle tool:

1. In the Tools panel, click the active edit-fill/stroke tool, and select the ink bottle tool, or press S.

2. Select new stroke attributes (see Chapter 2).

3. Click the ink bottle's hot spot in one of the following ways:

   ▸ Click directly on the stroke.

   ▸ If a shape has a stroke and a fill, and both are deselected, click the fill.

   ▸ If a shape has a stroke and a fill, and both are selected, click the fill.

   ▸ If a shape has a stroke and a fill, and only the fill is selected, click the stroke.

   The stroke takes on its new attributes **B**.

TIP To save time, you can copy the fill and stroke attributes of one element and apply them to another element. In the Tools panel, select the eyedropper tool, or press I. To copy a fill color or gradient, click the fill. To copy all attributes of a stroke, click the stroke. Flash automatically switches tools—the paint bucket appears for fills, the ink bottle for strokes. The attributes of the clicked item appear in all related panels. When you click a fill, for example, the fill type and fill color appear in the Tools panel, the Color panel, and the Property inspector. You can then use the loaded paint bucket or ink bottle tool to apply the attributes to another graphic element.

TIP To pick up the color of a stroke or fill and apply it to both strokes and fills, Shift-click with the eyedropper tool. Flash loads the selected color into the Fill Color and Stroke Color controls in the Tools panel, the Color panel, and the Property inspector.

For merge-shapes, drawing-objects, primitives

With nothing selected, click stroke or fill

With fill and stroke selected, click stroke or fill

For merge-shapes only

With only fill selected, click stroke

B You needn't select a stroke to change its attributes. Just click the stroke or the unselected fill with the ink bottle. Warning: If the fill is selected, you must click the stroke itself; you can't click the selected fill to change an unselected stroke.

Use Panels to Change Selected Fills and Strokes

You can choose new colors for the fills and strokes of selected graphic elements from any appropriate panel—Color, Swatches, or Tools—or the Property inspector. When you choose a new color from the Swatches panel, Flash uses the Color panel to determine whether that color applies to fills or strokes. When the Fill Color control is selected in the Color panel, Flash applies the swatch color to selected fills. When the Stroke Color control is selected, Flash applies the color to strokes.

When a selected merge-shape has a stroke or fill set to No Color, however, you can change that setting only by adding a fill or stroke with the paint bucket or ink bottle tool (see Chapter 2).

When your selected shape is a drawing-object or a primitive-shape, changing the fill or stroke attributes in the Color panel, Tools panel, or Property inspector adds the missing element **C**.

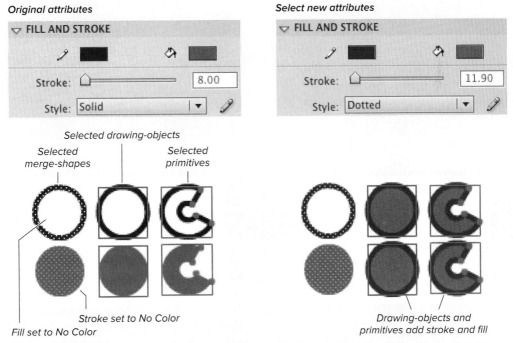

C When you use panel settings to change the attributes of a drawing-object or primitive-shape with a fill or stroke that was originally set to No Color, Flash adds the missing element, whereas doing the same for a selected merge-shape has no effect.

To modify gradient fills on the Stage:

1. On the Stage, select a graphic element that has a gradient fill.

2. In the Tools panel, from the transform-tools submenu, select the gradient-transform tool ⬛, or press F.

   Handles for manipulating the gradient appear around the selected fill **D**. Move the pointer over the fill and the gradient-transform icon ↖ appears.

3. To relocate a linear or radial gradient's center within a graphic element, do the following:

   ▸ Position the pointer over the center-point handle ⬜. The move pointer appears ✛.

   ▸ Drag the center-point handle to the new location **E**.

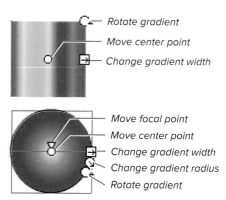

Rotate gradient
Move center point
Change gradient width

Move focal point
Move center point
Change gradient width
Change gradient radius
Rotate gradient

D Handles for transforming gradients appear around a selected item when you select the gradient transform tool. You can also select a gradient and activate its handles by clicking the item directly with the gradient-transform tool.

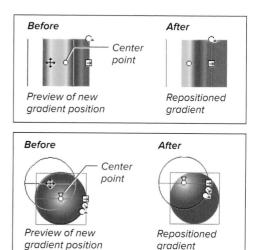

Before — Center point — After
Preview of new gradient position — Repositioned gradient

Before — Center point — After
Preview of new gradient position — Repositioned gradient

E Drag the center-point handle to reposition the center of the gradient within your shape.

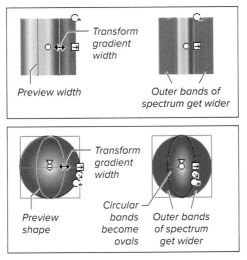

Transform gradient width

Preview width

Outer bands of spectrum get wider

Transform gradient width

Preview shape

Circular bands become ovals

Outer bands of spectrum get wider

F Using the gradient-transform tool to drag a selected gradient's handle inward creates a narrower area for displaying the gradient spectrum.

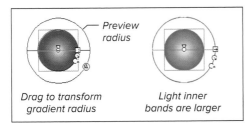

Preview radius

Drag to transform gradient radius

Light inner bands are larger

G With a radial gradient selected, drag the first round handle outward to create a larger radius.

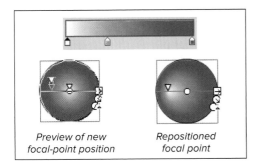

Preview of new focal-point position

Repositioned focal point

H This gradient blends from white (the leftmost gradient pointer) to purple, to blue. This order puts white at the center of a radial gradient, giving the illusion of highlighting on a three-dimensional object. Move the focal point to mimic changes in the way light hits the object.

4. To change the width of a linear or radial gradient, drag the square handle ⊟.

The pointer changes to a double-headed arrow. Drag toward the center point to compress the color transition; drag away from the center point to expand the transition **F**.

5. To change the overall size of a radial gradient, drag the radius handle ⊙ **G**.

The pointer icon changes to match the handle ⊙. Drag toward the center to shrink the gradient; drag away from the center to expand the gradient.

6. To change a radial gradient's focal point (the gradient's central color), do the following:

▸ Position the pointer over the focal-point handle ⊟. The pointer changes to match the handle ▽.

▸ Drag the focal-point handle to the desired location **H**.

TIP You can also use these techniques to modify a gradient stroke. Select the stroke, then select the gradient-transform tool to activate the transformation handles. (Alternatively, select the gradient-transform tool, and then click the stroke.)

TIP By default Flash spreads the full color spectrum of a locked gradient fill over the Pasteboard and the Stage. As a result, in some Stage views, a locked fill's gradient-transform handles may be completely out of view. If you click a gradient with the gradient-transform tool and nothing seems to happen, make sure you can see all sides of the Pasteboard. (Choose View > Pasteboard, if necessary.) Then choose a new magnification level. You may need to view the Stage at 50%—or even 25%—to see all the gradient-transform handles for a selected gradient.

To rotate a gradient fill:

1. With the gradient-transform tool selected in the Tools panel, click the fill or stroke containing the gradient you want to modify.

2. To change the gradient's orientation within the fill or stroke, drag the rotate handle ◐ ◐.

   The pointer changes to a circular arrow ◔. You can rotate the gradient clockwise or counterclockwise.

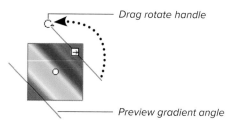

Drag rotate handle

Preview gradient angle

I As you drag the gradient's rotate handle with the gradient-transform tool, you spin the gradient around its center point.

TIP When you use the paint bucket tool to fill a shape, dragging within the shape (instead of simply clicking) rotates a gradient. To constrain the gradient angle to vertical, horizontal, or 45-degree angles, hold down the Shift key as you drag.

TIP Although you can rotate a radial gradient, it won't have much visible effect unless you have already changed the gradient's center point, width, or focal point.

To control gradient overflow:

1. Follow the steps in the preceding task to create a gradient that is narrower than the shape it sits in.

2. In the Color panel, in the Flow section **J**, do one of the following:

   ▸ To extend the colors in the leftmost and rightmost gradient pointers, select Extend Color (the button on the left).

   ▸ To repeat the gradient, but with the colors in reverse order, select Reflect Color (the center button).

   ▸ To repeat the gradient with colors in the original order, select Repeat Color (the button on the right).

   To activate the Flow buttons, your Publish Settings must be set to publish for Flash Player 8 or later (see Chapter 17).

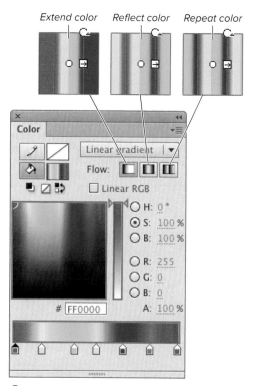

Extend color   Reflect color   Repeat color

J When you're set to publish your movie to Flash Player 8 or later (see Chapter 17), the Color panel's Flow section is active. You can choose how Flash fills out a gradient that is narrower than the shape it sits in.

About Curve and Corner Points

Flash's selection and subselection tools let you modify an element's curves and lines. With the subselection tool, you can move the curve and corner points that define the element's path and rearrange the curves' Bézier handles. When you drag a selection rectangle to enclose a merge-shape path with the subselection tool, Flash displays any curve points' Bézier handles. (Corner points have no handles.)

When you choose the selection tool, Flash hides all that technical stuff. You simply drag a line to reshape it. Still, the selection tool has its own hidden version of curve and corner points, which are evident in the icons that accompany the tool as it interacts with an unselected line or curve **A**.

| Over an empty spot | Over a selected line on the Stage |

| Over an unselected curve point | Over an unselected corner point |

A The icons appearing with the selection pointer indicate what is located beneath the pointer.

For the selection tool, corner points appear at the end of an unselected segment or at the point where two segments join to form a sharp angle. All of the other in-between points—even those in the middle of a completely flat line segment—are curve points. When you drag a curve point with the selection tool, you pull out a range of points in a tiny arc. When you drag a corner point with the selection tool, you pull out a sharp point.

Modifying Shapes: Natural Drawing Tools

You can edit all the strokes and fills you create in Flash after you've drawn them. You can edit deselected merge-shapes and drawing-objects in Flash's natural-drawing style, using the selection tool to change the path that defines the shape; or you can work directly with the path's anchor points and Bézier curves by using the subselection tool, and the various Bézier tools. (See "Modifying Shapes: Bézier Tools" in this chapter.) You can modify primitive-shapes by dragging their control points with the selection tool, or you can change their properties in the Property inspector.

Note: For the following tasks, make sure the item you want to modify is deselected. These techniques all deal with modifying strokes, but the same techniques work for modifying fills by reshaping their paths. (See "About Fill Paths" in this chapter.)

To activate the end of a segment with the selection tool:

1. Position the selection tool's pointer over the end point of a deselected line segment.

   The corner-point icon ✎⌐ appears.

2. Click the end point. The end of the segment becomes active.

3. Drag the end point to a new location **B**.

   As you drag, the end of the line changes to a small circle, showing that the line is active for modifications. Flash previews the modified segment as you drag.

4. Release the mouse button. Flash redraws the line segment.

To reshape a curve with the selection tool:

1. Position the selection tool's pointer over the middle of an unselected curve segment.

   The curve-point icon ✎⌐ appears.

2. Drag the curve to reshape it **C**. Flash previews the curve you're drawing.

3. Release the mouse button. Flash redraws the curve.

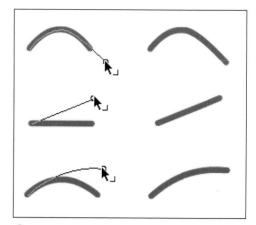

B Drag away from the existing curve or line segment to lengthen it (top). Reposition the end point to change the direction of the line (middle) or curve segment (bottom).

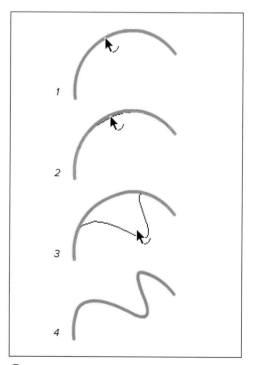

C Click the middle of a curve (1) to activate the curve segment for editing (2). Drag to reshape the curve (3). When you release the mouse button, Flash redraws the curve (4).

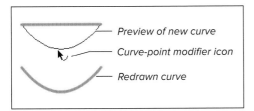

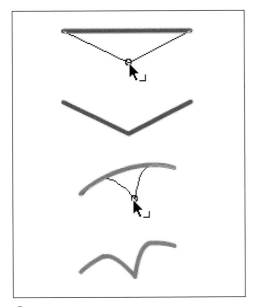

D Although this line doesn't look curved (top), Flash treats all its middle points as curve points. Drag one of those points to create a line that looks like a curve (bottom).

- Preview of new curve
- Curve-point modifier icon
- Redrawn curve

E Option-click (OS X) or Alt-click or Ctrl-click (Win) to create a new corner point for editing your line. Dragging a corner point from a straight-line segment creates a sharp V (top). Dragging a corner point from a curve creates a V with curving sides that comes to a sharp point (bottom).

To turn a straight-line segment into a curve segment with the selection tool:

1. Position the selection tool's pointer over the middle of an unselected line segment. The curve-point icon appears.

2. Drag the line to reshape it **D**. Flash previews the curve that you're drawing.

3. Release the mouse button. Flash redraws the line, giving it the curve you defined.

To create a new corner point with the selection tool:

1. Position the selection tool's pointer over the middle of an unselected line or curve segment. The curve-point icon appears.

2. Option-click (OS X) or Alt-click or Ctrl-click (Win) the line. After a brief pause, the arc changes to the corner-point icon ↖, and a circle appears where the pointer intersects the line. You're now activating a corner point.

3. Drag to modify the line or curve segment and add a new corner point **E**.

Modifying Shapes: Bézier Tools

The subselection tool lets you work with the anchor points of a path, moving them and manipulating their Bézier handles. Flash has two styles for displaying anchor points: hollow (the default) and solid. To set an anchor point style, from the Flash menu (OS X) or the Edit menu (Win), choose Preferences. From the Category list, choose Drawing. In the Pen Tool section, select/deselect the Show Solid Points checkbox, and click OK.

Note: The tasks in this book assume that Show Solid Points is selected.

To view a path and anchor points:

1. In the Tools panel, select the subselection tool ![icon], or press A. The pointer changes to a hollow arrow ↖.

2. On the Stage, click the line or curve you want to modify. Flash selects and highlights the path and anchor points. To manipulate a particular point, you must select it directly.

TIP When the subselection tool is selected in the Tools panel, use the Select All command—press Command-A (OS X) or Ctrl-A (Win)—to highlight the path and anchor points for all the graphic elements on the Stage and Pasteboard.

About Fill Paths

Although a fill shape without a stroke has no outline, it does have a path that defines its shape. The selection, pen, and subselection tools all work to reshape fill paths just as they do to reshape strokes, as outlined in the tasks in this chapter Ⓐ.

Ⓐ When you position the pointer over the edge of a deselected fill shape, the selection tool displays either the curve-point icon or the corner-point icon. Clicking the edge of the fill activates a portion of the path outlining the shape (top). Selecting the edge of a fill shape with the subselection tool highlights the full path and its anchor points. You can reposition anchor points and Bézier handles to modify the fill shapes (bottom).

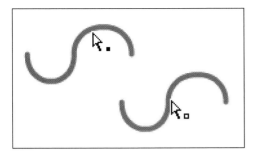

B A solid square appears next to the hollow arrow when the subselection tool is ready to select the entire path (top). When a hollow square appears (bottom), the tool is ready to select and manipulate a single anchor point.

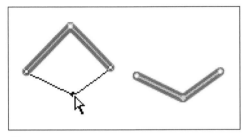

C Using the subselection tool, drag a corner point to reposition it.

To select an anchor point:

1. Using the subselection tool, move the pointer over the path you want to modify.

   A small solid square appears next to the hollow arrow when the pointer is above a curve or line segment. A small hollow square appears next to the hollow arrow when the pointer is directly above an anchor point **B**.

2. Click an anchor point. Flash highlights the selected point and displays its Bézier handles.

TIP You can directly select multiple points on a merge-shape path using the subselection tool. Draw a selection rectangle that includes the points you want to select. Flash highlights the entire path and selects any points that fall within the rectangle. This technique won't work on paths created as drawing-objects.

To move a corner point:

1. Use the subselection tool to highlight the path and anchor points of the element you want to modify.

2. Position the pointer over a corner point.

3. Drag the desired corner point to a new location. Flash redraws the path **C**.

TIP Corner points are often easy to identify without highlighting the path. You can drag such points without first highlighting the path. If you don't click precisely on the point, however, you'll move the whole path, not just the intended point.

To move a curve point:

1. Use the subselection tool to highlight the path and anchor points of the element you want to modify.

2. Position the pointer over a curve point. The anchor-point icon appears.

3. Drag the point to a new location **D**. Flash previews the new curve as you drag.

   After you move a curve point, the path remains selected, and the Bézier control handles extend so you can further manipulate the curve.

To reshape a curve with the Bézier handles:

1. With the subselection tool, click the curve you want to modify.

2. Click one of the anchor points that define the curve you want to modify. Bézier handles appear.

3. Drag one of the Bézier handles. The pointer changes to a solid arrowhead as you drag.

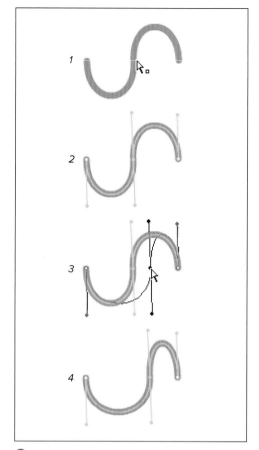

D When you select an anchor point (1), Flash highlights the entire path (2). You can drag the anchor point to modify the path (3). The path and anchor points remain highlighted when you're done (4).

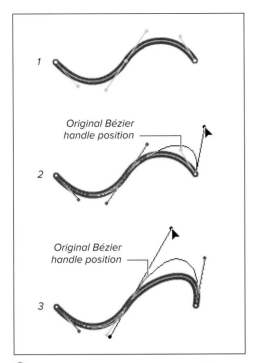

1

Original Bézier
handle position

2

Original Bézier
handle position

3

Ⓔ When you select anchor points, their Bézier handles appear (1). Leaning a Bézier handle away from a curve makes that curve segment more pronounced (2). Dragging the Bézier handle away from its anchor point makes the curve deeper (3).

4. To modify the curve, do one or more of the following:

   ▸ To make the curve bulge in the opposite direction, move the Bézier handle past the existing curve, opposite to the direction of the current bulge.

   ▸ To make the curve deeper, position the Bézier handle farther from the anchor point.

   ▸ To make the curve shallower, position the Bézier handle closer to the anchor point.

   Flash previews the new curve as you manipulate the Bézier handle Ⓔ.

TIP A curve point that connects two curve segments has two Bézier handles. By default, the handles act in concert as you move them, modifying the curves on either side of the anchor point. You can adjust just one handle (one curve) at a time. Using the subselection tool, Option-drag (OS X) or Alt-drag (Win) the handle. Or, with the anchor point selected and the Bézier handles extended, in the Tools panel select the convert anchor point tool. Use the caret pointer to drag a handle independently.

TIP You can move selected anchor points by pressing the arrow keys. To move in larger increments, hold down Shift with the arrow key.

To convert a corner point to a curve point:

1. Use the subselection tool to highlight the path and anchor points you want to modify.

2. In the Tools panel, from the Bézier-tool submenu, select the convert anchor-point tool **F**, or press C. The pointer becomes an upward-pointing caret ⌃.

3. Position the caret pointer over a corner point.

4. To activate Bézier handles, click the point, then drag away from it.

   Flash converts the corner point to a curve point that has Bézier handles **G**. As you drag, the handles extend and move, modifying the curve.

TIP You can also use the subselection tool to convert a corner point to a curve point. Position the tool's hollow-arrow pointer over a selected corner point, then Option-drag (OS X) or Alt-drag (Win) away from the point to pull out the Bézier handles.

TIP To quickly choose between the subselection tool and the four Bézier tools, press A to choose the subselection tool, P for the pen tool, = (equals sign) for the add–anchor-point tool, – (minus sign) for the delete–anchor-point tool, and C for the convert–anchor-point tool.

TIP The pen tool can perform many of the same functions as the other three Bézier tools (add anchor point, delete anchor point, and convert anchor point). As you position the pen pointer over the Stage and existing paths, the pointer icon changes, indicating the tool's current function. The ✎ pen adds anchor points, the ✎ pen converts curve points to corner points, and the ✎ pen deletes corner points.

TIP To temporarily access the delete–anchor-point tool while using the add–anchor-point tool, hold down the Option key (OS X) or Alt key (Win).

F In addition to the pen tool, the Bézier-tool submenu offers three other tools for modifying the anchor points and Bézier curves of a path. Click the current Bézier tool in the Tools panel to access a submenu showing all four tools.

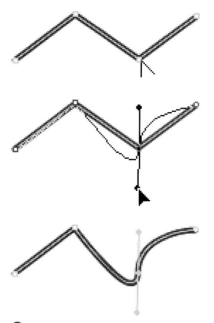

G To change a corner point into a curve point (with Bézier handles), use the convert–anchor-point tool (top) to drag out a corner point. You pull Bézier handles out of the point instead of relocating the point (middle). When you release the mouse button, Flash redraws the curve (bottom).

H Clicking a curve point with the convert–anchor-point tool (left) reduces the point to a corner point (right). Flash redraws the path accordingly.

I Click an anchor point with the delete–anchor-point tool to remove the point. Flash redraws the path accordingly.

To convert a curve point to a corner point:

1. Using the subselection tool, select the path you want to modify.

2. In the Tools panel, from the Bézier-tool submenu, select the convert–anchor-point tool, or press C.

3. Click a curve point on the selected path. Flash converts the curve point to a corner point, removing the Bézier handles and flattening the curved path **H**.

TIP When using the pen tool, you can access the convert–anchor-point tool temporarily by holding down the Option key (OS X) or Alt key (Win).

To delete an anchor point:

1. Using the subselection tool, select the path you want to modify.

2. In the Tools panel, from the Bézier-tool submenu, choose the delete–anchor-point tool, or press – (minus sign). The pointer becomes a pen with a minus sign.

3. Position the pointer over an anchor point and click. Flash removes the anchor point and reshapes the path to connect the remaining points **I**.

TIP While you can also delete anchor points by selecting them with the subselection tool and pressing Backspace or Delete, the results may surprise you. When a selected anchor point connects two segments, pressing Delete removes the anchor point and reshapes the path. When the selected anchor point lies at the intersection of three or more segments, however, Flash removes not only the anchor point, but also all the line and curve segments that directly attach to that point. You may wind up removing more than you intended.

To add a point within a path:

1. Use the subselection tool to select the path you want to modify.

2. In the Tools panel, from the Bézier-tool submenu, choose the add–anchor-point tool, or press = (equals sign). The pointer becomes a pen with a plus sign ✎₊.

3. Position the pointer over the path and do one of the following:

   ▸ Click between two corner points to create a new corner point.

   ▸ Click between two curve points to create a new curve point.

   ▸ Click between a corner point and a curve point to create a new curve point.

   Flash adds a new point 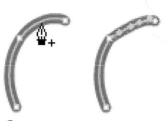.

 Position the add–anchor-point tool between existing anchor points (left). Click the path to add a new point (right).

K A slash appears when you position the pen pointer over a terminal anchor point (the first or last point in an open path). Clicking the point links the pen tool to that path. Then, clicking on the Stage creates a new point that extends the existing path.

To extend an existing path:

1. In the Tools panel, from the Bézier-tool submenu, choose the pen tool, or press P.

2. Position the pointer over the anchor point at either end of the path (a terminal anchor point). The pointer becomes a pen with a small slash 🖊.

3. Click the terminal anchor point. The pen links to that point as if you'd just placed it **K**.

4. Click to add points as you learned in Chapter 2.

   To create a single unified path, the pen tool and the existing path must be in the same drawing mode. If the existing path is a drawing-object and the pen is set to Merge Drawing mode (or vice versa), Flash places the points, but the segments remain separate.

   TIP To temporarily access the add–anchor-point tool while using the delete–anchor-point tool, hold down the Option key (OS X) or Alt key (Win).

   TIP While creating a new path, you can link to any existing path, provided the pen tool is in the same drawing mode as the existing path. When you're ready to link, position the pointer over a terminal anchor point in the path you want to join. When the pen is in Merge Drawing mode and you link to a merge-shape path, the 🖊 pointer appears. When the pen is in Object Drawing mode and you link to a drawing-object path, the 🖊 pointer appears. Click the existing terminal anchor point to join the paths.

Modifying Primitives

With Flash's rectangle- and oval-primitive tools, you create shapes with paths defined by a set of properties specific to that shape. You can't change the outline of a primitive-shape freely the way you can reshape the outline of a merge-shape or drawing-object. You can change the primitive's defining properties by dragging control points in the shape or by setting new values in the Property inspector.

To modify a rectangle-primitive:

1. Using the selection tool, select the rectangle-primitive you want to modify.

   The shape's bounding box highlights, and control points appear **Ⓐ**. Each corner has two control points. For sharp corners with a corner-radius setting of 0, the points sit directly on top of one another. For rounded corners, a control point appears at both ends of the arc that defines the corner. The two points work in concert—dragging one moves the other.

2. Position the pointer over one of the control points. The pointer becomes a solid arrowhead.

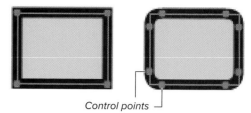

Control points

Ⓐ The rectangle-primitive has two control points for the corner radius of each corner. When the corner radius is set to 0, the corner is a sharp 90-degree angle, and the control points sit directly on top of one another.

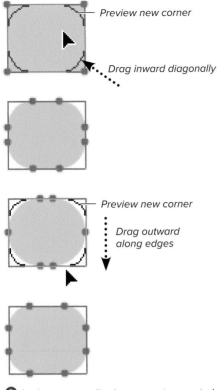

Preview new corner

Drag inward diagonally

Preview new corner

Drag outward along edges

B As the corner radius increases, two control points appear at the end of the arc defining the corner. Drag inward to round the corner more; drag outward to round it less.

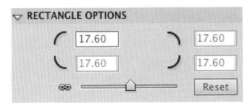

C The Rectangle Options section of the Rectangle Primitive Property inspector has fields for entering a precise corner-radius value for each corner of a selected rectangle-primitive. In the linked state 🔗, the Constrain Corner Radius modifier uses one value for all four corners. (Drag the slider to change the selected object interactively.) In the unlinked state 🔗, you can enter values for each corner separately to create a variety of shapes. (The slider is unavailable in this state.)

3. To modify the shape, do one of the following:

- ▶ To increase the radius (make the corner more rounded), drag the point inward.

- ▶ To decrease the radius (make the corner less rounded), drag the point outward.

You can drag diagonally toward the center of a shape, or you can drag vertically or horizontally along the edge containing the control point **B**.

TIP To set precise corner-radius values, select the rectangle-primitive on the Stage, then access the Rectangle Options section of the Rectangle Primitive Property inspector **C**. To create rounded corners, enter positive values in the Rectangle Corner Radius fields. To create indented corners, enter negative values. (For details about setting these properties, see Chapter 2.)

TIP You can't change a square or rounded corner to an indented corner by dragging the control points. You must enter a negative value in the Property inspector. Once the rectangle-primitive has an indented corner, however, you can drag its control points to adjust the size of the indent.

To modify an oval-primitive:

1. Using the selection tool, select the oval-primitive you want to modify.

   The shape's bounding box highlights, and control points appear **D**. Oval-primitives have four control points: one pair for the start and end angles of the outer oval, and another pair for the start and end angles of the inner oval. When the start angle and end angle of an oval have the same value, the control points lie directly on top of one another.

2. Position the pointer over a control point. The pointer becomes a solid arrowhead.

3. To modify the shape, do one or more of the following:

   ▸ To change the start angle, drag the control point clockwise or counter-clockwise around the perimeter of the oval **E**.

   ▸ To change the end angle, drag the control point clockwise or counter-clockwise around the perimeter of the oval.

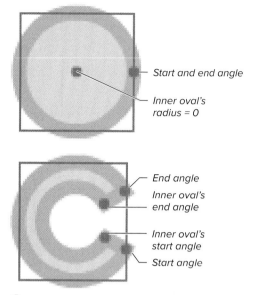

Start and end angle
Inner oval's radius = 0

End angle
Inner oval's end angle
Inner oval's start angle
Start angle

D An oval-primitive has control points for the start and end angles of the outer and inner oval shapes.

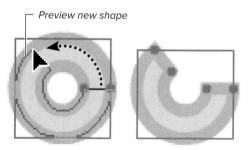

Preview new shape

E Drag the control points on the outer edge of an oval-primitive clockwise or counterclockwise to change the start and end angles of the shape.

Preview larger inner radius

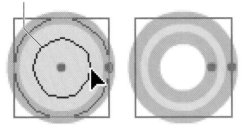

Preview smaller inner radius

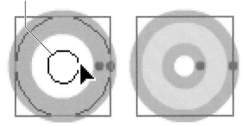

F You can drag the control points on the inner edge of an oval-primitive to resize the radius of the inner oval. Drag toward the center of the shape to close down the opening in the middle of the shape, and drag away from the center to open up a bigger space.

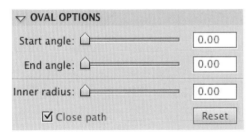

G The Oval Options section of the Oval Primitive Property inspector has fields for entering precise values for a selected oval-primitive's start angle, end angle, and inner radius. Drag the sliders to change the selected oval-primitive interactively.

▸ To increase the inner radius (to create a larger space inside the oval), drag outward **F**.

▸ To decrease the inner radius (to create a smaller space inside the oval), drag inward.

TIP To set precise values for the start angle, end angle, and/or inner radius, select the oval-primitive on the Stage, then access the Oval Options section of the Oval Primitive Property inspector **G**. (For details about setting these properties, see Chapter 2.)

TIP Although you can't alter the paths of primitives to create fanciful free-form shapes, you can use a primitive as the start of a shape with paths that can be freely modified. After you set the primitive's properties, convert the shape to a merge-shape or drawing-object. (See "Converting Shape Types" in this chapter.) Then modify the merge-shape or drawing-object using any of the techniques discussed in this chapter.

Converting Shape Types

Flash offers a variety of shape types: fills, strokes, merge-shapes, drawing-objects, primitives, and text. You can convert some shape types into others. For example, you can convert strokes to fills, merge-shapes to drawing-objects (and vice versa), and primitive-shapes to merge-shapes and drawing-objects. You can also convert text, a special type of fill, to a regular drawing-object fill (for TLF text) or merge-shape fill (for Classic text). You cannot, however, convert merge-shapes or drawing-objects to primitive-shapes.

To convert a stroke to a fill:

1. Select a stroke on the Stage.

2. Choose Modify > Shape > Convert Lines to Fills.

   Flash converts the stroke to a fill shape that looks exactly like the stroke. You can now edit the path of the "stroke's" outline as though you were working with a fill created with the brush tool 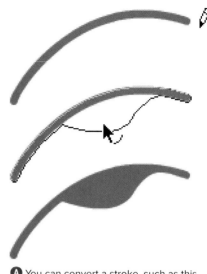.

Ⓐ You can convert a stroke, such as this line drawn with the pencil tool (top), to a fill. The fill's outline then has its own editable path (middle and bottom).

Selected merge-shape (fill and stroke)   *Converted to drawing-object*

B To convert the shape currently selected on the Stage into a drawing-object, choose Modify > Combine Objects > Union.

To convert a merge-shape or a primitive to a drawing-object:

1. On the Stage, select a single merge-shape or primitive-shape.

2. Choose Modify > Combine Objects > Union. Flash converts the selected shape to a drawing-object, and it remains selected **B**.

TIP The Modify > Combine Objects commands (Union, Intersect, Punch, and Crop) work on multiple selected drawing-objects and primitives. The last three commands work on overlapping drawing-objects or primitives. In effect, these commands convert the drawing-objects or primitives to merge-shapes (so they will interact) and then convert the resulting shape (or shapes) back into a drawing-object. Note that primitives lose their status as primitives when you combine them. (You'll learn more about combining shapes in Chapter 5.)

Converting Vector Shapes to Bitmaps

When creating Flash content, you may use images containing dozens, even hundreds, of shapes. Each one is a vector object that must be rendered for display. As a result, complex vector images may slow playback (especially on hardware with lower processing power, such as Android devices). They also can slow playback when you test a movie during authoring.

To address slowdown for static vector images at runtime, you can export them as bitmaps when you publish your movie (see Chapter 17).

To avoid slowdown during authoring, you can convert complex vector art on the Stage to bitmaps. Select the vector shapes that won't need to animate (a complex background image, for example), and then choose Modify > Convert to Bitmap. Flash encloses the selection in a bounding box, converts it to a bitmap, and places a copy of the bitmap in the library. Just be sure to wait until your vector image is complete before converting, or save a copy of it to modify and use later. For even better practice, create your artwork in a symbol. You can then convert an instance of the symbol to a bitmap. (You'll learn about creating symbols in Chapter 7.)

To convert a drawing-object or a primitive to a merge-shape:

1. On the Stage, select a drawing-object or primitive-shape.

2. Choose Modify > Break Apart, or press Command-B (OS X) or Ctrl-B (Win). Flash converts the selected drawing-object or primitive-shape to a merge-shape; it remains selected.

To convert a block of TLF text into individual drawing-objects:

1. Select a TLF text field on the Stage. If the selected field links to other TLF text fields with threaded text, Flash selects all of the linked fields.

2. Choose Modify > Break Apart, or press Command-B (OS X) or Ctrl-B (Win). Flash transforms each letter in the selection into a drawing-object and selects it **C**.

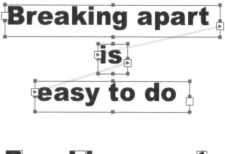

C With TLF text fields selected (top), you can transform each letter into a separate drawing object (bottom) by choosing Modify > Break Apart.

TIP You can transform Classic Text to simple graphic shapes, but it requires two steps. First, select the Classic text field on the Stage and choose Modify > Break Apart. Flash places each letter in a separate text field and selects them all. To transform those single-letter text fields into merge-shapes, select the text fields and choose Modify > Break Apart.

TIP Converting TLF text to drawing-objects can be useful when you have a small amount of text that must look exactly the same in the finished product as it did during the authoring phase, but you don't want to embed that font.

TIP You don't actually have to select a TLF text field; just position the text tool's I-beam cursor anywhere within the text field. When you choose Modify > Break Apart, Flash converts all the text in that text field, and any fields linked to it, to drawing-objects.

Complex Graphics on a Single Layer

When you create complex graphic elements in Adobe Flash Professional CS6, you must consider the fact that strokes and fills interact when they are created in merge mode on the same layer. Sometimes you want that interaction, sometimes you don't.

Think of creating a mouse's head. Using the oval tool, draw a large blue oval fill and add two smaller blue ovals for ears. When the tool is in Merge Drawing mode and you create the ovals on one layer, they combine into a single mouse-head shape. If you plan to animate the head as a unit—never changing the ears—a single unified shape might be just what you want. If you plan to animate the ears, a unified shape may be less desirable. To avoid redrawing the entire head each time you change an ear's position, you can prevent the merging. In this chapter, you'll see how graphic elements on one layer interact, and learn techniques to control or prevent that interaction.

In This Chapter

When Merge-Shapes Interact

In most vector-based graphics programs, each line or shape is a separate object. Adding a new object has no effect on objects created earlier. Overlapping objects have a stacking order, and higher objects obscure lower objects, but one element does not modify another. In Flash's Merge Drawing mode, however, lines (strokes) and shapes (fills) are raw, and they do modify one another.

When Merge-Shape Lines Intersect

Intersecting merge-shape lines on the same layer affect one another. When you draw two intersecting lines in Merge Drawing mode, the second line cuts—or, in Flash terminology, *segments*—the first line **A**.

You might expect that the second line to wind up on top of the first, but that's not always the case. To test this, draw a green line, draw a yellow line across it, then draw another green line that crosses the yellow line. The second green line jumps *behind* the yellow one when you release the mouse button. Flash creates a stacking order for merge-shape lines based on their creation order and color. If your lines and outlines don't stack up as you'd like, you may need to group items or create them on separate layers.

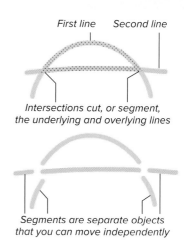

First line   Second line

Intersections cut, or segment, the underlying and overlying lines

Segments are separate objects that you can move independently

A When you draw one line across another in Merge Drawing mode, every intersection cuts the line into segments. This cutting happens even if the lines are the same color, but it's easiest to see with contrasting colors.

When Merge-Shape Lines and Fills Intersect

A fill without an outline still has a path. In Merge Drawing mode, fill paths can cut lines and outline strokes of other shapes. Placing merge-shape strokes over merge-shape fills can result in lots of little line segments and fill shapes. Try using the pencil and brush tools in Merge Drawing mode. When you paint a fill that intersects a line, the fill remains one solid object and cuts the line **B**. When you draw a line that intersects a fill, the line cuts the fill, and the path of the fill cuts the line **C**.

When intersecting fills created in Merge Drawing mode are the same color, the newer fill adds to the merge-shape. When fills of different colors interact, the newer fill replaces the older one.

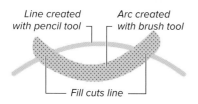

Line created with pencil tool   Arc created with brush tool

Fill cuts line

B When a merge-shape fill overlays a merge-shape line, the fill cuts the line. As the selection highlight shows, the fill remains one solid object.

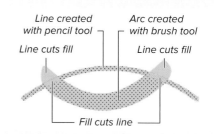

Line created with pencil tool   Arc created with brush tool

Line cuts fill   Line cuts fill

Fill cuts line

C When a merge-shape line overlays a merge-shape fill, the line's path cuts the fill, and the fill's path cuts the line.

Note for Working in this Chapter

Two of Flash's drawing tools—the brush tool and the eraser—offer special modes for use with multiple fills and strokes on a single layer. In this chapter, unless you're specifically requested to do otherwise, leave both tools at their default settings of Paint Normal (for the brush tool) and Erase Normal (for the eraser).

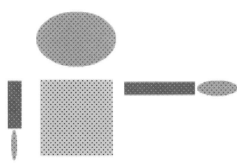

A The first step in grouping is selecting the shapes you want to include in the group.

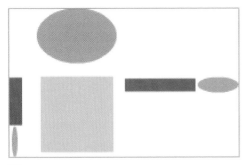

B The Modify > Group command unites multiple selected shapes within a single bounding box.

Working with Groups

A *group* is a virtual container that holds graphic elements. Groups prevent selected merge-shapes from interacting, lock down the attributes of shapes, and preserve spatial relationships among graphic elements. Although you can also group drawing-objects and primitive-shapes, the tasks in this section are intended to show the interaction with merge-shapes. Use the oval and rectangle tools to create objects to practice with. Make sure the Object Drawing button in the Tools panel is deselected.

To create a group:

1. On the Stage, select one or more items using any of the methods discussed in Chapter 4 **A**.

2. Choose Modify > Group, or press Command-G (OS X) or Ctrl-G (Win).

   Flash groups the items, placing them within a bounding box **B**. The visible bounding box indicates that the group is selected. When the group isn't selected, the bounding box is hidden.

TIP If you choose Modify > Group when nothing is selected, you immediately enter group-editing mode. In that mode, anything you draw on the Stage becomes part of a new group.

To return objects to ungrouped status:

1. Select the group that you want to return to ungrouped status.

2. Choose Modify > Ungroup, or press Shift-Command-G (OS X) or Ctrl-Shift-G (Win). Flash removes the bounding box and selects all the items.

Interactions between strokes and fills occur when you draw a shape, and also when you place a copy of a shape or move a shape. Be careful when pasting copies of merge-shape fills and strokes on a single layer. You can inadvertently add to or delete part of an underlying merge-shape. When you ungroup a grouped shape that overlaps merge-shapes on a single layer, the shapes will segment one another.

To prevent interaction between merge-shapes on one layer:

1. Draw a fairly large merge-shape oval with no stroke. Choose the oval tool, and click the Merge Drawing button in the Options section of the Tools panel. Set the stroke color to No Color and choose a fill color.

2. Select the oval you just drew.

3. To make the oval a grouped element, choose Modify > Group, or press Shift-Command-G (OS X) or Ctrl-Shift-G (Win).

4. Deselect the grouped oval.

5. Using the oval tool and a different fill color, draw a smaller oval in the middle of your first oval.

   When you finish drawing, the new oval disappears behind the grouped oval **C**. Grouped objects always stack on top of ungrouped objects.

6. Choose the selection tool, and reposition the large oval to make the small one visible **D**.

7. Deselect the large oval, and select the small oval.

8. To make the small oval a grouped object, Choose Modify > Group.

   Flash puts the small oval in a bounding box and brings it to the top of the stack **E**. The most recently created group is always on the top of the stack. Now the two ovals won't interact.

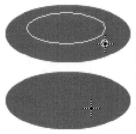

C When you draw a merge-shape on top of a grouped object, the ungrouped shape stacks beneath the grouped object when you release the mouse button.

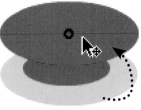

D Dragging the grouped oval reveals the ungrouped oval below.

E After grouping, the small oval—the most recently created group—pops to the top of the stack.

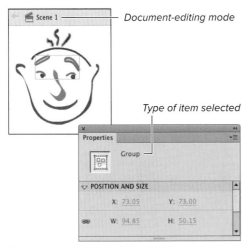

Document-editing mode

Type of item selected

Group

A The eyes and eyebrows of this figure are a selected group, and the Property inspector identifies them as such. You can use the hot-text controls in the Position and Size section to change the *x*- and *y*-coordinates and the height and width of the selected group's bounding box. The Edit bar indicates you are in document-editing mode.

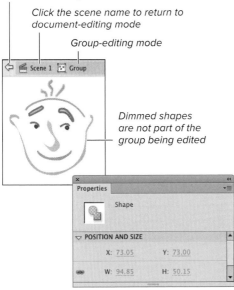

Click the Back button to return to document-editing mode

Click the scene name to return to document-editing mode

Group-editing mode

Dimmed shapes are not part of the group being edited

B In group-editing mode, the selected shapes (in full color) are editable; the dimmed items are there for context only.

Editing Groups

Although you can transform an entire group (scale, rotate, and skew it), you can't directly edit the individual shapes within a group. To do so, you must use the Edit Selected command.

To edit the contents of a group:

1. Select the group you want to edit **A**.

2. Choose Edit > Edit Selected.

   Flash enters group-editing mode. The Edit bar indicates that you're in group-editing mode **B**. The bounding box for the selected group disappears, and Flash dims all the items on the Stage that aren't part of the selected group. These dimmed items aren't editable but do provide context for editing the selected group.

3. Make changes to the contents of the group.

4. To return to document-editing mode, do one of the following:

   ▸ Choose Edit > Edit All.

   ▸ Double-click an empty area of the Stage or the Pasteboard.

   ▸ Click the current scene name in the Edit bar.

   ▸ Click the Back button in the Edit bar.

TIP To enter group-editing mode quickly, use the selection tool to double-click a grouped item on the Stage.

TIP By default, the Edit bar is visible. To hide it, choose Window > Toolbars > Edit Bar. When the Edit bar is hidden, it's harder to know when you're editing objects on the Stage in the main document and when you're editing objects within groups (or drawing-objects or symbols).

Controlling Stacking Order

Within a single Timeline layer, text fields, grouped objects, drawing-objects, and primitives stack as if they were sitting on sublayers above any ungrouped merge-shapes, which all reside on the lowest sublayer.

To change position in a stack:

1. On the Stage, create at least three graphic-objects, and select one. Use grouped shapes, drawing-objects, primitives, and/or text fields.

2. From the Modify > Arrange menu, choose one of the following:

   ▸ To move the selected item up one level, choose Bring Forward, or press Command–Up Arrow (OS X) or Ctrl–Up Arrow (Win) **Ⓐ**.

   ▸ To move the selected item down one level, choose Send Backward, or press Command–Down Arrow (OS X) or Ctrl–Down Arrow (Win).

   ▸ To bring the item to the top of the stack, choose Bring to Front, or press Option-Shift–Up Arrow (OS X) or Ctrl-Shift–Up Arrow (Win).

   ▸ To move the item to the bottom of the stack, choose Send to Back, or press Option-Shift–Down Arrow (OS X) or Ctrl-Shift–Down Arrow (Win).

Created 1st   Created 2nd   Created 3rd

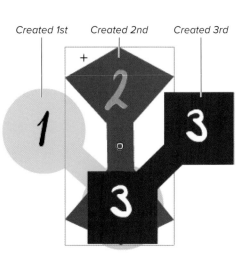

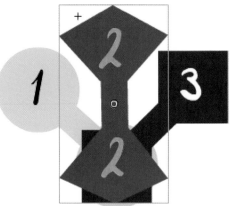

Ⓐ Each dumbbell-like shape is a separate group (top). Choose Modify > Arrange > Bring Forward to move a selected group up one level in the stacking order (bottom).

A Applying the Modify > Combine Objects > Union command to drawing-object or primitive-shape fills of the same color (left) melds the fills and creates a single drawing-object (right).

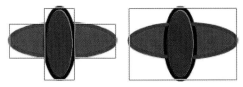

B Applying the Modify > Combine Objects > Union command to drawing-objects (or primitive-shapes) of different colors (left) causes the selected fills and strokes to replace and segment one another as merge-shapes would. The resulting shapes unite in a single drawing-object (right).

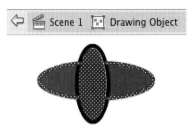

C You can edit the raw shapes that make up a drawing-object. On the Stage, double-click the drawing-object to open its container and access the shapes in drawing-object–editing mode. You can see how the shapes segment one another. Each chunk of stroke and fill is a separate shape.

Combining Drawing-Objects and Primitives

Drawing-objects and primitive-shapes don't interact with one another or with merge-shapes, even when they overlap. The Modify > Combine Objects command forces them to interact. In effect, the command converts selected objects to merge-shapes (so they can interact), and then converts those shapes to a drawing-object.

To unite multiple drawing-objects or primitives:

1. Use the drawing tools in Object Drawing mode, or the rectangle- or oval-primitive tools, to create overlapping shapes:

   ▸ Make two or more overlapping fills with the same colors.

   ▸ Make two or more overlapping shapes with fills and strokes. Use different colors for the fills and strokes in each shape.

2. Select the overlapping fills that are the same color.

3. Choose Modify > Combine Objects > Union. The two fills become a single drawing-object shape **A**.

4. Select the overlapping shapes of different colors.

5. Repeat Step 3.

   The fills and strokes of the shapes segment one another, but you wind up with a single drawing-object containing all those segmented shapes **B**.

TIP You can also use the Modify > Combine Objects > Union command to combine a mix of merge-shapes, drawing-objects, and primitives.

TIP To access and edit merge-shapes inside a drawing-object, double-click it **C**.

To use one drawing-object to remove part of another:

1. Use the drawing tools in Object Drawing mode, or the rectangle- or oval-primitive tools to create two or more overlapping shapes with a variety of fills and strokes.

2. Select the objects you created.

3. From the Modify > Combine Objects menu, choose one of the following:

    Intersect retains fills and strokes where all the selected shapes overlap, and deletes all other fills and strokes. The resulting shape(s) take stroke and fill attributes from the topmost shape.

    Punch uses the topmost shape like a cookie cutter to remove any shapes directly below it. (Imagine the shape left in the cookie dough after you've cut out a cookie.) The resulting shape(s) retain their original attributes.

    Crop uses the topmost shape like a cookie cutter to select a new shape from any shapes that lie below it. (This time your cookie cutter leaves you with the cookie itself.) The resulting shape(s) retain their original attributes **D**.

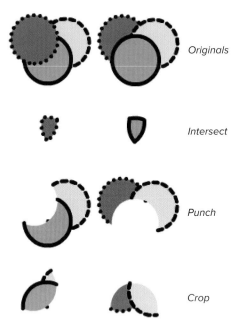

Originals

Intersect

Punch

Crop

D The last three commands in the Modify > Combine Objects menu have different results depending on which object is located on top of the stack. The Intersect command creates a new shape from the intersection of all selected shapes, using the top shape's attributes. With Punch, the top shape takes a bite out of the others and removes it; the remaining shapes keep their original attributes. With Crop, the top shape takes the same bite but this time removes everything else; the resulting shapes keep their original attributes.

TIP When you select merge-shapes, the Modify > Combine Objects menu offers only the Union command. You can choose this command instead of grouping merge-shapes. The Union command preserves the spatial relationships between shapes but gives you the ability to change fills and strokes directly on the Stage (as described in Chapter 4).

TIP If you choose Modify > Combine Objects > Intersect and your shapes disappear, they did not intersect anywhere. That result may seem self-evident, but when you've selected many shapes, or complex shapes, it may be hard to see.

Graphics on Multiple Layers

In Adobe Flash Professional CS6, you can create the illusion of three-dimensional depth by overlapping graphic elements. As you learned in Chapter 5, you can create this overlapping effect on one layer by stacking drawing-objects, primitive-shapes, groups, and symbols. The more elements the layer contains, however, the more difficult it becomes to manipulate and track their stacking order.

When you place items on separate layers, it's easy to control the way the items stack. You can make shapes appear to be closer to the viewer by putting them on a higher layer. Raw shapes on different layers don't interact, so you needn't worry about grouping merge-shapes or having one merge-shape inadvertently delete another. Additionally, you can hide and show layers—even organize layers in folders—and label them to make it easier to work with multiple layers and elements in a Flash document.

In This Chapter

Touring the Timeline's Layer Features

Flash graphically represents each layer as one horizontal section of the Timeline and provides controls for viewing and manipulating these graphic representations. Several handy features help you work with graphics on layers, such as viewing the items on layers as outlines and assigning colors to those outlines so you can easily see which items are on which layers. You can lock layers so that you can't edit their contents accidentally, and you can hide layers to make it easier to work with individual graphics within a welter of other graphics.

You can also create guide layers to help when positioning elements, mask layers for selectively hiding and revealing layer contents, and motion-guide layers for animating classic tween elements along a curving path. (You learn more about classic tween motion-guide layers in Chapter 9.) Figure **A** displays a road map to the important layer features in the Timeline.

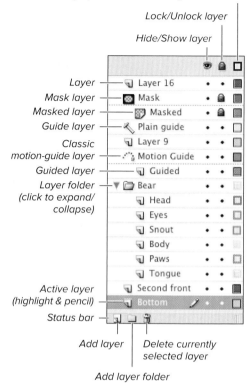

A The Timeline graphically represents all the layers in a Flash movie, and layer folders let you organize those layers in a complex movie. You can do much of the work of creating and manipulating layers and folders by clicking buttons in the Timeline.

About Layers

You can think of a Flash document as a stack of filmstrips: a sheaf of long, clear acetate strips divided into frames. Each filmstrip is analogous to a Flash layer. Shapes painted on the top filmstrip obscure shapes on lower strips. In areas where the top filmstrip is blank, elements from the lower strips show through.

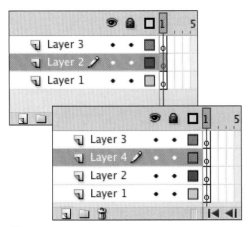

A Select the layer that should be located beneath the new layer (top). Flash inserts a new layer directly above the selected layer and gives the new layer a default name (bottom).

Why Use Folders?

Complex Flash movies contain dozens of layers. Viewing and navigating such hefty Timelines can be tedious and confusing. Organizing layers in folders helps manage a complex Timeline. You can, for example, place all the layers related to one character inside a folder. By collapsing the folder, you no longer see the layers and frames for that character's animation in the Timeline; but you can still view the character, and its animation, on the Stage. When you next need to work with that character's frames in the Timeline, you just expand the folder.

Creating and Deleting Layers and Folders

When creating a particular scene in your movie, you can add new layers and layer folders as you need them. Folders are really just another type of layer—one that holds no graphic content. Folders do not have frames (or keyframes) in the Timeline. (Keyframes are special frames in which you place your graphic elements; you'll learn about them in Chapter 8.)

To add a layer or a layer folder:

1. In the Timeline, to choose the new layer's location, select an existing layer or folder by clicking it. Flash always adds the new layer or folder directly above the one you selected. To add a layer or folder beneath the current bottom layer, create a new layer, then drag it to the bottom of the stack.

2. To add a layer, do one of the following:

   ▸ Choose Insert > Timeline > Layer.

   ▸ In the Timeline's Status bar, click the New Layer button ▣.

   Flash adds a new layer and gives it a default name, such as *Layer 4* **A**.

   Continues on next page

3. To add a folder, do one of the following:

   ▸ Choose Insert > Timeline > Layer Folder.

   ▸ In the Timeline's Status bar, click the New Folder button ▢.

   Flash adds a new layer folder and gives it a default name, such as *Folder 1* or *Folder 2* **B**. The folder is open by default, making it easy to place layers within it. (See "Organizing Layers" in this chapter.)

   TIP Flash assigns a number to default names based on the number of layers or folders already created in the active scene of the movie, not on the number of layers and folders that currently exist or their current positions.

   TIP Flash tracks layer and folder numbers separately. The first folder you insert among numerous layers is given the name *Folder 1.*

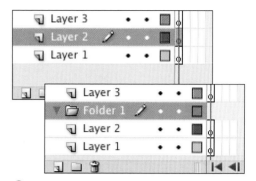

B Select the layer that should be below the new folder (top). Flash creates a new folder above the layer you selected (bottom). Flash names new folders based on the number of folders in the current scene of the movie.

To delete a layer or a folder:

1. In the Timeline, select the layer or folder you want to delete.

2. Click the Delete button 🗑.

   If your selection includes folders containing layers, a dialog warns that deleting the layer folder will also delete all the layers it contains.

3. To delete the folder and its layers, click Yes. Flash removes that layer (and all its frames) or that folder from the Timeline.

   or

   To cancel the delete operation, click No.

   TIP You can also select and delete multiple layers. To select noncontiguous layers or folders in Step 1 of the preceding task, Command-click (OS X) or Ctrl-click (Win) every layer or folder you want to remove. To select a range of layers, click the lowest layer you want to delete, then Shift-click the highest layer.

Setting Layer Properties

The Timeline represents each layer or layer folder as a horizontal field containing a name and three buttons that control the way the layer's or folder's contents look on the Stage. You can hide a layer or folder, lock a layer or folder (leaving the contents visible but uneditable), and view as outlines the items on the layer or within the folder.

To rename a layer or folder:

1. In the Timeline, double-click the layer or folder name. Flash activates the name's text-entry field.

2. Type a new name.

3. Press Enter, or click anywhere outside the name field.

To hide/show the contents of a layer or folder:

In the Timeline for the layer or folder that you want to hide or show, click the icon in the Eye column Ⓐ.

The layer or folder toggles between the hidden and visible states. A red *X* in the column indicates that the layer or folder is hidden. Its contents no longer appear on the Stage. A bullet indicates that the layer is visible. You decide how the hidden setting affects the final movie. When you publish a movie (see Chapter 17), you have the option to include or exclude the contents of hidden layers and folders.

Toggles visibility of the layer's contents

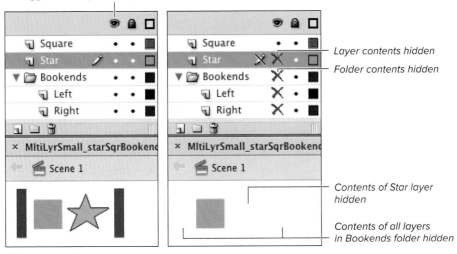

Layer contents hidden
Folder contents hidden

Contents of Star layer hidden

Contents of all layers in Bookends folder hidden

Ⓐ The column below the eye icon controls the visibility of layers. Each of the four graphic elements (left) is on a separate layer. The bars on either side of the image are in the Bookends folder. Hiding the Star layer makes the star disappear from the Stage. Hiding the Bookends folder also makes the bars disappear (right).

To lock/unlock a layer or folder:

In the Timeline for the layer or folder that you want to lock or unlock, click the icon in the Lock column **B**.

The layer or folder toggles between the locked and unlocked states. A padlock icon in the column indicates that the layer or folder is locked. Its contents appear on the Stage, but you can't edit them. A bullet indicates that the layer or folder is unlocked and its contents are editable. Locking a layer or folder has no effect on the final movie.

To view the contents of a layer or folder as outlines or solids:

In the Timeline for the layer or folder that you want to view as outlines or solids, click the icon in the Outline column (topped by a square icon ☐) **C**.

The layer or folder toggles between Outline mode and Solid mode. When the outline icon ☐ is visible, the contents of the layer or folder appear on the Stage as outlines. When the solid icon ■ is visible, the layer or folder contents appear in their complete forms. For regular layers, the outline square indicates the color Flash uses to create the outlines for the contents of that layer. (For layer folders, the color of the square has no meaning; the square just shows which mode the folder is in.) Placing a layer or folder in Outline mode doesn't affect the final movie.

> **TIP** Setting a folder to Outline mode displays the contents of all the layers within the folder as outlines. Click the outline square of individual layers within the folder to see that layer's content as solid shapes.

Locked layer
Unlocked layer

B The padlock icon indicates that a layer is locked. The contents of a locked layer appear on the Stage, but you can't edit them.

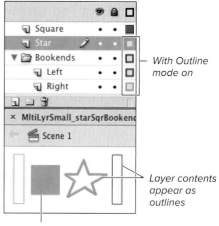

With Outline mode on

Layer contents appear as outlines

Contents of other layers appear as solids

C A hollow square in the Outline column indicates that graphic elements on that layer appear as outlines. Setting a folder to Outline mode automatically changes all the layers within it to Outline mode.

> **TIP** You can set layer properties in three ways: (1) click the layer-property control buttons in the Timeline; (2) control-click a layer (OS X) or right-click a layer (Win), and choose a command from the contextual menu for layers; or (3) set property values in the Layer Properties dialog. (To open the Layer Properties dialog, choose Modify > Timeline > Layer Properties, or double-click a layer's folded-page icon or folder icon in the Timeline.) All three methods let you set layer visibility, lock layer contents, or view layer elements as outlines. The Layer Properties dialog offers additional functions: creating plain guide layers, changing the height of a layer in Timeline view, choosing an outline color, and changing an existing layer from one type to another, while the contextual menu lets you create classic motion-guide layers.

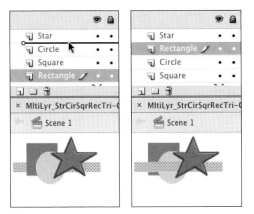

A The black bar with a small circle at its left end (left) represents the new location for the layer you're dragging (in the figure, it's the Rectangle layer). Release the mouse button to drop the layer into its new position. Flash selects the layer and its contents (right). The rectangle shape moves from the bottom of the heap, below the square, to just under the star.

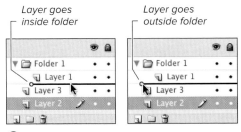

Layer goes
inside folder

Layer goes
outside folder

B When you position a layer below the last layer in an open folder, you must decide whether to place the dragged layer inside or outside the folder. As you drag into the open folder, the preview bar's circle automatically aligns with the right side of the target-folder icon (left), indicating that the dragged layer will go inside the target folder. To place the layer outside the folder, drag to the left until the preview bar's circle aligns with the left side of the folder icon (right). The option to drag to the left is available only when you place a layer at the bottom of the folder.

Organizing Layers

You can rearrange layers (and folders) by dragging them to new positions in the Timeline. Drag them into folders to create a visual hierarchy of layers.

To reorder layers (or folders):

1. In the Timeline, drag the desired layer (or folder). A black bar with a small circle previews the new location of the layer (or folder).

2. When the preview bar is in the layer order you want **A**, release the mouse button. Flash moves the layer (or folder) to the new location and selects it.

To move existing layers (or folders) into open folders:

1. Begin dragging the desired layer (or folder).

2. Position the preview bar directly beneath the target folder (or beneath a layer within the target folder other than the last layer).

    The preview bar's circle aligns with the right side of the target folder's icon.

    or

    Position the preview bar beneath the last layer within the target folder and drag to the right.

    The preview bar's circle aligns with the right side of the target folder's icon.

3. Release the mouse button. The dragged layer appears inside the target folder.

TIP To position a layer or folder directly below the last layer of an open folder without placing it inside the folder, drag to the left until the preview bar's circle aligns with the left side of the folder icon **B** and release the mouse button.

Cutting and Pasting Between Layers

You can create and place graphics only on the active layer of a document. But you can copy, cut, or delete elements from any visible, unlocked layer. You can select items on several layers, cut them, and then paste them all into a single layer; or cut items individually from one layer, and redistribute them to separate layers.

To copy and paste across layers:

1. Create or open a multilayer document.

    One layer should be empty. The others should contain at least one graphic object. For ease of use, work with drawing-objects, primitives, or grouped shapes.

2. On the Stage, select an object. In the Timeline, the layer highlights in blue.

3. Choose Edit > Copy, or press Command-C (OS X) or Ctrl-C (Win).

4. In the Timeline, select the empty layer.

5. Choose Edit > Paste in Center.

    Flash pastes the copy of the shape in the empty layer in the middle of the window **Ⓐ**. You can now move the shape to a new position, if you wish.

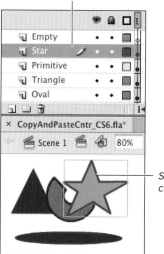

Active layer

Selected and copied object

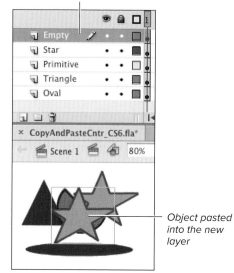

Select new active layer

Object pasted into the new layer

Ⓐ Copying an object from one layer to another involves selecting the object (top), copying it, selecting the target layer, and then pasting the copy there. The Edit > Paste in Center command positions the pasted object in the center of the document window (bottom).

Two Ways to Paste

Flash offers two pasting modes: Paste in Center and Paste in Place. Paste in Center puts elements in the center of the open document window. (Note that the center of the current window may not be the center of the Stage. To paste to the center of the Stage, you must center the Stage in the open window.) Paste in Place puts an object at the same *x*- and *y*-coordinates it had when you cut or copied it. Paste in Place is useful for preserving the precise relationships of all elements in a scene as you move items from one layer to another.

To cut and paste in place across layers:

1. Open or create a document that has several graphic objects on different layers, and one empty layer, named Empty.

2. Select two (or more) objects. The layer containing the last object selected becomes the active layer in the Timeline.

3. Choose Edit > Cut, or press Command-X (OS X) or Ctrl-X (Win). Flash removes the selected objects **B**.

Continues on next page

*Active layer is the layer
of the item last selected*

*Selected objects
from several layers*

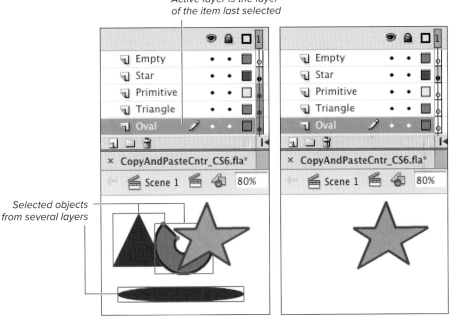

B The first step in consolidating items from several layers on a single new layer involves selecting all the items (left) and cutting them (right). You can then activate the new layer and paste the objects.

4. In the Timeline, select the Empty layer.

5. Choose Edit > Paste in Place. Flash pastes all the objects back into their original locations on the Stage but on a different layer **C**.

TIP To confirm that you've pasted all the selected objects on one layer, hide the Empty layer **D**.

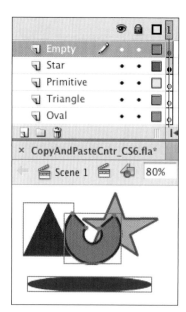

C The Paste in Place command positions each cut object at its original coordinates but on the new layer.

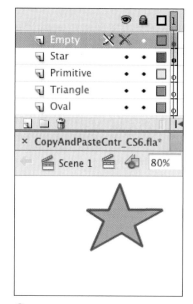

D Hiding the Empty layer confirms that all of the pasted objects were relocated to that layer.

Stay Aware of the Active Layer

A Flash document allows only one active layer at a time. Newly created shapes, pasted copies of objects, and symbol instances dragged from the Library all wind up on the active layer. Make sure that the desired layer is active when you start an operation. Clicking a layer in the Timeline activates the layer (and selects all the items on that layer on the Stage). Clicking an item on the Stage activates that item's layer in the Timeline. Unless you lock or hide layers, objects on all layers are available for editing. Simply editing a merge-shape or drawing object using the selection tool will not activate that shape's layer, nor will editing fills and strokes using the paint bucket and ink bottle tools.

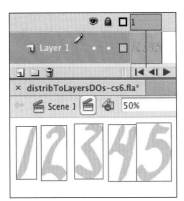

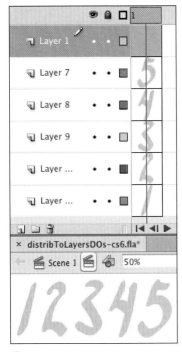

A With elements selected on the Stage (top), choose Modify > Timeline > Distribute to Layers, to automatically cut each element and paste it in place in a new layer (bottom).

Distributing Graphic Elements to Layers

Using the Cut and Paste in Place commands for numerous items can be tedious. Flash's Distribute to Layers feature automates this process, putting each element of a selection on a separate layer. This feature is handy when creating two types of animation—*motion tweening* and *classic tweening*—in which each animated element must be on its own layer. (You'll learn about classic tweening in Chapter 9 and motion tweening in Chapter 11.)

To place selected elements on individual layers:

1. Open or create a document that has several separate objects on one layer.

2. Choose Edit > Select All, or press Command-A (OS X) or Ctrl-A (Win).

3. Choose Modify > Timeline > Distribute to Layers, or press Shift-Command-D (OS X) or Ctrl-Shift-D (Win) **A**.

   Flash creates a layer for each object, adding the new layers to the bottom of the Timeline. Each object remains in the same location on the Stage, but on a separate layer.

TIP When you apply Distribute to Layers to a selected group, the various elements of the group remain joined. To distribute the elements separately, you must first break the group apart. The same procedure applies to symbols (see Chapter 7).

Working with Guide Layers

Flash offers two types of guide layers. Plain *guide* layers can contain any kind of content: lines, shapes, symbols, or text. The elements on a guide layer don't become part of the final movie. They just help you position items on the Stage. *Motion guide* layers contain a single line that directs the movement of an animated element in a classic tween (see Chapter 9).

To create a plain guide layer:

Control-click (OS X) or right-click (Win) a layer, and choose Guide from the contextual menu. The layer changes to a guide layer with a T-square icon before the layer name **A**.

To create a motion guide layer:

Control-click (OS X) or right-click (Win) a layer, and choose Add Classic Motion Guide from the contextual menu.

A new layer appears in the Timeline, linked to the layer you clicked **B**. A motion-guide icon and default name starting with *Guide:* identify the layer as a motion guide.

TIP When you've placed guide elements in a scene, lock the guide layer so you don't accidentally move the guide elements.

TIP When moving layers in the Timeline, it's easy to accidentally transform a plain guide layer into a motion guide layer. As you drag a motion guide layer directly beneath a plain guide layer, watch the preview bar and the icon in the plain guide layer. To preserve the plain guide layer, drag to the left until the preview bar's small circle aligns with the left side of the T-square icon. To transform the plain guide layer into a motion guide layer, drag to the right to align the circle with the right side of the T-square icon.

A In the Timeline, Flash identifies plain guide layers with a T-square icon. It's a good idea to rename the layer to further identify it as a guide.

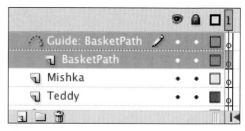

B Click a layer and, from the contextual menu for layers, choose Add Classic Motion Guide. The clicked layer indents below the new layer, indicating that the two are linked. A motion-guide icon and default name identify the new layer as a classic motion guide.

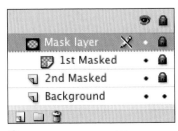

A The mask-layer icon ⊗ imitates the masking effect with a dark mask shape over a checkerboard pattern. Masked layers are indented; their layer icon has a checkerboard pattern ▧.

Working with Mask Layers

Mask layers let you hide and show elements on underlying layers. In the final movie, shapes on a mask layer become "holes" that let items on linked layers show through.

To create a mask layer:

Control-click (OS X) or right-click (Win) a layer, and from the contextual menu, choose Mask.

Flash defines the layer as a mask, links it with the layer directly below, and locks both layers so that masking is in effect **A**.

To add masked layers:

1. To link an existing unmasked layer to a mask, drag the unmasked layer directly below the mask layer or one of its linked layers.

   The preview bar automatically aligns with the masked-layer icon.

2. To add a new masked layer to a mask, select any of the mask's linked layers, and create a new layer. The new masked layer appears directly above the selected layer.

   TIP When you drag an unmasked layer beneath the lowest layer of the masked set and want to add it to the masked set, you must drag the preview bar to the right until the circle aligns with the masked layer's icon. (Dragging to the left to align the circle with the left side of the Timeline, places the unmasked layer below the set of masked layers, but outside the masked set.)

To create the mask shape:

1. Create one or more layers containing graphic content.

2. Create a mask layer and link the content layers to it.

   Make sure that the mask layer is selected, visible, and unlocked. It should be highlighted in the Timeline, and the Eye and Lock columns should contain bullets (not Xs or padlock icons).

3. Use the drawing tools to create a fill shape on the mask layer **B**. Flash uses only fills to create the mask and ignores any strokes on the mask layer.

   TIP You cannot create letter-shaped masks using TLF text. The rectangular bounding box of the text field—not the letterforms themselves—defines the mask. To create letterform masks, use a Classic text field. Alternatively, you can start with TLF text, break it down to drawing-objects (choose Modify > Break Apart), and convert it to a symbol (see Chapter 7). Or, you can fully break down the TLF text to merge-shapes (choose Modify > Break Apart twice), select the resulting merge-shape letters, and group them.

To see the mask's effect:

Lock the mask layer and all linked layers.

or

1. Control-click (OS X) or right-click (Win) a mask (or masked) layer.

2. From the contextual menu, choose Show Masking. Flash automatically locks the mask layer and all the layers linked to it.

   In document-editing mode, you must lock the mask layer and any masked layers beneath it to see the mask effect **C**. You can see the effect without locking the layers in one of Flash's test modes (see Chapter 8).

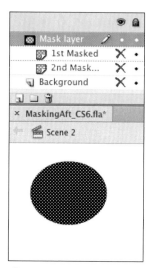

B Fill shapes—such as the oval on this mask layer—create "holes" that reveal content on the masked layers below. All mask shapes must be on the same sublevel of the mask layer. That is, you must use only one merge-shape or one graphic-object. To use multiple shapes, you must break them all down to merge-shapes, then combine them (by grouping, for example) or wrap up shapes and/or drawing-objects inside a symbol (see Chapter 7).

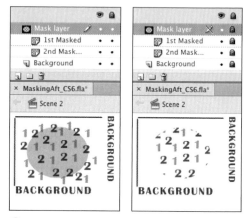

C After defining the mask and masked layers, you must lock them to see the mask in effect in document-editing mode. Using a transparent fill for the mask shape lets you see exactly what lies below the mask's "hole" when the layers are unlocked.

Working with Symbols

Ultimately, you'll want to animate the static graphics you've learned to create, and you'll probably want to use them again and again. Fortunately, you can save graphic elements for reuse by turning them into *symbols* and storing them in the *library* that is a part of each Flash document.

A symbol is just one type of library *asset*. The library also contains bitmaps, font symbols (embedded fonts), sounds, and video clips. Flash refers to each copy of a library asset that you use in a movie as an *instance* of that asset.

In this chapter, you'll work with libraries and create static (single-frame) graphic symbols. In later chapters, you learn about creating animated (multi-frame) graphic symbols, movie-clip symbols, and buttons (see Chapters 12 and 14) and adding sound and video (see Chapter 16).

Using the Library Panel

In the Library panel, you can view and organize all of the assets (symbols, font symbols, sounds, video clips, and bitmaps) used in a Flash movie. You'll see when an asset was last modified, what type of asset it is, and how many times it was used. The Library panel also contains a search feature for locating specific assets.

To open the library of the current document:

- Choose Window > Library, or press Command-L (OS X) or Ctrl-L (Win).

  The Library panel opens **Ⓐ**. The panel can display the library of any open Flash document.

TIP The Library panel displays the assets of just one document at a time. To view libraries for multiple documents simultaneously, you can open multiple Library panels. In the open Library panel, click the New Library Panel button ⬚ just below the panel menu. Flash opens the current library in a new panel window showing the assets of the same document. Then, choose a different library in one of the panels.

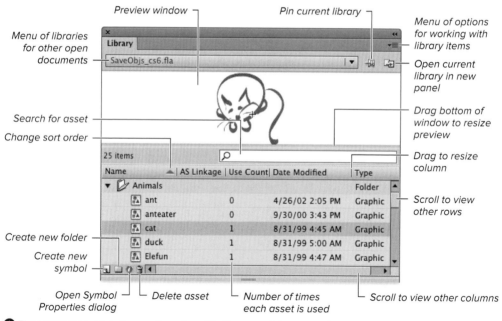

Ⓐ The Library panel lists the assets assigned to the current document. Items are sorted by the selected column (displaying a triangle in the column heading). Click the triangle to reverse the sort order.

B The Library panel contains the libraries of all the currently open documents. To view a different library without switching documents, choose another document from the menu.

To view the library of another open document:

1. With two or more Flash documents open, access the Library panel.

2. From the menu of open documents, choose the desired document **B**. The Library panel displays the assets of the selected document.

TIP You can organize a library using hierarchical folders. To create a new folder, click the New Folder button ▣ at the bottom of the Library panel, or choose New Folder from the panel menu.

To open the library of a closed document:

1. Choose File > Import > Open External Library, or press Shift-Command-O (OS X) or Ctrl-Shift-O (Win). The Open As Library dialog appears.

2. Find the file that contains the library you want to open. Select the file, and click Open.

   The Library panel appears, making those symbols available for use in other movies.

TIP Flash makes a set of *common libraries* available from the Menu bar—a sort of library of libraries. Flash installs with three common libraries. You can add your own by adding a folder named Libraries to the User-Level Configuration folder for your language installation. Any files you add to that Libraries folder also appear in the Common Libraries menu when you restart the application. Choosing an item from the Common Libraries menu opens only the library, and not the file itself. You might create a common library to make your favorite symbols, sounds, video clips, and bitmaps accessible from the Menu bar.

Creating Master Symbols

Flash's symbols allow you to encapsulate elements and reuse them throughout a Flash movie without increasing the movie's file size. You can create new symbols directly in the symbol editor. You can also select one or more elements on the Stage and convert them to a symbol. This method is useful when you want to create multiple graphic elements in context with one another, but make each element available as a separate symbol.

The following tasks create static graphic symbols. You can also create symbols containing animation (see Chapter 12) or symbols that act as buttons (see Chapter 14).

To create a new symbol:

1. To enter symbol-editing mode, do one of the following:

   ▸ Choose Insert > New Symbol, or press Command-F8 (OS X) or Ctrl-F8 (Win).

   ▸ From the Library's panel menu, choose New Symbol.

   ▸ Click the Library panel's New Symbol button **Ⓐ**.

   The Create New Symbol dialog opens **Ⓑ**.

2. Type a name for your symbol.

   A completed movie may have dozens, if not hundreds, of symbols; so assigning a brief descriptive name will help you (and others who may work on the project) remember each symbol's role.

3. From the Type menu, choose Graphic.

Ⓐ The folded-page icon at the bottom-left corner of the Library panel is the New Symbol button. Clicking the button is one way to enter symbol-editing mode and start creating a symbol from scratch.

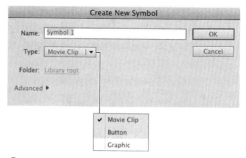

Ⓑ In the Create New Symbol dialog, name your symbol and choose a type. Click the Folder hot text to choose or create a library folder in which to place the symbol. Settings relating to the way the movie works at runtime, such as linkages for sharing and import/export, appear in the Advanced section of the dialog.

Back button (return to document-editing mode)

Current scene | Current symbol | List of scenes | List of symbols

Scene 1 | Wild

Registration crosshair for symbol being created

C In symbol-editing mode, the name of the current symbol appears in the Edit bar just above the Stage. A registration crosshair on the Stage and the disappearance of the Pasteboard are your clues that this is symbol-editing mode.

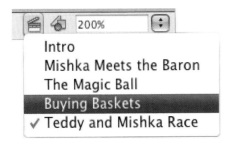

200%

Intro
Mishka Meets the Baron
The Magic Ball
Buying Baskets
✓ Teddy and Mishka Race

D Choose a scene from the Edit bar's Edit Scene menu to switch to that scene in document-editing mode.

4. Click OK.

Flash places a master copy of the symbol in the library and enters symbol-editing mode: the symbol's name appears in the Edit bar, a crosshair appears at the center of the Stage, and the Pasteboard disappears **C**. The crosshair indicates the symbol's registration point. (See the sidebar "Registration and Transformation Points for Symbols.")

5. Create Timeline layers and graphic elements on the Stage, just as you would in the regular editing environment.

6. To return to document-editing mode, do one of the following:

▸ Choose Edit > Edit Document, or press Command-E (OS X) or Ctrl-E (Win). Flash returns you to the current scene.

▸ In the Edit bar, click the Back button or the Current Scene link. Flash returns you to the current scene.

▸ In the Edit bar, choose a scene from the Edit Scene pop-up menu in **D**. Flash takes you to that scene.

TIP By default, Flash puts new master symbols at the root level of the library (the Folder hot text is *Library root*). Click the hot text to open the Move to Folder dialog, where you can select an existing folder or create (and select) a new folder as the destination for the symbol you're creating.

TIP When creating new symbols, consider how the registration point will work with your finished symbol. Will you be rotating the symbol around its center? If so, put the registration point at the symbol's center by positioning your elements evenly around the crosshair. Will you be animating the symbol as a character, such as a bird? Then you might place the registration point at a specific body part, say the tip of the beak, so you can orient the character naturally when animating it.

To convert existing graphics to symbols:

1. Select the graphic element(s) you want to convert to a symbol.

2. Choose Modify > Convert to Symbol, or press F8 on the keyboard. The Convert to Symbol dialog **E** opens.

3. Type a new name for your symbol.

4. From the Type menu, choose Graphic.

5. To set the symbol's registration point, click one of the squares in the registration grid **F**.

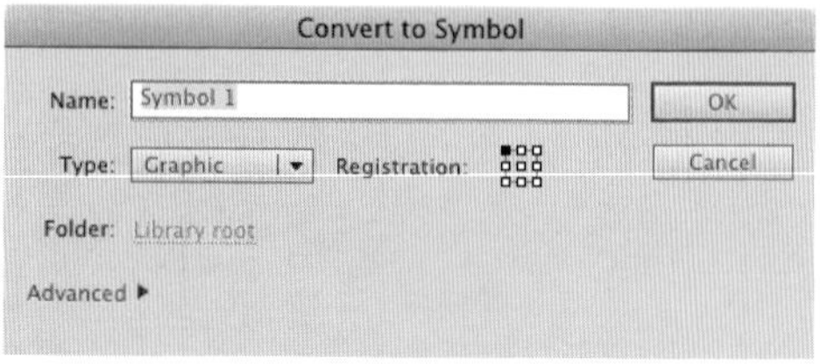

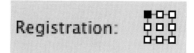

E To turn a selection into a symbol, choose Modify > Convert to Symbol. In the Convert to Symbol dialog, name your symbol, choose a type, and set the registration-point location.

Registration:

F By default, Flash registers a symbol by the upper-left corner of its bounding box. Click a different square on the registration grid—another corner, the center, or a side—to register the symbol by that point on the symbol's bounding box.

About Symbol Types

Each Flash symbol is, in fact, a Flash movie in miniature, complete with its own Timeline. To determine how a symbol's Timeline meshes with the Timeline of the movie in which that symbol appears, you specify a *type* for the symbol: graphic, button, or movie clip.

A graphic symbol's Timeline operates in lockstep with the main movie Timeline. Like any graphic element, a static graphic symbol occupies only one frame of the main movie Timeline. A three-frame animated graphic symbol occupies three frames (see Chapter 12).

Buttons have their own four-frame Timeline. A button instance occupies one frame of the main movie Timeline, and displays different content as a user's mouse interacts with the button (see Chapter 14).

Movie clips also occupy just one frame of the main movie Timeline, but have their own multiframe Timeline that plays independently of the main Timeline (see Chapter 12).

Selected merge-shape

Converted to a symbol

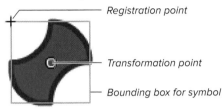

Registration point

Transformation point

Bounding box for symbol

G A selected merge-shape on the Stage is highlighted with dots. When you convert that shape to a symbol, the bounding box is the only item that is highlighted. A crosshair locates the symbol's registration point. A circle locates the symbol's transformation point.

6. Click OK.

The selected items on the Stage become an instance of the symbol, and a master copy of the symbol appears in the library. At the same time, a bounding box encloses the symbol instance, the transformation-point circle appears at the center of the symbol, and the registration crosshair appears in the location you selected in Step 5 **G**. You can no longer edit the item directly on the Stage, but must open it in one of Flash's symbol-editing modes.

TIP To quickly convert a graphic element to a symbol, select the elements on the Stage and drag the selection to the lower half of the document's Library panel. In the Convert to Symbol dialog, name and define your symbol as described in the preceding task.

TIP A graphic symbol can consist of one or more merge-shapes, drawing-objects, primitive-shapes, grouped shapes—you name it. You can even include symbols within symbols. Whatever is selected on the Stage when you choose Convert to Symbol becomes part of the symbol.

Registration and Transformation Points for Symbols

Flash uses the *registration point* (represented by a small crosshair) to *register* a graphic-object—that is, to locate the object via coordinates on the Stage during authoring and playback. For drawing-objects, primitives, groups, and text fields, the registration point is always the upper-left corner of the object's bounding box. For symbols the registration point works differently. The registration point stays the same for each instance of the same symbol, but you set that point's location. When you convert a selection to a symbol, you can choose from nine preset registration-point locations. When you create a symbol from scratch (or edit a symbol), you determine the point's location by positioning elements around the crosshair on the Stage.

Flash uses the *transformation point* (represented by a small circle) as the reference point for transforming a symbol instance. When you rotate a symbol, for example, the transformation point is the pivot around which the symbol spins. You can also use the transformation point for snapping operations. By default, Flash places the transformation point in the center of a symbol instance, but you can change that for individual symbol instances by dragging the circle to a new location using the free-transform tool.

Using Symbol Instances

A *symbol instance* is actually just a pointer to a *master symbol*—a full set of instructions that Flash uses to re-create the content you've defined as a symbol. Using symbols, therefore, helps keep file sizes small. When you convert a graphic on the Stage to a symbol, you have one symbol instance on the Stage. To use that symbol again, or if you created the symbol in symbol-editing mode, you'll need to move a copy from the library to the Stage.

To place a symbol instance in your movie:

1. In the Timeline, select the layer and keyframe where you want the graphic symbol to appear.

   Flash only places symbols in keyframes. If you select an in-between frame, Flash places the symbol in the preceding keyframe. (To learn more about keyframes, see Chapter 8.)

2. In the Library panel, click the desired symbol name. The selected symbol appears in the preview window.

3. Drag a copy of the symbol from the preview window to the Stage. A rectangular outline stands in for the symbol as you drag A.

4. Release the mouse button. Flash places an instance of the symbol on the Stage and selects that instance.

> **TIP** To quickly place a symbol instance, drag a symbol name directly from the Library panel to the Stage without using the preview window.

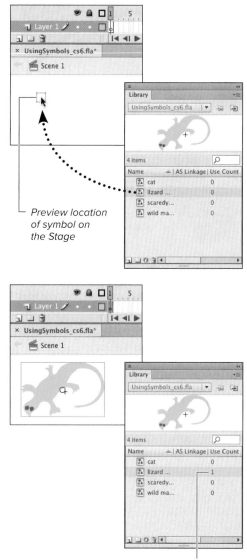

Preview location of symbol on the Stage

Use count updated

A When you drag a symbol from the Library panel to the Stage (top), Flash places the symbol on the Stage, selects it, and updates that symbol's use count in the Library panel.

To change the color of a selected symbol instance, access the Property inspector's Color Effect section. From the Style menu, choose a property to modify.

Deleting Master Symbols

Deleting master symbols from the library isn't difficult but does require some advance thought. You don't want to accidentally delete a symbol that's currently used in a movie, which is especially easy to do when you've nested symbols within symbols. Select the symbol in the Library panel, then look at the use-counts column. (If use counts don't appear in the panel, drag the bottom scroll bar to view them, or widen the panel.) If the use count is zero, feel free to delete the symbol by clicking the library's Delete button 🗑, choosing Delete from the panel menu, or pressing Delete. When the symbol is in use, it's best to track down exactly where the symbol instance appears before deciding whether it's safe to delete the master symbol.

Note that you can use the Movie Explorer panel to help find a symbol. To access the panel, choose Window > Movie Explorer, or press Option-F3 (OS X) or Alt-F3 (Win).

Modifying Symbol Instances

You can change the appearance of individual symbol instances without changing their master symbol. As with any other element, you can move, scale, or rotate an instance by manipulating it with the selection and free-transform tools. You can also modify a selected instance by altering values in the Info and Transform panels, or in the Position and Size section of the Property inspector (see Chapter 4).

You can change a symbol instance's color and transparency, but the method for doing so differs from the methods you've learned for assigning colors to merge-shapes, drawing-objects, and primitive-shapes. You modify the color, intensity, and transparency of a symbol instance in the Color Effect section of the Property inspector.

To change an instance's color properties:

1. On the Stage, select the symbol instance you want to modify.

2. In the Color Effect section of the Property inspector, from the Style menu Ⓐ, choose a color property to modify.

3. Adjust the selected color property, as described in the following tasks.

To change an instance's brightness:

1. In Step 2 of the preceding task, from the Style menu, choose Brightness. A Bright slider and a field for entering a brightness percentage appear **B**.

2. To change the symbol's brightness, drag the Bright slider or type a percentage in the brightness-amount field.

   A value of –100 makes the symbol black; a value of 0 leaves the symbol at its original brightness; a value of 100 makes the symbol white **C**.

To change the instance's tint:

1. In Step 2 of the first task in this section, from the Style menu, choose Tint. Tint settings appear **D**.

2. To choose a new color, do one of the following:

   ▸ Drag the Red, Green, and Blue sliders; or type new values in the Red Color, Green Color, and Blue Color fields.

   ▸ Click the Tint Color control, and choose a color from the pop-up swatch set.

3. Drag the Tint slider, or type a percentage in the Tint Amount field.

   The percentage indicates how much of the new color to blend with the existing colors. Applying a tint of 100 percent changes all the lines and fills in the symbol to the new color. Applying a lesser percentage mixes some of the new color with the existing colors in the symbol, almost like placing a transparent film of the new color over the symbol.

B Use the Brightness settings in the Color Effect section of the Property inspector to change the intensity of a symbol instance. A high value will make the symbol instance lighter; a low value will make it darker.

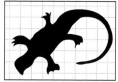 

–100 percent brightness setting *100 percent brightness setting*

C At its extremes, the Brightness setting lets you turn a symbol instance completely black or completely white.

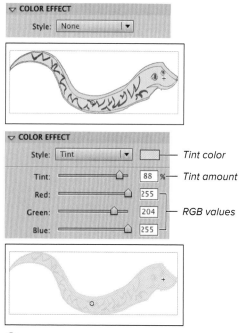

D Use the Tint settings in the Color Effect section of the Property inspector to change the color of a symbol instance. The original symbol (top) has no color effect applied. The modified symbol (bottom) has a pink tint applied.

Original

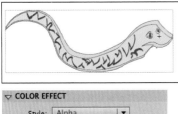

Alpha 33 percent

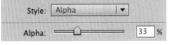

E To change the transparency of a selected symbol instance, access the Color Effect section of the Property inspector. From the Style menu choose Alpha, then drag the Alpha slider or edit the text field to enter a new alpha amount. A lower percentage makes the symbol instance more transparent.

To change the instance's transparency:

1. In Step 2 of the first task in this section, from the Style menu, choose Alpha. The Alpha settings appear **E**.

2. To change the amount of transparency, drag the Alpha slider, or type a new value in the alpha-amount field.

A value of 0 makes the symbol completely transparent; a value of 100 makes the symbol opaque.

About Advanced Effect Settings

The Advanced color-effect settings let you simultaneously change the RGB and alpha values for a selected symbol instance. The percentage hot-text controls (in the left-hand column) determine the percentage of the master symbol's original RGB and alpha values that are applied to the selected symbol instance. The offset hot-text controls (in the right-hand column) add to or subtract from the original alpha, red, green, and blue values **F**.

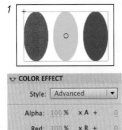

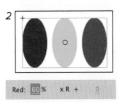

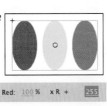

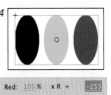

F Let's look at an example of the Advanced color-effect settings at work. The original ovals are pure red, pure green, and pure blue (1). Decreasing the red-percentage value affects only the red oval (2); a red-percentage of 0 would make the red oval totally black. The green and blue ovals had 0 percent red to start, so decreasing their red-percentage value has no visible effect. Increasing the red-offset value adds red to everything (3). Decreasing the red-offset value affects only the red oval (4).

Editing Master Symbols

Master symbols not only help you keep file sizes down, they also help you maintain graphic consistency. When you modify a master symbol in symbol-editing mode, the changes appear in every instance of that symbol in your movie. If, for example, you create a client logo as a symbol, when the client decides to change the logo's colors, you need to edit only the master symbol to update the logo everywhere it appears.

To enter symbol-editing mode from the Stage:

1. On the Stage, select the symbol you want to edit.

2. To open the symbol editor, do one of the following:

   ▸ Choose Edit > Edit Symbols, or press Command-E (OS X) or Ctrl-E (Win).

   ▸ Choose Edit > Edit Selected.

   ▸ From the pop-up list of symbols in the Edit bar, choose the symbol you want to edit .

   Flash opens the symbol editor in the current window. You can edit the symbol using any of the techniques you've learned for modifying graphics and creating and deleting content.

TIP The Edit in Place command lets you edit your master symbol on the Stage with all other items dimmed **B**. To execute the Edit in Place command, double-click a symbol instance on the Stage, or select the instance and choose Edit > Edit in Place. Any changes you make will affect all instances of that symbol.

A Choosing a symbol from the Edit Symbol pop-up menu in the Edit bar takes you into symbol-editing mode.

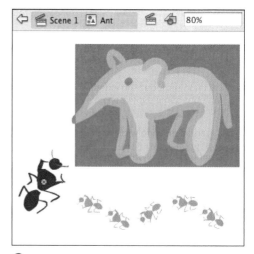

B The Edit in Place command lets you see your symbol instance in the context of other items on the Stage. The symbol instance appears in full color. (It's the large ant in this example.) The other elements on the Stage are dimmed. In this mode, changes made to the instance affect the master symbol and all the instances in the movie.

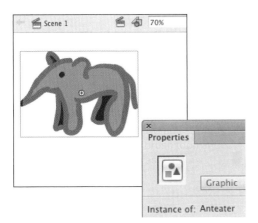

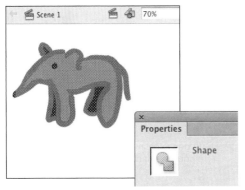

A The Property inspector reveals that the selected graphic is an instance of a symbol named Anteater (top). To break the link with its master symbol, choose Modify > Break Apart. The Property inspector reveals that the selection now consists of shapes and is no longer a symbol instance (bottom).

Converting Symbol Instances to Graphics

At times, you'll want to break the link between a placed instance of a symbol and its master symbol. For example, you may want to redraw the shape in a specific instance but not in every instance. To convert a symbol back to an independent shape or set of shapes, break it apart.

To break the symbol link:

1. On the Stage, select a symbol instance.

2. Choose Modify > Break Apart, or press Command-B (OS X) or Ctrl-B (Win) **A**.

   Flash breaks the link to the symbol in the library and selects the symbol's elements. The Property inspector no longer displays information about the instance of the symbol; it displays information about the selected shapes.

   If the original symbol contained any grouped elements, they remain grouped after you break the link, while ungrouped elements stay ungrouped. Any symbols that existed within the original symbol remain as instances of their respective master symbols. You can now edit these elements.

Converting Symbol Instances to Bitmaps

When you preview your movie using the Control > Test Movie/Test Scene command, playback may bog down when you are using complex vector images. You can avoid the slowdown by converting non-animated images to bitmaps. In Chapter 4, you converted a complex vector graphic directly to a bitmap during authoring. To ensure that you always have a copy of the vector graphic (should you need to edit it later), you can first convert it to a symbol, and then convert an instance of the symbol into a bitmap. Select the symbol instance on the Stage and choose Modify > Convert to Bitmap. You can also Command-click (OS X) or Ctrl-click (Win) the instance and choose Convert to Bitmap from the contextual menu. In Chapter 12 you'll learn to create movie-clip symbols, which offer additional options for converting vectors to bitmaps for efficient playback.

Swapping Symbols

You can replace one symbol instance with another while retaining all the modifications you made in the original symbol instance. For example, if you want to change a logo in just a few places on your site, you can create the new logo as a separate symbol and swap it with specific instances.

To switch symbols:

1. On the Stage, select the symbol instance you want to change.

2. Do one of the following:

   ▸ Choose Modify > Symbol > Swap Symbol.

   ▸ In the Property inspector, click the Swap button **Ⓐ**.

   The Swap Symbol dialog opens, listing all the symbols in the current document's library **Ⓑ**. The name of the symbol you're modifying is highlighted, and a bullet appears next to the name in the Symbol list.

3. From the Symbol list, select the replacement symbol. The original symbol remains bulleted. The new symbol is highlighted and appears in the preview window.

4. Click OK. Flash places the new symbol in the old symbol's location and applies any modifications you previously made for that instance **Ⓒ**.

TIP To quickly swap symbols, double-click the new symbol's name in the **Swap Symbol** dialog. Flash replaces it and closes the dialog.

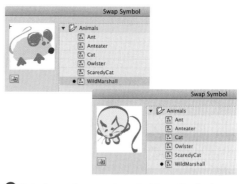

Ⓐ Click the Swap button in the Property inspector to replace a selected symbol with a different symbol from the same document.

Ⓑ Select a replacement symbol from the list in the Swap Symbol dialog, and click OK to exchange one symbol for another. A bullet appears beside the original symbol's name. The selected symbol name is highlighted, and the symbol appears in the preview window.

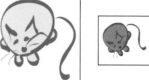

Ⓒ When you swap symbols, any modifications made to the selected instance on the Stage will also apply to the replacement instance. Here, original master symbols appear on the left, while instances used on the Stage appear on the right. Applying the Swap Symbol command to the mouse instance (which was tinted, scaled, and rotated) swaps in an instance of the cat with the same modifications.

Frame-by-Frame Animations

Frame-by-frame animation was the standard technique prior to computer animation. This hand-drawn method simulates motion using a sequence of still images that show progressive stages of a movement.

Traditional animators, such as those who worked for Walt Disney Studios, drew thousands of images, each slightly different from the next, to reflect every movement in the cartoon. Animating those drawings meant photographing the drawings as a sequence of motion picture film frames. Traditional animators painted characters (or parts of characters) and other elements of a scene on transparent sheets called *cels.* They stacked the cels to create a composite image for the frame. This cel technique allowed animators to reuse parts of an image that stayed the same in more than one frame.

With Adobe Flash Professional CS6, you can apply frame-by-frame animation techniques to create your own animated content.

In This Chapter

Touring the Timeline's Animation Features

The Timeline represents every element of a movie and is the framework for building content. In Flash CS6, the Timeline appears in an independent panel that displays information about the open and active document. You'll use this panel extensively as you create animations.

For a new Flash document, the Timeline displays a single layer with hundreds of little boxes. The first box has a solid black outline and a hollow bullet. A bullet identifies a frame that has been defined as a *keyframe* (a container for graphics, sound, or video). A hollow bullet indicates a *blank keyframe* (the container is empty), and a solid bullet indicates a keyframe with content. The rest of the Timeline boxes have gray outlines to indicate undefined placeholder frames, or *protoframes*. Every fifth protoframe is tinted gray. As you create animation, you will convert protoframes into *frames* (or *in-between frames*) and *keyframes*, thereby creating *spans*. A span consists of a key-frame plus any in-between frames that follow it.

Although you'll work solely with *keyframe spans* in this chapter, Flash CS6 can create three types of spans.

- *Keyframe spans* are used in frame-by-frame animation, classic tweening (Chapter 9), and shape tweening (Chapter 10).

- *Tween spans* are used in motion tweening (Chapter 11).

- *Pose spans* are used in inverse kinematics (Chapter 13).

Keyframe spans have black outlines in the Timeline along with a hollow rectangle in the last frame of the span. When the keyframe at the beginning of a span has content, the in-between frames in the span continue to display that content on the Stage. If you've set Frame View to Tinted Frames (the default), the in-between frames of a keyframe span with content also have a gray tint in the Timeline. Figure **A** shows a Timeline with a variety of defined frames and spans.

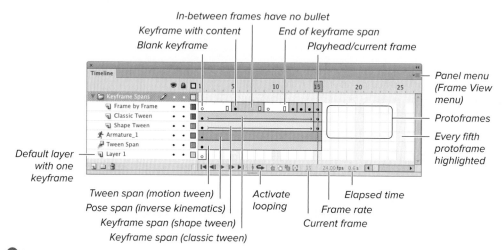

A Similar to an interactive outline, the Timeline represents all the scenes, frames, and layers of a Flash movie. Frames appear in chronological order. Click any frame in the Timeline to go directly to that frame and view its contents on the Stage.

Choosing Frame Views

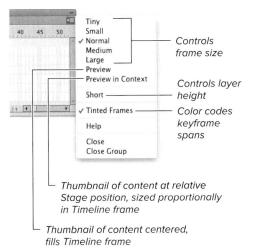

The Timeline is the framework that contains all the still images that make up an animation. The Timeline displays the layers and frames of the currently active document. New documents automatically start with a Timeline containing one layer and a blank keyframe as the first frame. You define keyframes and frames to contain content and tweens.

Tiny
Small
✓ *Normal*
Medium — *Controls*
Large — *frame size*
Preview
Preview in Context
Short — *Controls layer*
height
✓ *Tinted Frames* — *Color codes*
Help — *keyframe*
spans
Close
Close Group

Thumbnail of content at relative Stage position, sized proportionally in Timeline frame

Thumbnail of content centered, fills Timeline frame

Ⓐ The Timeline's panel menu lets you control the size and appearance of frames in the Timeline.

To view frames at different sizes:

- In the Timeline, from the panel menu (also known as the Frame View menu in this panel), choose a display option **Ⓐ**.

   Flash resizes the frames in the Timeline to reflect your choice **Ⓑ**.

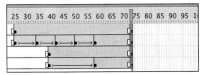

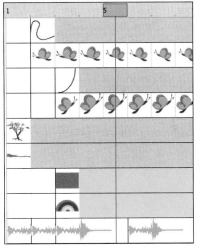

Ⓑ Each Frame View option is useful in its own way. Let's compare two options: In Tiny mode (above), the Timeline appears as a minimal graph, helping you to see the larger sweep of a long movie, but making it harder to see the details of each keyframe. In Preview mode (right), the Timeline displays thumbnails of each keyframe's content, giving you useful visual cues.

To hide/show color coding for frames:

- In the Timeline, from the panel menu, choose Tinted Frames.

  When Tinted Frames is active (the default setting), Flash color-codes keyframe spans in the following ways: spans containing static content are gray, spans containing classic tweens are bluish-purple, and spans containing shape tweens are light green.

About File Size and Animation Style

One way to create the illusion of motion in Flash is to use frame-by-frame animation to display a series of still images. Each image requires a separate keyframe. Each keyframe slightly increases the file size of the published movie (the SWF file), which in turn affects the download time for people viewing your movie over the web.

In general, you should strive to keep SWF files as small as possible. Therefore, you may want to limit the use of frame-by-frame animation. Use it when you can best control subtle movement and shape changes by redrawing the graphic elements in each frame. Otherwise, use Flash's classic-tweening, shape-tweening, motion-tweening, and inverse-kinematic features.

For learning purposes, in this chapter you create a bouncing ball by placing a shape in multiple keyframes. You could minimize file size by converting the ball shape to a symbol and reusing it in each keyframe (adding keyframes with the same symbol adds little to the size of the file). In the real world, however, if you can use a symbol, it's more efficient to use one of Flash's tweening methods.

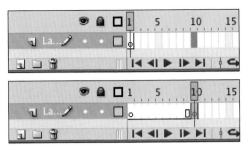

(A) To add a blank keyframe, select a protoframe in the Timeline (top), and choose Insert > Timeline > Blank Keyframe. The new blank keyframe appears at the frame you selected, and defined frames fill out the preceding keyframe span. A hollow rectangle indicates the last frame of the span.

Context Menu for Frames

The tasks in this section access frame-related commands from the Menu bar. However, those frame commands are also available from a contextual frame menu that you can open by Control-clicking (OS X) or right-clicking (Win) a frame in the Timeline.

Creating Keyframes

Flash offers two commands for creating keyframes. Choose Insert > Timeline > Blank Keyframe to define a keyframe that's empty; use this command when you want to completely change, replace, or remove the contents of the Stage. Choose Insert > Timeline > Keyframe to define a keyframe that duplicates the content of the preceding keyframe in that layer; use this command when you just want to modify the content of the preceding keyframe.

To add a blank keyframe to the end of your movie:

1. Create a new Flash document. By default the document has one layer and a blank keyframe at Frame 1.

2. In the Timeline, click Protoframe 10.

   The playhead doesn't move into the protoframe area, but Protoframe 10 highlights as the current selected frame.

3. Choose Insert > Timeline > Blank Keyframe.

   The Timeline updates **(A)**. A hollow rectangle appears at Frame 9. A black line separates Frame 9 from Frame 10, indicating where one keyframe span ends and the next begins. The gray bars that originally separated Protoframes 2–9 become tick marks, and the gray highlight disappears from Frame 5.

To create a blank keyframe within a keyframe span:

1. Continuing with the ten-frame movie from the preceding task, in the Timeline, select Frame 1.

2. Draw a shape on the Stage.

   Flash updates the Timeline, and Frame 1's bullet changes from hollow to solid **B**.

   With Tinted Frames active, Frames 1–9 turn gray, indicating a keyframe span. A hollow rectangle marks the end of the span. Keyframe 1's content remains visible through Frame 9 in this layer.

Frame 10's bullet remains hollow, indicating that the frame has no content.

3. In the Timeline, in the area above the layers, click the number 5 or drag the playhead to Frame 5.

   On the Stage, this in-between frame displays the content of the preceding keyframe, Frame 1.

4. Choose Insert > Timeline > Blank Keyframe.

   The current in-between frame—where the playhead is currently located—becomes a keyframe and all content is removed from the Stage **C**.

B When you place content in a keyframe, a solid bullet appears at that frame in the Timeline. The gray tint indicates the in-between frames that display content from the span's initial keyframe. The hollow square indicates the end of the span. The hollow circle indicates a blank keyframe.

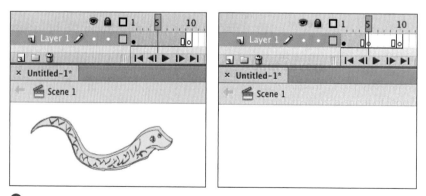

C When you convert an in-between frame that displays content into a blank keyframe, Flash removes all content from the Stage. Frames 6–9 are tinted, which indicates that they display the content of the span's initial keyframe, Frame 1 (left). A blank keyframe inserted at Frame 5 becomes the new initial keyframe of a span containing Frames 6–9 (right). Because there is no content in the span's initial keyframe, the tint disappears.

To duplicate the contents of the preceding keyframe:

1. Open a new Flash document and place content in Keyframe 1.

2. In the Timeline, select Frame 3.

3. Choose Insert > Timeline > Keyframe.

   Flash creates a new keyframe that duplicates the content of Keyframe 1. In the Timeline, a hollow rectangle appears at Frame 2 and a solid bullet at Frame 3 **D**. The content of Frames 1 and 3 is totally separate.

Content of the first keyframe   Current frame   Duplicate of the first keyframe

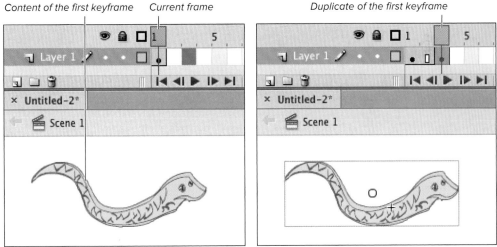

D With Frame 3 selected (left), the Insert > Timeline > Keyframe command duplicates the content of the preceding keyframe in that layer (Frame 1) and uses that content to create a new keyframe (right).

Insert Keyframe vs. Convert to Keyframes

Whether you should insert or convert keyframes depends on how many frames you have selected when you issue the command and how many frames you want to create. The Insert commands create a single keyframe regardless of the number of selected frames; the Modify commands create multiple keyframes, one for each selected frame.

With a single frame selected, the Insert > Timeline > Keyframe command and the Modify > Timeline > Convert to Keyframe (F6) command work identically. If you select one protoframe, or one in-between frame, both commands transform the selected frame to a keyframe that duplicates the content of the preceding keyframe. When an in-between frame or a protoframe follows the selected keyframe, both commands transform that following frame to a keyframe that duplicates the content of the selected frame. Neither command has any effect when another keyframe directly follows the selected keyframe.

With multiple protoframes or in-between frames selected, the Insert > Timeline > Keyframe command creates a single keyframe, usually at the location of the playhead. The remaining selected frames become in-between frames.

With multiple protoframes or in-between frames selected, choosing Modify > Timeline > Convert to Keyframes turns every selected frame into a keyframe.

The commands for blank keyframes work similarly. Choose Insert > Timeline > Blank Keyframe to create one keyframe at the playhead's location and turn the remaining frames into in-between frames. Choose Modify > Timeline > Convert to Blank Keyframes (F7) to turn each of the selected frames into a blank keyframe.

These commands work a bit differently when used within the tween span of a motion tween (see Chapter 11) or within the pose span of an inverse kinematics tween (see Chapter 13).

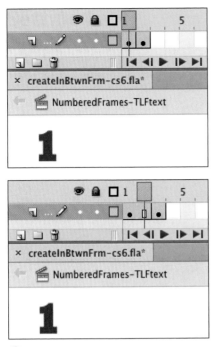

Creating In-between Frames

Frames that appear between keyframes are tied to the preceding keyframe. They display its content and add a space in which to create classic tweens and shape tweens. Flash shows the connections between these frames by tinting them and placing a hollow rectangle at the end of the keyframe span.

To add in-between frames:

1. Create a Flash document that has keyframes and content in Frames 1 and 2.

2. In the Timeline, position the playhead at Keyframe 1.

3. Choose Insert > Timeline > Frame, or press F5. Flash adds an in-between frame Ⓐ. Your movie now contains a keyframe at Frame 1, an in-between frame at Frame 2, and another keyframe at Frame 3.

Ⓐ With the playhead at Frame 1 (top), the Insert > Timeline > Frame command adds a new in-between frame at Frame 2.

What Are Keyframes and In-between Frames?

Traditional cel animation required veritable armies of artists to create the enormous number of drawings that the technique entails. To keep costs down, animation studios devised an assembly line workflow. It started with models sheets to define the look and movement patterns of each character. Then came storyboards that outlined the dramatic action within and across scenes. Eventually, individual artists drew and painted hundreds of cels, each slightly different, to bring the animation to life.

To make hand-drawn animation more efficient, lead animators drew keyframes that defined the *movement extremes* (crucial body positions within a movement), while other animators filled in the movement between those extremes by drawing in-between frames.

Keyframes define a significant change to a character or graphic. Imagine a 25-frame sequence in which a bear starts out facing the audience and then quickly turns to the right to look at a leaping salmon. This scene requires two keyframes—the bear face-on and the bear in profile—connected by 23 in-between frames.

Flash doesn't use the term *in-between frames;* it uses *frame* for frames that aren't defined as *keyframes, property keyframes,* or *pose frames.* However, for clarity, this book does refer to *in-between frames.*

Selecting Frames in Keyframe Spans

In Preferences, you can choose one of two methods for selecting frames in the Timeline. Frame-based selection, the default, treats every frame individually; clicking a frame selects just that frame. Span-based selection groups frames as members of a *keyframe span* (the keyframe plus any in-between frames that follow it and display its content); clicking one frame in the middle of a span selects the entire span.

Except where noted, the examples in this book use the default frame-based selection.

To choose a selection method:

1. Choose Flash > Preferences (OS X) or Edit > Preferences (Win). The Preferences dialog opens.

2. From the Category list, select General. The General settings appear on the right side of the dialog **Ⓐ**.

3. In the Timeline section, choose one of the following frame-selection methods:

   ▸ To manipulate keyframe spans in the Timeline, select the "Span based selection" checkbox **Ⓑ**.

   ▸ To manipulate individual frames in the Timeline, deselect the "Span based selection" checkbox **Ⓒ**.

Ⓐ The method for selecting frames in the Timeline is a Preferences setting. To enable a single-click to select an entire span, in the Timeline section of the dialog, select the "Span based selection" checkbox.

Timeline: ☑ Span based selection

Ⓑ To work with keyframe spans as a unit in the Timeline, select the "Span based selection" checkbox in the General section of the Preferences dialog.

Timeline: ☐ Span based selection

Ⓒ To work with individual keyframes in the Timeline, deselect the "Span based selection" checkbox in the General section of the Preferences dialog.

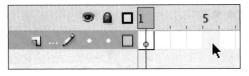

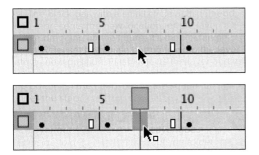

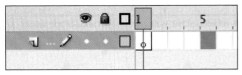 Both frame-selection methods treat protoframes identically for selection. Click a protoframe (top) to select it.

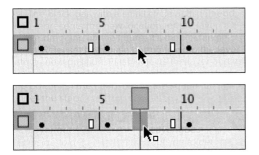 Using frame-based selection, click a frame in the middle of a keyframe span (top) to select only that frame (bottom).

To select undefined frames:

To select protoframes with either selection method, do one of the following:

- To select one protoframe, click it **D**.

- To select two protoframes and all the frames between them, click the first protoframe, and then Shift-click the last protoframe.

- To select noncontiguous protoframes, Command-click (OS X) or Ctrl-click (Win) the protoframes.

To select frames in keyframe spans—frame-based method:

In the Timeline—with frame-based selection active—do one of the following:

- To select a keyframe, click it.

- To select the last frame in a keyframe span, click it.

- To select a single frame within a keyframe span, click that frame **E**.

- To select an entire keyframe span, double-click any frame in the span.

- To add frames to your selection, Shift-click the additional frames. Flash selects all the frames between the last selected frame and the frame you Shift-clicked.

- To select a range of frames, click the first frame of the range, then Shift-click the last frame in the range; or starting with no frames selected, drag through the range of frames.

To select frames in keyframe spans—span-based method:

In the Timeline—with span-based selection active—do one of the following:

- To select a keyframe, click it.

- To select the last frame in a keyframe span, click it.

- To select one in-between frame, Command-click (OS X) or Ctrl-click (Win) that frame.

- To select an entire keyframe span, click a middle frame in the keyframe span 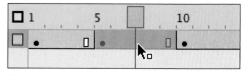; or Shift-click the first or last frame in the span.

- To add other spans to your selection, Shift-click any frame in each additional span. The selection can include non-contiguous spans .

- To select a range of frames, Command-drag (OS X) or Ctrl-drag (Win) through the frames.

TIP Both selection methods let you select all the frames in a layer by clicking the layer name. The span-based method also lets you select all the frames in a layer by triple-clicking: first double-click a frame (its span is selected after the first click), then click that selected span a third time. There's no need to rush that third click—the double-click primes the span, so when you later click anywhere in that selected span, Flash selects all the frames in that layer.

TIP Both selection methods let you select noncontiguous frames by Command-clicking (OS X) or Ctrl-clicking (Win) each frame that you want to include. This technique does not work within the tween span of a motion tween or within an inverse-kinematics pose span.

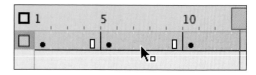

F Using span-based selection, clicking a frame in the middle of a keyframe span (top) selects the whole span (bottom).

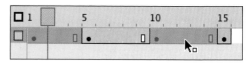

G Using span-based selection, you can Shift-click to select keyframe spans that aren't contiguous.

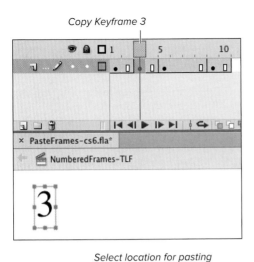
Copy Keyframe 3

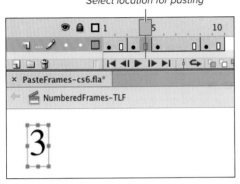
Select location for pasting

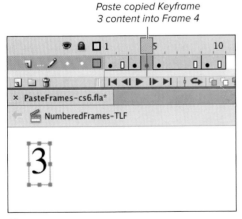
Paste copied Keyframe
3 content into Frame 4

Ⓐ When you paste a frame with new content into an in-between frame, Flash converts the frame to a keyframe.

Manipulating Frames in a Layer

You can't copy or paste frames using the standard Copy and Paste commands for graphic elements. The Edit > Timeline submenu provides commands specifically for copying and pasting frames. In addition, you can relocate selected frames to new locations by dragging them in the Timeline.

For the following tasks, open a new Flash document. Create a ten-frame movie with keyframes at Frames 1, 3, 5, and 9. Using the text tool, place a text field in each keyframe, and enter the number of the frame in the text field; this technique makes it easier to see what's happening as you practice. Create two copies of this practice document (choose Edit > Save As). Name them PasteFrames.fla and DragFrames.fla.

To copy and paste a single frame:

1. Open the PasteFrames.fla document, and in the Timeline, select Keyframe 3.

2. Copy the selected frame to the Clipboard by choosing Edit > Timeline > Copy Frames, or pressing Option-Command-C (OS X) or Ctrl-Alt-C (Win).

3. In the Timeline, select Frame 4 as the location to paste the copied frame.

4. Choose Edit > Timeline > Paste Frames, or press Option-Command-V (OS X) or Ctrl-Alt-V (Win) to paste the copied frame into Frame 4 **Ⓐ**.

Continues on next page

5. Select Frame 5 and paste another copy **B**.

Flash replaces the content of Keyframe 5 with the content of Keyframe 3.

6. Select Protoframe 12 and paste another copy.

Flash extends the movie to accommodate the pasted frame. Note that the playhead won't move to Protoframe 12 until after you've pasted the copy.

> **TIP** You could copy and paste multiple frames by selecting a range of frames in Step 1.

> **TIP** To copy and paste the content of a keyframe, you can also copy an in-between frame that displays that content. When you paste, Flash creates a new keyframe.

> **CAUTION** Flash always replaces the content of the selected frame with the pasted frame (or, for multiple-frame pastes, with the first pasted frame). If you're not careful, you may overwrite the content of keyframes you intend to keep. To be safe, always paste frames into in-between frames, protoframes, or blank keyframes. You can later delete any extra, unwanted keyframes.

To drag frames to another location:

1. Open the DragFrames.fla practice file, and in the Timeline, select the keyframe span that starts with Keyframe 5 and ends with Frame 8.

2. Position the pointer over the selected frames.

3. Drag the selected frames.

A dark blue outline appears around the selection highlight as you drag. Use the dark-blue rectangle to preview the new location in the Timeline for the selected frames.

Keyframe 5 selected

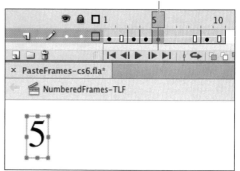

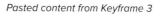

Pasted content from Keyframe 3

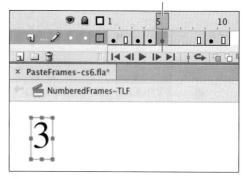

B When you paste a frame with new content into a keyframe, the keyframe's content is replaced.

Standard Layer Operations

In Flash CS6 you can copy and paste an entire Timeline layer into a new layer. You can also cut and duplicate layers. You'll learn more about multiple-layer editing techniques in Chapter 12.

Select and drag: either selection style

Selected frames

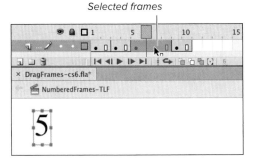

Preview of new frame location

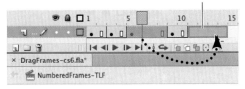

After drag: frame-based selection style

Original keyframe removed   Frames in new location

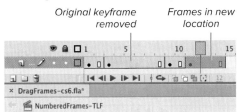

After drag: span-based selection style

Original keyframe retained, content removed   Frames in new location

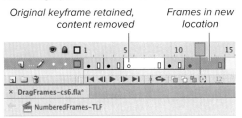

Ⓒ You can drag a range of selected frames to change its location in the Timeline. The Timeline updates in different ways depending on which frame-selection method is active. Frame-based selection removes selected keyframes from their original locations, leaving only in-between frames. Span-based selection retains the original keyframes but removes their contents.

4. To move the selected frames to the end of your movie, drag the rectangle into the area of protoframes, and release the mouse button.

   Flash adds frames to the end of the movie that display the content from Frames 5–8. With frame-based selection, Flash completely removes the content from Frames 5–8 and adds those frames to the preceding span. With span-based selection, Flash removes the content but leaves a blank keyframe at Frame 5 Ⓒ.

5. To move the selected frames to the beginning of your movie, drag the selected frames to Frame 1 and release the mouse button.

   With both selection styles, the dragged frames replace the contents of Frames 1–4. There is no longer a keyframe at Frame 5.

TIP To drag a copy of selected frames in the Timeline, Option-drag (OS X) or Alt-drag (Win) the frames.

TIP No matter which frame-selection method you use, pressing the Command key (OS X) or Ctrl key (Win) lets you temporarily access some of the functionality of the other method. With span-based selection, pressing the modifier key allows you to select individual frames using the arrow pointer. With frame-based selection, pressing the modifier key allows you to extend keyframe spans using the double-headed arrow pointer.

TIP Using the double-headed arrow pointer to resize one span amidst others can get a bit tricky. The expanding span cannot remove the content of other keyframes, but it can squeeze and shorten a neighboring span by using up its in-between frames. When you reduce the size of a span by dragging, Flash creates blank keyframe spans to cover any gaps between the end of the span you're resizing and the beginning of the neighboring span.

Removing Frames

You can remove frames using one of two commands: Clear Keyframe or Remove Frames. Clear Keyframe converts a keyframe or a range of frames to in-between frames and deletes the content from the Stage without changing the number of frames in the movie. Remove Frames fully deletes frames from the Timeline (thereby reducing the number of frames in the movie) and also deletes any associated content. For the following tasks, use the same type of practice document you created in "Manipulating Frames in a Layer" in this chapter.

To remove keyframe status from a frame:

1. In the Timeline, select Keyframe 5.

2. Choose Modify > Timeline > Clear Keyframe, or press Shift-F6.

   Flash removes the bullet from Frame 5 in the Timeline (indicating that the frame is no longer a keyframe) and removes the graphic elements it contained. Frame 5 becomes an in-between frame, displaying the contents of Keyframe 3 **A**. The total number of frames in the movie remains the same.

> **TIP** Don't confuse Clear Keyframe with the Clear Frames command, which has a similar name but a very different function. The Clear Frames command (choose Edit > Timeline > Clear Frames) removes all content from the Stage for a selected frame (or range of frames) by converting the selection to an empty keyframe (or an empty keyframe span). Any unselected in-between frames following your selection become a keyframe span and continue to display their original contents.

Before clearing the keyframe
Selected keyframe is Frame 5

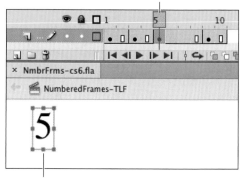

Content of selected keyframe

After clearing the keyframe
Frame 5 becomes an in-between frame

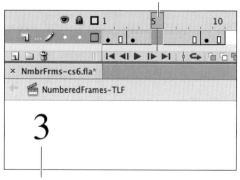

Frame 5 displays the content of the preceding keyframe

A The Modify > Timeline > Clear Keyframe command removes the contents of the selected keyframe from the Stage and converts the keyframe to an in-between frame. The Clear Keyframe command doesn't change the overall length of the movie.

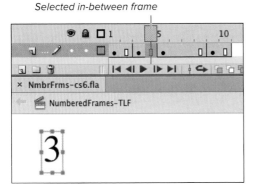

Selected in-between frame

After deleting

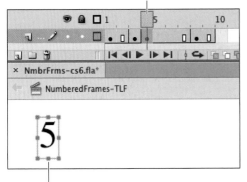

Content originally in Keyframe 5 is now in Keyframe 4

B The Edit > Timeline > Remove Frames command deletes selected frames from the movie and reduces its length.

To delete a frame from a keyframe span:

1. With your practice file in its original state (keyframes at 1, 3, 5, and 9), select Frame 4 in the Timeline. Frame 4 is an in-between frame associated with Keyframe 3.

2. Choose Edit > Timeline > Remove Frames, or press Shift-F5.

   Flash deletes Frame 4, reducing the overall length of the movie by one frame **B**. The content that was in Keyframe 5 moves back one frame to become the new Keyframe 4.

3. Select Keyframe 3, and choose Edit > Timeline > Remove Frames again.

   Flash deletes the selected keyframe and its content, and reduces the length of the movie by one frame. The content that was in Keyframe 4 moves back one frame to become Keyframe 3.

TIP Flash doesn't let you use Clear Keyframe to remove keyframe status from the first frame of a movie, but you can delete it. If you select all the frames in one layer and choose Edit > Timeline > Remove Frames, Flash removes all the defined frames in the Timeline, leaving only protoframes. You must then add a keyframe at Frame 1 to place content on that layer.

To delete a range of frames:

1. Using your practice file in its original state (keyframes at 1, 3, 5, and 9), in the Timeline, select Frames 3–6.

2. Choose Edit > Timeline > Remove Frames.

   Flash deletes all the selected frames 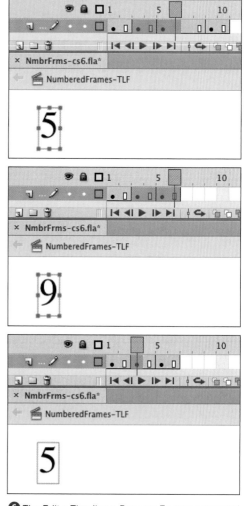. The content of the fully selected span (Frames 3 and 4) is completely removed. The content of the partially selected span (Frames 5 and 6) is retained, but the span is shortened.

TIP With frame-based selection active, you can quickly replace the contents of one keyframe with the contents of another keyframe. Select an in-between frame that displays the contents you want to copy. Drag that source frame over the keyframe whose contents you want to replace. Flash replaces the contents of the target keyframe with the contents of the source keyframe.

C The Edit > Timeline > Remove Frames command can delete a range of frames. Because an entire keyframe span (Frames 3 and 4) is included in this selection (top), Flash not only reduces the number of frames but also removes the content of that keyframe span (middle). Where only part of a span is selected (originally Frames 5 and 6), the span is shortened, but the content remains (bottom).

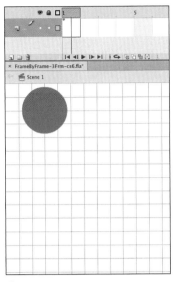

(A) In Keyframe 1, using the oval tool, draw a large circular fill near the top of the Stage. This shape will become a bouncing ball.

Inserted keyframe

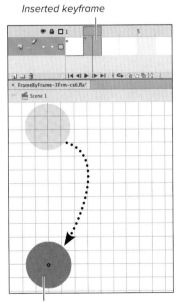

Drag to reposition ball

(B) Choose Insert > Timeline > Keyframe to duplicate the ball from Keyframe 1 in Keyframe 2. Then drag the ball to reposition it.

Making a Simple Frame-by-Frame Animation

A time-honored example of frame-by-frame animation is a bouncing ball. A crude, frame-by-frame animation of a bouncing ball takes just three frames, each one showing the ball in a different position.

To set up the initial keyframe:

1. Create a new Flash document, and name it FrmByFrmBounce. Choose View > Grid > Show Grid to help position graphics in this task.

2. In the Timeline, select Keyframe 1. From the panel menu, choose Preview in Context mode.

   This setting makes it easy to keep track of what you do in the example.

3. Near the top of the Stage, using the oval tool, draw a large circle (the ball) **(A)**.

To create the second keyframe:

1. In the Timeline, select Protoframe 2.

2. Choose Insert > Timeline > Keyframe.

   Flash creates Keyframe 2, duplicating the ball from Keyframe 1.

3. In Keyframe 2, select the ball and reposition it at the bottom of the Stage **(B)**.

To create the third keyframe:

1. In the Timeline, select Protoframe 3.

2. Choose Insert > Timeline > Keyframe.

   Flash creates Keyframe 3, duplicating the ball from Keyframe 2.

3. In Keyframe 3, select the ball and reposition it, placing the ball roughly two-thirds of the way back up the Stage, almost back to the original position **C**.

   That's it. Believe it or not, you have just created all the content you need to animate a bouncing ball. To see how it looks in motion, in the Timeline click Keyframes 1, 2, and 3 in turn. As Flash changes the content of the Stage at each click, you'll see a very crude animation.

Inserted keyframe

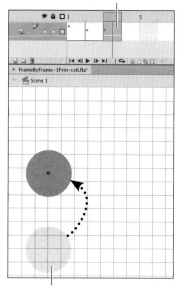

Drag to reposition ball

C Choose Insert > Timeline > Keyframe to duplicate the ball from Keyframe 2 in Keyframe 3. Drag the ball to reposition it again.

Smoother Frame-by-Frame Animation

To smooth the crude movement of your ball, you need to move it in smaller increments. This means adding more keyframes (see "Creating Keyframes" in this chapter) and repositioning the ball slightly in each one **D**. The smoothest frame-by-frame animations make tiny changes to graphic elements over numerous keyframes. Adding keyframes does increase file size, though not as much as adding multimedia elements such as sound and video.

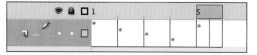

D With frames set to Preview in Context, the Timeline shows the location of the ball in this frame-by-frame animation. The ball moves from the top of the Stage to the bottom in a single frame (left). Adding more keyframes and moving the ball in smaller increments creates a smoother downward bounce (right).

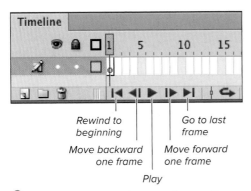

Rewind to beginning

Go to last frame

Move backward one frame

Move forward one frame

Play

A Five standard buttons for controlling media playback appear in the Status bar at the bottom of the Timeline.

B To access a separate panel of controller buttons, choose Window > Toolbars > Controller. Opening the Controller panel allows you to place playback-control buttons wherever it's most convenient on your desktop.

Previewing the Action

To preview animation in Flash's authoring environment, you can use media navigation buttons to move the playhead through the Timeline and display frames in sequence. You can play all the Timeline frames, or select a subset of frames that can loop on command. You can also enter a test mode in which Flash exports the file and runs it in Flash Player.

To control the playhead's movement:

- Access the Timeline and click the button for the command you want to use **A**.

or

- Choose Window > Toolbars > Controller to open a separate panel of playback-control buttons **B**.

TIP You can use keyboard commands to move the playhead one frame at a time. To move the playhead one frame forward, press the . (period) key; to move one frame backward, press the , (comma) key.

TIP To scrub (scroll quickly) through the movie, drag the playhead backward or forward in the Timeline. Flash displays the content of each frame as the playhead moves through it.

TIP A set of five playback-control buttons also appears at the bottom of the Motion Editor panel.

TIP The Control menu in the Menu bar also offers playback commands that duplicate the functions of the playback-control buttons.

To play a selection of frames in the Flash editor:

1. To activate looping, in the Timeline, click the Loop button 🔄.

   Frame-range markers appear at the top of the panel, indicating which frames will loop during playback ⓒ.

2. To set the range of looping frames, drag the left ⁑ and right ⁑ markers until the gray bar covers the desired frames.

3. To play the looping frames, do one of the following:

   ▸ Press Enter.

   ▸ Click a Play button ▶ at the bottom of the Timeline, at the bottom of the Motion Editor, or in the Controller panel.

   Flash plays the selected frames repeatedly.

4. To stop playback, do one of the following:

   ▸ Press Enter.

   ▸ Deselect the Loop button.

   ▸ Click a Pause button ⏸.

   As long as the Loop button is active in the Timeline, all playback controls and Play commands will play only the selected frames.

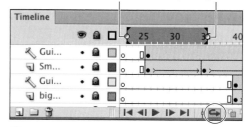

Drag to change range

ⓒ When you click the Loop button, frame-range markers appear in the Timeline. To determine which frames loop repeatedly when you issue a Play command, drag the handles to resize the marker range. As you create and refine animation segments, it's often more efficient to review a small movement sequence by looping a range of frames, rather than manually scrubbing through those frames, or playing the entire movie.

About Setting Frame Rates

Frame rate controls how fast Flash delivers images. Flash CS6 lets you assign frame rates as low as 0.01 frames per second (fps) and as high as 120 fps. Flash's default rate, 24 fps, matches the standard rate for film.

If your target audience is likely to view your content over the Internet or on a mobile device, their system or device won't necessarily be able to achieve a fast frame rate even if you assign one to your movie. For an audience using low-bandwidth connections or devices with low processing power, consider using a frame rate of 15 fps, or even 12 fps.

The animations you create for the tasks in this book are short—usually 24 frames or less. That makes it easy to show you all of the frames in one screen shot. When you start testing those movies, they'll zip by in the blink of an eye. To make it easier to see what's happening, set a very low frame rate for these animations (5–10 fps).

To play all frames in the Flash editor:

Make sure the Timeline's Loop button is deselected and do one of the following:

- To play the frames once, choose Control > Play, or press Enter.

  The Play command in the Control menu changes to a Stop command, which you can choose to stop playback at any time.

- To play the frames repeatedly, choose Control > Loop Playback.

  A checkmark appears by the menu choice. Now, clicking the Play button plays the movie repeatedly until you issue a Stop command.

To play frames in Flash Player:

Choose Control > Test Scene, or press Option-Command-Enter (OS X) or Ctrl-Alt-Enter (Win).

Flash exports your movie to a Flash Player (SWF) file and opens it in a separate window. Flash stores the SWF file at the same hierarchical level of your system as the original Flash (FLA) file. The SWF file retains the name of the FLA original, but with the name of the current scene appended and the extension changed to .swf. (That is, an Intro scene named MyMovie.fla becomes MyMovie_Intro.swf.)

TIP You can also choose **Control > Test Movie** to preview your movie; it just takes a bit of extra work to choose an application from the Test Movie submenu. The offerings in the submenu depend on the document's current Publish settings (see Chapter 17). For tasks in this book, choose > In Flash Professional. (The movie will open in a Flash Player window.) Once you've chosen the test method you prefer, you can test quickly using keyboard commands. Press Command-Enter (OS X) or Ctrl-Enter (Win) to activate the playback application currently selected in the submenu.

To adjust frame rate via the Status bar:

1. In Document Editing mode, access the Timeline.

2. In the Status bar, enter a Frame Rate value between 0.01 and 120 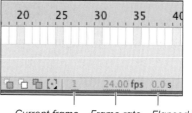.

Current frame   Frame rate   Elapsed time

D The Status bar contains a Frame Rate hot-text control for entering quick adjustments to the playback speed of your movie.

Warnings When Testing TLF Text

As you learned in Chapter 3, TLF text requires that a *TLF SWZ file*—a file that contains special ActionScript instructions—be available to the player at runtime to display the TLF text correctly. You have several ways to ensure that the end user has access to that file. With default Publish settings, Flash player accesses the TLF SWZ file as a shared runtime library and will look for the library on the Adobe server. If Flash Player can't locate that SWZ file, the player checks for the file on the local machine.

When you use the Test Scene command (or the Test Movie > In Flash Professional command) to preview a movie containing TLF text, Flash creates a copy of the TLF SWZ file and the SWF movie file in one folder. As you develop and test, the TLF SWZ shared runtime library is always available to the Flash player, and you'll see your TLF content play regardless of whether or not you are con-nected to the Internet. When you are working offline, however, Flash may display an error mes-sage in the Output panel, such as **Error opening URL 'http://fpdownload.adobe.com/pub/swz/ crossdomain.xml'**.

The message results from the default setting that allows Flash to look in various places for the TLF SWZ. Think of it as a reminder that the fast, easy, guaranteed access you have to the TLF SWZ dur-ing testing won't necessarily be true for your audience. (Flash Authoring assumes by default that you will deploy your published SWF to a publicly accessible web server with the TLF SWZ file. If that's not the case, you can change the Publish settings to work with other deployment methods.)

In addition, as you test, Flash checks to see whether your content includes items that might benefit from streaming (such as large animations). When it finds such content, a warning dialog reminds you that the default Publish settings don't allow you to stream content with TLF text. For the exercises in this book, you can safely dismiss these warnings. However, when creating your own content, you'll need to pay attention to these reminders and evaluate which publishing options work best for your delivery platform and target audience. (You'll learn more about working with Publish Settings in Chapter 17.)

Five-Frame Bounce

For the tasks in this section and the rest of this chapter, create a five-frame movie of a bouncing ball using the techniques in "Making a Simple Frame-by-Frame Animation" in this chapter. Name the movie 5FrameBounce. In Keyframe 1 place the ball at the top of the Stage; in Keyframes 2 and 3 place the ball at two places in its descent; in Keyframe 4 place the ball at the bottom of the Stage; and in Keyframe 5 place the ball roughly half-way back to the top Ⓐ. To make it easier to see what's happening, use a fairly low frame rate—say, 5 fps.

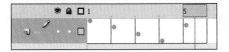

Ⓐ With the Timeline set to Preview in Context, you can see the relative positions of the ball in every keyframe.

Varying Frame-by-Frame Rate

Frame rate in Flash is constant—the rate you set for the document remains in effect for the entire movie. You can control the tempo of any movement by changing the number of frames it takes to complete the animation of that movement. If a ball's downward bounce takes 20 frames and its upward bounce takes 10, the ball seems to drop slowly and rebound quickly. One way to slow the action is to add keyframes, but doing so increases file size. Sometimes you can add in-between frames to slow the action. In-between frames add little to the exported movie's file size.

To add in-between frames:

1. Create a five-frame bouncing-ball movie (see the sidebar "Five-Frame Bounce").

2. Choose File > Save As, and make a copy of the file. Give the file a distinguishing name, such as BounceSlower.

3. In the BounceSlower Timeline, Control-click (OS X) or right-click (Win) Frame 1 to access the contextual menu for frames.

Continues on next page

4. Choose Insert Frame.

Flash inserts an in-between frame at Frame 2 and pushes the keyframe that was there to Frame 3 **B**.

5. Repeat Steps 3–5 for the second and third keyframes in the movie.

You now have keyframes in Frames 1, 3, 5, 7, and 8 **C**.

6. Choose Control > Test Scene.

Flash exports the movie to a SWF file and opens it in Flash Player. Play through the regular five-frame bouncing ball animation, and then play through the movie you just created (Bounc-eSlower). You can see that the action in the movie with added in-between frames feels different from the action in the movie in which one keyframe directly follows another. The added frames slow the motion.

CAUTION Keep in mind that this example serves to illustrate a process. In most animations, you shouldn't overuse this technique. When you add many in-between frames, you'll slow the action too much and destroy the illusion of movement. Experiment with it yourself. Add another three to five frames between the first three keyframes to see the effect on playback speed. The ball no longer seems to bounce, it moves down in small spurts and jumps back to the top.

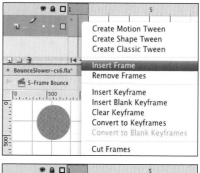

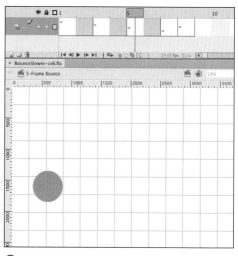

B Select a frame; Ctrl-click (OS X) or right-click (Win), and choose Insert Frame from the contextual menu (top). Flash inserts an in-between frame directly after the selected frame (bottom).

C With in-between frames separating the initial keyframes, the first part of the animation moves more slowly than the second.

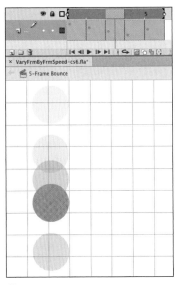

A In Onion Skin mode, Flash displays the content of multiple frames but dims everything that's not on the current frame. The range markers in the Timeline indicate how many frames appear as onion skins.

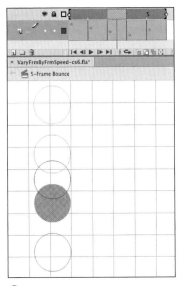

B In Onion Skin Outlines mode, Flash displays the content of multiple frames, but uses outlines for content outside the current frame.

Using Onion Skinning

In frame-by-frame animation, you make incremental changes to the graphic elements in each keyframe, positioning the elements in each frame to make the smoothest movement. To make this task easier, Flash's onion skinning feature displays the graphic elements of a keyframe in the context of elements in surrounding frames.

Onion skinning displays dimmed or outline versions of content in surrounding frames. (You can set the number of frames Flash displays at once.) The buttons for turning on and off the various types of onion skinning appear in the Status bar at the bottom of the Timeline.

To turn on onion skinning:

- In the Status bar of the Timeline, click the Onion Skin button .

  The content of the frames included in the marker range appears in a dimmed form **A**. You can't edit the dimmed graphics—only the full-color graphics in the current frame can be edited.

To turn on outline onion skinning:

- In the Status bar of the Timeline, click the Onion Skin Outlines button .

  The content of all the frames included in the marker range appears in outline form **B**. You can't edit the outline graphics—only the solid graphics that appear in the current frame can be edited.

To adjust the number of frames displayed in onion skinning:

1. In the Status bar of the Timeline, click the Modify Markers button 🔲.

   A pop-up menu appears, containing commands for setting the markers' function **C**.

2. To onion-skin frames on either side of the current frame (where the playhead is located), do one of the following:

   ▸ To onion-skin two frames on either side of the current frame, choose Marker Range 2.

   ▸ To onion-skin five frames on either side of the current frame, choose Marker Range 5.

   ▸ To onion-skin all the frames in the movie, choose Marker Range All **D**.

TIP Flash moves the markers around in the Timeline as you move the playhead. Flash always includes onion skins (either solid or outline) for graphics in the selected number of frames before the current frame and after it.

TIP The contents of locked layers do not appear in onion skin views.

TIP You can prevent the markers from moving each time you select a new frame in the Timeline. Drag the markers to encompass the frames you want to see together. From the Modify Markers menu, choose Anchor Markers. As long as you keep selecting frames inside the anchored range, the anchored set of frames remain in Onion Skin mode.

TIP The markers for looping and for onion skinning look identical but are actually separate items. The frame-range markers—which identify the frames that loop when you issue a Play command—do not respond to the settings in the Marker Range menu. You must always drag the markers that define the set of looping frames; the markers for looping are always anchored and don't follow the playhead.

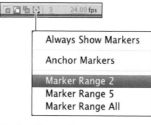

Marker Range 2

Marker Range 5

C In the Modify Markers pop-up menu, you can set the number of frames that appear as onion skins.

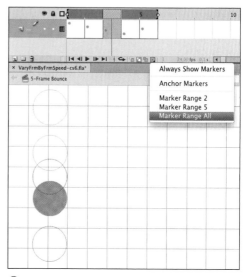

D The Marker Range All setting extends the markers to enclose all the frames of the Timeline. You see the content of all frames on the Stage. In Onion Skin Outlines mode, only the content of the current frame is solid.

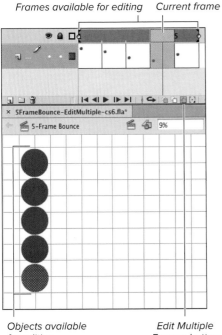

Frames available for editing   *Current frame*

Objects available for editing

Edit Multiple Frames button

Ⓐ In Edit Multiple Frames mode, Flash displays and makes editable all the graphics in the frames within the Timeline's current marker range. This makes it possible to move an animated graphic to a new location on the Stage in every keyframe at the same time.

Editing Multiple Keyframes

If you decide to change an animated element's position, you must change every keyframe in which that element appears. Repositioning the items one at a time is not only tedious but also can introduce errors. You may miss a keyframe, and you can easily move the animated elements out of alignment. Flash solves this problem by letting you move elements in multiple keyframes simultaneously. The same markers used for onion skinning apply to Edit Multiple Frames mode. You can edit the content of any keyframe that falls within the range of frames selected by the markers.

Editing multiple keyframes is especially important for frame-by-frame animation, shape tweens, and classic tweens. For motion tweens, it's easy to reposition the tween target in every frame of the animation simply by moving the motion path (see Chapter 11).

To relocate animated graphics on the Stage:

1. Open the five-frame animation of the bouncing ball that you created earlier in this chapter (5FrameBounce).

2. In the Timeline, in the Status bar, click the Edit Multiple Frames button 🖿 **Ⓐ**.

    On the Stage, Flash displays the graphic content of frames within the marker range and makes all that content editable simultaneously. (When the Edit Multiple Frames button is deselected, only the current frame's content is editable.)

3. From the Modify Markers menu, choose Marker Range All.

Continues on next page

Now you can see the five circles that represent the ball in each phase of its bounce. You can edit any of those circles, even if the playhead is not currently at the keyframe containing that circle.

4. Using the selection tool, draw a selection rectangle that includes all the visible circles on the Stage **B**.

5. Drag the selection to the opposite side of the Stage **C**.

In just a few steps, you've relocated the bouncing ball. Imagine how much more work it would be to select each keyframe separately, move the circle for that frame, select the next keyframe, line up the circles precisely in the new location, and so on.

TIP When you select Edit Multiple Frames, Flash no longer displays onion skinning for keyframes; onion skinning does appear for in-between frames with tweened content. If you find it confusing to view solid graphics in multiple keyframes, turn on Outline view in the Layer Properties section of the Timeline **D**.

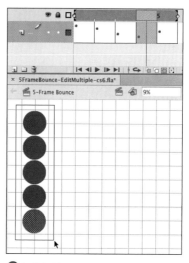

B In Edit Multiple Frames mode, you can use the selection tool to select graphics in any of the frames within the marker range.

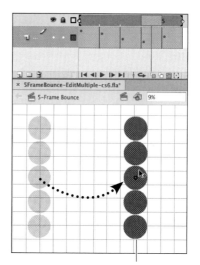

Flash previews the old and new locations as you drag selected graphics

C In Edit Multiple Frames mode, you can relocate an animated graphic completely, moving it in every keyframe with one action.

Outline-mode toggle

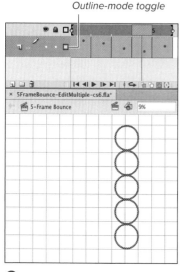

D Turn on Outline mode to make it easier to work with graphics in multiple frames.

Animation with Classic Tweening

In Chapter 8, you created a three-frame animation of a bouncing ball by changing the position of the ball graphic in each of the three keyframes. Animating movement and changes to shapes by hand (frame by frame) is labor-intensive. Adobe Flash Professional CS6 reduces the number of frames you must draw when you use a process called *tweening*.

Flash does three types of tweening: classic, shape, and motion tweening. This chapter introduces classic tweening.

Classic and shape tweening both use keyframe spans to create animation. To set up the keyframe span, you place one version of a graphic element in an initial keyframe, and a second version in an ending keyframe. When you assign tweening to the keyframe span, Flash creates a series of incremental images that fill in the animation. The number of in-between frames determines the number of images in the series and the length of the animation.

In This Chapter

When to Use Classic Tweening

Tweening reduces the amount of labor involved in creating animated sequences. Instead of drawing the graphics for every frame of a movie, you create the essential frames—the keyframes—and let Flash do the drawing. Flash performs several types of tweening: classic tweening, shape tweening (see Chapter 10), and motion tweening (see Chapter 11). Flash also uses another type of animation, inverse kinematics, which is similar to tweening in that it animates by incrementally changing a structure composed of shapes or symbols (see Chapter 13). Each tween method has its own requirements and benefits.

Here are some things to consider about classic tweening and motion tweening:

Classic tweening works only with symbols. You can use classic tweening to animate changes to the properties of a symbol instance on the Stage. Such properties include the symbol's location on the Stage (position), the symbol's size (scale), whether the symbol changes its orientation to the Stage (rotation), and so on. You can't change an element's outlines using classic tweening; for that, you must use shape tweening (see Chapter 10) or inverse kinematics (see Chapter 13).

Motion tweening also works only with symbols and involves changing their properties. So how do you decide whether to use classic or motion tweening?

Classic tweening supports some workflows often used by character animators. Because you set up initial and ending keyframes in classic tweening, you can map out a complete animation quickly by placing all the keyframes first and assigning classic tweening later, a process known as *blocking*. Classic tweening knits those segments together seamlessly, interpolating changes from one keyframe to the next and from that keyframe to the next, and so on.

That's not so easy with motion tweening. Each motion-tween span is an independent segment of animation with a single keyframe. If you want the segments to link smoothly, you need to do a bit of extra work to make sure the position of a tweened object at the end of one span matches precisely with its counterpart in the next tween span.

Classic tweening also takes advantage of a graphic symbol's ability to display different frames of its Timeline. Character animators use this feature to turn multiframe graphic symbols into miniature libraries, building a set of facial expressions or gestures into a single symbol, then displaying just the image that's needed at any given time. (You'll learn about creating multiframe, animated, graphic symbols in Chapter 12.)

Classic tweening's multiple-keyframe approach also lets you interpolate between two different color effects (one applied to the symbol instance in the initial keyframe of the tween, the other applied to the symbol instance at the end). In motion tweens, each tween span has just one symbol instance, so Flash can't interpolate changes to color effects.

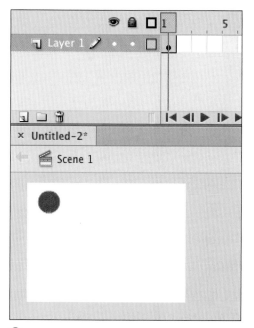

Creating a Bouncing Ball with Classic Tweening

You create classic tweens using pairs of keyframes. The first keyframe shows a graphic object—a symbol—in its original state; the second keyframe shows the same symbol, but with modifications. You then issue a command to link the two keyframes in a classic-tween span. You can use classic tweening to create the same type of bouncing ball you made in Chapter 8. This time you use a symbol for the ball graphic.

To prepare content for classic tweening:

1. In Keyframe 1 of a new document, place an instance of a symbol that represents a ball near the top of the Stage **A**.

Continues on next page

Which Frames Contain Tweening?

The Timeline provides visual cues to indicate which frames contain tweens.

An arrow in a keyframe span indicates the presence of a classic tween or shape tween. (The arrow doesn't appear when you choose Preview or Preview in Context in the Timeline's panel menu.)

A dotted line in a frame shows that it is set to contain a classic tween or a shape tween, but also indicates that something is wrong and Flash can't complete the tween. These tweens are called *broken tweens* **B**.

When you choose Tinted Frames in the panel menu, a light bluish-purple tint indicates the frames that contain a classic tween. If Tinted Frames is inactive, the frames are white, and a red arrow indicates the presence of a tween.

B An arrow in a keyframe span indicates that the frames contain a proper tween sequence. With Tinted Frames active as the Timeline view, a light bluish-purple tint is applied to the tween span (left). If Tinted Frames is not active, the tween span displays a red arrow (middle). A dotted line indicates that the keyframe span is set to tween, but Flash has found a problem (right).

For example, use the oval tool to draw a circle shape, then convert it to a symbol (see Chapter 7) and name it **MyBall**. Flash could convert the shape for you, but it's best to do the conversion yourself. (See the sidebar "Classic Tween Symbols: Best Practice.")

2. Command-click (OS X) or Ctrl-click (Win) Frames 5 and 10, and press F6.

Flash creates Keyframes 5 and 10, duplicating Keyframe 1. (To review creating keyframes, see Chapter 8.) By changing the position of the ball in those keyframes, you show Flash how to create the animation.

3. To set the ball's position for the low point of the bounce, in the Timeline, move the playhead to Keyframe 5. On the Stage, drag the ball symbol to the bottom of the Stage.

4. To set the ball's position for the rebound, move the playhead to Keyframe 10. Drag the symbol to position it slightly above mid-Stage, almost back to its starting point.

You have just set up a frame-by-frame animation much like the one you created in Chapter 8, except that the keyframes are farther apart **C**. In Keyframe 1, the ball is at the top of its bounce; in Keyframe 5, the ball is at the bottom of its bounce; and in Keyframe 10, the ball is almost back to the top of its bounce. To have Flash interpolate the changes and create a smoother animation than in the frame-by-frame exercise, you need to apply tweening to the keyframe spans.

Original keyframes

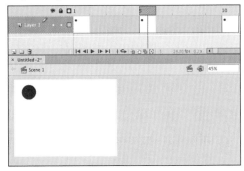

Symbol in new position in Keyframes 5 and 10

C The initial keyframes for a classic tween are similar to those of a frame-by-frame animation. The difference is that the content of the keyframe must be a symbol. Reposition the symbol in Keyframes 5 and 10 to set up a bounce.

D You can select any frame in a keyframe span to assign classic tweening.

E Flash adds information to the Timeline to indicate which frames contain classic tweens. Here, a light bluish-purple tint and an arrow signify a completed classic tween.

F With two motion-tween sequences, you can create a bouncing ball: one sequence shows the downward motion, and the other shows the rebound.

To apply classic tweening:

1. To apply classic tweening to the first half of the ball's bounce, in the Timeline, select any of the frames in the first keyframe span—1, 2, 3, or 4 **D**.

   Flash automatically selects the ball symbol. To define a classic tween, the item to be tweened must be selected.

2. Choose Insert > Classic Tween.

   Flash defines Frames 1–4 as a classic tween, and updates the Timeline **E**. These in-between frames no longer display the content of the preceding keyframe. Instead, they display the incrementally changed tween content that Flash creates. This tween content is shielded so you can't select it.

3. To define the classic tween for the second half of the ball's bounce, in the Timeline, Control-click (OS X) or right-click (Win) any of the frames in the second keyframe span—5, 6, 7, 8, or 9— and choose Create Classic Tween from the contextual menu.

   Flash creates the second half of the ball's bounce with another classic tween **F**.

The Many Ways to Position Tweened Symbols

In the preceding task, you positioned a classic-tween symbol by dragging it directly on the Stage, but you also could have used the Property inspector or the Info panel to do the job. The trick is to make sure that the symbol is selected.

In Step 3 of the task, for example, instead of moving the playhead to Keyframe 5, you can select the keyframe in the Timeline, which also selects the contents of that frame on the Stage. In the Info panel you can enter new values for the symbol's *x*- and *y*-coordinates to change the ball's position.

Although the Info panel recognizes a symbol selected this way, the Property inspector does not. When you select a keyframe in the Timeline, the Property inspector displays the properties of the frame itself, and not its content (even though that content is selected on the Stage). To allow the Property inspector to focus on a classic-tween symbol, you must select that symbol directly—for example, by clicking it with the selection tool. You can then access the Property inspector and use the X and Y hot-text controls in the Position and Size section to position the symbol on the Stage.

TIP When you choose Preview or Preview in Context from the Timeline's panel menu, the tweening arrow doesn't appear in frames containing tweens. Nor can you see the incremental steps that Flash creates for the tween. But if you turn on onion skinning, you can see the interpolated content for all the in-between frames in position on the Stage **G**.

TIP Oddly enough, although you can't select a symbol on an in-between frame of a classic tween, you can drag it or edit it. Dragging a symbol on an in-between frame, even a tiny bit, creates a new keyframe. Double-clicking a symbol on an in-between frame opens that symbol in symbol-editing mode. Be careful not to unintentionally move your mouse when you double-click, or you will create an additional keyframe.

TIP In this simple example, the ball moves at a constant rate through each half of its bounce. If you wanted the ball to slow down as it reached the top of its upward rebound, you could use *easing* to vary the rate of change in the ball's position. For a quick introduction to easing, see Chapter 12.

Range of frames displayed as onion skins

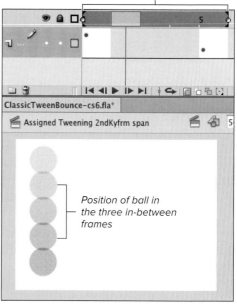

Position of ball in the three in-between frames

G Turn on onion skinning to preview the positions of a classically tweened symbol on the Stage.

Classic Tween Symbols: Best Practice

Classic tweens work only with symbols, and each keyframe of the tween can contain just one symbol instance. If you issue the command to create a classic tween when you've selected other types of graphic objects (merge-shapes, drawing-objects, primitive-shapes, groups, or text), Flash automatically converts the objects into a pair of symbols—one for the initial keyframe of the tween, and the other for the ending keyframe. Flash does not display a warning dialog. It just adds generically named symbols (for example, Tween 1 and Tween 2) in the library and creates the tween. Unless you immediately rename the tween symbols to something more easily identifiable, you may find the names confusing if you later need to edit your tween.

Also, if you accidentally put more than one object on the layer you're using for the classic tween, Flash combines the objects into one symbol instead of warning you that the tween can have only one object per layer.

For best results (and to avoid unwanted surprises), before you apply tweening, convert the graphic element (or elements) you want to tween into a symbol.

Adding Keyframes to Classic Tweens

After you have set up a classic tween, Flash creates new keyframes when you drag a classic-tween symbol to a new Stage position in an in-between frame. You can also add new keyframes by choosing Insert > Timeline > Keyframe.

To add keyframes by repositioning a classic-tween symbol:

1. Create a ten-frame classic tween of a bouncing ball, following the steps in the preceding task.

2. In the Timeline, select Frame 3.

   On the Stage, you see the ball symbol in one of the in-between positions Flash created.

3. Using the selection tool, drag the ball to a new position.

   Flash inserts a new keyframe at Frame 3 and splits the preceding five-frame tween into separate tweens **A**. The new keyframe contains another instance of the ball symbol.

To add keyframes by command:

1. Continuing with the document from the preceding task, select Frame 7.

2. Choose Insert > Timeline > Keyframe.

   Flash creates a new keyframe at Frame 7. A new instance of the symbol appears on the Stage in the position Flash created for it in that in-between frame. You can now change the symbol's position (or change other properties of the symbol).

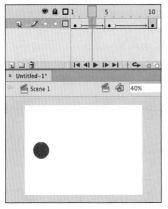

In the selected frame, the symbol appears in its tweened position.

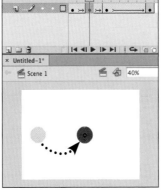

Repositioning the symbol creates a new keyframe.

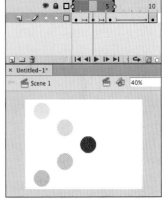

Onion-skin view of other tween positions for the symbol

A In a classic-tween span, when the playhead is at an in-between frame, you can create a new keyframe by repositioning the tween symbol on the Stage. Repositioning the ball in an in-between frame that's part of a classic tween creates a new keyframe and a revision of the tweened frames.

Moving Symbols in Straight Lines

In the preceding tasks, you created a well-behaved bouncing ball that moves up and down. To animate a ball that bounces around like crazy, you must add keyframes and place the ball symbol in various locations. The symbol moves in a straight line from one position to the next, but to livelier effect.

To move an item from point to point:

1. To set up an open-ended classic tween, in a new Flash document or on a new layer, do the following:

   ▶ In Keyframe 1, place an instance of a ball symbol.

   ▶ In the Timeline, select Frame 20, and choose Insert > Timeline > Frame. Flash creates a keyframe span by defining 19 in-between frames.

   ▶ In the Timeline, select any frame in the keyframe span (Frames 1 through 20) and choose Insert > Classic Tween. Flash assigns classic tweening to the keyframe span, but the dotted line in the Timeline indicates that the tween isn't yet complete **A**. You must create keyframes that describe the ball's motion.

2. In the Timeline, position the playhead at Frame 5.

3. On the Stage, drag the ball symbol to a new position.

   Flash creates a new keyframe at Frame 5 and completes a classic tween for Frames 1 through 4 **B**.

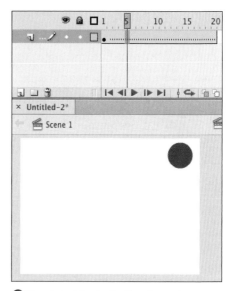

A The dotted line in the Timeline indicates that these 20 frames contain a classic tween that is broken. It has no ending keyframe to define changes to the tween symbol.

Completed classic-tween segment

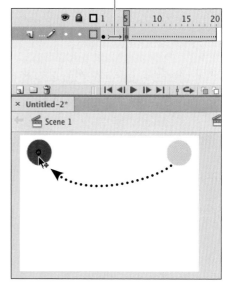

B When the playhead is at an in-between frame of a classic-tween span and you move the tween symbol to a new position on the Stage, Flash creates a new keyframe and completes a new tween segment.

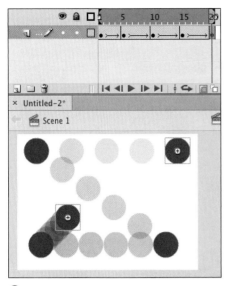

C By stringing classic tweens together, you can animate a symbol that moves from point to point. In the Status bar, click the Onion Skin button to see the ball in all the tweened positions. (The Edit Multiple Frames button is selected to make the keyframe elements stand out.)

4. Repeat this repositioning process (Steps 2 and 3) for Frames 10, 15, and 20.

You now have a ball that bounces around wildly **C**.

5. To end the classic tween, do the following:

▸ Select the last keyframe in the series.

▸ Choose Insert > Remove Tween.

If you don't remove tweening from the last frame, any subsequent frames that you add will also be set to classic tween, which may create unexpected results.

TIP To animate frenetic bouncing, move the symbol a longer distance in a small number of in-between frames. To slow the action, move the symbol a short distance or use a larger number of in-between frames.

TIP To add more frames, after performing Step 4, select Frame 30 or Frame 40, and choose Insert > Timeline > Frame. Flash makes all the newly defined frames part of the classic tween. Now you can add keyframes by following the procedure described earlier in this task. Just be sure you end up with a keyframe as the last frame in the series. If you have more frames than you need, you can remove them.

Moving Symbols Along a Path

In the preceding task, you made a ball move all over the Stage in short point-to-point hops. A ball does sometimes behave this way, but other animations may require movements that are softer—trajectories that are arcs, not straight lines. You could achieve this effect by stringing together many point-to-point keyframes, but Flash's classic tweening offers a more efficient method: the *motion guide*. Motion guides describe the exact path an animated graphic-object takes. Unless you have a special need to use a classic tween, motion tweening makes it even easier to move objects along a path (see Chapter 11).

To add a motion-guide layer:

1. In a new Flash document or on a new layer, create a ten-frame classic tween.

   In the first keyframe, place the symbol to be tweened in the top-left corner of the Stage. In the last frame, place the symbol in the bottom-right corner of the Stage. Your document should resemble  **A**.

2. Select the layer that contains the symbol you want to move along a path.

3. Control-click (OS X) or right-click (Win) the layer-name area and choose Add Classic Motion Guide from the contextual menu. Flash adds the classic motion-guide layer directly above the layer you clicked **B**.

4. In the Timeline, select Keyframe 1 of the motion-guide layer.

5. To create a path for the tweened symbol to follow, use the pencil tool to draw a line on the Stage **C**.

A To animate a symbol to follow a path, first set up a classic tween. Initially, the symbol moves from its beginning position to its ending position in a straight line. (Onion Skin mode and Edit Multiple Frames are selected to show the entire tweened movement.)

B When you choose Add Classic Motion Guide from the contextual menu, Flash creates a motion-guide layer with a default name (*Guide:* plus the name of your originally selected layer). Flash indents the originally selected layer and links it to the motion-guide layer. Flash defines the linked layer as a guided layer.

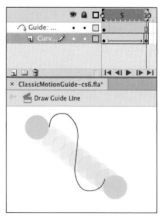

C A path on a motion-guide layer controls the movement of a classic-tween symbol on a linked layer.

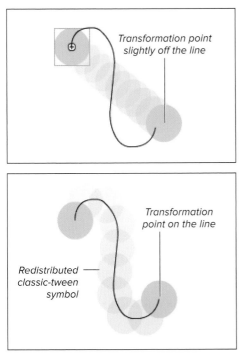

Transformation point slightly off the line

Transformation point on the line

Redistributed classic-tween symbol

D To follow the motion guide, each instance of the classic-tween symbol must have its transformation point sitting directly on the motion-guide line. (The transformation point appears as a small white circle.)

Guiding Motion for Multiple Classic Tweens

You can use a single classic motion-guide layer to control the movement of classic-tween symbols on several layers. Each motion-guide layer governs any layers linked to it. Each symbol in one of these *guided layers* must follow the same movement path.

When you want multiple classic-tween symbols to follow different paths, you must create multiple motion-guide layers within your Flash document. Each motion guide governs the actions of classic-tween symbols on its own set of linked layers.

TIP You could use any of the drawing tools—except the oval- or rectangle-primitive—to draw the motion guide in Step 5. Any merge-shape or drawing-object path (whether a stroke or a fill) on a motion-guide layer can control the motion of classically tweened symbols on linked layers. But it's easiest to visualize the motion when you draw lines (strokes).

To connect tweened elements to a motion guide:

1. Continuing with the document from the preceding task, choose View > Snapping > Snap to Objects.

   For Flash to move a classic-tween symbol along a motion guide, the transformation point of the symbol (displayed as a small white circle) must be centered on the line. The Snap to Objects setting helps you position the symbol correctly. (To learn more about the transformation point, see Chapters 4 and 7.)

2. In Keyframe 1, use the selection tool to position the classic-tween symbol so its transformation point lies directly over the beginning of the motion guide.

   As you drag, the snapping ring enlarges slightly as it approaches any snapping elements you have set. For example, with Snap to Objects active, the ring grows larger when the point is centered over the motion guide.

3. In Keyframe 10, drag the classic-tween symbol to position its transformation point directly over the end of the motion guide.

   Flash redraws the in-between frames so that the symbol follows the motion guide **D**. Flash centers the classic-tween symbol over the motion guide in each in-between frame. In the final movie, Flash hides the guide.

Continues on next page

TIP After you draw the motion guide, lock the motion-guide layer to avoid accidentally editing the guide as you snap the classic-tween symbol to it.

TIP When you select the initial keyframe of a classic tween in the Timeline, the Tweening section of the Frame Property inspector contains a Snap checkbox. Select it to force a classic-tween symbol's transformation point to snap to the end of the guide.

TIP For best tweening results, a motion guide's path should be open. When you draw a motion guide as an outline shape with the rectangle or oval tool, use the eraser tool to create a small break in the outline.

About Motion Guides and Orient to Path

Being round and symmetrical, a ball looks natural following a motion guide whether the guide is a gentle arc or a complex curve. Other symbols may require rotation to appear natural as they move along the motion-guide path. For example, you might want a living creature to face in the direction it's moving, rotating slightly to match the twists and turns of its path.

If the motion guide is a simple arc, rotating the symbol instances in the initial and ending keyframes of a classic tween to align with the motion guide is usually enough to make the movement appear natural.

When the curve is complex—an *S* shape, for example—that change in orientation may not be sufficient **E**. In that case, you can force a classic-tween symbol to rotate to preserve its orientation to the motion guide, through all its curves. Select any frame in the classic-tween span to access the Frame Property inspector; in the Tweening section, select the Orient to Path checkbox **F**.

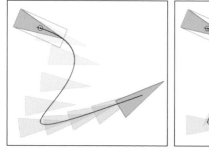

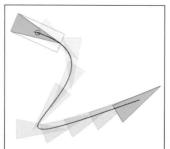

E The triangle has been rotated in the initial and ending keyframes to align with the motion guide, but that rotation doesn't provide enough information to keep the triangle aligned in the midsection of the curve (left). When Orient to Path is active, the arrow rotates to align better with the path at every frame (right).

F To force a classic-tween symbol to face the direction of movement, select the Orient to Path checkbox in the Tweening section of the Frame Property inspector.

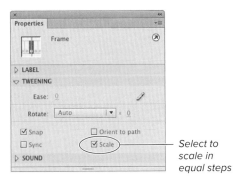

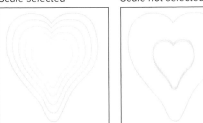

Select to scale in equal steps

Scale selected · Scale not selected

A To resize a classic-tween symbol in equal steps, in the Tweening section of the Frame Property inspector, select the Scale checkbox. When the checkbox is not selected, the symbol remains at roughly its original size through all the frames of the keyframe span (Frames 1 through 4) and suddenly changes to the new size at the final keyframe (Frame 5).

Animating Size Changes

In classic tweening, you can animate changes in the size of a symbol from one keyframe to another by changing the symbol's Horizontal Scale and/or Vertical Scale properties. To enable the symbol to grow or shrink smoothly in a classic tween, you must select the Scale checkbox in the Frame Property inspector.

To grow or shrink a classic-tween symbol:

1. In a new Flash document or on a new layer, in Keyframe 1, place a symbol instance on the Stage.

2. To create a keyframe that defines the end of a growing sequence, select Frame 5 in the Timeline; then choose Insert > Timeline > Keyframe, or press F6.

   Flash duplicates the symbol from Keyframe 1 in the new keyframe.

3. Select any of the frames in the keyframe span (Frame 1, 2, 3, or 4).

4. Choose Insert > Classic Tween. The classic-tween arrow and color coding now appear in the keyframe span.

5. With the frame you selected in Step 3 still selected, access the Frame Property inspector.

6. In the Tweening section, make sure the Scale checkbox is selected (the default) **A**.

   When Scale is selected, Flash increases the size of the symbol instance in equal steps from Keyframe 1 to Keyframe 5.

Contnues on next page

7. With the playhead at Keyframe 5, select the symbol instance and make it bigger.

8. To add the ending keyframe for a shrinking sequence, select Frame 10 in the Timeline and press F6. Flash duplicates the symbol from Keyframe 5 in the new keyframe.

9. Select any of the frames in the keyframe span (Frame 5, 6, 7, 8, or 9).

10. Choose Insert > Classic Tween.

The classic-tween arrow and color coding now appear in the second keyframe span (Frames 5 through 9).

11. With the playhead at Keyframe 10, select the symbol instance and make it smaller. Flash creates a tween that shrinks your graphic in five equal steps **B**.

TIP As long as you don't change the settings in the Frame Property inspector, the Scale checkbox remains selected, and Flash updates the tween whenever you change the content in one of the keyframes in the sequence. The Frame Property inspector needn't be open to fine-tune the size of your scaling graphic.

B To animate shrinking in a classic tween, make the tween symbol smaller in the ending keyframe of the sequence than in the initial keyframe. Turn on Onion Skin mode to see the size of the symbol Flash creates for each in-between frame.

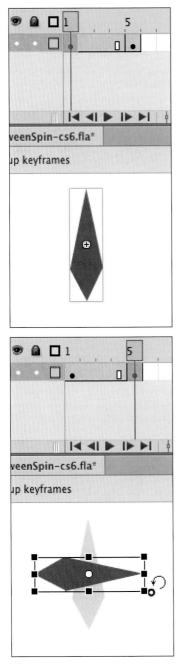

veenSpin-cs6.fla*

ıp keyframes

A To prepare a rotational classic tween, in the keyframe that ends the sequence, rotate the item to its ending position.

Rotating and Spinning Graphics

With classic tweening, you can make a symbol spin by changing its Rotation property. When you create a classic tween for rotation, you must not only create beginning and ending keyframes (as you did when animating changes to position and size), you must also specify the direction of rotation and the number of times to spin.

To rotate a symbol less than 360 degrees:

1. In a new Flash document or on a new layer, in Keyframe 1, place a symbol instance on the Stage. For this task, use a shape that makes the rotation visible, such as a triangle or an arrow.

2. In the Timeline, select Frame 5, and choose Insert > Timeline > Keyframe, or press F6. Flash duplicates the symbol from Keyframe 1 in the new keyframe.

3. On the Stage, in Keyframe 5, rotate the symbol instance 90 degrees clockwise **A**.

4. In the Timeline, select any of the frames in the first keyframe span (Frame 1, 2, 3, or 4).

Continues on next page

5. Choose Insert > Classic Tween.

6. With the frame you selected in Step 4 still selected, access the Frame Property inspector's Tweening section.

7. From the Rotate menu **B**, choose one of the following options:

Auto rotates the graphic in the direction that requires the smallest movement **C**.

CW rotates the graphic clockwise.

CCW rotates the graphic counterclockwise.

8. To rotate less than 360 degrees, use the hot-text control to the right of the Rotate menu to enter a Rotation Count of 0.

Flash tweens the symbol to rotate around its transformation point. Each in-between frame shows the symbol rotated a little more.

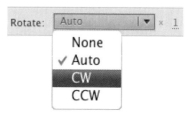

B The Rotate menu in the Tweening section of the Frame Property inspector lets you choose the rotation direction of a classic tween.

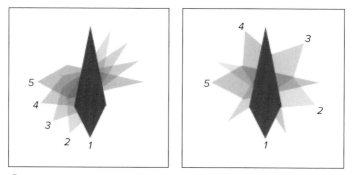

C When rotating a symbol with a classic tween, you can specify the direction of the rotation as clockwise or counterclockwise. You can also choose Auto to let Flash pick the rotation direction that involves the smallest change and produces the smoothest motion. Compare the degree of change in each frame (numbered 1–5 above) between rotating an arrow clockwise from 12 o'clock to 3 o'clock (left) and rotating the arrow counterclockwise to reach the same position (right).

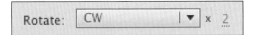

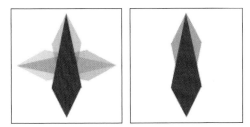

D In the Frame Property inspector, use the hot-text control to the right of the Rotate menu to set the number of times a classically tweened item should spin.

E Compare a single rotation (left) with a double rotation (right) in the same number of frames.

To spin a symbol 360 degrees:

1. Follow Steps 1 and 2 of the preceding task to create a five-frame sequence with identical keyframes in Frame 1 and Frame 5.

   There's no need to reposition the graphic because the beginning and ending frames of a 360-degree spin look exactly the same.

2. In the Timeline, select any of the frames in the first keyframe span (Frame 1, 2, 3, or 4).

3. Choose Insert > Classic Tween, and access the Frame Property inspector.

4. In the Tweening section, from the Rotate menu, choose a direction of rotation.

5. Using the Rotate Count hot-text control to the right of the Rotate menu, enter the number of times the symbol should spin **D**.

   Flash creates new positions for the symbol to rotate it completely the specified number of times in the current span of frames. The symbol tweens differently depending on the number of rotations you choose and the number of frames in the span **E**.

Animating Color Effects

When you use classic tweening to animate changes to symbol instances in keyframes, you can also tween changes in color, by applying a color effect to the symbol instance.

To change a symbol's color over time:

1. In a new Flash document, create a five-frame classic tween.

2. With the playhead at Keyframe 5, select the symbol and access the Property inspector.

3. To change the symbol's color (see Chapter 7), in the Color Effect section of the Property inspector, from the Style menu, choose new settings.

   Flash recolors the symbol in three transitional steps—one for each in-between frame 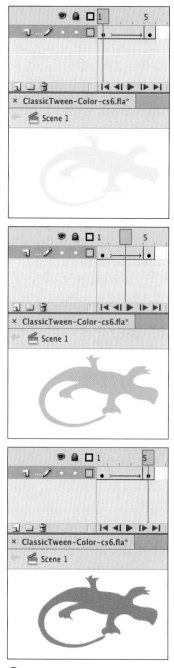.

4. To tween additional color changes, add tween segments by doing the following:

   ▸ In the Timeline, select Frame 10 and press F6 to duplicate the preceding keyframe. Select any of the frames in the second keyframe span (Frame 5, 6, 7, 8, or 9) and choose Insert > Classic Tween. Select the symbol in Frame 10 and repeat Step 3.

TIP You can use classic tweening to change a symbol's transparency (Alpha), thereby making that symbol appear to fade in or out.

Ⓐ In a classic tween, you can change the color of a symbol, as well as its position. Flash creates transitional colors for each in-between frame

Animation with Shape Tweening

Shape tweening in Adobe Flash Professional CS6 works much like classic tweening. You set up a keyframe span (the graphic content of the beginning and ending keyframes must be different in some way), then you define the keyframe span as a shape tween. Flash redraws the graphics for each in-between frame, making the incremental changes that transform the first shape into the final one. Shape tweens can animate changes that redefine the shape of a graphic element as well as its size, color, location, and so on.

Flash can shape-tween more than one graphic on a layer, but the results can be unpredictable. When several shapes are on a layer, Flash pairs beginning and ending shapes according to its rules, generally transforming near shapes, but not necessarily the pairing you have in mind. By limiting yourself to a single shape tween on each layer, you determine exactly which shapes transform to which.

Note: Unless otherwise indicated, you can perform the tasks in this chapter using merge-shapes, drawing-objects, or primitive-shapes.

In This Chapter

Creating a Bouncing Ball with Shape Tweening

Although shape tweens can animate changes to many graphic properties—color, size, location—the distinguishing function of shape tweening is transforming one shape into another. Although you could use a shape tween to replicate the simple bouncing-ball animation you created in Chapters 8 and 9, a better use of shape tweening for a bouncing ball would be to flatten its curve as it strikes the ground.

To prepare content for shape tweening:

1. In Keyframe 1 of a new document, create a bouncing-ball shape near the top of the Stage. Use the oval tool in either Merge mode or Object Drawing mode to draw a circle.

2. Command-click (OS X) or Ctrl-click (Win) Frames 5 and 10, and press F6. Flash creates Keyframes 5 and 10, duplicating the content in Keyframe 1 **A**.

3. In Frame 5, drag the ball to the bottom of the Stage, the low point of the bounce.

4. Using any of the techniques you learned in Chapter 4, reshape the circle by elongating the ball sideways and flattening it on the bottom **B**.

5. In Frame 10, drag the ball to a position slightly above mid-Stage, almost back to the starting point.

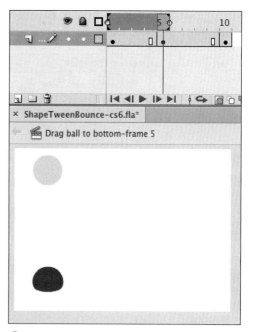

A To begin setting up a bouncing-ball shape tween, create Keyframes 1, 5, and 10, just as you did when creating classic tweens in the previous chapter. However, the ball must be a shape, not a symbol instance.

B Changing the shape of the ball graphic in the keyframe at the bottom of the bounce makes the movement appear more natural. The ball seems to respond to gravity by flattening on contact with something solid, such as the floor. (Turn on onion skinning to see the beginning and ending keyframes.)

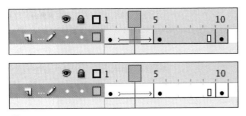

C With Tinted Frames active (choose it from the Timeline's panel menu), Flash tints the frames containing a shape tween with a light green (top). If Tinted Frames is inactive, the frames are white, and the arrow that indicates the presence of a tween changes from black to green.

To apply shape tweening:

1. To define the shape tween for the first half of the ball's bounce, in the Timeline, select any frame in the first keyframe span (Frame 1, 2, 3, or 4).

   Note that the ball is selected automatically. When you define a shape tween, the element to be tweened must be selected.

2. Choose Insert > Shape Tween. Flash creates a shape tween in Frames 1–4 and color-codes those frames in the Timeline **C**.

Continues on next page

When to Use Shape Tweening

Use shape tweening when you want to animate changes to the outline of a merge-shape or drawing-object. You can use shape tweening to modify a shape slightly (to make a box bulge outward on one side, for example) or to completely transform a shape (for example, to turn Cinderella's pumpkin into a coach). You have full control over the shape at key points in the transformation because you draw the shapes in the initial and ending keyframes. In addition, you can improve the transitions with shape hints, a technique you'll learn in this chapter.

In some cases, you may find Flash's interpolation of the changes unsatisfactory. If a single shape tween fails to give you the results you want, try breaking the transformation into smaller segments by adding more keyframes at critical points within the tween. You can then modify those keyframe shapes precisely.

If you still can't get the result you want using shape tweens, you may need to use frame-by-frame animation and draw each stage of the transformation yourself. Depending on the shapes and transformations involved, *inverse kinematics*—another technique for animating changes to a shape's outline—may help you to accomplish your goals (see Chapter 13).

3. In the Tweening section of the Frame Property inspector, from the Blend menu **D**, choose one of the following options:

- **Distributive** smoothes out the in-between shapes.
- **Angular** preserves sharp corners and straight lines as one shape transforms into another.

4. To define the shape tween for the second half of the ball's bounce, in the Timeline, select any of the frames in the second keyframe span (5, 6, 7, 8, or 9).

5. Repeat Steps 2 and 3. Flash creates the second half of the ball's bounce with another shape tween **E**.

D When you select any frame in a shape-tween span, shape-tween settings appear in the Tweening section of the Frame Property inspector. To determine how Flash handles changes to the corners of a graphic as it transforms, choose a setting from the Blend menu.

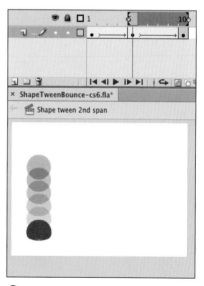

E With onion skinning turned on, you can see the in-between frames created for the shape tween in the second keyframe span (the rebound). This animation looks similar to the bouncing ball created with a classic tween. In this case, the change in the object's shape creates the illusion of impact.

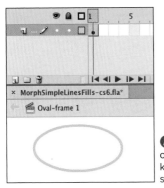

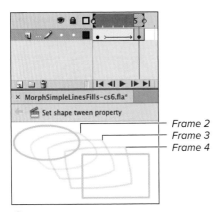

A Draw an oval in the first keyframe of the shape tween.

B Draw a rectangle in the second keyframe of the shape tween.

Frame 2
Frame 3
Frame 4

C When you define Frames 1–4 as a shape tween, Flash creates the three intermediate shapes that transform the oval into a rectangle. Turn on onion skinning to see the shapes for the in-between frames.

Morphing Simple Strokes and Fills

Shape tweens can transform fill shapes and outlines (strokes). In this section, you try some shape-changing tasks using both types of shapes.

To transform an oval into a rectangle:

1. In a new Flash document or on a new layer, in Frame 1, draw an outline oval on the Stage **A**.

2. In the Timeline, select Frame 5, and choose Insert > Timeline > Blank Keyframe. Flash creates a keyframe but removes all content from the Stage.

3. On the Stage, in Frame 5, draw an outline rectangle **B**. Don't worry about placing the rectangle in exactly the same location on the Stage as the oval; you'll adjust the position later.

4. In the Timeline, select any of the frames in the keyframe span (1, 2, 3, or 4).

5. Choose Insert > Shape Tween. The oval transforms into the rectangle in three equal steps—one for each in-between frame **C**.

Continues on next page

6. To align the oval and rectangle, do the following:

  ▸ In the Timeline's Status bar, click the Onion Skin button or the Onion Skin Outlines button. Flash displays all the in-between frames.

  ▸ In the Timeline, move the playhead to Frame 1.

  ▸ On the Stage, position the oval so that it aligns with the rectangle 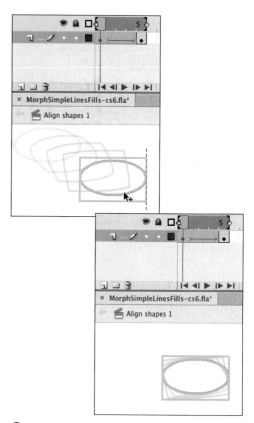 **D**. The oval transforms into a rectangle, remaining in one spot on the Stage.

To transform a rectangle into a free-form shape:

1. In a new Flash document or on a new layer, in Frame 1, draw a rectangular fill on the Stage.

2. In the Timeline, select Frame 5, and choose Insert > Timeline > Blank Keyframe.

3. On the Stage, in Frame 5, use the brush tool to paint a free-form fill. Keep the fill simple—a blob with gentle curves.

4. In the Timeline, select any of the frames in the keyframe span (1, 2, 3, or 4).

5. Choose Insert > Shape Tween.

Flash transforms the rectangle into the free-form fill in three equal steps—one for each in-between frame **E**.

D Use onion skinning to help position the key-frame shapes. With Frame 1 selected, drag the oval to center it within the rectangle (top). Doing so makes the oval grow into a rectangle without moving elsewhere on the Stage (bottom).

E Flash transforms a rectangle into a free-form blob with shape tweening.

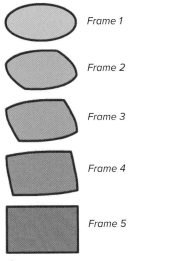

Frame 1

Frame 2

Frame 3

Frame 4

Frame 5

Ⓐ Flash transforms a fill shape with an outline stroke in five frames. The shape tween not only changes the graphic's shape, but also its color.

Shape-Tweening Multiple Shapes

When using classic tweening (see Chapter 9) and motion tweening (see Chapter 11), you are limited to one item per tween, meaning just one item per layer. With shape tweening, however, Flash can handle multiple items on a layer. Flash does a good job of shape-tweening items that fit together simply, such as a single fill shape outlined with a stroke. For the most predictable results with more complex shapes, you should limit yourself to one item per layer (see "When Multiple-Shape Tweens on a Single Layer Go Bad" in this chapter.)

To shape-tween fills with strokes (outlines):

1. Follow the steps in the preceding tasks to create a shape tween of an outline oval transforming into a rectangle.

2. Fill each shape with a different color. Flash tweens the fill and the stroke together and tweens the change in color Ⓐ.

When Multiple-Shape Tweens on a Single Layer Go Bad

When you're shape-tweening stationary elements, you can probably get away with several shape tweens on the same layer. But if the elements move around much, Flash can become confused about which shape goes where.

While you may intend the paths of two shapes to cross, Flash may create the most direct route between a starting shape and an ending one. Figure ⑧ illustrates the problem. For simple shapes, you can tag beginning and ending shape pairs with shape hints to help the shapes transform as you intend, but the safest practice is to put each shape tween item on its own layer.

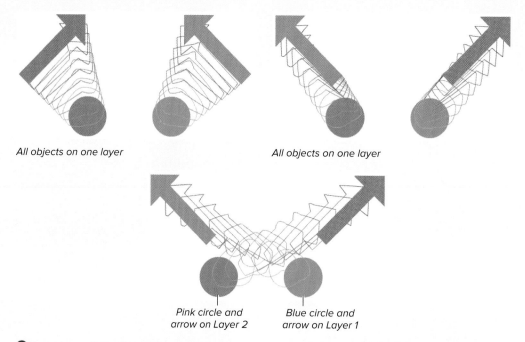

All objects on one layer   *All objects on one layer*

Pink circle and   *Blue circle and*
arrow on Layer 2   *arrow on Layer 1*

⑧ Tweening multiple shapes with paths that don't cross in a single layer can work fine. In the image on the upper left, both objects are on the same layer, and the pink circle transforms into the pink arrow without a hitch. In the upper right image, both objects are on the same layer, but Flash transforms the pink circle into the blue arrow and the blue circle into the pink arrow because it sees that as the most direct path. When you want to create diagonal paths that cross, you should put each object on its own layer, as in the image on the bottom.

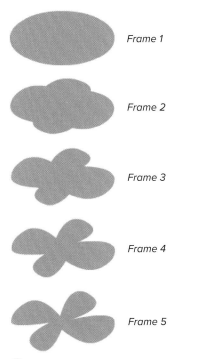

Frame 1

Frame 2

Frame 3

Frame 4

Frame 5

A Flash handles the tween from an oval to a simple flower shape without requiring shape hints.

Transforming a Simple Shape into a Complex Shape

The more complex the shape you tween, the more difficult it is for Flash to create the expected result. You can improve tweening results by adding *shape hints* to link points on the original shape to points on the final shape.

To shape-tween a more complex shape:

1. In a new Flash document, or on a new layer, create a five-frame shape tween.

   In Keyframe 1, draw an oval fill with no stroke; duplicate it in Keyframe 5, then apply shape tweening to the keyframe span.

2. Modify the ending shape.

   In the Timeline, move the playhead to Frame 5. Using the selection tool or subselection tool, drag four corner points toward the center of the oval to create a flower shape. (To review shape editing, see Chapter 4.)

3. Play the movie to see the shape tween in action.

   Flash handles the tweening for this change well **A**. It's fairly obvious which points of the oval should move in to create the petal shapes. If you modify the shape further, however, Flash has difficulty creating appropriate transitions to the new shape. That's when you need to use shape hints.

To use shape hints:

1. Using the animation you created in the preceding task, add another shape-tween segment. Duplicate the flower shape in a new keyframe by selecting Frame 10 and choosing Insert > Timeline > Keyframe (or pressing F6). Select any frame in the keyframe span (Frame 5, 6, 7, 8, or 9) and choose Insert > Shape Tween.

2. In Keyframe 10, edit the flower to add a stem. Reshape the flower's path using the selection tool or the pen and subselection tools, or use the brush tool to paint a stem the same color as the flower.

3. Play the movie. The addition of the stem makes it difficult for Flash to create a smooth tween that looks right 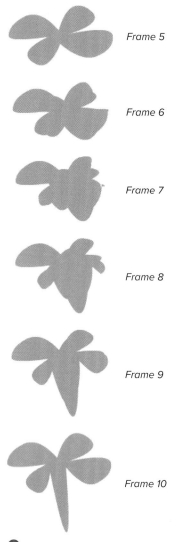.

4. To begin adding shape hints, move the playhead to Keyframe 5, the initial keyframe of this tweening sequence.

5. Choose Modify > Shape > Add Shape Hint, or press Shift-Command-H (OS X) or Ctrl-Shift-H (Win). Flash places a shape hint ● in the center of the object in the current frame.

6. To identify an area that tweens badly, use the selection tool to drag the shape hint to a problem point on the edge of the shape.

   As you drag, Flash previews the hint's position with a circle icon; the circle becomes darker and thicker when it connects with the path. Don't worry about getting the shape hint in exactly the right spot; just make sure it's on the path. You can fine-tune its position later.

Frame 5

Frame 6

Frame 7

Frame 8

Frame 9

Frame 10

B The addition of a stem to the flower overloads Flash's capability to create a smooth shape tween. Frames 7 and 8 are particularly bad.

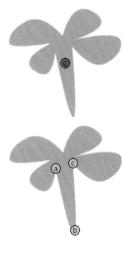

Areas of change

C Start adding shape hints in the first keyframe of a tween sequence. Flash places each new hint in the center of the tweened object (top), and you must drag each hint into position (middle). Distribute multiple hints in alphabetical order along the object's path, placing them on crucial points of change (bottom). Here, the three points with hints *a*, *b*, and *c* define the points from which the stem of the flower will grow.

D To complete the placement of shape hints, select the second keyframe of your tween sequence. Flash stacks up hints corresponding to the ones you placed in the preceding keyframe (top). You must drag each hint into the correct final position (bottom).

7. Repeat Steps 5 and 6 until you have placed shape hints on all the problem points of your shape in Keyframe 5 **C**.

   Each new shape hint you add contains the next letter in the alphabet. You must place the hints in alphabetical order around the edge of the shape. (Flash does the best job when you place shape hints in counterclockwise order, but you can also place them in clockwise order.)

8. In the Timeline, move the playhead to Keyframe 10. Flash has already added shape hints to this frame; they stack up in the center of the shape.

9. With the selection tool, drag each shape hint to its position on the path of the new shape.

   Keep the hints in the same order (counterclockwise or clockwise) you chose in Step 7 **D**. When the end-of-tween shape hint is sitting on a path, the hint changes from red to green. If you select the initial keyframe of the span, you can see that the associated beginning-of-tween hint has turned yellow.

10. To evaluate the improvement in tweening, play the movie.

Continues on next page

11. To fine-tune the shape hints' positions, select one of the tween's keyframes; then in the Timeline's Status bar, select Onion Skin Outlines and set the range markers to cover the tween span.

Where the onion skin outlines reveal rough spots in the tween, adjust the hint positions **E**. Repositioning the hints changes the shapes in the in-between frames. You may need to adjust the shape hints in both keyframes. If you still can't get a smooth tween, try adding more shape hints.

TIP To remove a single shape hint, make the initial keyframe the current frame. Select the shape hint you want to remove, and drag it out of the document window. Or, Control-click (OS X) or right-click (Win) the shape hint, and choose Remove Hint.

TIP To remove all shape hints at the same time, make the initial keyframe the current frame, and choose Modify > Shape > Remove All Hints. Or, Control-click (OS X) or right-click (Win) any shape hint, and choose Remove All Hints.

TIP When you select a shape with the selection tool, Flash hides any visible shape hints. To view the hints again, choose View > Show Shape Hints, or press Option-Command-H (OS X) or Ctrl-Alt-H (Win).

TIP In Windows, when you work with a shape that already has hints, you can add a new hint quickly by Ctrl-clicking any of the existing shape hints.

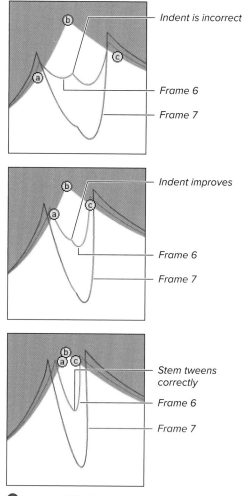

Indent is incorrect

Frame 6

Frame 7

Indent improves

Frame 6

Frame 7

Stem tweens correctly

Frame 6

Frame 7

E It can be difficult to match points exactly in the two keyframes when you initially place the shape hints. After you've positioned the hints in the beginning and ending keyframes of a sequence, turn on onion-skin outlines to see where you need to adjust the placement of the hints. With the initial placement, the stem starts growing with an indent at the bottom (top). Moving the hints closer together improves the tween (middle). When the onion-skin outlines reveal a smooth tween, you're done (bottom).

Animation with Motion Tweening

In a classic tween, you create animation by setting up a series of keyframes. Each of those keyframes contains a separate instance of the symbol you want to animate. You manipulate each symbol individually to change its properties. Flash calculates any differences in the symbols' properties at each keyframe (position, size, rotation, and so on) and uses that information to create a series of images in which the symbol changes incrementally.

Motion tweens work somewhat differently. You set up a single keyframe, with a single symbol instance, then define a motion-tween span. Within that span, *property keyframes* indicate changes to the symbol's properties. Again, Flash animates the symbol instance—known as the *tween target* or *target instance*—by creating a series of images that change the tween target's properties over time.

In This Chapter

Creating a Bouncing Ball with Motion Tweening

It's easy to do a version of the standard bouncing-ball animation with motion tweening. You start with a single instance of the ball, place it in a tween span in the Timeline, and tell Flash how to move that instance by adding position keyframes.

To set up a motion tween:

1. Open a new Flash document. The document contains one layer and one keyframe (Frame 1).

2. To preset the motion tween's duration, select the frame that marks your desired span length—for this task, select Frame 10—and choose Insert > Timeline > Frame **Ⓐ**.

3. In the Timeline, select Keyframe 1.

4. Place an instance of a symbol that represents a ball near the top of the Stage. For example, use the oval tool to draw a circle shape, then convert it to a symbol (see Chapter 7) and name it **MyBall**.

5. To apply motion tweening to the target symbol, do one of the following:

   ▶ In the Timeline, select Keyframe 1 (the one containing **MyBall**) or any frame in the keyframe span (Frames 1–10). Flash selects the symbol on the Stage.

   ▶ On the Stage, select the symbol you want to animate (**MyBall**). Flash selects the entire keyframe span in the Timeline.

Ⓐ To specify the length of a motion tween (in frames), define a keyframe span of that length in the Timeline. The end-of-span rectangle and gray tint (in Tinted Frames mode) identify the keyframe span.

Motion-Tween Symbols: Best Practice

Flash can create motion tweens using symbols or text fields (either TLF or Classic). When you attempt to apply motion tweening to other types of content, a dialog appears asking if you want Flash to convert the content to a symbol for you. If you answer OK, Flash creates the symbol with a generic name and carries out the motion tween. This is an improvement over Flash's automatic creation of symbols for classic tweens (where Flash just creates the symbol without any warning). Still, it's a good idea to decline Flash's automated conversion so you can name the symbol meaningfully and make sure that the symbol includes what you want it to include. If you encounter this dialog, cancel it and create your own symbol.

 When the playhead is within a keyframe span, choosing Insert > Motion Tween converts that span to a tween span and adds an icon 🏃 to the layer name to indicate that this layer contains motion tweening. Tween spans are always tinted a light blue, which appears even when you deselect Tinted Frames in the Frame View menu.

Applying Tweening to Multiple Items

You can apply the Insert > Motion Tween command to a selection that includes multiple items, and even to items on multiple layers. Flash uses the following process when creating tween spans for the selected items.

When a selection contains multiple items on the same layer—or includes one or more items that are not symbols or text fields—Flash must convert the selection to a symbol before creating the tween span. (See the sidebar "Motion-Tween Symbols: Best Practice.") If the selected items are on a layer with unselected items, Flash converts the selection to a symbol, pulls the symbol into a new layer, and creates the tween span in the new layer. (The unselected items remain on their original layer.) If the selection includes all the items on a single layer, Flash creates the tween span in that layer. When you select multiple symbols and/or text fields, each residing on its own layer, Flash creates a separate tween span for each selected object on its original layer.

6. Choose Insert > Motion Tween.

Flash converts the keyframe span to a *tween span* **B**. The symbol in a motion tween is called the *tween target*. The target in this example, **MyBall**, appears through all the frames of the span. To animate **MyBall**, you must add property keyframes within the tween span.

TIP Defining a keyframe span (Step 2 in the preceding task) is optional. If you apply motion tweening to a single keyframe, Flash creates a tween span with a default length. (See the sidebar "About Tween-Span Length and Location" in this chapter.)

TIP You can apply motion tweening directly to an object on the Stage. (For best results, you should apply motion tweening only to a symbol or text field. See the sidebar "Motion-Tween Symbols: Best Practice.") Using the selection tool, Control-click (OS X) or right-click (Win) the object to be tweened. From the contextual menu, choose Create Motion Tween.

About Tween-Span Length and Location

The Insert > Motion Tween command creates tween spans of different lengths depending on the arrangement of frames in the active layer. If you want Flash to create a tween span with a specific number of frames, you must first set up a keyframe span with that number of frames.

Before creating motion tween

After creating motion tween

When the target symbol is in Keyframe 1 of a layer with no other defined frames, Flash creates a one-second tween span based on the current frame rate (at the default 24-fps frame rate, the resulting tween span contains 24 frames).

Before creating motion tween

After creating motion tween

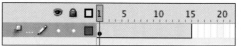

When the target symbol is in a keyframe span, Flash converts that span to a tween span with the same number of frames.

Before creating motion tween

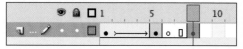

After creating motion tween

You can't mix motion tween spans with other types of tween spans on a single layer. When the target symbol is on a layer containing other types of tweens, Flash pulls the target symbol to a new motion-tween layer, at the same frame number, and creates the tween span. (Here the tween span is just one frame long.)

Before creating motion tween

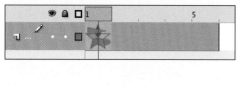

After creating motion tween

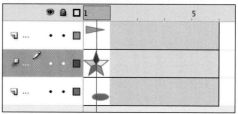

Each tween span is limited to one object. When you apply motion tweening directly to an object on the Stage (such as the star) and other objects are in the same frame on the same layer (such as the triangle and oval), Flash pulls the selected object out to a new motion-tween layer and inserts new layers in the Timeline hierarchy as needed to preserve the stacking order of the objects.

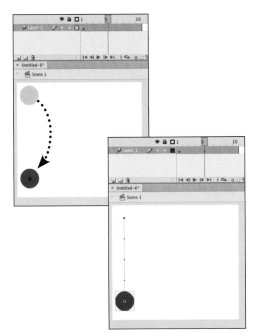

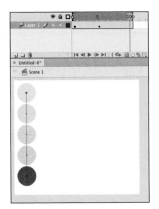

C When you change the position of the tween target on the Stage (top), Flash adds a property keyframe (represented by a small diamond icon ◆) and creates a motion path on the Stage (bottom).

D The motion path maps the movement of the tween target in a motion tween. Viewing the path gives you a general impression of the motion sequence, but it's also good to play the animation to see how it's working. Here, onion skinning allows you to see the interpolated changes to the tween target.

To change the tween target's position for the downward bounce:

1. Continuing with the file you created in the preceding task, set the tween target's position for the low point of the bounce by moving the playhead to Frame 5 in the Timeline.

2. Using the selection tool, drag the tween target (**MyBall**) to the bottom of the Stage.

   In the Timeline, Flash adds a diamond icon to the tween span at Frame 5. The diamond indicates a property keyframe—in this case a position keyframe. (See the sidebar "About Property Keyframes" in this chapter.) The motion path for the tween appears on the Stage **C**.

3. To view the animation, move the playhead to Frame 1 and choose Control > Play, or press Enter. The ball moves from the top of the Stage to the bottom in five frames, then sits at the bottom for five frames **D**.

4. Save your document as a template for future use; name it DownBounceMaster. Be sure to close the template document before moving on to the next task. (For detailed instructions about templates, see Chapter 1.)

TIP When the tween target has focus (for example, when you click the symbol on the Stage using the selection tool), you can change the target's position by changing its *x*- and *y*-coordinates in the Position and Size section of the Property inspector, or in the Info panel. When you select a tween span in the Timeline, the symbol is also selected, but the span has focus. Properties of the motion-tween object appear in the inspector.

To change the tween target's position for the upward bounce:

1. Using the DownBounceMaster template that you created in the preceding task, open a new document.

2. To set the ball's position for the rebound, select Frame 10 in the Timeline.

   The playhead moves to that frame, and Flash selects the tween target, making it ready for you to manipulate.

3. Position the tween target two-thirds of the way up toward the original position. You can drag the symbol, press the arrow keys to move it, or change its coordinates in the Property inspector or the Info panel.

   Flash adds a second position keyframe to the tween span at Frame 10, and adds a new segment to the motion path on the Stage **E**. In this case, the new segment lies directly over the original path.

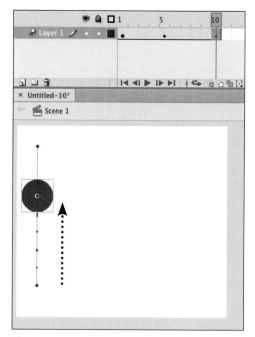

E The position of the playhead in a tween span tells Flash where to add a property keyframe for any changes you make to the selected tween target. In this figure, the tween target was dragged to a new location.

About Property Keyframes

Flash's Motion Editor displays each tweenable property in a separate graph. By viewing the graph, you can see the exact values for tweened properties at every frame in a selected tween span. The Timeline is less precise. A diamond icon ◆ appears in a frame when you've assigned a value to any property in that frame. By assigning a value—for example, by manipulating the tween target on the Stage, or by entering a value in the Motion Editor—you create a *property keyframe*. You can set the Timeline to display the property keyframe diamonds or to hide them. (See the sidebar "Hiding Property Keyframes" in this chapter.)

The Motion Editor displays curves for all tweenable properties. For example, the Basic Motion section of the panel includes separate curves for the horizontal and vertical positions of an object. The Timeline lumps the two into one property keyframe type: *position.* The Timeline can display diamonds representing six properties: Position, Scale, Skew, Rotation, Color, and Filter. When talking about the Timeline, the tasks in this book refer to these general categories when mentioning the presence of a property keyframe. For example, Frame 5 contains a *position keyframe* and a *rotation keyframe.* When talking about the Motion Editor, tasks refer to the specific property curves— for example, the X curve and the Rotation Z curve each have a property keyframe at Frame 5.

About Motion Presets

The *motion preset* is a form of reusable animation. A preset is basically a copy of a tween span with its motion path, property keyframes, and easing intact, but waiting to be assigned a tween target. The preset contains all the information about how the animated item moves, which properties change and when, how long the change takes, and so on. The only thing missing is the symbol.

To use a motion preset, access the Motion Presets panel. (If it's closed, choose Window > Motion Presets.) The panel looks something like a library panel. Motion presets appear in hierarchical folders in a scrolling list, and a window at the top previews the animation of a selected preset. Flash CS6 includes a number of default presets, and you can also save custom presets. Open the folder containing the desired preset, and choose a preset name. On the Stage, select the item you want to animate; then in the Motion Presets panel, click the Apply button. Flash turns the selected item into a tween target and creates a motion-tween layer and tween span, just as when you choose Insert > Motion Tween. However, the motion preset creates the tween span and all the property curves necessary to create the animation. When you click the Apply button, Flash begins the animation with the tween target at its current Stage position. To put the tween target through its motion so that it ends up at its current position, Shift-click Apply.

You can save your own motion tweens as presets. In the Timeline, select a tween span. In the Motion Presets panel, click the Save Selection As Preset button ⊡ in the panel's lower-left corner. Enter a name in the Save Preset As dialog and click OK. Flash adds your preset to the Custom Presets folder in the panel.

4. Choose Control > Test Scene, or press Option-Command-Enter (OS X) or Ctrl-Alt-Enter (Win) to preview the animation.

   The ball moves from the top of the Stage to the bottom, then rebounds almost back to the top. If you let the animation loop, the ball bounces continually.

5. Save the document as a template for future use; name it FullBounceMaster. Then close the template document.

TIP In this task you create the rebound by adding a second position keyframe. This method makes it easy to know that a change takes place at this point in the Timeline. The drawback to this method is that the motion path for the rebound lies directly on top of the motion path for the downward bounce, so it can be difficult to manipulate the overlapping segments of the motion path. More advanced animators can achieve the same result by adding easing to create the rebound motion. You can see an example of using easing to create motion in the default motion preset named **Bounce-Smoosh. (See the sidebar "About Motion Presets.")**

Working with Motion-Tween Paths

With motion tweens, whenever you change the tween target's position, Flash creates a motion path and adds a control point to the path at the frame where the change occurs. (See the sidebar "About Frame Points and Control Points" in this chapter.) Initially, a motion path consists of straight-line segments. To make a symbol follow a curve, you must edit the motion path.

To reposition a motion path:

1. Select the motion path on the Stage. Using the selection tool, for example, click directly on the motion path.

2. To change the motion path's position, do one of the following:

- ▸ Use the selection tool to drag the motion path to a new location 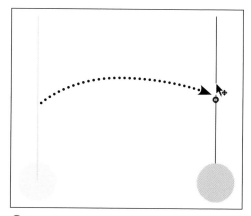.

- ▸ Press the arrow keys to move the selected path.

- ▸ Access the Motion Tween Property inspector, and in the Path section, use the X and Y hot-text controls to enter new values for the *x*- and *y*-coordinates of the upper-left corner of the path's bounding box. The tween target is connected to the path; the entire animation sequence moves to the new location.

A You can relocate an entire motion-tween animation on the Stage by dragging a selected motion path with the selection tool.

TIP Depending on the particular motion path and tween target, it may be difficult to select just the path. You can select both the tween target and the path, for example, by drawing a selection rectangle that includes the path and the tween target. You're ready to drag the selection or move it by pressing the arrow keys.

TIP If you select both the path and the tween target, you have access to the Mixed Property inspector, which has no Path section. Changing the X and Y values in the Mixed inspector's Position and Size section does move the motion path and tween target, but the values apply to the bounding box of the entire selection. To change the properties of the motion path alone, deselect the tween target.

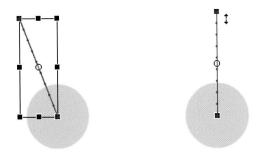

B Flash's free-transform tool activates a transform box around a selected motion-tween path (left). For horizontal or vertical paths, the path activates without a box (right). The tool works on the motion path as it would on any other object. Drag the handles to resize, rotate, or skew the bounding box containing the path.

Properties	
Motion Tween	

▷ EASE	
▷ ROTATION	
▽ PATH	
X: 49.0	Y: 48.0
W: 194.0	H: 320.0
▷ OPTIONS	

C The Path section of the Motion Tween Property inspector contains hot-text controls governing the properties of the motion path's bounding box. By changing the values for W (width) and H (height), you change the width and height of the path's bounding box, thereby increasing or decreasing the path length.

To resize the path:

1. Using the DownBounceMaster template you created earlier in this chapter, open a new document. It contains a motion path with two control points corresponding to the two position keyframes you created for the ball's movement.

2. Select the motion path on the Stage.

3. In the Tools panel, select the free-transform tool. Flash activates a transform box for the motion path, just as it would for a regular path **B**.

4. Using the techniques you learned in Chapter 4, manipulate the resize handles to change the length (and/or orientation) of the path.

   or

   Select the tween span in the Timeline and do the following:

   ▸ Access the Motion Tween Property inspector.

   ▸ In the Path section, use the W and H hot-text controls to enter new values for the width and height of the motion path's bounding box **C**.

TIP You can also access the Path section of the Motion Tween Property inspector after selecting the motion path on the Stage.

To reshape a motion path by moving the tween target:

1. Using the FullBounceMaster template you created earlier in this chapter, open a new document. The motion path contains three control points.

2. Move the playhead to the frame where you want to add or change the tween target's position. For this task move the playhead to Frame 10.

3. Using the selection tool, drag the tween target (the symbol instance `MyBall`) to a new position—for example, to the bottom-right corner of the Stage. Flash redraws the motion path 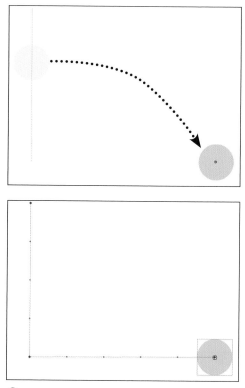 **D**.

4. Play through the movie. Instead of bouncing, the ball drops down and moves to the right.

To reshape a motion path by moving control points:

1. Continue with the file you created in the preceding task. Using the subselection tool ⬧ on the Stage, position the pointer over a control point ◦—for example, the point corresponding to the ball's final position.

   The pointer icon contains a hollow square ⬚ when the tool is on a control point.

D Changing the position of the tween target changes the motion path. When you move the tween target in a frame with an existing position keyframe, Flash moves the control point of the motion path on the Stage.

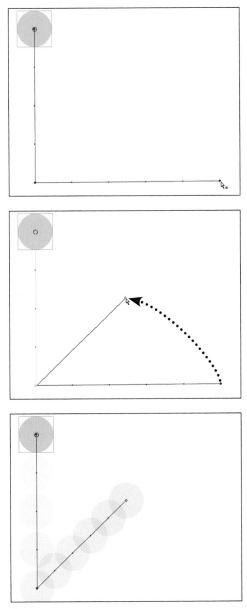

2. Drag the control point to a new location—for example, to the middle of the Stage. Flash previews the new motion path as you drag.

3. Play through the movie. Now, the ball drops down and makes a short hop **E**.

TIP The pointer icon contains a solid square when the subselection tool is positioned over the path but not over a control point. Dragging with the solid-square icon active moves the entire motion path.

About Frame Points and Control Points

A *motion path* is a graphic representation of changes in the tween target's position over time. The path is also an object similar to one you'd create with Flash's drawing tools, but with some important differences. A merge-shape or drawing-object Bézier path consists of anchor points connected by line segments and curves. A motion path is also a Bézier path, but one that consists of *frame points* representing frames in the tween, and *control points* (similar to anchor points) representing the position keyframes in the tween.

Tween spans with up to 100 frames use frame points ⊷ to indicate each frame in the tween; in frames where the tween target changes position, a control point ⊷ replaces the frame point. Tween spans longer than 100 frames use frame points ⊷ to represent a group of frames, for example, every fifth frame. (Note that the exact number of frames represented depends on the length of the tween span.) To view control points ⊷, select the motion path with the subselection tool.

E When you position the subselection tool over a control point in a motion path, a hollow-square modifier-icon appears (top). You can drag the control point to reposition the tween target on the Stage at that frame (middle). Flash redraws the motion path when you release the mouse button (bottom). Here, onion skinning shows the new motion of the ball.

To transform a straight-line motion path to an arc:

1. Continuing with the file you created in the preceding task, select the subselection tool.

2. On the Stage, position the pointer over the motion path's initial control point. This control point corresponds to the keyframe at the beginning of the motion-tween span.

3. To extend Bézier handles for modifying the path, Option-drag (OS X) or Alt-drag (Win) the control point. Drag in the direction you want the curve to grow **F**. Flash redraws the motion path to create a curve.

TIP To gain more control over the curve of the path—for example, making the ball follow an S curve—repeat Step 3 for all the control points in the motion path, and adjust the Bézier handles to achieve the desired curves.

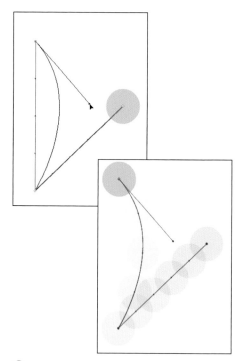

F Use the subselection tool to Option-drag (OS X) or Alt-drag (Win) Bézier handles from the control points in a motion path (top). Reposition the handles to transform a straight-line motion path into a curved path (bottom).

Modify Motion Paths the Natural Way

You can modify a motion path using the selection tool. The technique is similar to the way you modify lines with natural drawing tools as described in Chapter 4.

Make sure the motion path is deselected. Position the selection pointer over the motion path, between two control points. When the curve point icon appears in the pointer ⬐, drag that segment of the motion path to create a curved segment. To further refine the curve, switch to the subselection tool and click a control point. Bézier handles extend from the two control points that define the curve segment.

Although the selection tool can transform the motion-path segment into an arc, it can't create angular changes to the path. When you edit a merge-shape or drawing-object path, you can Option-drag (OS X) or Alt-drag (Win) to add new corner points, but this method doesn't add control points to a motion path. To add control points, you must add position keyframes. (See the task, "To add control points to a motion path.")

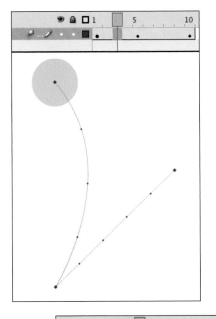

To add control points to a motion path:

1. Continuing with the file from the preceding task, select Frame 3 in the Timeline.

2. Control-click (OS X) or right-click (Win) the selected frame and choose Insert Keyframe > Position from the contextual menu.

   Flash adds a position keyframe to Frame 3, and a new control point appears on the Stage in the middle of the motion path 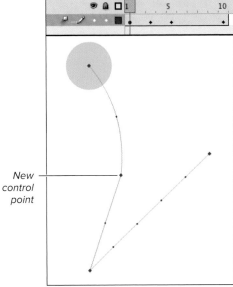. The tween target moves to that point on the motion path.

3. Repeat Steps 1 and 2 to add as many control points as you like.

   You can then use the techniques in the preceding tasks to reposition the new control point(s) or activate the Bézier handles to reshape each segment of the motion path.

TIP When you add control points, it doesn't matter what is selected in the Timeline. Flash always adds the new position keyframe at the current playhead location. When you remove control points, however, you need to pay attention to the Timeline selection. To achieve reliable results for both actions, train yourself to select the correct frame, then Control-click (OS X) or right-click (Win) that frame to open the contextual menu.

New control point

G To add new control points to a motion path, you must create a new position keyframe. One way to do so is to Control-click (OS X) or right-click (Win) a selected frame (top) within the tween span, and choose Insert Keyframe > Position from the contextual menu. Flash adds a property-keyframe diamond icon to the Timeline (bottom).

To remove control points from a motion path:

1. Continuing with the file from the preceding task, select Frame 3 in the Timeline.

2. Control-click (OS X) or right-click (Win) the selected frame and choose Clear Keyframe > Position from the contextual menu.

3. Flash removes the position keyframe from the selected frame. (Note that when multiple frames are selected, the Clear Keyframe command removes all keyframes of the selected type from all the selected frames.)

TIP In the Timeline, the property keyframe's diamond icon ◆ does not indicate the type of property (or properties) changing at any given frame. If a diamond appears in the Timeline for a frame where you'd like a control point, but the motion path displays only a frame point ┈, you need to add a position keyframe **ⓗ**.

TIP Here's a quick way to add a position keyframe without actually changing the tween target's position in that frame (a useful trick for creating curves in sections of the motion path that currently lack control points). In the Timeline, move the playhead to the desired frame. On the Stage, select the tween-target symbol. Press the Up Arrow key, then press the Down Arrow key. Flash adds a position keyframe to account for the change in the position property even though the tween-target symbol winds up in its original position.

TIP To quickly delete all position keyframes, select the motion path and press the Delete key. Flash deletes the path and all its position keyframes. All other property keyframes remain; so, for example, the tween target might grow or rotate or change color, but it stays in one place while doing so. If you subsequently add a motion path to the span, those same property changes take place and the tween target moves along the new path.

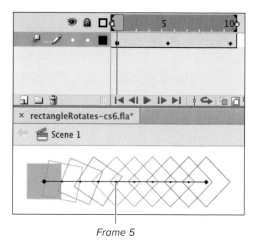

Frame 5

ⓗ Frame 5 of this Timeline contains a property-keyframe diamond, but the fifth dot in the motion path is just a small, frame dot. This fact indicates that the diamond icon represents a property other than position. Here, onion skinning reveals that the tween target is rotating as well as moving to the right. The diamond represents a rotation keyframe.

TIP You can also add a position keyframe using the Motion Editor. (See "Motion Editor Basics" in this chapter.)

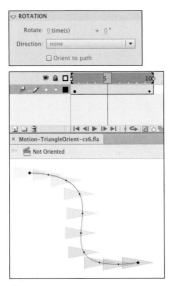

A The Motion Tween Property inspector displays attributes of the tween. In the Rotation section, when the Orient to Path checkbox is deselected (top), the tween target maintains its original orientation to the Stage throughout the motion tween (bottom).

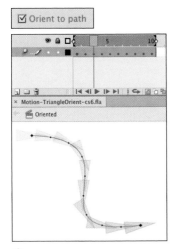

B When Orient to Path is active, the tween target maintains its original alignment to the motion path throughout the motion tween. Flash adds a rotation keyframe to every frame of the tween span.

Orienting Tween Targets to Curves

By default, a tween target keeps its original orientation to the Stage even when following a curving motion path. To create more natural movement, you can force a tween target to rotate and preserve its orientation to the motion path in each frame of a tween.

To orient a tween target to a curving path:

1. Create a ten-frame motion tween of a symbol that follows a curving path. To see the effect clearly, use a symbol that's not circular.

2. Turn on onion skinning to see how the tween target moves along the path without orientation A.

3. In the Timeline, select any frame in the tween span and access the Motion Tween Property inspector.

4. In the Rotation section of the inspector, select the Orient to Path checkbox B.

   Flash adds a rotation keyframe to every frame in the tween span, adjusting the degree of rotation in each frame to preserve the tween target's original alignment with the path.

Swapping Tween Elements

Flash treats a motion tween as an object, making it easy to swap elements in the tween span. You can replace the tween target with another symbol and retain all the property changes of the original tween. You can also change the motion path by pasting a different path into the tween span. The new path can be a motion path from another tween span, or a merge-shape or drawing-object path.

To swap a tween target:

1. Open a new document using the FullBounceMaster template that you created in the preceding section. It contains a ten-frame motion tween of a bouncing ball, using a symbol named **MyBall**.

2. Create a new symbol. For example, convert a square shape into a symbol named **MySquare**. (For details about creating symbols, see Chapter 7.)

3. In the Timeline, select any frame within the motion-tween span and access the Library panel. If it's not open, choose Window > Library.

4. Drag a copy of **MySquare** from the library to the Stage. A dialog asks if you want to replace the existing tween target 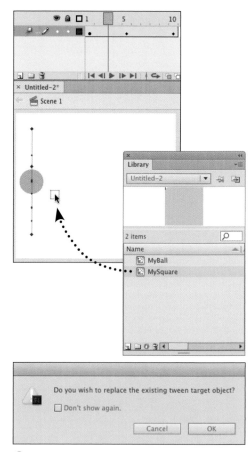.

A Whenever a motion-tween layer is the active layer and the playhead is in a tween span, dragging a symbol from the library to the Stage (top) opens a dialog asking if you want to replace the original tween target with the object you're dragging (bottom).

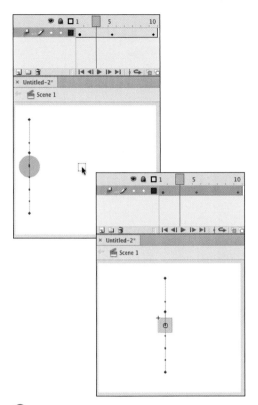

5. Click OK.

Flash removes the original symbol (**MyBall**) and substitutes an instance of **MySquare**. The Tween span retains all its property keyframes. The tween target moves to the Stage position where you dragged the new symbol, and the motion path moves to match **B**.

TIP Pasting a copied symbol instance to the Stage with the motion-tween span active also opens a dialog asking if you want to replace the existing tween target. Depending on which Paste command you used, when you click OK, Flash pastes the symbol in its original location or in the center of the Stage and moves the motion path to link up with the new tween target. If the location of the tween is important, be sure to use the Edit > Paste in Place command.

TIP To swap symbols and preserve the tween target's original stage position, select just the tween target on the Stage and click the Swap button in the Property inspector.

B When you swap tween targets by dragging a new symbol to the Stage (top), the size and shape of the motion path and the locations of the frame dots and control points stay the same, but the path moves to hook up with the new symbol wherever you placed it (bottom). Reposition the path if necessary.

Hiding Property Keyframes

By default, the Timeline displays all six types of property keyframes. When you create property changes for individual properties in different frames, the Timeline may resemble a diamond bracelet with property-keyframe markers in almost every frame. To reduce the clutter, you can choose which types of property keyframes appear in the Timeline. Control-click (OS X) or right-click (Win) any frame in a motion-tween span and choose View Keyframes from the contextual menu. A submenu lists all six property types, plus All and None. You can select or deselect one property each time you access the menu. When you deselect a type, Flash stops displaying that type in the Timeline. If your Timeline seems light on property keyframes, or you're trying to insert property keyframes using the contextual menu and not seeing the results in the Timeline, try choosing to view that property type again. (You can also verify the location of the property keyframes in the Motion Editor.)

To swap a motion path:

1. Continuing with the document you created in the preceding task, add a new layer and create a second motion tween.

   Layer 1 already contains a motion tween that moves the symbol **MySquare** vertically in straight lines. In Layer 2, create a motion tween that moves the symbol **MyBall** along a curved path. Name the layers Move Ball and Move Box to remind you which tween is on which layer **C**.

2. In the Tools panel, choose the selection or subselection tool.

3. On the Stage, click directly on the motion path for **MyBall** and choose Edit > Copy, or press Command-C (OS X) or Ctrl-C (Win). Flash copies the motion path to the Clipboard.

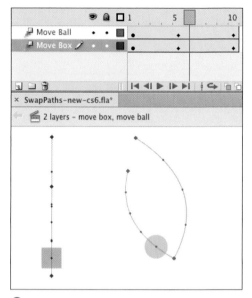

C Give the Move Ball and Move Box motion tweens very different motion paths to make it easy to see the difference when you swap one for the other.

Drawing New Motion Paths

In addition to copying and pasting motion paths between motion spans, you can copy and paste a regular merge-shape or drawing-object path created with Flash's drawing tools (see Chapter 2). This swap option makes it possible to create motion paths using Flash's Bézier tools, which are designed for creating precise curves. You simply draw a path, copy it, then paste it into a tween span. The pasted path becomes the new motion path. There are two things to keep in mind: you can't draw directly in a motion-tween span, and you can't use a closed path as a motion path.

To draw a new path for a motion tween, you must work in a keyframe that's not part of a motion-tween span. An easy way to do that is to add a new layer and work in the initial blank keyframe. Alternatively, you could open a new document and work there.

When you try to paste a closed path—for example, an outline oval—into a motion-tween span, a warning dialog informs you that a motion guide must have two end points. To fulfill this requirement, use the oval tool to draw a circular stroke, then use the eraser tool to delete a tiny portion of the stroke. The path is now open, and you can use it to move a tween target around a circular path.

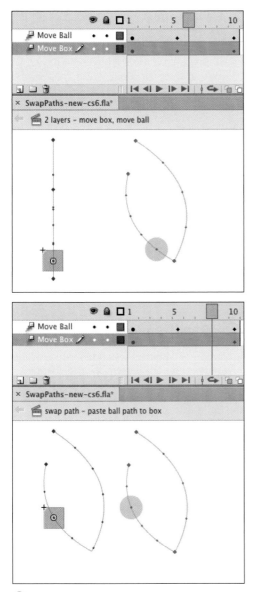

D Pasting a motion path removes any position keyframes in the middle of the target span. Flash creates one position keyframe in the last frame of the span and spreads the animation over the whole span. In this example, the original path in the Move Box layer has a position keyframe at Frame 5 (top). After you paste the copied path, that position keyframe disappears (bottom).

4. To select a tween target to receive the new motion path (**MySquare**), do one of the following:

   ▸ On the Stage, click **MySquare**.

   ▸ In the Timeline, click the tween span in the Move Box layer.

5. Choose Edit > Paste in Center, or press Command-V (OS X) or Ctrl-V (Win).

   Flash pastes the ball's motion path into the square's span, distributing the movement over the full length of the target span using roving keyframes (see the sidebar "About Roving Keyframes," in this chapter). The pasted path has just two position keyframes: the initial keyframe and the last keyframe of the span **D**.

6. Play through the animation.

   MySquare and **MyBall** now trace the same path in different areas of the Stage, but the timing is different. **MyBall** reaches the lowest point of its curve at Frame 5 where there's a position keyframe; **MySquare** reaches the same point somewhere between Frames 6 and 7.

TIP To make two tween targets follow the same path, in Step 5, choose Edit > Paste in Place, or press Shift-Command-C (OS X) or Ctrl-Shift-C (Win). Flash positions the pasted motion path in the same Stage location as the copied path and moves the tween target so that its transformation point connects with the pasted path.

TIP When multiple layers contain tween spans with tweens at the same frame, you can choose to view all the motion paths or just one. In the Timeline, select any frame in any tween span, then access the Motion Tween Property inspector. From the panel menu, select Always Show Motion Paths to simultaneously display all paths in the current span (where the playhead is located). Deselect the option to display only the active layer's path.

Motion Editor Basics

Flash's Motion Editor is a complex and powerful tool that graphically presents information about motion-tween animation. The horizontal axis of the graph represents frame numbers (or, in essence, time); the vertical axis represents the value of the property being graphed. Editing those graphs changes the animation. *Motion Editor* is a bit of a misnomer because it not only controls the position of the tween target (which creates the motion) but also controls various other tweenable properties. Many of the sophisticated techniques this panel offers are beyond the scope of a *Visual QuickStart Guide,* but using the Motion Editor to create simple animation is a good way to start learning to work with it.

TIP Some properties in the Color Effect and Filters categories can't be graphed as curves. If you've applied one of these properties to a tween target, that property appears in the Graph column as a property keyframe on a flat gray line with a value of zero. Tint Color in Color Effect is one example: there is no "red-ness" value that Flash could graph along the vertical axis. Tint Amount, which does have a corresponding value (a percentage), gets its own row with a graph in the Tint subcategory of the Motion Editor.

To view property curves:

1. Access the Motion Editor.

2. To display the property curves for a motion tween, do one of the following:

   ▸ In the Timeline, select the tween span or any frame in the span.

   ▸ On the Stage, select the motion path.

   ▸ On the Stage, select the tween target.

   The graphs for the tweenable properties appear in the Motion Editor. (See the sidebar "Motion Editor vs. Timeline.")

TIP The arrow keys act as shortcuts for navigating the Motion Editor. To move up and down the rows, press the Up Arrow and Down Arrow keys. Flash selects the next row in turn. The selected row retains its current state. If the next row is a category row in its collapsed state, the row stays collapsed. If the next row is a property within an expanded category, the row remains it at its current size. To change a row's state, press the Right Arrow and Left Arrow keys. To expand a category row, press the Right Arrow key; to collapse the row press the Left Arrow key. To make the current property row taller, press the Right Arrow key; to make the row shorter, press the Left Arrow key.

Motion Editor vs. Timeline

The fundamental tool for working with frame-by-frame animation and shape and classic tweening is the Timeline with its layers and frames. The keyframes displayed in the Timeline show where the key points of change occur. Motion tweens are also Timeline based, but they allow you to control changes to individual properties. As a result, you can have many more key points of change to track in an animation segment. The Timeline presents a limited amount of information concerning the type of change happening at any given frame and a limited amount of control over those changes.

Continues on next page

Motion Editor vs. Timeline *(continued)*

To see more detail and gain full control over the property keyframes in a motion-tween span, you must use the Motion Editor.

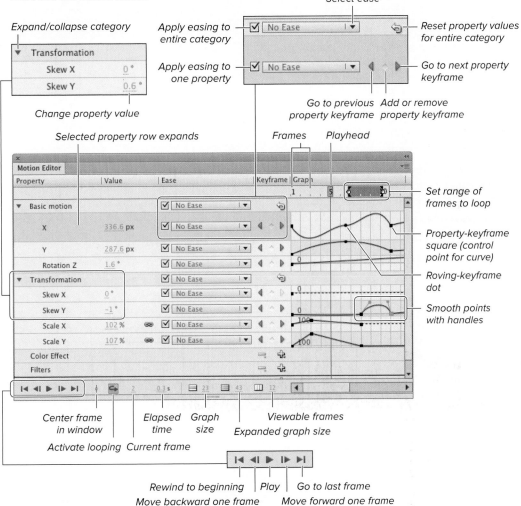

Select ease

Expand/collapse category

Apply easing to entire category — Reset property values for entire category

Apply easing to one property — Go to next property keyframe

Change property value

Go to previous property keyframe   Add or remove property keyframe

Selected property row expands   Frames   Playhead

Set range of frames to loop

Property-keyframe square (control point for curve)

Roving-keyframe dot

Smooth points with handles

Center frame in window   Elapsed time   Graph size   Viewable frames

Expanded graph size

Activate looping   Current frame

Rewind to beginning | Play | Go to last frame

Move backward one frame   Move forward one frame

The Motion Editor contains its own version of the Timeline and its own playhead. The Motion Editor shows information for just one motion-tween span at a time. Each tweenable property has its own row. If the property can be graphed as a curve, the row contains a graph with Bézier curves representing the changes to that property within the selected motion-tween span. Property keyframes appear in the graph as control points (black squares) defining the shape of the curve. The horizontal axis of the graph represents time/frame numbers, while the vertical axis represents the value of the property being graphed.

To customize graph views:

1. Access the Motion Editor and select a tween span.

2. To set the size of the rows containing the property graphs, do one of the following:

   ▸ To set the minimum row height for all properties, use the Graph Size hot-text control.

   ▸ To determine how much a row enlarges when you select it, set the Expanded Graph Size hot-text control to the desired row height in pixels .

3. To see more (or fewer) frames in the panel, use the Viewable Frames hot-text control to set the number of frames displayed **B**.

   Unlike the Timeline, which displays all the frames in a layer, the Motion Editor only shows the frames of the selected tween span. The maximum value for Viewable Frames is the number of frames in the span.

TIP To set Viewable Frames to quickly show all the frames in a span, enter a number that's bound to exceed the number of frames in the span—for example, 99,999. Flash changes the value to the actual number of frames and sizes the graph accordingly.

TIP Clicking an expanded, tall row reduces it to the default height.

Set minimum row height   Set expanded row height

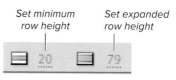

A Hot-text controls in the Motion Editor let you set the size of the rows and, thereby, the size of the graphs. Clicking anywhere in the gray area of the row to the left of the graph expands the row to the current maximum setting.

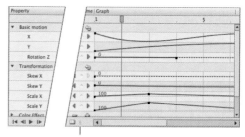

Viewable Frames

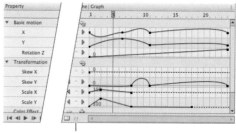

Viewable Frames

B The Motion Editor can display one frame of the selected tween span, several frames (top), or all the frames in the span (bottom). Use the Viewable Frames hot-text control to set the number of frames that appear in the Graph column.

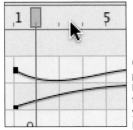

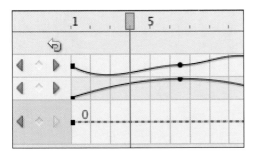

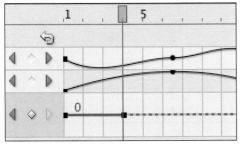

C To position the playhead in the Motion Editor, click a tick mark for the frame location you want, or drag the playhead to the frame.

D When the current frame has no property keyframe (top), the Add or Remove Keyframe button is ghostly gray ■ and quite hard to see. When the frame has a property keyframe, the button turns yellow ◇. Property keyframes in the graph appear as black squares (or dots if the keyframe is set to roving).

To add keyframes to a property curve:

1. In the Graph column of the Motion Editor, move the playhead to a frame that lacks a property keyframe **C**.

   You can drag the Motion Editor playhead to a new location, or click directly on the frame number or on a tick mark above the graphs.

2. In the row containing the property curve you want to change, click the gray Add or Remove Keyframe button **D**.

   A property keyframe (represented by a black square) appears in the graph. Flash connects the property keyframes with a solid line.

TIP Instead of clicking the Add or Remove Keyframe button, you can Control-click (OS X) or right-click (Win) the property curve at any frame and choose Add Keyframe from the contextual menu.

TIP When you hold down the Command key (OS X) or Ctrl key (Win) and position the pointer over the property curve, the pointer changes to a pen with a plus sign 🖊₊. Click the graph to add a new control point.

TIP Flash updates the Motion Editor graphs when you change the tween target's properties using any method, but the Motion Editor need not be open. If, for example, the playhead is sitting at a frame that lacks property keyframes for X and Y positions, and you move the tween target by dragging it on the Stage or by changing its *x*- and/or *y*-coordinates in the Property inspector or Info panel, Flash adds property keyframes to the X and Y graphs in the Motion Editor.

To remove keyframes from a property curve:

- Repeat Steps 1 and 2 of the preceding task, except this time be sure to move the Motion Editor's playhead to a frame that contains a property keyframe. Flash removes the black square from the graph and redraws the curve segment **E**.

TIP When you hold down the Command key (OS X) or Ctrl-key (Win) and position the pointer over a control point in a property curve, the pointer changes to a pen with a minus sign ✑₋. Click the control point to remove it.

TIP When you Control-click (OS X) or right-click (Win) a property keyframe in a property curve, the contextual menu includes the Remove Keyframe command.

TIP You can remove all property keyframes from all the graphs in a category by clicking the Reset Values button ⟲ in the main category row of the Motion Editor.

To navigate the property keyframes:

- To move the Motion Editor's playhead from one property keyframe to the next in a property curve, click the Go to Previous Keyframe/Next Keyframe buttons ◄ ᐱ ▶ in the row containing the desired property curve.

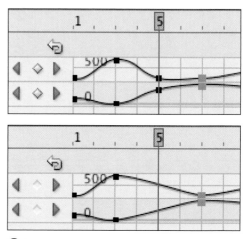

E Click a yellow Add or Remove Keyframe button (top) to remove the property change at the current frame. Flash removes the property keyframe square from the graph and redraws the curves. On the Stage, the tween target no longer displays changes to the specified property at that point in the animation.

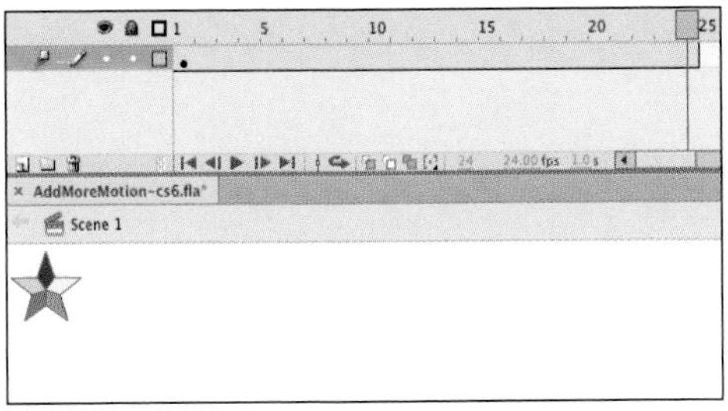

A Create a motion tween for working with the Motion Editor. Here, an instance of the symbol **MyStar** is the tween target for a 24-frame motion tween.

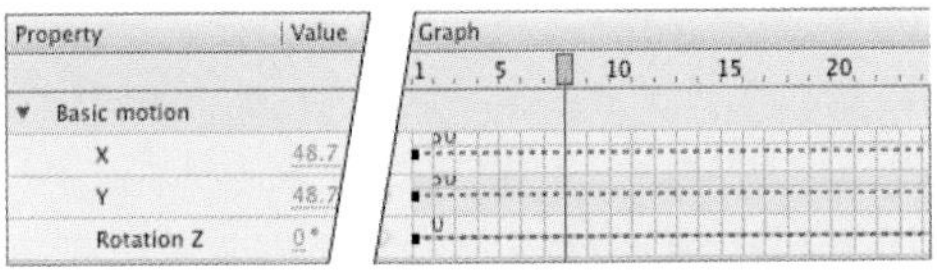

B The Motion Editor displays the properties of the tween span currently selected in the Timeline. For a two-dimensional tween, the Basic Motion category contains graphs for three properties: X (horizontal position), Y (vertical position), and Rotation Z (the degree of rotation applied to the tween target).

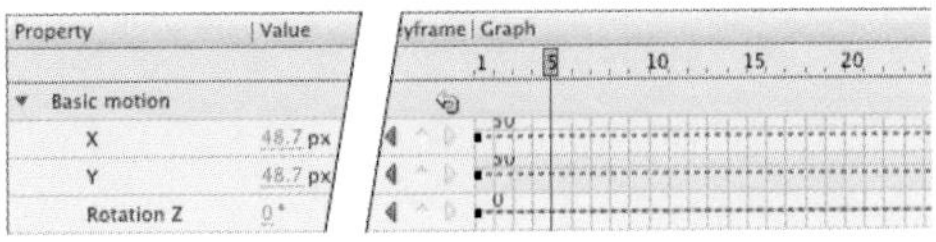

C To add a property keyframe to a specific frame, move the playhead to that frame in the Graph column of the Motion Editor.

Adding More Motion

In the first section of this chapter, you added position keyframes to the motion-tween span by dragging the tween target (the symbol named **MyBall**) on the Stage. However, you can also use the Motion Editor to add position keyframes and assign values for the *x*- and *y*-coordinates of the tween target.

To create motion by adding position keyframes in the Motion Editor:

1. Create a 24-frame motion tween.

Open a new Flash document (with default settings). In Layer 1, select the empty Frame 1 (the default blank keyframe), and place an instance of a symbol named **MyStar** on the Stage. Select **MyStar** and access the Property inspector. In the Position and Size section use the hot-text controls to place the symbol near the upper-left corner of the Stage. Set the values for X (horizontal position) and Y (vertical position) to 50 pixels. Choose Insert > Motion Tween. Flash creates a default motion-tween span 24 frames long. Your document should resemble figure **A**.

2. In the Timeline, select any frame in the tween span and access the Motion Editor's Basic Motion category **B**.

3. In the Graph column, move the Motion Editor's playhead to Frame 5 **C**.

You may need to scroll the graph to see Frame 5. The graph contains a black square representing the initial keyframe at Frame 1. The dotted lines in the Basic Motion graphs indicate that the tween span contains no position or rotation keyframes that create movement.

Continues on next page

4. In the X row, click the Add or Remove Keyframe button.

Flash adds a property keyframe to both the X and Y graphs at Frame 5 (the current frame) and completes the first segment of the two property curves, changing the dotted line to a solid black line **D**.

5. To move the tween target to the right, use the hot-text control to increase the X value from 50 to 500.

Flash redraws the property curve **E**. When the document's units of measure are set to pixels, the tween target moves 450 pixels to the right.

6. To move the tween target downward, repeat Steps 3–5 for Frame 15, this time increasing the Y value from 50 to 300. The tween target moves 250 pixels toward the bottom of the Stage.

7. To move the tween target diagonally, repeat Steps 3–5 for Frame 20, this time changing the values for X and Y.

Set both values to 100 to move the tween target diagonally toward the upper left corner of the Stage.

8. Repeat Steps 3–5 for Frame 10, this time setting the X value to 350 and the Y value to 150.

Each time you add property keyframes to the X and Y graphs, their curves update in the Motion Editor, and the motion path updates on the Stage **F**. You can refine the animation by adding

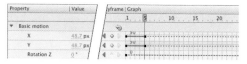

D After you add a property keyframe, a new control point appears in the property curve. Adding a property keyframe to the X curve (horizontal position) simultaneously adds one to the same frame of the Y curve (vertical position). Flash links the X and Y values because they translate to *x*- and *y*-coordinates for the tween target's registration point.

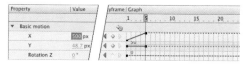

E Changing the value for a control point in the X row moves the tween target horizontally on the Stage. Flash updates the motion path on the Stage and completes a segment of the X and Y property curves in the Motion Editor.

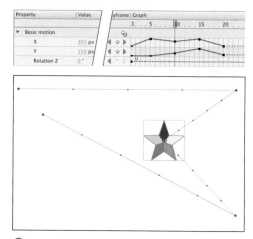

F The X and Y property curves in the Motion Editor show all the points of change in the tween target's position; the motion path on the Stage shows the same thing. The squares in the path are control points corresponding to the property keyframes in the curves.

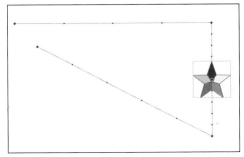

Removing a property keyframe from the X (and Y) property curve in the Motion Editor removes a control point from the motion path on the Stage. Flash redraws the motion path and the property curves.

(or removing) property keyframes at any point in the curve. You can add a property keyframe within an existing curve segment (between property keyframes), or add a property keyframe in the dotted-line section of the graph to create a new curve segment.

TIP In Step 6, using a higher value to position a symbol lower on the Stage may seem counterintuitive (especially when you're using the Y hot-text control interactively—dragging down in the hot-text control moves the symbol up on the Stage.) It's all due to the way Flash tracks elements. (See "How Flash Tracks Elements" in Chapter 4.)

To edit motion by removing position keyframes in the Motion Editor:

1. Continuing with the file you created in the preceding task, place the Motion Editor's playhead at Frame 10.

2. In either the X or Y row, click the yellow Add or Remove Keyframe button.

   Flash removes the black square from both graphs, redraws the X and Y curves in the Motion Editor, and redraws the motion path on the Stage **G**. The curves and motion path return to the state they were in before you completed Step 8 in the preceding task.

3. Save this document as a template and call it MovingStarMaster.

Animating Other Property Changes

You can use the Motion Editor to add property keyframes for all the properties that you animate with motion tweens. The process is similar to adding property keyframes for Stage position; however, the specific settings and graphs are different. In the following tasks, you'll create some basic property keyframes to animate changes in size, rotation, and color.

To rotate the tween target:

1. Using the MovingStarMaster template that you created in the preceding task, open a new document, select the tween span, and access the Basic Motion section of the Motion Editor.

2. Move the Motion Editor's playhead to Frame 5.

3. Change the Rotation Z value to enter the degree of rotation. For this task, enter 90 degrees. Positive values create clockwise rotation; negative values, counterclockwise.

   Flash adds a property keyframe to the Rotation Z graph and updates the curve 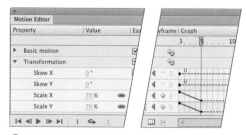.

A You can use the Rotation Z hot-text control in the Motion Editor to add a bit of spin to the tween target.

Manipulating Tween Targets to Add Property Keyframes

In Chapter 9, you placed symbol instances in keyframes on either end of a keyframe span to create a classic tween. You then changed the properties of the symbols by directly manipulating the symbol instances—for example, using the free-transform tool to change a symbol's size. You can use those same techniques with motion tweening. Whenever you manipulate a tween target on the Stage, Flash translates your changes into property keyframes. You saw Flash add position keyframes to the Timeline when you created the bouncing ball earlier in this chapter. The technique works for any property that you can tween in a motion tween. Flash creates property keyframes in both the Timeline and the Motion Editor when you make changes to the Tween target on the Stage. For example, open a new document using the DownBounceMaster template. Move the playhead to Frame 7. Using the free-transform tool, change the size of the tween target (**MyBall**). Flash adds a scale keyframe at Frame 7 in the Timeline and adds a property keyframe at Frame 7 of the property curves for Scale X and/or Scale Y in the Motion Editor.

B Onion skinning reveals that the tween target rotates when you add a property keyframe at Frame 5 of the Rotation curve in the Motion Editor.

4. Step through the animation, moving the playhead one frame at a time.

   The star rotates 90 degrees in five steps (Frames 1–5) **B** and retains its rotated position for the rest of the tween.

5. Save this document as a template, name it RotateStarMaster, then close the file.

TIP In the preceding task, the star stops rotating at Frame 5. If you want the star to resume rotation in later frames, you need to add more rotation keyframes. If you want the star to rotate continuously throughout the tween to reach **90 degrees**, place the rotation keyframe at the end of the tween span, or apply the rotation to the entire tween span using the Motion Tween Property inspector. (See "About Autorotation in Motion Tweens" in this chapter.)

A Note About Editing Motion

Often, the easiest way to create and edit the movement of a tween target is to drag the target instance on the Stage. Dragging automatically creates a new position keyframe at the current frame, and dragging lets you interactively check and adjust the tween target's position and relationship to other elements. When you need to position a tween target precisely, you can enter x- and y-coordinates for the tween target's registration point using the Property inspector, the Motion Editor, or the Info panel. Which method is best? In part, it depends on your working style. But there's another issue to consider. The behind-the-scenes math that the Motion Editor performs to calculate and draw the motion path works somewhat differently than the math in all the other methods. (To see the differences in action, try dragging a tween target to various spots on the Stage. For each location, check the X and Y values in the Property inspector and the Motion Editor to observe that the values often differ slightly.) Using the hot-text controls and graphs in the Basic Motion section of the Motion Editor can have unexpected results for the motion path on the Stage. And as a practical matter, the graphs in the Motion Editor are small and difficult to deal with compared with the motion path on the Stage. The tasks in this section show you how to use the Motion Editor by adding keyframes and changing the X and Y values to move the tween target in straight lines around the Stage. To move a tween target in more complex ways, and to edit the motion path after you've created position keyframes, it's best to work directly with the tween target and motion path on the Stage, or to use the Property inspector or the Info panel to enter specific x- and y-coordinate values.

To change a tween target's scale:

1. Repeat Steps 1 and 2 of the preceding task. This time, access the Transformation section of the Motion Editor.

2. To change the size of the tween target, access the Scale X and Scale Y rows and do one of the following:

   ▸ To preserve the tween target's aspect ratio, with Link Values active ∞, use the Scale X or Scale Y hot-text control to enter a new percentage **C**. Changing one value correspondingly changes the other value. Larger values increase the size of the tween target; smaller values reduce it.

   ▸ To change the tween target's vertical and horizontal dimensions independently, set the Link Values modifier to Unlinked mode ⋕. Then use the Scale X or Scale Y hot-text control to enter new percentages independently.

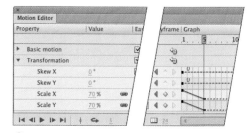

C The Link Values modifier in the Scale rows of the Motion Editor works just like the Constrain/Unconstrain modifier in the Transform panel. With ⋕ active, you can change the X and Y values independently. With ∞ active, changing one value changes the other as well, preserving the tween target's aspect ratio.

About Autorotation in Motion Tweens

For the tasks in this section, you rotate the motion-tween target by creating rotation keyframes in the Motion Editor. You must specify a precise degree of rotation, entering negative values to rotate the tween target counterclockwise and entering positive values to rotate it clockwise. When you created classic tweens (see Chapter 9), you let Flash automatically spin objects by entering values in the Rotate section in the Tweening area of the Frame Property inspector. The technique also works for a motion-tween target. Select the tween span in the Timeline to see the properties of the motion tween. In the Rotation section of the Motion Tween Property inspector, use the Rotation Count and Additional Rotation hot-text controls to set the number of times the tween target rotates. (Set Rotation Count to 0 when you want the target to rotate less than 360 degrees.) There's just one little quirk to keep in mind: when you create rotation for the tween target via the Property inspector, Flash spreads the rotation out over the entire tween span. Even when you specifically select a single frame earlier in the tween span, Flash adds the rotation keyframe to the last frame in the current span. If you want the rotation to end at an earlier frame, you must select the rotation keyframe and drag it from the last frame of the tween span to the desired frame. (See "Modifying Tween Spans" in this chapter.)

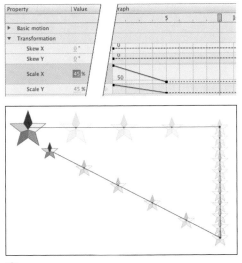

Property		Value		Graph					
						5			1
▶	Basic motion								
▼	Transformation								
	Skew X	0 °			0				
	Skew Y	0 °			0				
	Scale X	45 %							
	Scale Y	45 %			50				

D Onion skinning reveals the interpolated steps that change the tween target's size when you add a property keyframe to the Scale X curve in the Motion Editor. With Link Values active, a Scale X value of 45 percent shrinks the star while retaining its aspect ratio.

A Note About Rotation and 3D Tweening

In the preceding task, you learned about rotation in two dimensions (rotation along the *z*-axis). When you create a motion tween, Flash also lets you create rotation in three-dimensional space (rotation along the *x-*, *y-*, and *z*-axes). To access those properties, Control-click (OS X) or right-click (Win) a motion-tween span in the Timeline and choose 3D Tween from the contextual menu. The additional rotation properties appear in the Basic Motion section of the Motion Editor. Animated 3D rotations are beyond the scope of a *Visual QuickStart Guide*.

3. Play through the animation.

The star moves around the Stage. By the time it reaches the end of its horizontal motion (at Frame 5), the star has changed to the new size you specified in Step 2 **D**. Note that it keeps this new size for the remainder of the animation, or until you add another scale keyframe. The position keyframes that exist at Frames 15 and 20 have no effect on the size of the star.

TIP When the Motion Editor has focus, issuing a Play command—for example, clicking the Play button or pressing Enter—causes the playhead to loop through frames, even when the Loop button is deselected and Loop Playback is deselected in the Control menu. To stop playback, issue a Stop command—for example, by clicking the Pause button or pressing Enter a second time. To play the movie just once, select the Timeline panel to give it focus.

TIP The graphs for the skew property are also located in the Transformation section of the Motion Editor. You can add new keyframes to the Skew X and/or Skew Y graphs. Then use the Skew X hot-text control to change the horizontal skew of the tween target. Use the Skew Y hot-text control to change the vertical skew. Skew values are always set independently.

To change a tween target's color:

1. Continuing with the file from the preceding task, with the tween target (**MyStar**) selected on the Stage, in the Graph column of the Motion Editor, move the playhead to Frame 12.

2. In the Color Effect row, click the plus icon ⊕ to access the Add Color menu and choose the desired effect **E**.

   The Add Color menu offers the same effects you used to modify symbol instances in Chapter 7. For this task, choose Tint. A new subcategory—Tint—appears in the Color Effect section of the Motion Editor with rows and graphs for Tint Color and Tint Amount.

3. To change the tween target's color, do the following:

   ▶ In the Tint Color row, use the color control to choose a color.

   ▶ In the Tint Amount row, use the hot-text control to specify how much of the tint to apply to the tween target. For this task, choose 90 percent.

4. Play through the animation. **MyStar** changes from its original color to its new color in 12 steps, then keeps its new color for the rest of the tween **F**.

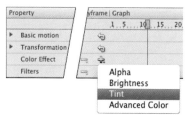

E Access the Add Color menu ⊕ in the Motion Editor's Color Effect row to apply a color effect to your tween target.

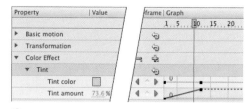

F New property curves appear in the Motion Editor when you choose an option from an Add menu. When you choose Add Color > Tint, curves appear for Tint Color and Tint Amount. Changing the values of those properties at Frame 12 in the Motion Editor adds new property keyframes to their graphs, updates those curves, and changes the star color over the first 12 frames of the animation.

Editing Curves in the Motion Editor

The graphs in the Motion Editor show changes to each property as a Bézier-style curve. The horizontal axis of the graph shows frame numbers (time), and the vertical axis shows the property values. You can edit most property curves inside the Motion Editor in ways similar to those you learned for editing Bézier paths (Chapter 4). The exceptions are the X and Y property curves that define the motion path. While curves do appear in the Motion Editor for the X and Y properties, you can change them only by editing the motion path on the Stage.

The Motion Editor uses special terminology. Property keyframes appear as *control points* that define the curve (similar to anchor points in a Bézier path). As you change a property in various frames of a motion tween, new control points appear in that property curve. Initially, each control point is a *corner point,* and the curve consists of straight line segments. You can convert the control points to *smooth points* (similar to curve points in a Bézier path), then drag handles to shape the curve on either side of the control point. When you drag a control point horizontally, the property keyframe moves to a new frame in the tween; when you drag a control point vertically, the value of the property changes.

By default, as you drag, a tool tip appears showing the frame number and current value of the control point. To hide these tips, in the Motion Editor's panel menu, deselect Show Tooltips.

Here are some ways to work with property curves in the Motion Editor:

 To select a control point, click it. Flash highlights the point in green. To select multiple points in one property curve, Shift-click each point. To deselect a point, Shift-click it.

 To move a control point to a different frame number, drag the point horizontally.

 To change the control point's value, drag the control point vertically (drag up to increase the property value and drag down to decrease it). The graph scrolls as you drag, making it hard to work with when the Motion Editor is docked and/or set to a small size. To make the graphs easier to work with, undock the Motion Editor and size it fairly large.

 To adjust a curve, select a smooth point to view its handle(s). Drag a handle to adjust the curve on that side of the control point. The steeper the curve, the faster that property changes.

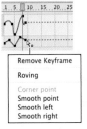 *To convert a corner point to a smooth point (or vice versa),* Control-click (OS X) or right-click (Win) the control point and choose an option from the contextual menu. The menu options vary depending on the type of point you click and its location. Smooth options appear when you click a corner point. Choosing Smooth Point adds handles to both sides of the point; Smooth Left adds a handle to the left; and Smooth Right adds a handle to the right. Corner options appear when you click a smooth point. Choosing Corner Point removes the handles from both sides of the control point; Linear Left removes the left-side handle; Linear Right removes the right-side handle. Left-side and/or right-side options appear only if a graph segment exists on that side of the point. You can also Option-drag (OS X) or Alt-drag (Win) a corner point to convert it, extend its handles, and begin shaping the curve.

Modifying Tween Spans

The selection styles for working with key-frame spans (frame-based and span-based) also affect your work with tween spans, but there are a few new twists to learn. No matter which selection style you use, when the pointer hovers near the outside edge of the span, the icon becomes a resize pointer ⟷ that lets you change the size of a span by dragging its first or last frame. When you do, the entire motion-tween object changes. Flash adjusts the position of any property keyframes within the tween span—spreading the animation out or squeezing it down—to fit the new span proportionally.

To select tween spans:

- Do one of the following:
  - ▸ In frame-based selection mode, double-click a frame in the tween span.
  - ▸ In span-based selection mode, single-click any frame within the tween span.

  Flash selects the entire span and highlights it **Ⓐ**.

TIP After you've selected a tween span, you can add a contiguous span to the selection by Shift-clicking it.

To select one frame in a deselected tween span:

- Do one of the following:
  - ▸ In frame-based selection mode, click the desired frame.
  - ▸ In span-based selection mode, Command-click (OS X) or Ctrl-click (Win) the desired frame.

TIP In frame-based selection mode, you must position the pointer carefully to select just the first or last frame of a tween span. When the pointer hovers near the left edge of the first frame, or the right edge of the last frame, the resize pointer ⟷ appears. Clicking the first or last frame with the resize pointer selects the entire tween span.

TIP Even when you work in frame-based selection mode, a selected tween span operates as if it were in span-based selection mode. As long as the dark-blue highlight is present, you must Command-click (OS X) or Ctrl-click (Win) to select one frame within the span and deselect the others.

Ⓐ Flash tints tween spans light blue. Selected spans highlight in a darker blue.

Original span   *Ready to resize*

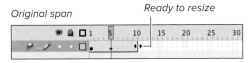

Drag right to enlarge

Resized span, with redistributed property keyframe

B Resizing a tween span by dragging doesn't merely add or remove frames at the end of the span. The animation contained in the tween span expands or contracts as an object. Flash redistributes the property keyframes to preserve the proportions of the tween. The original tween span has a property keyframe roughly at midspan, and so does the resized span. Flash does its best to maintain the relative positions of the property keyframes within the span. In the original span, 4 frames come before the property keyframe and 5 come after it. When you double the length of the span, Flash doubles the number of frames before the property keyframe to 8; that leaves 11 frames that come after. That's slightly more than double, but necessary to fill out the 20 frames.

To select multiple frames in a tween span:

- In frame-based selection mode, when the span is deselected, drag through the range of frames you want to select.

- In span-based selection mode (or in frame-based mode if the whole span is selected), Command-drag (OS X) or Ctrl-drag (Win) through the desired frames.

To resize a tween span and redistribute animation:

1. Position the pointer over the last frame in the tween span. The resize pointer ⟷ appears.

2. To lengthen the span, drag to the right; to shorten the span, drag to the left.

   Flash treats the span and the animation it contains as an object, and proportionally redistributes property keyframes within the span **B**.

> **TIP** You can also resize a tween span by dragging the first frame in the span.

> **TIP** Increasing the size of the span can overwrite frames and keyframes within other spans on the same layer, just as it does with keyframe spans (see Chapter 8). Reducing the size of the span creates new empty keyframe spans.

To extend or trim a tween span without redistributing animation:

1. Position the pointer over the right edge of last frame in the tween span, and wait until the resize pointer ⟷ appears.

2. To extend the span by adding in-between frames at the end, Shift-drag to the right.

3. To trim frames from the end of the span, Shift-drag to the left. Flash cuts any property keyframes in the trimmed section along with the in-between frames **C**.

TIP You can also add in-between frames to the end of a tween span by selecting a proto-frame in the same layer, and choosing Insert > Timeline > Frame (or pressing F5). Flash extends the span to the selected frame.

TIP If you select frames within a tween span and press F5, Flash increases the size of the span by adding that number of in-between frames. Where Flash adds the frames depends on the precise location of your selection in relation to any property keyframes.

TIP When the playhead is within a dese-lected tween span, pressing F5 adds one in-between frame at the playhead location

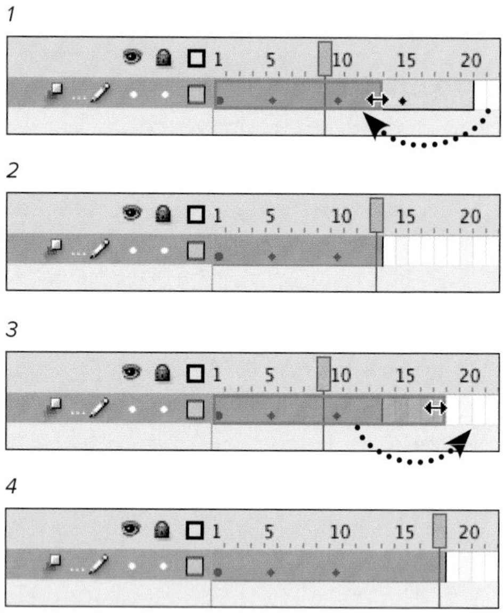

1

2

3

4

C Shift-drag the end of a tween span to resize it without redistributing its property keyframes. Shift-drag to the left (1) to clip off the end of the span (2). Shift-drag to the right (3) to add in-between frames at the end of the span (4).

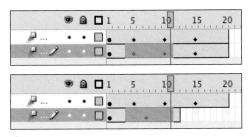

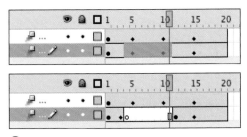

D The Edit > Timeline > Remove Frames command shortens the tween span by removing the selected frames, including any property keyframes in the selection.

E When you cut selected frames from a tween span (instead of removing them), Flash transforms them into an empty keyframe span. When you cut frames midspan, the empty keyframe span winds up in the middle. The remaining frames from the original tween span become a second tween span.

To shorten a tween span by removing internal frames:

1. Select one or more contiguous frames within the tween span.

2. Choose Edit > Timeline > Remove Frames, or press Shift-F5. Flash deletes the frames—removing any property keyframes that fall within the selection—and shortens the tween span by the number of frames selected **D**.

> **TIP** The contextual menu for tween spans also contains a Remove Frames command.

To cut frames out of a tween span:

1. Select one or more contiguous frames within a tween span.

2. Choose Edit > Timeline > Cut Frames, or press Option-Command-X (OS X) or Ctrl-Alt-X (Win).

   Flash converts the selection to an empty keyframe span with a blank initial keyframe. Other frames in the selection become in-between frames. Flash converts any frames that follow the selection into a second tween span based on the original tween target, possessing all the properties that were applied at that frame **E**.

> **TIP** You can split or combine tween spans. To divide a span, select the frame at which the span should split. Control-click (OS X) or right-click (Win) the selected frame and choose Split Motion from the contextual menu. To combine spans, in the Timeline, Shift-click one or more contiguous tween spans in a layer. Control-click (OS X) or right-click (Win) any of the selected frames, and from the contextual menu, choose Join Motions. Flash creates a single tween span using the tween target from the earliest span.

To move tween spans by dragging:

- Select the span and drag it to the right or left within the Timeline layer.

  Depending on the configuration of elements in the layer, Flash resizes other spans, removes their contents, and/or creates blank keyframe spans in the original tween span's location **F**. If you drag a tween span so that it completely covers another keyframe or span, Flash deletes the covered item. Flash creates an empty keyframe span at the end of the layer to retain the layer's original number of defined frames.

TIP You can drag a tween span to a different layer.

TIP Option-dragging (OS X) or Alt-dragging (Win) a tween span creates a copy of the span, which you can place elsewhere in the same layer or in a different layer.

TIP You can also drag one or more property keyframes within a tween span. Select the frame containing the property-keyframe ◆ you want to move (or select a range of frames with property keyframes) and position the pointer over the selection. When the pointer with the hollow square ▫ appears, drag the selection to a new position in the Timeline. Remember that a small diamond icon ◆ may represent more than one property. Dragging a selection repositions the property keyframes for all the properties associated with each diamond.

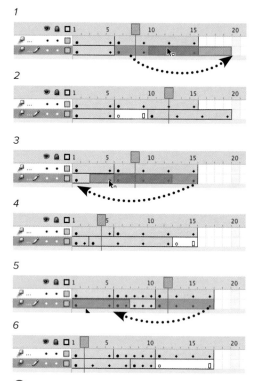

F Drag a selected motion-tween span in the Timeline to relocate the span in the same layer, or in a different layer. The results vary depending on the elements in the layer. Dragging a tween span to the right into the protoframe area (1) creates a new keyframe span to account for the "gap" between the first span and the new location of the second span (2). Dragging a tween span to the left, into the preceding span (3), shortens preceding span (4). Dragging a tween span so that it completely covers another span (5) replaces the covered span and its contents with the dragged span (6).

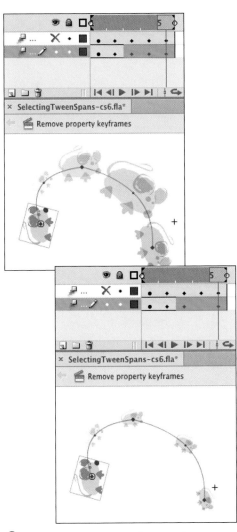

G To remove a property keyframe, in the Timeline, select one or more frames in the tween span and access the contextual menu for frames. This motion tween contains keyframes for multiple properties. The property that changes at Frame 4 is Scale. With Frames 3–5 selected (top), choosing Clear Keyframe > Scale removes all the scale property keyframes from the selected frames, and the small diamond icon ⬧ no longer appears in Frame 4. The diamonds that remain in Frames 3 and 5, represent other properties that change in those frames.

To remove property keyframes:

1. To remove property keyframes from a single frame, select that frame.

   or

   To remove property keyframes from a range of frames, select those frames.

2. To access the contextual menu for frames, Control-click (OS X) or right-click (Win) the selected frame.

3. Choose Clear Keyframe.

4. From the submenu that appears, choose one of the following:

   ▸ To remove one category of property keyframes at a time, choose a type: Position, Scale, Skew, Rotation, Color, or Filter.

   ▸ To remove all categories simultaneously, choose All.

   Flash removes the property keyframe(s) from the selection in the Timeline, updates the property curve in the Motion Editor, and updates the tween target and/or motion path on the Stage **G**.

TIP When you are working with the Timeline, and you want to remove more than one category of property keyframes but retain others, you must repeat the removal process for each category.

TIP In the Motion Editor, to remove all the keyframes from all the property curves in one category, click the Reset button ⟲ in the main category row.

TIP Be careful when using the contextual menu's Clear Keyframe commands, as they remove all the property keyframes of a selected type from all selected frames. If you select the entire span, the commands delete all property keyframes of the selected type throughout the span.

About Roving Keyframes

The number of frames in an animation segment affects how fast or slow an object seems to move. An object that covers lots of ground in a few frames seems to move quickly. One that goes a short distance over many frames seems to move slowly.

When you resize a tween span in the Timeline, Flash redistributes the tween span's position keyframes to retain the span's original proportions of fast and slow movement. For example, start with a 15-frame motion tween of a ball, add a position keyframe at Frame 5, and move the ball 100 pixels to the right; add another position keyframe at Frame 15, and move the ball 50 pixels down. The movement to the right (the first third of the tween) seems faster than the movement down (the last two-thirds). If you stretch the span in the Timeline to 30 frames (see the tasks in "Modifying Tween Spans" in this chapter), the first position keyframe is placed at Frame 9, preserving the feeling that the first third of the movement is faster than the rest.

As you adjust tween spans to fine-tune the animation in a motion tween, you may produce undesirable changes of speed. Setting keyframes to *roving* redistributes position keyframes to maintain a uniform speed.

To turn on roving keyframes in the Timeline, Control-click (OS X) or right-click (Win) the tween span, and from the contextual menu, choose Motion Path > Switch Keyframes to Roving. To turn off roving, access the contextual menu for the tween span and choose Motion Path > Switch Keyframes to Non-Roving. In the Motion Editor, you can set individual position keyframes to roving. Roving keyframes appear as dots instead of squares in the property curve. Control-click (OS X) or right-click (Win) a control point in either the X or Y property curve and select Roving from the contextual menu. Flash changes the control points to dots in that frame for both the X and Y curves. To turn off roving, repeat the process and deselect Roving in the menu.

Roving keyframes relinquish their specific frame-number assignment and allow Flash to distribute motion evenly across the tween span. Returning to the original 15-frame example above, the ball moves a total of 150 pixels over 15 frames. When you change the tween span to use roving keyframes, Flash redistributes the motion so the ball moves 10 pixels in each frame. The ball now starts moving down between Frames 10 and 11 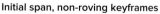.

While the span is set to roving keyframes, Flash redistributes any positional changes made to the tween target, so the action unfolds at a constant rate. If you later return the tween span to non-roving keyframes, Flash updates the Timeline with position keyframes that reflect the redistribution. In the 15-frame example, if you return the tween span to non-roving keyframes, Flash captures the redistribution by adding a position keyframe at Frame 10.

Initial span, non-roving keyframes

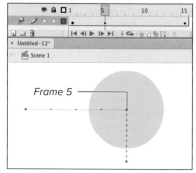

Span set to roving keyframes

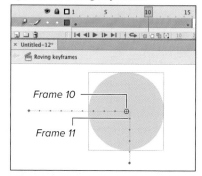

H When you first activate roving keyframes for a span, Flash removes the position keyframes in the middle of the span, and places one property keyframe at the end so that motion is distributed evenly.

The Insert > Keyframe Conundrum

When you create classic tweens and shape tweens, pressing F6 is a great timesaver that lets you duplicate the preceding keyframe quickly to create tween segments. By habit, you might reach for F6 while working in a motion tween, but pause first to evaluate your needs.

There is only one true keyframe in each motion-tween span: the first frame of the span. All the other "keyframes" are property keyframes controlling changes to individual properties. (The contextual menu for tween spans adds to the confusion with its Insert > Keyframe command, but the submenu makes it clear that you're inserting property keyframes.) Pressing F6 within a tween span creates *property* keyframes for every property that exists at that point.

Four of the properties represented by the diamond icon ◆ in the Timeline— Position, Scale, Skew, and Rotation—are always present in the initial keyframe of the tween span, even before you change any property. These properties allow Flash to describe the tween target. At a minimum, pressing F6 creates property keyframes for these four properties. If you've added the Color and Filter properties to the tween, pressing F6 also creates their property keyframes.

When you need to change every property at one point, creating all those control points at once can be helpful. Often, however, you just wind up with excess control points with values that don't change, and it may be harder to edit the property curves to create subtle changes. You can move an excess control point to a different frame (or delete the point), but that's a tedious process in long animations, where a tween span may contain hundreds of frames.

Copying Frames and Properties

You can reuse all or part of a motion tween by copying and pasting frames from the tween span into other frames in the Timeline.

To copy and paste a complete motion tween:

1. In the Timeline, select the full tween span.

2. Choose Edit > Timeline > Copy Frames, or press Option-Command-C (OS X) or Ctrl-Alt-C (Win).

3. In the Timeline, do one of the following:
   ▸ Create a new layer and select its initial blank keyframe or one of its protoframes.
   ▸ Add a new blank keyframe to the end of an existing layer containing a motion tween, and select it.
   ▸ Select a protoframe at the end of a layer containing other motion tween(s).
   ▸ Select a frame or range of frames within an existing tween span.

4. Choose Edit > Timeline > Paste Frames, or press Option-Command-V (OS X) or Ctrl-Alt-V (Win).

   Flash pastes a tween span with the same content and property changes. The initial keyframe of the pasted tween is in the selected frame; the pasted tween extends for the same number of frames as the original. When you paste a tween span into the middle of another tween span, Flash divides the span where you paste and may overwrite some of it. When you paste a tween span into a blank keyframe span, Flash adds the empty in-between frames to the end of the pasted motion tween.

To copy and paste property keyframes:

1. Open a new document using the RotateStarMaster template that you created earlier in this chapter.

2. Add a new layer. In Keyframe 1, place an instance of a different symbol, **MySquare**, in the lower-left corner of the Stage, and name the layers Square and Star.

3. On the Stage, select the **MySquare** instance and choose Insert > Motion Tween. Flash creates a second motion tween; currently the tween span contains no property keyframes.

4. In the Timeline, in the Star layer, select Frame 17. Flash can copy properties from only one frame at a time.

5. Control-click (OS X) or right-click (Win) the selected frame, and from the contextual menu, choose Copy Properties.

6. In the Square layer, select Frame 5, access the contextual menu, and choose Paste Properties.

   Flash creates a new property keyframe at Frame 5 of the Square layer, using the property settings that existed at Frame 17 of the Star layer 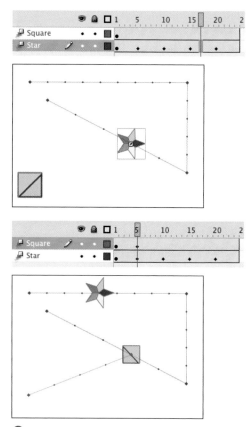.

A The properties for **MyStar** at Frame 17 (top) were copied and pasted onto **MySquare** at Frame 5 (bottom). **MySquare** moves to the same position **MyStar** has at Frame 17 and rotates 90 degrees.

> **TIP** The Copy Properties command captures property values for all the property types that exist for the selected tween target at the frame where you copy. The Paste Properties command, however, pastes only those properties that already exist in the tween you're pasting to.

Recycling Animation

Reusing tweens can increase the efficiency of your workflow. You can copy and paste entire tween spans, or just a few frames. When pasting only in-between frames, Flash creates a new initial keyframe. The tween target has the properties it had in the first selected frame. If the target was turning from red to blue in the pasted tween, the tween target starts with the same purple color it had in the first frame of the selection.

Intermediate Animation Tasks

You've learned to manipulate shapes and symbols—animating them one at a time, in a single layer—but Adobe Flash Professional CS6 is capable of much more complicated animation techniques. To create complex animated movies, you need to work with multiple shapes or symbols and multiple layers. You may even want to use multiple scenes to organize long animations.

In this chapter, you work with multiple layers in the Timeline, stack animations on the various layers to create more-complex movement, and save animations as reusable elements for easy manipulation—either as animated graphic symbols or as movie-clip symbols. With these techniques, you can really start to bring your animations to life.

In This Chapter

Working with Frames in Multiple Layers

As your animation grows more complex, you can organize it by adding layers to your document. You can cut, copy, and paste multiple selected frames across multiple layers. You can also insert frames, keyframes, and blank keyframes into selected keyframe spans, tween spans, and layers.

To copy and paste layers:

1. Control-click (OS X) or right-click (Win) the name of the layer you want to copy. Flash selects the layer and all of its frames and opens the contextual menu for layers.

2. Choose Copy Layers.

3. Control-click (OS X) or right-click (Win) the name of the layer that should be directly below the pasted layer.

4. From the contextual menu, choose Paste Layers.

   Flash creates a new layer above the layer you clicked 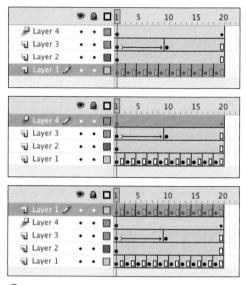. The pasted layer has the same properties as the copied layer (name, type, outline color, and layer height) and contains the same frames, keyframes, content, and animation.

TIP You can paste layers into the same scene as the copied layer, into a different scene, or into a different document.

TIP Choose Duplicate Layers in Step 2, to automatically copy the layer and paste it into a new layer directly above the clicked layer. Flash adds the word *copy* to the duplicate layer's name.

A To copy a layer, with all its properties and content, Control-click (OS X) or right-click (Win) the layer name, then choose Copy Layers from the contextual menu. Flash selects the clicked layer and all its frames (top). To paste, select the layer that should lie below the pasted layer (middle). Then Control-click (OS X) or right-click (Win) the selected layer name and choose Paste Layers. The pasted layer appears above the currently selected layer. The new layer contains all the frames and content of the copied layer (bottom).

Click to deselect frames

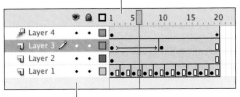

Click to deselect frames

B Clicking any gray area in the Timeline deselects all frames. To move the playhead and deselect frames, click one of the numbers above the frames. To leave the playhead in place, click the gray area at the bottom of the Timeline.

Begin selection

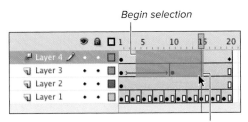

Drag to opposite corner

C In frame-based selection mode, starting with all frames deselected, simply drag across layers to select a range of frames in those layers. In span-based mode, Command-drag (OS X) or Ctrl-drag (Win).

Layers to Play With

To practice working with frames and layers, create a document with four layers, each with 20 defined frames. Add content that helps you understand what's going on. Use the text tool, for example, to place the frame number in every other frame of Layer 1 and to place a text block with the layer name in Layers 2, 3, and 4. Set up a motion tween by selecting Frame 1 in Layer 4 and choosing Insert > Motion Tween. Set up a classic tween by selecting Frame 10 in Layer 3, choosing Insert > Timeline > Keyframe, then selecting any frame in the preceding keyframe span (Frames 1–9) and choosing Insert > Classic Tween.

To select specific frames in several layers:

1. Create a practice document containing multiple layers and tweens. (See the sidebar "Layers to Play With.")

2. To deselect all frames, in the Timeline, click in the gray area above or below the layers and frames **B**. Deselecting frames prevents you from accidentally moving selected frames or adding them to a selection.

3. In the Timeline, draw a selection rectangle that encompasses all the desired frames **C**.

   In frame-based selection mode, drag diagonally from the first frame through all the desired frames. In span-based selection mode, Command-drag (OS X) or Ctrl-drag (Win). Flash highlights the selected frames as you drag.

TIP You can also select a range of frames on multiple layers by clicking. Imagine the rectangle you would create to select a range of frames by dragging (as in Step 3 above). In frame-based selection mode, click the frame at one corner of that imaginary rectangle and then Shift-click the frame in the diagonally opposite corner. In span-based selection mode, hold down a modifier key—Command (OS X) or Ctrl (Win)—when you click and Shift-click.

TIP Do not use the click/Shift-click method if your selection would end with a frame set to motion tweening; you'd just wind up selecting the ending frame.

TIP In span-based selection mode, when you have a series of back-to-back classic tweens or shape tweens, clicking a frame in any of the spans selects the entire series, including the span that follows the ending keyframe of the last tween in the series.

To copy selected frames:

1. Continuing with the practice document from the preceding exercise, select Frames 5–10 in all four layers.

2. Choose Edit > Timeline > Copy Frames, or press Option-Command-C (OS X) or Ctrl-Alt-C (Win). Flash copies the frames and layer information to the Clipboard.

To replace the content of frames with a multiple-layer selection:

1. Continuing with the document from the preceding task, select Frames 15–20 on all four layers.

2. Choose Edit > Timeline > Paste Frames, or press Option-Command-V (OS X) or Ctrl-Alt-V (Win).

    Flash pastes the copied Frames 5–10 into Frames 15–20 in each of the four layers 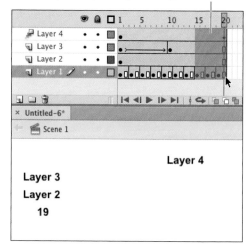. The numbers on the Stage in Layer 1 now start over with the number 5 in Frame 15, 7 in Frame 17, and 9 in Frame 19. Flash created a new keyframe at Frame 15 of Layer 2, a new classic-tween keyframe span in Layer 3, and a new motion-tween span in Layer 4.

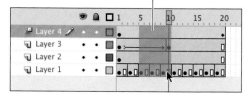

Copy selected Frames 5–10

Prepare to paste by selecting Frames 15–20

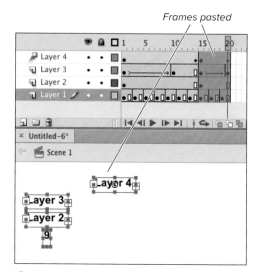

Frames pasted

D Pasting copied frames into existing frames replaces their content. Here, the content copied from Keyframe 9 winds up in Keyframe 19 and continues to show in Frame 20, where the playhead is.

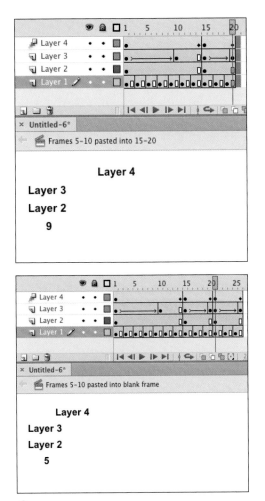

To paste a multiple-layer selection into blank frames:

1. Continuing with the document from the preceding task, select Frame 21 on all four layers.

2. Choose Edit > Timeline > Paste Frames, or press Option-Command-V (OS X) or Ctrl-Alt-V (Win).

   Flash pastes the copied Frames 5–10 into Protoframes 21–26 in each of the four layers ⓔ. Layer 1 now displays the number 5 in Frame 21, 7 in Frame 23, and 9 in Frame 25. Flash created a new keyframe at Frame 21 in Layer 2, a new classic-tween keyframe span in Layer 3, and a new motion-tween span in Layer 4.

   TIP You can also paste a multiple-layer selection into a new document, scene, layer, or symbol. Select the initial blank keyframe and choose Edit > Timeline > Paste Frames. Flash adds layers to accommodate the copied frames and layers.

ⓔ Pasting a multiple-layer, multiple-frame selection at the end of a set of defined frames (top) extends the Timeline to accommodate the new frames and layers (bottom).

Animating on Multiple Layers

To animate multiple objects simultaneously using classic or motion tweens, each object must be on a separate layer because each motion-tween or classic-tween segment is restricted to a single object. Although you can create shape tweens and frame-by-frame animations using more than one object per layer, it's usually best to keep each animated object on a separate layer. The tasks in this section introduce you to tweening items on multiple layers simultaneously.

Working with Multiple-Layer Classic Tweens

For the tasks in this section, you'll combine three simple classic tweens on three layers to create a game of Ping-Pong. The first step is to create the symbols and layers. One layer contains a Ping-Pong ball symbol; the other layers each contain a paddle symbol.

To set up the graphics layers:

1. Open a new Flash document, and add two new layers.

2. To help keep track of the elements, rename the top layer Ball, the middle layer 1st Paddle, and the bottom layer 2nd Paddle.

3. Create the graphics as symbols (see Chapter 7).

   Create a symbol named **PingPongBall** containing an appropriate graphic element. (For example, use the oval tool to draw a circular fill.) Create two symbols—**1stPaddle** and **2ndPaddle**— each containing a paddle graphic. (For example, use the rectangle tool to draw a rectangular fill.) Place each symbol in the layer that has the same name. Your file should look like **A**.

4. Save the file as a template named Ping-PongSetupMaster. Be sure to close the template file before continuing. You can use the same initial graphic setup to create a classic-tween or motion-tween version of the Ping-Pong animation.

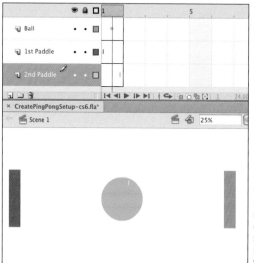

A When you use classic or motion tweening to animate several symbols simultaneously, each symbol must be on a separate layer. Descriptive layer names help you keep track of what goes where.

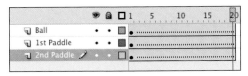

B To set up classic tweens in multiple layers with a single command, first select the desired frame in each layer, then choose Insert > Classic Tween.

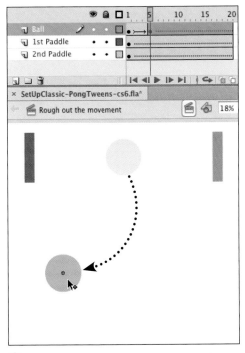

C The frames on all three layers have been set to classic tweening, but the tweens are broken, as indicated by the dotted lines. You must add keyframes and content to complete the tween.

D Moving a symbol instance in a frame that's defined as part of a classic tween causes Flash to make the layer containing the symbol the active layer. Flash creates a keyframe in that layer for the symbol's new position, thus completing one tween sequence.

To set up a classic tween in all layers with one command:

1. Using the PingPongSetupMaster template you created in the preceding task, open a new document.

2. In the Timeline, select Keyframe 1 in all three layers **B**.

3. Choose Insert > Classic Tween. Flash sets all three frames to be classic tweens.

4. In the Timeline, select Frame 20 in all three layers.

5. Choose Insert > Timeline > Frame, or press F5. Flash extends the classic tween through Frame 20 on all three layers. A dotted line across the frames indicates that the tween is incomplete **C**. To move the ball and paddles around the Stage, you must complete the classic-tween sequence by adding keyframes and repositioning the symbol instance in each one of them.

To rough out the movement— classic tweening:

1. Continuing with the file from the preceding task, in the Timeline, move the playhead to Frame 5.

2. On the Stage, drag the ball into position to connect with one of the paddles for the first hit.

   Ball becomes the active layer. At Frame 5, Flash creates a new keyframe containing another instance of the `PingPongBall` symbol in its new location **D**.

Continues on next page

Flash completes the tween in the first keyframe span (Frames 1–4) of the Ball layer, which displays the completed-tween arrow. The broken-tween line remains in all the other frames.

3. On the Stage, reposition the first paddle so that it connects with the ball for the first hit.

   Flash makes 1st Paddle the active layer and creates Keyframe 5, containing another instance of the **1stPaddle** symbol in its new location **E**.

4. In the Timeline, move the playhead to Frame 10.

5. On the Stage, drag the ball into position to connect with a paddle for the second hit. Flash makes Ball the active layer and creates Keyframe 10, containing another instance of the **PingPongBall** symbol in its new location. Flash completes the classic tween between Keyframe 5 and Keyframe 10 of the Ball layer.

6. On the Stage, reposition the second paddle so that it connects with the ball for the second hit. Flash makes 2nd Paddle the active layer and creates Keyframe 10, containing another instance of the **2ndPaddle** symbol in its new location **F**.

7. Repeat Steps 1–6, creating Keyframes 15 and 20 to make the ball connect with each paddle one more time.

8. Play the movie to see the animation in action.

TIP In the preceding task, all the frames in all the layers are set to classic tweening. If you later add more frames, they will also be set to classic tweening. To completely end the tween sequences, you need to remove the tween from the last keyframe in each layer. Select the final keyframes and choose Insert > Remove Tween.

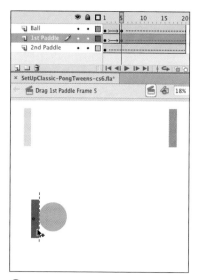

E As you reposition the paddle, Flash selects Frames 5–20, but the completed tween segment appears correctly in Frames 1–4.

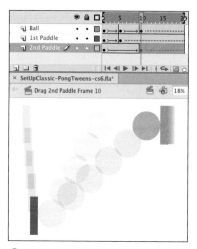

F Moving an element in another frame creates another tween. Here, the paddle on the right side appears to move more slowly than the paddle on the left side because Flash is creating a ten-frame tween for the right paddle, which moves a short distance. The left paddle tweens in five frames and moves a greater distance. (Here, onion skinning is turned on to make the tweened shapes visible.)

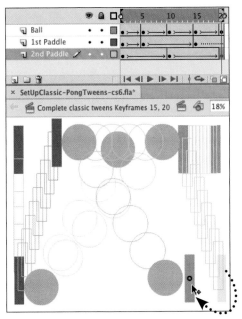

× SetUpClassic-PongTweens-cs6.fla*

Complete classic tweens Keyframes 15, 20   18%

G You can easily fine-tune the location of objects in classic tweens by turning on Onion Skin Outlines and Edit Multiple Frames. Here, the paddle on the right moves diagonally. If you want it to move vertically, vertically align the paddle graphics in the first and final frames, and then reposition the ball in each keyframe so that it contacts a paddle.

To adjust the movement— classic tweening:

1. Continuing with the file from the preceding task, in the Status bar, click the Onion Skin Outlines button and the Edit Multiple Frames button to activate these modes.

   Position the frame-range markers to cover all 20 frames or choose Onion All. With Edit Multiple Frames active, the symbol instances in keyframes appear as solid objects, while the interpolated tween graphics appear as onion outlines.

2. Reposition the symbol instances as necessary to fine-tune the motion **G**. For example, using the selection tool, drag a symbol instance on the Stage. Or, to change the symbols' *x*- and *y*-coordinates, select the instance and enter new X and Y values in the Position and Size section of the Property inspector.

TIP After you define a keyframe span as a classic tween, any slight change you make to the tweened symbol instance in an in-between frame creates a new keyframe. Even clicking the symbol and holding down the mouse button for more than a second or two creates a new keyframe. To avoid accidentally changing the positions of objects or creating new keyframes, lock or hide the layers that you're not working on.

TIP Motion tweens are not as delicate as classic tweens. In an in-between frame you can click and hold on a tween target without fear of accidentally creating a property keyframe. After you've finished positioning elements on a layer, however, it's a good idea to lock that layer to prevent unintended changes.

Working with Multiple-Layer Motion Tweens

In this section, you'll combine three simple motion tweens on three layers to create a game of Ping-Pong much like the classic-tween animation you created in the preceding tasks. As in that animation, one layer contains the ball, and the other layers each contain a paddle.

To set up a motion tween in all layers with one command:

1. Using the PingPongSetupMaster template you previously created, in "To set up the graphics layers," open a new document.

2. To define the length of the motion tween, in the Timeline, select Frame 20 in all three layers.

3. Choose Insert > Timeline > Frame, or press F5. Flash defines in-between Frames 2–20 in all layers. Frame 20 is selected in all three layers.

4. Choose Insert > Motion Tween.

    Flash creates a 20-frame motion-tween span in each layer 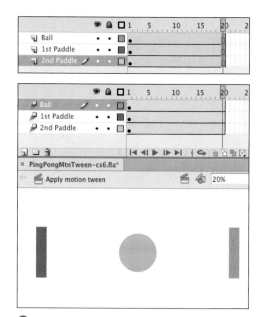. Frame 1 of each layer is a keyframe containing the span's tween target. (In the top layer, for example, it's an instance of the **PingPongBall** symbol.) To animate the symbols' movement around the Stage, you must add position keyframes to each tween span. You can do this by repositioning the tween targets at specific frames.

H When one frame is selected in keyframe spans on multiple layers (top), choosing Insert > Motion Tween converts all the spans to tween spans. The blue tint and lack of an end-of-span rectangle identify this as a tween span (bottom).

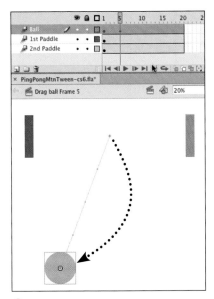

I Dragging a symbol on the Stage in a motion tween adds a position keyframe at the current frame and creates a motion path.

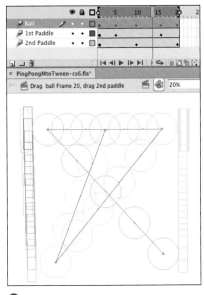

J By repositioning all of the tween targets in the appropriate frames, you create the same type of Ping-Pong animation in a motion tween that you created earlier in a classic tween.

To rough out the movement— motion tweening:

1. Continuing with the file from the preceding task, in the Timeline, move the playhead to Frame 5.

   The method you used to create keyframes within a classic tween also works to create position keyframes in a tween span. Dragging a symbol instance to a new location on the Stage creates a new position keyframe in the Timeline at the current frame (where the playhead is located).

2. On the Stage, drag the ball into position to connect with one of the paddles for the first hit.

   Ball becomes the active layer. Flash creates a position keyframe at Frame 5. Note that no other property changes exist currently for this frame. Flash creates a motion path from the ball's original location to its new location in Frame 5 **I**.

3. Follow Steps 3–8 of "To rough out the movement—classic tweening," in the preceding section.

   On the Stage, reposition the tween targets **PingPongBall**, **1stPaddle**, and **2ndPaddle** in Frames 5, 10, 15, and 20. Flash adds position keyframes and extends the motion path for each tween target after you move it **J**.

To adjust the movement— motion tweening:

1. Continuing with the file from the preceding task, to view and manipulate the motion paths of multiple tween targets simultaneously, do the following:

   ▸ Using the selection tool **⬚** or subselection tool **⬚**, click any motion path on the Stage. The Motion Tween Property inspector displays properties for motion tweening.

   ▸ In the Property inspector, from the panel menu, choose Always Show Motion Paths.

   Viewing multiple motion paths gives you access to every control point, not just those on the path in the active tween span. Viewing all the paths gives you a context for adjusting the target symbols' relative positions on the Stage **Ⓚ**.

2. To adjust a tween target's position at a specific frame, do the following:

   ▸ Move the playhead to the desired frame in the Timeline or Motion Editor. Each tween target appears on its motion path at the associated frame point or control point.

   ▸ Using the selection tool, drag the tween target to a new location on the Stage **Ⓛ**. Note that if the target you drag does not have a position keyframe, Flash creates a new position-property keyframe in the Timeline and property keyframes in the X and Y curves in the Motion Editor.

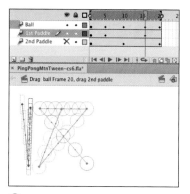

Ⓚ When Always Show Motion Paths is active, Flash displays the paths of all motion tweens in all visible layers at the current frame. Here the layer named 2nd Paddle is hidden, so its object and path do not appear on the Stage.

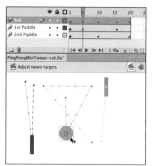

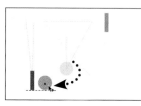

Ⓛ The Ball and 1stPaddle tweens each have a position keyframe at Frame 5; their tween targets appear on the Stage as solid objects centered over the control point for Frame 5. The 2ndPaddle tween has no position keyframe at Frame 5; its tween target appears on the Stage as a solid object centered over the frame point for Frame 5. When you drag the ball symbol, Flash moves the control point in the motion path.

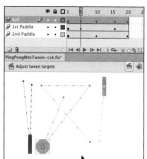

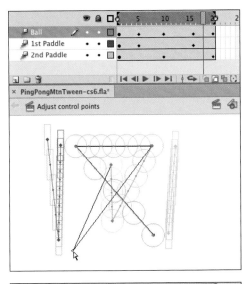

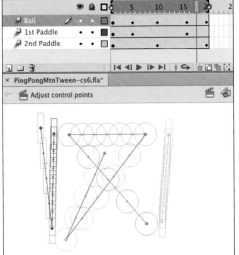

 To view more context for adjusting the position of multiple motion tweens, turn on onion skinning. You can then use the subselection tool to reposition any control point in any visible motion path. Because you are adjusting the control point, and not the tween target, you don't need to move the playhead to a specific frame, and you can't accidentally add new position keyframes. The oval outline for the control point disappears as you drag (top). Check the relative position of the control point and other objects on the Stage. After you release the mouse button, the control point onion skin reappears. Check the positioning, and drag the control point again, if necessary.

3. To roughly position all tween targets in context, at any position keyframe, do the following:

   ▸ In the Status bar, click the Onion Skin Outlines button 🔲 to activate onion skinning. Position the range markers to cover the tween span or choose Marker Range All. The onion outlines let you see how the tween targets relate to one another as they follow their motion paths.

   ▸ Using the subselection tool, drag any control point on the Stage. Flash previews the new motion path as you drag the control point. Release the mouse button to redraw the motion path and the outlines . There is no preview for a tween target's onion outline. You must estimate the position for the control point.

4. Save the file as a template named Ping-PongRallyMaster. Be sure to close the template file before continuing.

TIP With Edit Multiple Frames active, Flash displays the content of all the keyframes within the range markers. When positioning graphics on multiple layers for classic tweening, you need to have Edit Multiple Frames active to see (and manipulate) the symbol instances in all the keyframes of the tween simultaneously. With motion tweening, that's unnecessary and may be confusing. Each motion tween has just one keyframe at the beginning of the tween span. Even when the playhead is in a property keyframe later in the tween span, the solid symbol always appears at the initial control point of the motion path.

TIP When the tweened objects are close to the desired positions, turn off onion skinning. Then use the methods you learned in Chapter 11 to make tiny adjustments. For example, move the playhead to the frame where an object needs adjustment. Select the object, then press the arrow keys to precisely position the object.

Working with Multiple-Layer Shape Tweens

When working with complex shape tweens, remember that Flash deals most reliably with a single shape tween on a layer. In the following tasks, you create a multipart, multilayer graphic, and you shape-tween the whole package simultaneously.

To create shape tweens on separate layers:

1. Open a Flash document and create three layers: Top Flame, Middle Flame, and Bottom Flame.

2. Create one shape on each layer. For an animated flame, create three concentric ovals, using different fill colors and no stroke. Draw a large oval in the Bottom Flame layer, a medium oval in the Middle Flame layer, and a small oval in the Top Flame layer. Your file should look something like **N**.

3. Select Frame 5 in all three layers.

4. Choose Insert > Timeline > Keyframe. For each layer, Flash creates a keyframe with the same content as in Keyframe 1.

5. In the Timeline, select any of the frames in the Keyframe 1 span (1, 2, 3, or 4) in all three layers.

N Create each part of a multiple-element shape tween on a separate layer. Name the layers to help you track what goes where.

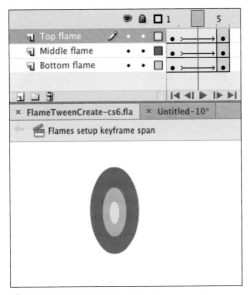

O You can assign shape-tweening to keyframe spans in multiple layers simultaneously. Select one frame in each keyframe span, then access the contextual menu for frames, and choose Create Shape Tween.

6. Control-click (OS X) or right-click (Win) the selected frames and choose Create Shape Tween from the contextual menu.

   Flash creates shape tweens in Frames 1–4 on all three layers **O**. To create flickering flames, you need to reshape the ovals in Keyframe 5.

7. In the Timeline, move the playhead to Keyframe 5.

8. On the Stage, edit the ovals to create flame shapes.

9. Play the movie to see the animation in action. Flash handles the shape-tweening of each layer separately. For comparison, try creating the oval and flame shapes on a single layer and then shape-tweening them **P**.

10. Click the Onion Skin Outlines and Edit Multiple Frames buttons to activate these modes; then reshape the flame objects as necessary to fine-tune the motion.

Each object on a separate layer

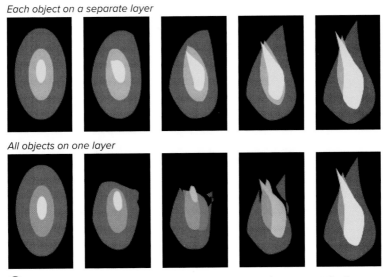

All objects on one layer

P Whether you use merge-shapes or drawing objects, when you put the three flames on separate layers (top), Flash does a reasonable job of tweening even if you don't add shape hints. With all three flame shapes placed on a single layer (bottom), Flash has difficulty creating the tweens. (The background in this document was set to black to make the shapes easier to see in each phase.)

Reversing Animation

Sometimes, you can save effort by creating just half the animation you need and letting Flash do the rest of the work. Think of a candle flame that grows and shrinks. The shrinking phase is the reverse of the growing phase. The technique for reversing animation is the same for shape tweens and classic tweens; you can reverse the animation of motion tweens in a variety of ways.

To reverse the frame order for shape (or classic) keyframe spans:

1. Open the document you created in the preceding section. This movie spans five frames on three layers. The first keyframe shows a flame as three concentric oval shapes; the final keyframe shows the flame in a taller, flickering configuration.

2. In the Timeline, select all five frames on all three layers.

3. In one of the selected frames, Control-click (OS X) or right-click (Win) to access the contextual menu for frames, then choose Copy Frames.

4. In the Timeline, select Frame 6 in all three layers.

5. In one of the selected frames, Control-click (OS X) or right-click (Win) to access the contextual menu for frames, and choose Paste Frames. Your movie now contains two back-to-back animation sequences of the growing flame (A).

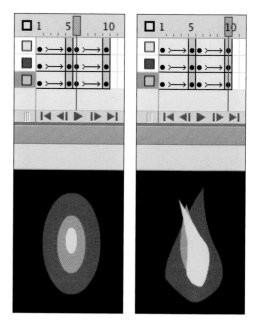

(A) After you paste the copied selection, the second tween sequence starts with the oval flame (left) and ends with the tall, flickering flame (right).

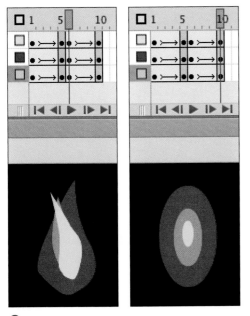

B After you reverse the frames, the second tween sequence starts with the flickering flame (left) and ends with the oval flame (right).

6. In the Timeline, select Frames 6–10 on all three layers.

7. Choose Modify > Timeline > Reverse Frames. Flash reverses the tween in the second sequence so that the flame starts tall and winds up as ovals in the final keyframe **B**.

TIP You can also use this technique to change the direction of frame-by-frame animation. Select the full range of keyframes that creates the movement you want to reverse, then choose Modify > Timeline > Reverse Frames.

TIP In the preceding task, you wind up with back-to-back duplicate keyframes (Frames 5 and 6 both contain the tall flame). You can remove the duplicate content and convert one of those keyframes to an in-between frame. Doing so has little effect on the motion, but removing duplicates reduces the number of vector shapes to be rendered in the published movie. To add the in-between frame to the first tween segment, select Frame 5 in all three layers, and press Shift-F6 to issue the Clear Keyframe command. To add the in-between frame to the second segment, select Frame 6 in all three layers and press Shift-F6. Because Frame 6 is the initial keyframe of this tween segment, issuing the Clear Keyframe command also removes the tween. While Frame 6 is still selected, choose Insert > Shape Tween.

To reverse the direction of motion for motion tweens:

1. Using the RotateStarMaster template you created in Chapter 11, open a new document. This single-layer file contains a 24-frame animation of a rotating star that moves to three new locations on the Stage.

2. To duplicate the motion tween, in the Timeline, Control-click (OS X) or right-click (Win) the layer name and choose Duplicate Layer from the contextual menu. The duplicate layer stacks above the original.

3. Name the layers Original Path and Reversed Path. Placing the motion tweens on separate layers helps you compare the original with the reversed version.

4. On the Stage, select the topmost motion path and drag it to a new location. Separating the paths makes it easier to compare the animation. Your document should look something like **C**.

5. In the Timeline, in the Reversed Path layer, Control-click (OS X) or right-click (Win) anywhere within the tween span.

6. From the contextual menu, choose Motion Path > Reverse Path. Flash reverses the path by reversing the graphs for the X and Y property curves in the Basic Motion section of the Motion Editor **D**.

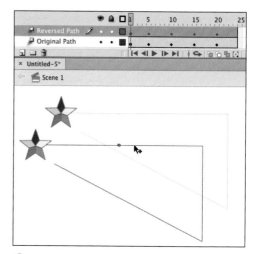

C To make it easier to compare duplicated motion tweens, drag the topmost motion path to a different area of the Stage.

Original motion tween

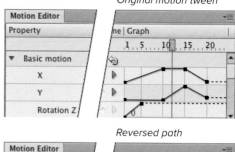

Reversed path

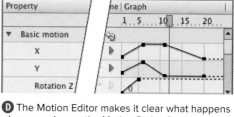

D The Motion Editor makes it clear what happens when you choose the Motion Path > Reverse Path command: Flash flips the direction of the X and Y property curves. (The Rotation Z property remains unchanged.)

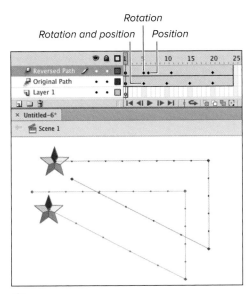
Rotation

Rotation and position | Position

When you reverse a motion tween by using the Motion Path > Reverse Path command, Flash flips the X and Y property curves, resulting in new locations for property-keyframe diamonds in the Timeline.

7. Play through the animation.

The two stars start from opposite ends of their respective motion paths and move in opposite directions. That's the result of reversing the property curves for X and Y. The Reverse Paths command has no effect on any other property curves. Both stars complete their rotations at Frame 5. Note that when you apply the Reverse Path command to complex tweens, Flash may redistribute position keyframes in the Timeline, while keeping other property keyframes in their original locations **E**.

TIP Another way to reverse the direction of motion is to flip the motion path itself. For example, select the motion path on the Stage, then choose Modify > Transform > Flip Horizontal (or Flip Vertical). You can also use the free-transform tool to change the direction of the path.

To reverse the order of all property keyframes:

1. Open a document containing a motion tween.

2. In the Timeline, Control-click (OS X) or right-click (Win) anywhere in the tween span.

3. From the contextual menu, choose Reverse Keyframes. Flash reverses the graphs for all of the property curves in the Motion Editor. (See the sidebar "The Mystery of Motion Reversal Explained" in this chapter.)

TIP Using the Reverse Keyframes command may yield unexpected results when you apply it to tweens in which some property curves lack a property keyframe in the final frame of the tween span. That's because when reversing the property curves, Flash ignores any in-between frames at the end of the Motion Editor graph (the dotted-line portion of the property curve). To force Flash to flip the entire graph, add a property keyframe to the last frame of the tween.

The Mystery of Motion Reversal Explained

Imagine animating a small red square that moves from left to right, doubles in size, and turns blue. You could reverse it in two ways: reverse the path to move a small red square from right to left (where it doubles in size and turns blue), or reverse the keyframes to move a large blue square from right to left (where it turns red and shrinks to half its size).

The results are straightforward for a simple animation with just a few changes, especially if the changes take place in just two keyframes, one at the beginning of the tween span and one at the end. But if changes take place throughout the tween, and property keyframes are in the middle of the tween span, Flash must decide exactly where to make the desired changes. The results can be complex and somewhat unexpected, especially when viewed in the Timeline.

To reverse motion tweening, Flash simply flips the property curve that appears in the Motion Editor graph. When you choose Motion Path > Reverse Path, Flash flips the X and Y curves in the Basic Motion section; when you choose Reverse Keyframes, Flash flips all the property curves.

Reversing a tween span that ends with in-between frames (where the property curve is a dotted line in the Motion Editor graph) can be especially confusing. Flash treats the curve from the first control point (the span's initial keyframe) to the last control point as an object and flips that. Flash excludes any in-between frames at the end of the tween span (where the property curve is a dotted line). This may make position keyframes appear in seemingly unexpected places in the Timeline when you reverse the animation **F**.

Timeline

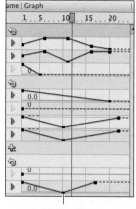

F When you use the Motion Path > Reverse Keyframes command, the number of property-keyframe diamonds in the Timeline may appear to increase. That's because one diamond can represent multiple properties. The Motion Editor shows what happens.

Motion Editor

Original

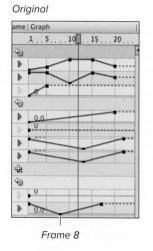

Frame 8

Reversed Path

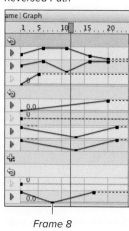

Frame 8

Reversed Keyframes

Frame 10

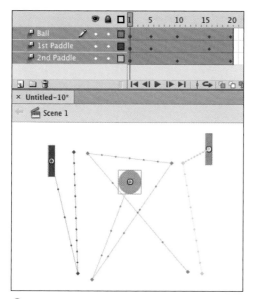

A To convert an existing animation to a symbol, first select all the frames in all the layers that make up the animation sequence. (This example uses the PingPongRally animation created in the section "Working with Multiple-Layer Motion Tweens" in this chapter.)

B You set a new symbol's type in the Create New Symbol dialog. Animated graphic symbols play in sync with the main movie that contains them. One frame in the main movie's Timeline displays one frame of the graphic symbol's Timeline. Movie clips operate from their own independent Timeline.

Saving Animations As Symbols

In Chapter 7, you created symbols to save graphic elements for reuse and to keep file sizes small. You can do the same thing with an entire multiple-frame, multiple-layer animation sequence, converting it to an animated graphic symbol or a movie-clip symbol. Reusing a symbol that holds animation adds little to the size of the published SWF movie file. Re-creating identical animation sequences—even if you animate symbols instead of raw shapes—increases the size of the SWF file somewhat. In addition, by wrapping up a complex animation in a symbol, you reduce the number of frames and layers you have to view in the Timeline.

To convert full layers of animation to a graphic symbol:

1. Using the PingPongRallyMaster template you created earlier in this chapter, open a new document. The file has three layers, each containing a 20-frame motion tween.

2. To select every frame in multiple layers, Shift-click the layer names **A**.

3. Choose Edit > Timeline > Copy Layers.

4. Choose Insert > New Symbol, or press Command-F8 (OS X) or Ctrl-F8 (Win).

5. In the Create New Symbol dialog, type a name for your symbol, `Rally-01-GraphicSymbol`.

6. From the Type menu, choose Graphic **B**.

7. Click OK. A new symbol appears in the library and Flash switches to symbol-editing mode, in which the symbol name appears in the Edit bar.

Continues on next page

8. In the symbol Timeline, select Layer 1 or Keyframe 1, and choose Edit > Timeline > Paste Layers.

The layers that you copied from the main movie Timeline are pasted above Layer 1 in the symbol Timeline **C**. You can adjust or edit the animation sequence at this point, if you'd like.

9. To return to document-editing mode, choose Edit > Edit Document, or click the Back button.

10. Save the file for later use, and name it AnimGraphicSymbol.

> **TIP** You can convert just part of an animation into a symbol. Follow the steps above, with these differences: In Step 2, select the frames that carry out just that segment of animation you want to include in the symbol. In Step 3, choose Edit > Timeline > Copy Frames. In Step 8, in the symbol Timeline, select Keyframe 1 or select a protoframe where you'd like the animation to start, and then choose Edit > Timeline > Paste Frames.

To convert an animation into a movie-clip symbol:

- Follow the steps in the preceding task, but this time, in Step 6, choose Movie Clip as the symbol type **D**. Save this file as MovieClipSymbol.

> **TIP** To make a movie clip that contains exactly the same frames as an existing animated graphic symbol, select the animated graphic symbol in the Library panel. From the panel menu, choose Duplicate. In the Duplicate Symbol dialog, rename the symbol and set its type to Movie Clip.

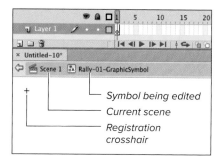

All layers of animation pasted into Timeline

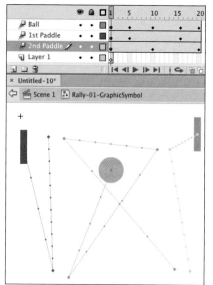

C When you create a new symbol, Flash switches to symbol-editing mode, making the new symbol's Timeline available for editing (top). Paste the layers and frames of your animation into the symbol's Timeline to create the animated symbol (bottom).

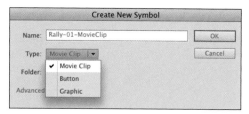

D To define a symbol that has an independent Timeline, choose Movie Clip from the Type menu in the Create New Symbol dialog. The entire movie-clip symbol runs in a single frame of the parent movie.

Symbols Reduce Layer Buildup

For tweened animations, you generally need to place each object on a separate layer. To animate a person, for example, you would create separate layers for the head, the torso, each arm, and each leg. For complex motion, you might even create separate layers for the eyes, mouth, fingers, and toes. Add some other elements to this character's environment, and you wind up dealing with many layers.

Turning an animation sequence into a symbol in effect collapses all those layers into one object. The process is a bit like grouping, but for Timeline layers instead of shapes. On the Stage, the symbol exists on a single layer, but that layer contains all the layers of the original animation.

How Do Animated Graphic Symbols Differ from Movie-Clip Symbols?

Flash provides for two kinds of animated symbols: graphic symbols and movie clips. The difference is subtle. An animated graphic symbol is tied to the Timeline of the parent movie in which it is used. A movie-clip symbol runs on its own independent Timeline. When the playhead stops moving in the parent movie's Timeline, an animated graphic symbol stops playing, but a movie-clip symbol continues to play.

Think of the frames of an animated graphic symbol as a tray of slides, and a movie-clip symbol as a film loop. The animated graphic symbol projects its slides, one per frame, in lockstep with the frames of its hosting movie (its parent Timeline): to see the next frame of the symbol, you move to the next frame in the parent Timeline. Like a tray of slides, an animated graphic symbol has no sound track. If you use sounds in an animated graphic symbol, those sounds don't play when you place the symbol into the parent Timeline.

In effect when you publish the parent movie, a graphic symbol's frames merge with the parent's frames; the graphic symbol's Timeline "disappears." Any interactivity created by frame scripts in the graphic symbol disappears as well.

Movie-clip symbols nested inside graphic symbols do retain the interactivity of their frame scripts. Just be aware that when the graphic symbol's Timeline disappears, the relationships of nested Timelines shift.

As you work in a Flash file (FLA), the relationship is Main movie (parent of graphic symbol) > graphic symbol (parent of nested movie clip) > nested movie clip. In the published file (SWF), the relationship is Main movie (parent of nested movie clip) > nested movie clip. The graphic symbol's Timeline is no longer available as the parent Timeline for nested movie-clips. Nested movie clips containing ActionScript code that refers to **parent** in a target path now affect the *parent* Timeline of the graphic symbol, not the Timeline of the graphic symbol itself. This fact of publishing can lead to unexpected results, particularly when you convert movie clips to graphic symbols and vice versa. (To learn more about ActionScript 3.0 and interactivity, see Chapter 15.)

A movie-clip symbol can project all its frames one after another, over and over, in a single frame of the parent Timeline. Movie clips do have a sound track and do retain their interactivity. (To learn more about sound, see Chapter 16.)

Here's one more thing to know about the two symbol types: because movie clips run on their own Timeline, they don't display their animation in the Flash authoring environment. On the Stage, a movie-clip symbol displays only its first frame. Animated graphic symbols, which use the same Timeline as the main movie, display their animation in the authoring environment.

Using Animated Graphic Symbols

To use an animated graphic symbol, choose a target keyframe span by selecting its keyframe (or any in-between frame within the span), then place an instance of the symbol on the Stage. The Timeline containing that target span is known as the *parent Timeline* or *parent movie*. The parent movie displays the animation inside the graphic symbol, but only within the frames of the target keyframe span.

To place an instance of an animated graphic symbol:

1. Open the AnimGraphicSymbol file you created earlier, and choose Insert > Scene.

   The new scene's Timeline has one layer with a blank keyframe at Frame 1. Working in a separate scene makes it easy to compare the animation created directly in the movie's main Timeline with the animation created in a graphic-symbol and then placed into the movie's main Timeline (the parent Timeline).

2. Access the Library panel and select the symbol named **Rally-01-GraphicSymbol**. The first frame of the animation appears in the preview window 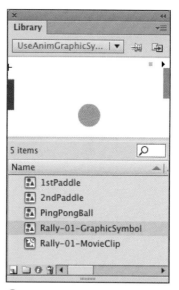.

3. Drag a copy of the symbol to the Stage.

   Flash places the symbol in Keyframe 1. You can see only the first frame of the animation **B**. The animation is 20 frames long, so you must have at least 20 frames to view the symbol in its entirety.

4. In the Timeline, select Frame 20, and choose Insert > Timeline > Frame, or press F5.

A Select the animated graphic symbol you want to use, and then drag a copy to your Flash document to place an instance on the Stage.

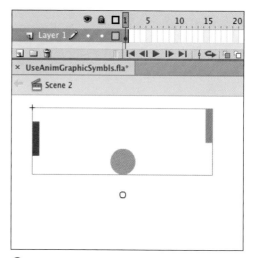

B When you drag an instance of the animated graphic symbol to the Stage, you see the symbol's first frame with its graphics selected. You will need to add frames to the keyframe span to allow the full animation of the symbol to play in the main movie.

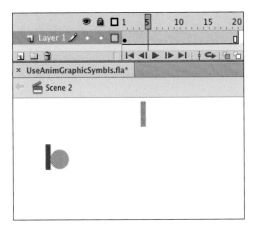

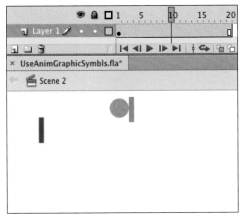

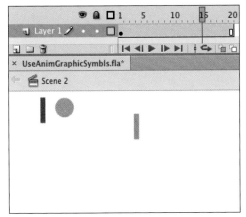

C Frames 1–20 are just regular defined frames that haven't been assigned any kind of tweening, but they display 20 frames of animation from the graphic symbol in Keyframe 1.

5. Play the scene. Flash displays each frame of the animated graphic symbol in a frame of the parent movie. Frame 2 of the symbol appears in Frame 2 of the movie, Frame 5 of the symbol appears in Frame 5 of the movie, and so on **C**. If the layer containing the animated–graphic-symbol instance in the parent Timeline has fewer frames than the symbol requires, Flash truncates the symbol's animation. If the layer has more frames than the symbol requires, by default, Flash repeats the graphic-symbol animation to fill those extra frames.

TIP By default, Flash loops the animation of graphic symbols to fill any extra frames in the keyframe span in the parent Timeline. To prevent looping to fill the span, select the graphic-symbol instance and access the Property inspector. In the Looping section, from the Options menu, choose Play Once.

TIP To display just one frame of the selected animated graphic symbol, choose Single Frame from the Options menu, then enter the desired frame number in the First field.

TIP Character animators can take advantage of a graphic symbol's ability to display a single specified frame instead of looping to create a *chart* of features for a character. Each frame of the symbol holds a different version of a feature—the eye in a snake character, for example. Frame 1 of the SnakeEyes symbol contains an open eye; Frame 2, that same eye half closed; Frame 3, the eye fully closed. To animate the snake's facial expressions, create a classic tween using the SnakeEyes symbol. At each keyframe of the tween you set the Single Frame option to display the appropriate eye position. To see this technique in action, check out Adobe's Lip Sync template. (Choose File > New, and in the New From dialog, click the Templates tab. In the Category column, select Sample Files; and in the Templates column, select Lip Sync.

Using Movie-Clip Symbols

To use a movie-clip symbol, select a keyframe (or an in-between frame within a keyframe span) and place an instance of the movie clip on the Stage. In the parent movie, the animation inside the movie-clip symbol loops until an instruction stops the clip playback. During authoring, a movie clip displays only Frame 1. To view the symbol's full animation in context with other elements, you must export the movie.

To place an instance of a movie clip:

1. Open the MovieClipSymbol file you created earlier, and choose Insert > Scene.

2. Access the Library panel and select the symbol named **Rally-01-MovieClip**.

3. Drag a copy of the selected symbol to the Stage. The symbol appears in Keyframe 1 Ⓐ. You needn't add frames to accommodate the animation, but you must export the movie to see it.

> **TIP** When you select a movie-clip symbol, the upper-right corner of the Library's preview window contains playback control buttons (▪ ▶). Click the Play button to preview the full animation of movie-clip symbol.

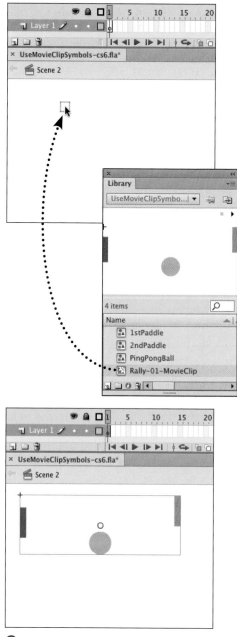

Ⓐ Drag an instance of your movie clip from the Library panel to the Stage (top). Flash places the instance in Keyframe 1 (bottom).

Exporting SWF Movie

Stop

B The Exporting SWF Movie dialog contains a progress bar and a button for canceling the export.

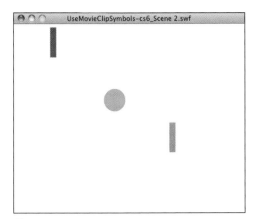

UseMovieClipSymbols-cs6_Scene 2.swf

C Flash Player displays your movie in a regular window. To exit the Player, close the window.

To view the movie-clip animation in context:

1. Continuing with the movie you created in the preceding task, choose Control > Test Scene.

   Flash exports the movie to a Flash Player format file, adding the name of the scene and the .swf extension to the filename and using the current publishing settings for all the export options. (For more information on publishing settings, see Chapter 17.) During export, Flash displays the Exporting SWF Movie dialog **B**. When it finishes exporting the movie, Flash opens the SWF file in Flash Player so you can see the movie in action **C**.

2. When you've seen enough of the movie in test mode, click the movie window's Close button (OS X) or Close box (Win) to exit Flash Player.

Using Easing in Tweens

By default within each segment of tweened animation, Flash transforms the tweened object from its original state to its final state at a constant rate.

Easing allows you to vary that rate, making changes start slowly and finish rapidly and vice versa. When you select a span containing tweening, you can assign it a single Ease value in the Property inspector. This Ease value applies equally to all properties. To set different rates of change for different properties, you must apply custom easing. (See the sidebar "About Custom Easing" in this chapter.)

To apply easing to the span:

1. In the Timeline, select one or more frames in a tween that's at least ten frames long, and access the Property inspector.

2. To make the animation start slowly and then accelerate (*ease in*), do one of the following:

   ▸ For classic and shape tweens, in the Frame Property inspector's Tweening section, enter a negative Ease value.

   ▸ For motion tweens, in the Motion Tween Property inspector's Ease section, enter a negative Ease value.

   The word *in* appears next to the Ease hot-text control 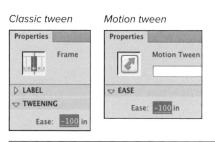.

Classic tween   *Motion tween*

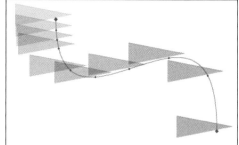

A A negative Ease value makes changes in the initial frames of the tween smaller and changes toward the end larger. The animation seems to start slowly and then speed up. The lower the Ease value, the greater the rate of acceleration.

Classic tween   *Motion tween*

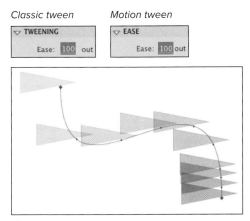

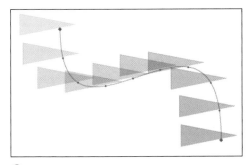

B A positive Ease value makes changes at the end of the animation smaller and changes in the initial frames larger. The animation seems to start quickly and then slow down. The higher the Ease value, the greater the rate of deceleration.

C With an Ease value of 0, Flash distributes the tweening changes evenly across the in-between frames. The effect is that of animation moving at a constant rate.

3. To make the animation start quickly and then decelerate (ease out), enter a positive Ease value **B**.

The word *out* appears next to the Ease hot-text control.

TIP An Ease value of 0 causes Flash to display the whole animation at a constant rate **C**.

Using Custom Easing to Create Motion

In classic tweens and motion tweens, you can use custom easing to make an object move. (See the sidebar "About Custom Easing" in this chapter.) Imagine, for example, a simple tween that moves an object from the left side of the Stage to the right in 20 frames. Now apply custom easing to the X property curve (horizontal position). Adjust the curve so that Frame 5 carries out 100 percent of the object's possible horizontal change and Frame 10 carries out just 50 percent. The oval now moves to the right side of the Stage at Frame 5, back to mid-Stage at Frame 10, then back to the right side at Frame 20.

To see this technique in a motion tween, check out the motion preset named Wave. (You'll find it in the Motion Presets panel, in the Default Presets folder.) After you apply the Wave preset to a symbol, open the Motion Editor and view the Y property curve (vertical position). Wave uses easing in the Y curve to make the tween target move up and down repeatedly, although the curve has just three *y*-position keyframes.

About Custom Easing

You can create custom easing for classic tweens and motion tweens, but not for shape tweens or IK poses. For classic tweens, custom easing is the only way to control the speed of individual property changes within a single keyframe span. For motion tweens, you can use the Motion Editor to create separate easing curves for each property. These advanced techniques are beyond the scope of a *Visual QuickStart Guide,* but here's a brief look at how to access the controls.

Classic easing To create custom easing for a classic tween, select any frame in the keyframe span. In the Tweening section of the Frame Property inspector, click the Edit Easing button ✎, to the right of the Ease hot-text control. The Custom Ease In/Ease Out dialog graphs the selected tween's property changes over time ❶. The horizontal axis represents each frame in the tween, while the vertical axis represents the amount of change. Editing the graph is similar to editing a Bézier path. Click the line (or curve) to add control points, then position the tangent handles. To ease all properties simultaneously, select the "Use one setting for all properties" checkbox. To set easing values for individual properties, deselect the checkbox. To view and edit a specific property (Position, Rotation, Scale, Color, or Filters), choose it from the Property menu.

Continues on next page

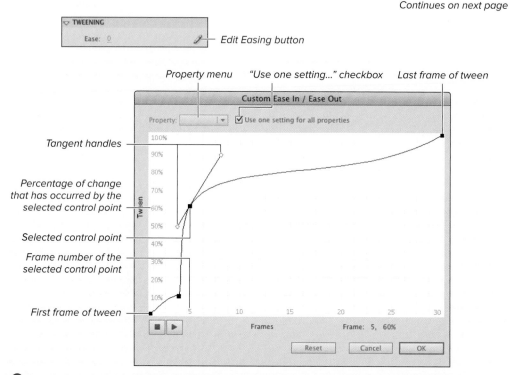

❶ For classic tweens, click the Edit Easing button (the pencil icon) in the Tweening section of the Frame Property inspector (top) to access the Custom Ease In/Ease Out dialog (bottom). Custom easing lets you control easing precisely, frame by frame, by creating a curve that defines the rate of change in each frame. Click anywhere on the line (or curve) to add a new control point with handles. Without easing, the rate is constant, starting at 0 percent in the first frame of the tween and reaching 100 percent in the last frame of the tween.

About Custom Easing *(continued)*

Motion easing You create custom easing for motion tweens in the Motion Editor, where you'll find a special Eases category. To view and work with an easing curve in the Motion Editor, you must bring the ease into the Eases category by selecting it from the Add Ease menu ⊕. A row with a graph for that ease appears in the Eases category. Flash includes a number of preset easing curves for common situations, such as Simple, Stop and Start, and Bounce. To create a custom easing curve, choose Custom from the Add Ease menu. Flash adds a new row with a graph for your custom easing curve **E**.

To apply an easing curve to a property—either a preset curve or one of your own devising—you must choose the easing curve from the Selected Ease menu in the row for the property you want to control. The Selected Ease menu in each row lists all the easing curves currently available in the Eases category. If you don't see the curve you want in a specific Selected Ease menu, you need to add the curve to the Eases category.

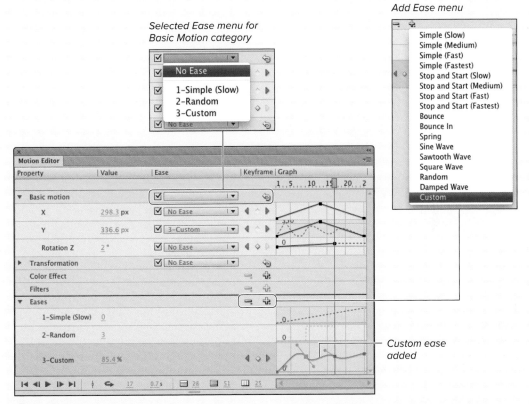

Add Ease menu

Selected Ease menu for Basic Motion category

Custom ease added

E The Motion Editor's Eases category (the last category in the Motion Editor) is the place to create custom easing curves. To begin the process, click the Add Ease menu (the plus sign) in the Eases row and choose Custom. You can then modify the graph in the Custom row. To apply the custom curve to a property curve, select the custom easing curve from the Selected Ease menu in the row of the property you want to control. You can create multiple custom curves to apply to different properties in the same motion tween.

Re-creating Classic and Motion Tweens

Flash offers three commands that will help you reduce repetitive animation work. Copy Motion, Paste Motion, and Paste Motion Special streamline the process of animating multiple objects that go through the same "motions."

To copy motion:

1. Create a ten-frame animation using either classic tweening (Chapter 9) or motion tweening (Chapter 11).

   You can copy the animation from multiple keyframe spans set to classic tweening, so long as the keyframe spans are contiguous in one layer. You can only copy the animation from one motion-tween span at a time.

2. In the Timeline, to select the animation, do one of the following Ⓐ:

   Classic tween Select one or more frames in a keyframe span set to classic tweening. The frames must be contiguous and must all be set to classic tweening. You can also select multiple

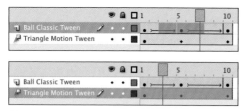

Ⓐ You can copy the animation of multiple contiguous classic-tweens by selecting at least one frame in each keyframe span (top). To copy the animation of a motion tween, you must select all the frames in the tween span (bottom).

contiguous classic-tween keyframe spans to copy the full range of motion. Do not, however, include the final keyframe of a classic tween if that keyframe is not highlighted as having the classic-tween property.

Motion tween Select the entire tween span. Flash can copy the motion of just one tween span at a time.

3. Choose Edit > Timeline > Copy Motion.

   Flash copies the changes in properties that define the tween for each selected (or partially selected) span. For classic tweens, Flash copies x-position, y-position, horizontal scale, vertical scale, rotation and skew, color, filters, and blend mode. For motion tweens, Flash copies all the properties of the tween that you can access via the Motion Editor.

About Copy Motion

Flash's Copy Motion command copies the following information that defines a classic-tween or motion-tween sequence: changes to a tweened object's properties (such as position, rotation, scale); duration of the tween (the number of frames it takes); and other tween settings (such as Easing). The Paste Motion command lets you apply that information to a different object (let's call it the *tween object*) to change its properties in the same way over the same number of frames using the same Tween settings. The Paste Motion Special command lets you apply changes to the tween object's properties selectively. The Copy Motion As ActionScript 3.0 command translates classic- and motion-tween animation to ActionScript 3.0–generated animation.

Selected tween object   *Selected keyframe*

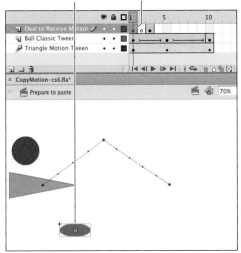

B To apply the copied motion tween to a new tween object, select the symbol on the Stage (or select its keyframe in the Timeline).

Motion pasted   *Copied span*

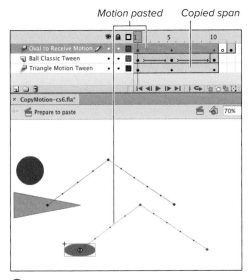

C The Paste Motion command pastes the tween sequence(s) of the copied motion into the Timeline for the selected tween object. The command preserves any existing unselected frames and keyframes in the Timeline, pushing them to later frames.

To apply copied motion to a different tween object:

1. To select the object that will reenact the copied motion, do one of the following:
   - On the Stage, select the object **B**.
   - In the Timeline, select a keyframe containing the object.

   The selected object must be one that can be tweened in the same way as the original tween object. (A merge-shape, for example, can't be used in motion tweening.) For best results, apply the copied motion only to an object isolated on its own layer.

2. Choose Edit > Timeline > Paste Motion.

   For classic tweens, Flash inserts the same number of keyframe spans into the Timeline (with the same number of frames and keyframes) as you copied. For motion tweens, Flash inserts a tween span of the same length—with the same property keyframes—as the tween span you copied. The selected target keyframe and all subsequent frames move to later frames in the Timeline **C**.

3. Play the movie. The tween object that received the copied property changes moves and transforms in the same way as the original.

TIP You can paste classic tween properties selectively. Choose Edit > Timeline > Paste Motion Special. In the Paste Motion Special dialog, select any of the following checkboxes: X position, Y position, Horizontal Scale, Vertical Scale, Rotation and Skew, Color, Filters, and Blend Mode. When you have copied a motion tween, you can't paste properties selectively because the Paste Motion Special command is unavailable; but after you paste the motion, you can edit all of the properties in the Motion Editor.

A Note About Display Options for Buttons and Movie Clips

When you select an instance of a movie-clip or button on the Stage, the Property inspector includes a Display section **D**. The Visible checkbox and Render menu offer settings that can optimize the movie for playback, an important consideration when you deliver content to mobile devices. The Blending menu lets you choose a blend mode to control the interaction of graphics in different layers and sublayers.

D Display section in Property Inspector

Let's take a brief look at why you might want to work with the Visible checkbox and Render menu.

Setting Visibility

During playback, some symbols should be available only at specific times. For example, a certain button symbol might appear only when a checkbox is selected. There are a couple of ways to do this using Timeline animation techniques. When the symbol should appear, you can add a keyframe and place an instance of the symbol on the Stage. When the symbol should disappear, you can add a keyframe and remove the symbol from the Stage. Alternatively, you could make the symbol "invisible," setting its alpha property to 0 percent. Flash must still draw the "invisible" object during playback and calculate the alpha setting, but that takes time and processor power. To save processor time you can set the symbol's visibility property. By default, all symbols are set to be visible. For a frame where the symbol should disappear, select the symbol instance on the Stage, then in the Property inspector's Display section, deselect the Visible checkbox. At runtime, Flash skips rendering that instance.

Rendering As Bitmaps

In general, Flash Player can copy pixels to the screen faster than it can calculate the curves of vector images and then render them. So why not convert all complex vector images to bitmaps, as you learned to do in Chapter 7? There are drawbacks to animating bitmap images. For example, the image may lose fidelity, especially if you rotate the bitmap or scale it up. The options in the Rendering menu give you more control when converting vector artwork to bitmaps. To use them, select the symbol instance on the Stage. Then, in the Display section of the Property inspector, choose a style from the Rendering menu.

- *Original (No Change)* Flash Player renders the vector images to the screen. Use this setting for button symbols and movie clips containing animated vector artwork that must retain its high image quality during animation.

- *Cache as Bitmap* Flash Player initially renders the symbol instance's vectors to a bitmap image and caches the image in memory. This is a good setting for symbols that animate infrequently and in simple ways, such as occasionally changing location. For such animations, the player can simply redraw the cached bitmap in the new spot. For other types of animation, the player must render the changed vector shapes, redraw the bitmap, and cache it. For symbols that constantly transform in ways that require redrawing, it is faster for the player to animate the original vectors than to constantly redraw them and cache a new bitmap.

- *Export as Bitmap* Flash Player converts the symbol instance to a bitmap at runtime. The symbol retains all of its editable vector shapes in the authoring environment. This is a good setting when you want the speediest animation at runtime, but you don't need the highest image quality as the symbol animates.

Intro to Inverse Kinematics

Inverse kinematics (IK) is a method of animating objects and shapes that relies on a skeleton-like structure (an *armature*) with multiple linked segments (*bones*). Once you set up the structure, you can manipulate it to create various configurations, or *poses*.

Imagine manipulating a human skeleton; if you raise the hand and bring it in toward the torso, the forearm also raises, and the elbow bends. Similarly, if you move one bone in an IK armature, connected bones move in response.

Flash interpolates changes between poses to create animation. You can use IK armatures to link multiple symbol instances, thereby controlling their movement in relation to one another. You can also use IK armatures within a single shape, controlling the way the shape's outline changes.

While the process of creating natural-looking movement with IK animation is complex and far beyond the scope of a *Visual QuickStart Guide,* the tasks in this chapter introduce you to creating armatures and poses using Flash's IK tools.

In This Chapter

Using Armatures to Connect Symbols

When you use IK armatures to connect two or more symbol instances, the whole structure moves together, something like a marionette puppet. You can link symbol instances in linear or branching fashion or use a combination, in which one or more branches extend in linear fashion.

A simplified cartoon body, for example, might have three bones branching from the base of the neck: one connects to the head, a second connects to the right shoulder, a third to the left shoulder. Each shoulder bone could connect in linear fashion to bones for the upper arm, forearm, and hand.

Note: For the tasks in this section, you'll create a linear armature. Make sure that any artwork you're planning to connect in symbol form has been converted into a movie-clip symbol before you start linking with the IK bone tool.

When to Use Inverse Kinematics

Flash's inverse-kinematics tools let you animate natural motion without redrawing lots of shapes or repositioning multiple symbols. Use IK's skeleton-like armatures when you want to animate symbols that have a permanent relationship—for example, the parts of a person or creature that can only bend in certain ways; or the parts of an engine or machine that move in predictable, constrained ways, like pistons, cogs, and flywheels. Another reason to use IK is to create shapes with moving, transforming outlines, where the changes can be controlled by an internal structure, such as a wiggling worm, or a blade of grass that bends in the wind.

About Transformation Points in IK

The IK bone tool offers two methods for positioning transformation points when connecting symbol instances. In the tool's default mode, you automatically create new transformation points as you create the bones. The locations where you place the bone's head and tail points become new transformation points for the symbol instances linked by the bone. To retain each symbol instance's existing transformation point, do the following: choose Flash > Preferences (OS X) or Edit > Preferences (Win); in the Preferences dialog, choose Drawing from the category list; in the IK Bone Tool section, deselect the Auto Set Transformation Point checkbox. With Auto Set deselected, the head point and tail point snap to the existing transformation point in their respective symbol instances when you create a new bone.

Note: For the tasks in this chapter use the bone tool the default Drawing Preferences, Auto Set Transformation Point.

Ⓐ The first step in creating an IK animation with symbol instances is to place instances on the Stage. Arrange the symbol instances in the relative positions they should have in the animated character or element that you're creating.

Ⓑ When the pointer is over a symbol instance, the pointer's bone and plus sign change to white, indicating that you can begin creating an IK bone. Click to place the head of the bone. In Flash's default IK drawing style, Flash moves the transformation point (the point of rotation) to the spot you click. Then drag to start drawing the bone.

Ⓒ As long as the pointer is within the symbol instance where you placed the head of an IK bone, the pointer is black with a No-symbol to indicate that you can't end the bone in this area.

Bone Views

The default graphic representation of an IK bone is a bulky item, especially if you're using it with small, delicate artwork. After creating the first IK bone in an armature, you can view bones in an outline form or as a single line. To change the look of the bones, select the armature, for example, by selecting the pose span in the Timeline. Open the Property inspector. In the Options section, from the Style menu, choose Wire (the outline form), Solid (the default, triangular form), or Line (a 1-pixel line). To hide bones completely, choose None.

To link symbol instances in a linear armature:

1. Place instances of a movie-clip symbol on the Stage and arrange them in the desired configuration, for example, in a line **Ⓐ**.

   For this task, use four instances of an oval symbol named `myOval`. Arrange them in a row to create a chain that can curl up or down from one end.

2. In the Tools panel, click the current IK tool, and from the submenu, select the bone tool 🖋 (or press M). The pointer icon changes to a black bone with a plus sign ⁺, indicating that you are ready to begin placing bones.

4. To begin drawing the first bone in the chain (the *parent bone*), position the pointer over the first symbol instance **Ⓑ**. The pointer changes to a white bone with a plus sign ⁺, indicating that you are within a symbol where you can start a bone.

5. To place the head of the bone, click inside the symbol instance.

6. To draw the bone, drag toward the second symbol instance in the chain.

   The pointer changes to a black bone with a No symbol ⁺, indicating that you are within the symbol instance containing the head of the bone; the tail of the bone must be in a different instance **Ⓒ**.

Continues on next page

7. To complete the first bone (and create the *tail* point), drag the pointer into the second symbol instance and release the mouse button.

As the pointer moves into the area of a different symbol instance, the icon changes to a white bone with a plus sign 🐾, indicating that you can complete the IK bone **D**.

When you release the mouse button, Flash draws a bone connecting the two symbol instances and pulls them out of their current layer(s) and into a new layer, called a *pose layer*. Flash gives the pose layer a default name (see the sidebar "About Pose Layers") and assigns the movie-clip symbol instances default names, identifying them as IK nodes (see the sidebar "About IK Instance Naming," in this chapter).

8. To begin drawing the second bone in the chain (a *child* bone), click the tail of the first bone you created. When the pointer is over the tail point, the icon changes to a white bone with a plus sign 🐾, indicating that you're ready to add another bone.

Original Timeline

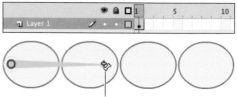

End parent bone

Layer created after bone completion

Some content remains in Layer 1

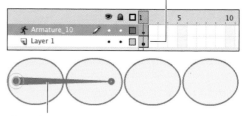

Completed parent bone

D The pointer changes to a white plus sign and bone when it moves into a symbol instance other than the one where you started. Release the mouse button to place the tail of the bone (the second point of rotation). When the bone is complete, Flash pulls the connected symbol instances into a special armature layer in the Timeline.

About Pose Layers

When you connect the first two symbol instances of an IK chain with the bone tool, Flash pulls the instances into a new layer, known as a *pose layer* and gives the layer a default name—for example, Armature_1. The pose layer lies directly above the layer that originally held the symbol instance that now contains the bone's head. As you continue to add symbol instances to the chain, Flash pulls each new addition into the existing pose layer; each added IK node stacks above the nodes already on the pose layer.

When you first create an IK armature, the pose layer consists of a one-frame pose span that is tinted olive green and contains a diamond icon ◆. The diamond indicates the presence of an IK armature in a particular configuration, or *pose*. You can define more frames to extend the span or drag to extend the span, then add poses at later frames to create motion over time. (See the section "Working with Poses" in this chapter.)

Click to begin child bone

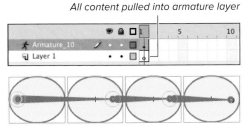

Drag to new instance

E To connect a child bone, position the pointer over the tail of the parent bone, click, and drag into a different symbol instance.

All content pulled into armature layer

F As you complete more bones, Flash pulls the newly connected symbol instances into the same armature layer with the others.

9. Click and drag to connect with the third symbol instance. Flash completes the second bone and pulls the third symbol instance into the armature layer **E**.

10. Repeat Steps 8 and 9 to add a bone connecting the third and fourth symbol instances **F**. Flash completes the third bone and pulls the fourth symbol instance into the armature layer.

You're ready to manipulate the armature and create poses (see the section "Working with Poses" in this chapter).

TIP Symbol instances in an IK armature can be overlapping or separate.

TIP You can use any type of symbol instance—graphic symbols, movie clips, or buttons—in an IK animation. Graphic symbols do not have instance names, so Flash doesn't label the connected instances as IK nodes. You cannot create a runtime IK animation, using graphic symbols. For the tasks in this book, use movie clips.

TIP In Step 5, the spot you click becomes the head of the first bone in a chain of bones. Take a moment to consider the placement of the head. In an IK arm, the head of the parent bone corresponds to a shoulder joint. If you plan to overlap the upper arm with the character's torso, then you probably want to place the joint in that area of overlap. If the upper arm will sit next to the torso, but not overlap it, you might want to place the joint closer to the edge of the upper-arm symbol.

TIP Note that the four-node chain you created in the preceding task has just three bones. The number of bones in a linear armature is always one less than the number of nodes in that armature.

TIP You don't need to be precise in positioning the head of a child bone. Whenever the pointer is within the area of the node containing the parent's tail point, the pointer changes to a white bone with a plus sign. Clicking anywhere within the node automatically connects to the tail point in that node.

Anatomy of an Armature

A linear armature contains a chain of bones in a hierarchical structure 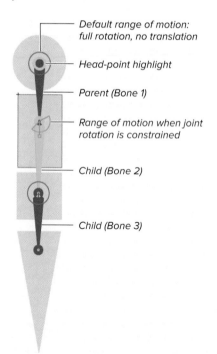. The first bone is known as the *parent* bone; all the bones that extend from it are known as *child* bones. The spot you click to begin drawing a bone becomes the *head* of the bone. The spot where you release the mouse button to complete the bone becomes the *tail*. In a linear armature, the bones link head-to-tail. After you create one bone, you place the head of the next bone directly over the tail of the preceding bone. The head and tail are both points of rotation, or *joints*, and they coincide with the transformation points of the symbol instances in which they reside. By default, Flash relocates the transformation point whenever you click the bone tool within a symbol instance, placing the transformation point where you place the head of the bone. (You can change that Preferences setting so that Flash snaps the head and tail points to the symbol instances' existing transformation points. See the sidebar "About Transformation Points in IK" in this chapter.) By default, the head and tail points allow bones to rotate through 360 degrees, like the hands of an analog clock.

All movement in an IK armature happens at the joints, and each joint has three movement properties: rotation, *x*-translation, and *y*-translation. The term *rotation* is straightforward; it refers to circular movement around the head point. In IK the term *translation* refers to linear movement: *x*-translation is movement along the *x*-axis of the bone, and *y*-translation is movement along the *y*-axis of the bone.

Continues on next page

Default range of motion: full rotation, no translation

Head-point highlight

Parent (Bone 1)

Range of motion when joint rotation is constrained

Child (Bone 2)

Child (Bone 3)

G In a linear armature, Flash highlights each head point with a range-of-motion icon. When you join multiple symbols in an armature, the first child bone starts at the tail of the parent bone; that point is also the head of the child bone. Click a bone to select it and view its properties in the Property inspector.

Anatomy of an Armature *(continued)*

You set the movement properties for a bone's head in the Property inspector. Rotation is fully enabled by default; but you can disable it, or constrain it to create a joint that bends in only one direction, like an elbow or a knee. Both types of translation are disabled by default, but you can fully enable *x*- and/or *y*-translation, or constrain them.

You cannot disable or constrain movement at a tail point. In a linear armature, most of the joints containing a tail point also contain a head point; you can constrain the joint by constraining the head. The symbol instance that comes at the end of the armature chain, however, contains a tail point that stands on its own. The final symbol instance in an IK chain can always move freely and rotate 360 degrees around its transformation point.

Branching armatures do not have a hierarchical structure. All the bones branch from a single spot—known as the *root* of the branches—and are known as *sibling* bones **(H)**. The location of the head joint is the same for all siblings. Although the bones are separate, their head joints must have identical rotation and translation settings. Flash handles that automatically, updating the joint properties of all sibling bones whenever you change one of the sibling's properties.

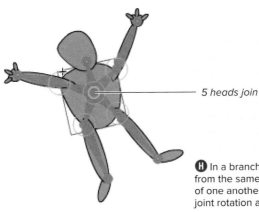

5 heads join

(H) In a branching armature, all of the bones start from the same spot, or root. The heads stack on top of one another, and all have the same settings for joint rotation and joint translation.

About IK Instance Naming

When you create an IK armature by connecting movie-clip or button symbol instances, Flash gives each instance—or *node*—a default instance name, starting with **ikNode_1**, **ikNode_2**, and so on. (Graphic symbols do not have an instance name.) Any new IK nodes you create in the same document are assigned the next sequential number.

The bones in an IK armature also get a default instance name that includes a number, but the numbering is not what you might expect. The first IK bone you create in a document gets the name **ikBoneName_3**, the next bone in the same chain of bones becomes **ikBoneName_4**, and so on. If you create another chain in the same document, the first bone in that chain starts with a number three greater than the number of the previous bone you created.

Creating IK Shapes

An IK armature inside a shape works something like a hand in a sock puppet. The armature can be linear or branching or a combination of the two styles.

To combine linear and branching armatures inside a shape:

1. Using Flash's drawing tools, on the Stage, create a shape to which you want to add an internal armature structure.

   For this task, draw a rounded rectangle, making it fairly long and narrow (see Chapter 2). You'll create an armature that has two linear chains that branch from a central point, allowing the shape to curl up or down from either end.

2. In the Tools panel, select the bone tool 🖉.

3. To begin drawing the first bone in the chain (the parent bone), click the spot where the armature should start—for example, the center of the rectangle **A**.

   Flash places the head of the parent bone. The head and tail points of each bone create points of rotation (places where the shape can bend). The shape as a whole pivots around the head of the parent bone in the chain.

4. To complete the bone, drag to the first spot where your shape should be able to bend, then release the mouse button.

   For this example, plan to place three bones in each half of the rectangle. Flash pulls the shape into a new pose layer and converts the shape to an IK shape.

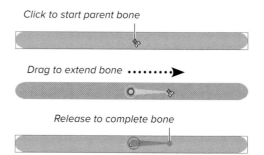

Click to start parent bone

Drag to extend bone

Release to complete bone

A Adding bones within a shape is very similar to adding bones between symbol instances, except that all the bones stay within the same shape.

Using Shapes with IK

The steps for creating the chain or branches are quite similar to those for connecting symbols. The difference is that you place all the bones within a single shape. You can use a merge-shape, drawing-object, or primitive-shape, with or without a stroke. Once you add IK bones to the shape, Flash converts it to a new type of shape, an *IK shape*.

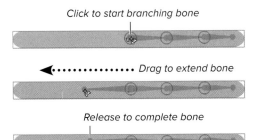

Click to start branching bone

◀·············· Drag to extend bone

Release to complete bone

B To begin the branching bone, position the pointer over the head of the parent bone in the existing chain, then drag to the left.

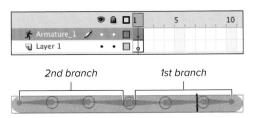

2nd branch   1st branch

C Your finished shape has two branches that start from the center of the shape. Each branch then continues with a linear chain of IK bones. This arrangement allows the two halves of the rectangle to curve independently, thus creating more complex poses.

5. To add the second bone in the chain, position the pointer over the tail of the first bone you created, and click.

   To add a bone to the armature within a shape, the pointer must be directly over the bone you're adding to. The ✛ pointer changes to the ✛ pointer when you're directly over the tail (or head) of an existing bone. Flash places the second bone's head.

6. To complete the second bone, drag to the spot where the bone should end, and release the mouse button.

7. Repeat Steps 5 and 6 to create the third bone, this time starting at the tail of the second bone.

8. To create another IK chain that branches from the first, click the parent bone you created in Steps 3 and 4.

9. To begin drawing the first bone (parent) of the second branch, drag in a different direction from the parent bone in the existing chain **B**. For this example, drag to the left.

10. Repeat Steps 5 and 6 to create a three-bone chain in the left side of the rectangle **C**.

   You're ready to manipulate the armature and create poses. (See "Working with Poses," in this chapter.)

TIP In the preceding task, you created two branches from the same root. You can also create branches farther down the chain. Just begin drawing a new bone by clicking the head of any bone in the chain. In an IK shape, drag the first bone in the new branch in a different direction within the shape. In an armature connecting nodes, drag the first bone in the new branch to a symbol instance that's not yet part of the armature.

Working with Poses

When you first create an armature, the pose layer contains a pose span with one pose frame (the frame with the diamond icon ◆). Similar to keyframes, pose frames mark key points of change that enable Flash to create IK animation. Each pose frame acts a bit like a property keyframe in a motion tween, giving Flash information about the position and rotation of each element in the armature. Flash creates a series of images that interpolate the changes required to transform the armature from one pose to the next. The property settings for the bones, and the way you set up the armature, restrict how the elements can move. To create IK animation, you must extend the pose span, add poses at the desired frames, select the armature to view and activate the bones, and manipulate the armature to put the elements into poses. To reposition the elements within the selected armature, use the selection tool.

Move Those Bones

Dragging a highlighted bone causes it to rotate around its head; moving the highlighted bone can also push on any bones that are higher up the chain, causing them to rotate as well. When a bone is set to allow x- and/or y-translation, you can also drag the bone along those axes. Any constraints you've put in place on how each bone moves will govern the ways you can interact with the bones as you drag them on the Stage. As you manipulate a highlighted bone, any child bones that are located lower in the hierarchy simply come along for the ride, retaining their current orientation with respect to their parent bone(s).

Putting an Armature Through Its Paces

When the pose span contains just the initial pose frame, you can edit its armature—change the arrangement of IK nodes, change the length of a bone, or change the number of bones. When the span contains additional poses at later frames, the spatial relationships between nodes and the dimensions of the bones are locked.

To avoid the extra work of setting up poses, and then deleting them because you run into a problem, it's helpful to try manipulating your armature in lots of ways before creating the real poses for your animation. Give the armature a good workout, dragging the bones around to create all the positions you may want to animate.

You could manipulate the armature in the initial frame of the pose span, before adding new poses or extending the span. If you do find a problem, however, it can be difficult to return the underlying shape or symbol instances to the precise starting arrangement. To make it easy to revert to the original pose, extend the pose span by a few frames. Then move the playhead to the end of the span and start manipulating the armature to see how the pieces move together. Flash adds a pose at the current frame. Continue putting the armature through its poses, until you find a problem, or until you're sure everything is OK. If it turns out that you need to edit the armature, you need remove only one pose. The first frame of the pose span contains the original pose with the symbol instances or shape arranged in the original position. Now you can edit the armature as you like and test again.

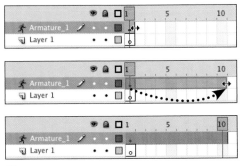

A To extend a pose span, position the pointer over the black bar at the right side of the pose span (top). When the resize pointer appears, drag the end of the span to the desired frame (middle). Flash extends the pose span and selects it (bottom).

B A diamond icon in the pose span indicates a frame where you can manipulate the IK armature and change its position. (Note that when the playhead is at the pose frame, the diamond looks more like a dot. Move the playhead and you'll see a diamond just like the one in the span's first frame.)

To define the pose span's length:

- Do one of the following:
  - In the Timeline, in the pose layer position the pointer over the black bar at the outside edge of Frame 1. When the resize pointer ↔ appears, drag to extend the pose span to the desired frame **A**.
  - Click the protoframe that should mark the end of the span and choose Insert > Timeline > Frame, or press F5.

  Flash extends the olive-green highlight of the pose span through the selected frame.

To create a new pose frame via Timeline command:

- In the Timeline, within the armature layer, Control-click (OS X) or right-click (Win) the desired frame and choose Insert Pose from the contextual menu.

  When you click a frame inside the pose span, Flash adds a diamond-shaped pose icon to that frame **B**. If you click a protoframe following the existing pose span, Flash extends the pose span to the frame you click and adds the diamond icon. You can now manipulate the IK armature to the desired configuration.

> **TIP** You can also create a new pose by manipulating an armature on the Stage, analogous to the way you can add keyframes to classic tweens or add property keyframes to motion tweens by manipulating symbol instances on the Stage within the defined span containing the tween. You click the desired frame within the pose span or move the playhead to the desired frame. Then use the selection tool to manipulate the armature on the Stage. Flash adds a pose diamond to the current frame.

To view an armature:

- Using the selection or subselection tool, do one of the following:
  - ▸ For an armature connecting IK nodes, click any node (any connected symbol instance).
  - ▸ For an armature within an IK shape, click anywhere within the shape.

  Flash selects the IK nodes or IK shape and makes the bones visible **C**. Icons indicating range of motion appear at each joint.

To manipulate the armature to create a pose:

1. In the Timeline, move the playhead to the desired frame in a pose span.

2. Select the armature you want to pose.

3. Using the selection tool, position the pointer over a bone. A black bone icon appears in the pointer ⤵ to indicate that you're ready to manipulate the armature **D**.

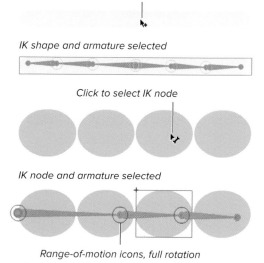

Click to select IK shape

IK shape and armature selected

Click to select IK node

IK node and armature selected

Range-of-motion icons, full rotation

C Clicking an IK shape or an IK node with the selection tool activates the bones of the armature so that you can manipulate them to create poses.

D To interact with a specific bone, click it with the selection tool, then drag it to position it. The bone rotates around its head. Other bones and nodes move in response if their joint settings allow for movement.

IK nodes

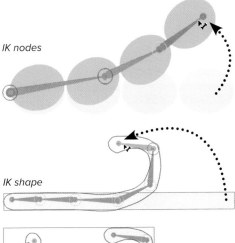

IK shape

E To manipulate an armature, use the selection tool. You can drag bones and nodes to position them and reconfigure the armature. In an IK shape, dragging the bones changes the contours of the shape.

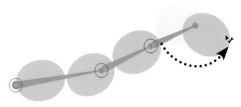

F You can also manipulate an IK armature by dragging nodes with the selection tool. The final node in an IK armature rotates freely when you drag that node

4. Click a bone to activate it for rotation. Flash highlights it in a different color than the other bones in the armature.

5. To reposition the selected bone, drag it **E**.

   The bone rotates and/or moves, and the armature changes in response to your manipulation. The precise ways that the structure can move depend on the settings you've created for each bone in the Property inspector (see the sidebar "Move Those Bones," in this chapter). If the bone is in an armature connecting IK nodes, the node containing the head moves along with the bone.

6. To reposition an IK node, drag directly on the symbol instance.

   If the IK node contains the head of a bone, the symbol instance and that bone rotate around the head point (the transformation point) according to the settings for that bone. If the IK node contains just a tail (that is, if the IK node is the last element in a linear armature), the node rotates around the tail point **F**.

TIP You don't have to select an individual bone to drag it. You can simply drag a bone in one step. Selecting the bone first highlights it and lets you see that you are working with the right portion of your armature.

TIP As you manipulate an armature to create new poses, remember that Flash is not recording the action. You need to create poses at key positions for your IK elements so that Flash can interpolate between poses to animate the movement you want. For example, just because you rotated a bone clockwise to reach a certain position doesn't mean Flash chooses that direction when it creates the animation. You may need intermediate poses to ensure that things move in the ways you intend.

To remove a pose from the pose span:

1. Move the playhead to the frame containing the pose.

2. Control-click (OS X) or right-click (Win) the frame containing the diamond icon.

3. From the contextual menu, choose Clear Pose.

TIP You can't remove the pose from the first frame of a pose span.

TIP You can remove poses from multiple selected frames as long as the selection excludes the initial pose. In the Timeline, select the frames with poses you want to eliminate, access the contextual menu from any frame in the selection, then choose Clear Pose.

TIP When the whole span (including the first frame) is selected, the contextual menu's Clear Pose command is available only if the playhead is located at a frame with a pose. In that case, the command removes that pose.

More IK Tasks

To learn more about working with Flash's inverse-kinematics tools, see bonus materials available on the companion website, www.peachpit.com/flashcs6vqs.

Saving IK as Symbols

To get the most value from your IK animations, you may want to incorporate them into symbols that you can animate with tweening. You might, for example, create a wiggly worm using an IK shape, put that animation into a movie-clip symbol, then use an instance of the worm symbol in a motion tween. The motion tween can make the constantly wiggling worm wander around the Stage, change size or color, and so on. One option for converting an IK animation into a symbol is to select the IK shape or all of the IK nodes (selecting the pose span in the Timeline automatically selects all the IK elements) and then choose Modify > Convert to Symbol, or press F8. Another option is to Control-click (OS X) or right-click (Win) the selected IK shape or any of the selected IK nodes, and from the contextual menu, choose Convert to Symbol. In the Convert to Symbol dialog that appears, you can name the symbol and choose its type, library location, and so on (see Chapter 7). You can also choose Insert > New Symbol, or press Command-F8 (OS X) or Ctrl-F8 (Win) to create a new symbol and paste a copied armature layer or pose-span frames into the symbol's Timeline. (Remember that you must drag an instance of the new symbol to the Stage to use it.) To see the symbol's IK animation, you must view the movie in Flash Player.

When saving IK animation in a symbol, you should always choose Movie Clip or Graphic as the Type. (Flash will transform an IK animation into a button, but the pose span overwrites the Up, Over, Down, and Hit frames, and the resulting button won't work.)

Building Buttons for Interactivity

After you master Flash Professional CS6's drawing and animating tools, you can create movies that play from beginning to end. However, to create interactive environments that transform viewers into users, you must add interface elements that enable user control.

The most common interface element is a button. Buttons have two levels of interactivity: first, responding to user input with visual feedback—for example, changing color when the pointer enters the button area; second, carrying out tasks—such as switching to a new scene when a user clicks the button.

In this chapter, you'll set up the first level of interactivity using button symbols and button components. You'll also set up a movie-clip symbol that can act as a visually responsive button. For these elements, built-in coding takes care of the first level of button interactivity. To achieve the second level of interactivity—making buttons respond in new ways and carry out tasks—requires scripting. You'll learn some ways to do that in Chapter 15.

Creating Button Symbols

A button symbol is a Flash movie with four frames. The first three are the Up, Over, and Down keyframes, which represent the button's three possible states. The fourth, the Hit keyframe, defines the button's active area. In the published movie, the graphic content of the first three frames appears when the user interacts with the symbol. If one of the button-state keyframes is blank, the button displays no new content during that state. If the Hit frame is blank, the content of the nearest preceding keyframe determines the button's active area.

Building Basic Buttons

To create the most basic button symbol, place simple shapes in each of the keyframes. Change the shapes and colors, or add internal elements to distinguish the graphics for the various button states. When you complete all four keyframes, the button is ready to use. Return to document-editing mode, and drag an instance of the button symbol from the Library panel to the Stage.

To build a basic button symbol:

1. Open the document in which you want to add buttons, and choose Insert > New Symbol, or press Command-F8 (OS X) or Ctrl-F8 (Win).

2. In the Create New Symbol dialog that appears, in the Name field, enter the name, `MyBasicButton`.

3. From the Type menu, choose Button 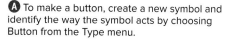.

A To make a button, create a new symbol and identify the way the symbol acts by choosing Button from the Type menu.

A Note About Touch Screens

The prevalence of mobile devices has made touch-sensitive screens a primary input device. Tapping and pinching, swiping and tilting are gestures we now rely on to access and navigate the web, work in apps, play games, and so on.

In current configurations, touch devices have no equivalent to the Over state of a button symbol in Flash. Whether your finger taps the screen where a button is or merely rests on it gently, the device records a click (the Down state). When you use Flash's four-frame (three-state) button symbols in content created for touch-screen devices, be sure to make the Down state visually distinct from the Up state.

ActionScript 3.0 handles many touch-screen gestures, which means you can use movie-clip symbols to create user-interface elements for touch-screen input. A discussion about designing good UI elements for touch devices is beyond the scope of a *Visual QuickStart Guide,* but in this chapter you create movie-clip symbols that can act as buttons. In Chapter 15, you will script the actions of these buttons. Flash CS6 *code snippets* features help with scripting, some even creating code that responds to basic touch actions.

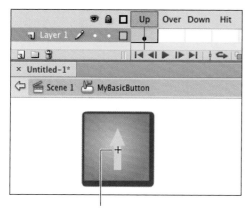

B The Timeline of every button symbol contains four frames: Up, Over, Down, and Hit. Flash automatically puts a blank keyframe in the Up frame of a new button symbol.

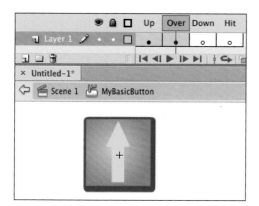

Registration crosshair marks the center of the symbol's Stage

C When a button is waiting for the end user to notice and interact with it, the contents of the Up keyframe appear.

D When the end user's pointer rolls over or pauses over the button, the contents of the Over keyframe appear.

4. Click OK. A new symbol appears in the Library panel and you enter symbol-editing mode. The Timeline contains the four frames that define the button: Up, Over, Down, and Hit. By default, the Up frame contains a blank keyframe **B**.

5. To create the button's Up state—the way the button looks onstage waiting to be clicked—do the following:

   ▸ In the Timeline, select the Up keyframe.

   ▸ On the Stage, create new graphic elements or place a symbol instance **C**. To center the graphic elements or symbol instance around the crosshair in the middle of the Stage, use the Align panel and select the Align to Stage checkbox. The crosshair becomes the symbol's registration point.

6. To create the button's Over state—the way the button looks when a pointer is placed over it—do the following:

   ▸ In the Timeline, select the Over frame.

   ▸ Choose Insert > Timeline > Keyframe to duplicate the contents of the Up keyframe. Duplicating the preceding keyframe helps ensure that the button elements align, and the button doesn't appear to jump around as it changes states.

   ▸ Edit the contents to create an appropriate Over state. For a simple change, enlarge an element within the button graphic or symbol **D**.

Continues on next page

7. To create the button's Down state—the way the button looks when the user clicks it—do the following:

   ▸ Select the Down frame.

   ▸ Choose Insert > Timeline > Keyframe to duplicate the Over keyframe.

   ▸ Edit the contents to create an appropriate Down state. For a simple change, darken the background of the button graphic or symbol or change an element within it **E**.

8. To create the button's Hit graphic—the element that defines the button's active area—first select the Hit frame in the Timeline; then press F6.

   Flash duplicates the Down keyframe. When you use a graphic with the same shape and size for all three states of your button, you can safely use a copy of any previous keyframe as the Hit graphic.

   Optionally, you can edit the Hit graphic to make it a single color **F**. Doing so helps remind you that end users won't see this graphic.

9. Return to document-editing mode, for example, by clicking the Back button in the Edit bar. The main Timeline appears.

   Now you can use the button symbol in your movie just as you would use any other symbol.

TIP Button symbols have just four frames, but there's no restriction on adding layers. Use symbols for the various elements that make up your button, and keep each element (especially any text) on a separate layer. That way, you can easily swap symbols to change the look of your buttons even after you've placed them in a project. This method streamlines the process of updating or revising your Flash content.

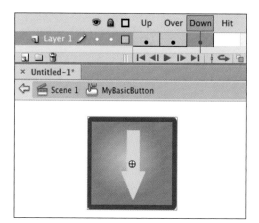

E When the end user clicks the button, the contents of the Down keyframe appear.

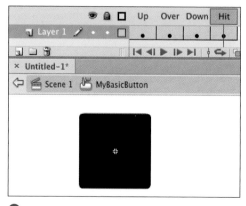

F The graphic in the Hit keyframe need not be a fully detailed image; it just needs to be a silhouette of the button shape. That shape defines the active button area. Here, the Hit keyframe contains a copy of the Down keyframe in which all elements have been changed to black.

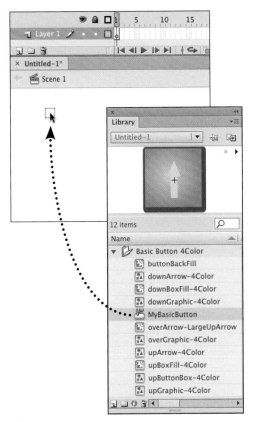

G To incorporate a button symbol into your Flash movie, drag an instance of the button from the Library panel to the Stage.

To place the newly created button in your movie:

- Continuing with the file from the preceding task, drag an instance of the button **MyBasicButton** from the Library panel to the Stage **G**.

TIP To create a consistent look on a website, you may want to reuse a set of buttons over and over. You can even reuse buttons in several projects with only slight changes. To save time, devote one document to buttons, and always create your button symbols there. Then you can copy a button from this master button file to your current Flash document and tweak the button in that document

To preview button states on the Stage:

- Choose Control > Enable Simple Buttons.

  Flash displays the Up, Over, and Down states as you move the pointer over the button and click. When Enable Simple Buttons is active, you can't select buttons or work with them. To deactivate Enable Simple Buttons, choose Control > Enable Simple Buttons again.

TIP You can preview the Up, Over, and Down states of your button symbol by selecting it in the Library panel and then clicking the Play button in the preview window. Flash displays each frame in turn.

Building Shape-Changing Button Symbols

Button graphics can emulate real-world switches or toggles. In a game, you can disguise buttons as part of the scenery—making the blinking eye of a character a button, for example. When the Up, Over, and Down keyframes of your button symbol contain graphics of different shapes and sizes, however, you need to create a graphic for the Hit state that covers all of the other states.

To build a button that changes shape:

1. Follow Steps 1–4 in the task "To build a basic button symbol" in this chapter. Name the button **MultiShapeBtn**.

2. To prepare each button frame to receive varying content, in the Timeline, select the Over, Down, and Hit frames; and choose Modify Timeline > Convert to Blank Keyframes, or press F7 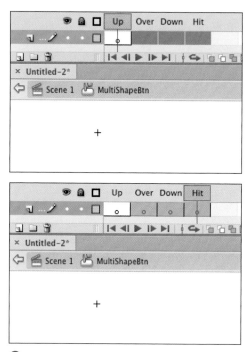.

3. To create the button's Up state, in the Timeline, select the Up keyframe and place the appropriate Up-state content on the Stage. For this task, use a circular shape.

4. Repeat Step 3 for the Over and Down keyframes. For this task, use a square for the Over keyframe and a star for the Down keyframe.

H Select the Over, Down, and Hit frames of a button symbol, then convert them to blank keyframes. The frames are ready for you to add content for each button state.

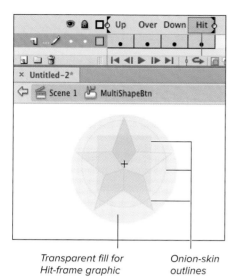

Transparent fill for Hit-frame graphic   *Onion-skin outlines*

I The silhouette in the Hit keyframe should encompass all possible button areas in all three button modes. For example, if you duplicate only the circle as the Hit graphic for this button, you exclude the tips of the star. As the user moves the pointer over the tips, the button returns to its Over phase; the user can't click the tips to activate the button. If you duplicate only the star, the user may roll the pointer over several areas of the circle and never discover that it's a button.

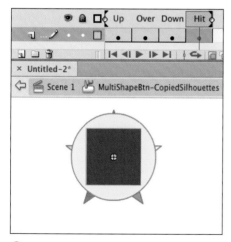

J By copying the graphic in each of the button states and using the Paste in Place command to place them in the Hit keyframe, you create a perfectly positioned silhouette that incorporates all the possible button areas.

5. To create the Hit graphic do one of the following:

▸ Draw a simple geometric shape that's large enough to cover all areas of the button in all of its states. Turn on onion skinning so that you can see exactly what you need to cover and how to position the Hit graphic **I**.

▸ Use Flash's Edit > Copy and Edit > Paste in Place commands to copy the graphic elements from the first three keyframes of the button and paste each of them into the Hit keyframe of the button. The graphics stack up in the Hit keyframe, occupying the exact area needed to cover the button in any phase of its operation **J**.

6. Return to document-editing mode (for example, by choosing Edit > Edit Document).

7. Drag a copy of the **MultiShapeBtn** symbol from the Library panel to the Stage.

8. To view and interact with the button in Flash Player, choose Control > Test Scene.

TIP To create a silhouette slightly larger than the objects in the Up, Down, and Over frames, in the Hit frame, select the stack of copied objects from the earlier frames and convert those objects to raw shapes by choosing Modify > Break Apart. Keep issuing the Break Apart command until all parts of the objects are reduced to raw shapes. Merge the shapes by applying a single fill and stroke color to them; then select the resulting shape, and choose Modify > Shape > Expand Fill. Enter a Distance value of 1 or 2 pixels, select the Expand radio button, and click OK.

Creating Fully Animated Button Symbols

The button symbols you created in the preceding tasks are animated in the sense that they change as the user interacts with them. Flash also lets you create fully animated button symbols—for example, a glowing light bulb. To make fully animated buttons, you place different movie clips in the button's Up, Over, and Down keyframes. Each movie clip contains its own animation sequence.

To create a fully animated rollover button:

1. Follow Steps 1 and 2 in the task "To build a button that changes shape" in this chapter. Name the button **FullAnimBtn**.

2. To create the button's Up state, in the Timeline, select the Up keyframe, and place an instance of a movie-clip symbol on the Stage. The movie clip shown in this example animates a spinning pentagon **K**.

3. Repeat Step 2 for the Over keyframe. The movie clip shown in this example animates a pentagon unfolding into a star **L**.

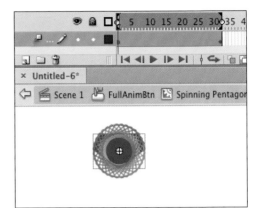

K The animation of the symbol in the Up keyframe plays when the button is in the Up state, when the end user is not interacting with the button in any way. Here, onion skinning in symbol-editing mode reveals all the frames of a spinning-pentagon; the animation was created with a motion tween.

L The animation of the symbol in the Over keyframe plays when the user's pointer rolls or rests over the button area. Here, the Preview mode of the Timeline shows the frame-by-frame animation of a pentagon shape that turns into a star.

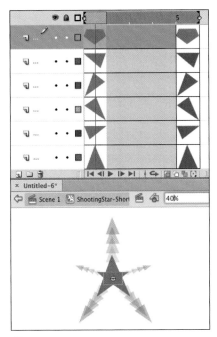

ⓜ The animation of the symbol in the Down keyframe plays when the user clicks inside the button area. Here, onion skinning in symbol-editing mode reveals all the frames of a classic tween that animates a star flying apart.

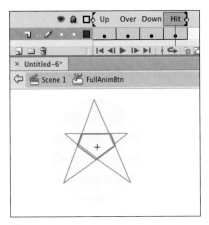

ⓝ When you're creating a graphic for a Hit keyframe, use onion skinning to see the initial keyframe of the movie clip in each button frame. Here, the graphic in the Hit keyframe is a transparent fill, which also helps you position the graphic to cover the graphics in the other keyframes.

4. Repeat Step 2 for the Down keyframe. The movie clip shown in this example animates a star flying apart **ⓜ**.

5. To create the button's Hit graphic, in the Timeline, select the Hit keyframe and create a shape that covers all areas of the button in all three states (Up, Over, and Down). An oval or rectangle often works well for this purpose **ⓝ**. Your goal is to create a graphic that's slightly larger than the silhouette of the animated items. During playback, as the user moves the pointer into the area of the Hit graphic, the button switches to the Over state. During the Over state, the oval is big enough to encompass all points of the star, and during Down state, the user can let the pointer drift a fair amount without exiting the area of the button.

6. Return to document-editing mode.

7. Drag a copy of the **FullAnimBtn** symbol from the Library panel to the Stage.

TIP You can place a movie-clip instance in the Hit keyframe of your button, but only the visible content from the clip's first frame determines the Hit area.

TIP With buttons enabled, in document-editing mode, Flash previews the first frame of the animations in the Up, Over, and Down keyframes of your fully animated button symbol.

TIP Because the movie clips play in their own Timeline, animated buttons continue to display their animation, even when you pause the main movie.

Using Button Components

Creating button symbols is just one way to add UI elements to a movie. You can add a variety of UI elements—including buttons— by using the *components*. (See the sidebar "About Components" in this chapter.)

To place an instance of the button component:

1. Open a Flash document and access the following panels: Components, Library, and the Property inspector.

2. In the Components panel, expand the User Interface folder 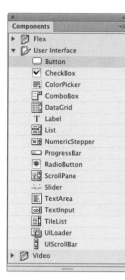.

3. Drag an instance of **Button** to the Stage. The button component and a folder named Component Assets are added to the document's library .

To preview the component instance:

- To interact with a button component and see all its states, view your document in Flash Player, for example, by choosing Control > Test Scene.

  As with other movie-clip symbols, during authoring, a button component on the Stage displays just its first keyframe. A button component's current parameter settings govern the button's initial state . To test the fully enabled button, you must view it in Flash Player.

A The Components panel lists the default components that come with Flash, including three categories of components for ActionScript 3.0: Flex, User Interface, and Video. Buttons are found under User Interface.

B A component is a special form of movie clip. When you drag an instance of the button component from the Components panel to the Stage, the button becomes an asset (its type is **Component**) in the Library panel of that document.

C The Control > Enable Simple Buttons command lets you interact with a button *symbol* during authoring to view all its states. This command has no effect on button *components*. During authoring, a component instance always displays its initial state, and you can drag that instance, as you would any other object on the Stage.

Modifying Button Components

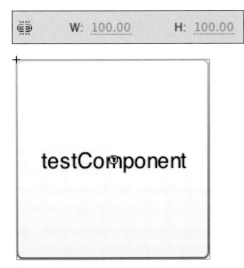

A To change the dimensions of a selected button-component instance, access the Position and Size section of the Property inspector. Use the W and H hot-text controls to enter new width and height values.

W: 100.00   H: 100.00

testComponent

B In Unconstrain mode, you can set a selected component's width and height values independently, thereby changing the aspect ratio. In this example, entering 100 pixels for width and height changes the rectangular button component into a square. In Constrain mode, Flash preserves the component's original aspect ratio, so entering a new value for one dimension changes the value for the other dimension proportionally.

The Component Parameters section of the Property inspector offers seven modifiable parameters for the button component. In the following tasks, you'll use three of them to change the button's label and set the button to work as a toggle.

To modify button-component dimensions:

1. On the Stage, select an instance of the button component.

2. In the Position and Size section of the Property inspector, use the W and H hot-text controls to enter new values for width and height **A**. For this task, set the modifier to Unconstrain mode and enter an H value of 100 to match the current W value.

   On the Stage, the button's dimensions change to match the new values **B**. The bounding box of the button component defines the active area of the button. As you change the dimensions, Flash automatically changes the Hit area for the button component to match.

> **TIP** You can rotate or skew a button component with the free-transform tool or in the Transform panel. You should know, however, that Flash creates the button's label text using device fonts, which can't be rotated or skewed. If you rotate or skew a button component, its label text disappears.

> **TIP** You can position a selected button component precisely by entering *x*- and *y*-coordinate values in the Info panel or in the Position and Size section of the Property inspector.

To modify button-component labels:

1. On the Stage, select an instance of the button component.

2. To view the component's parameters, access the Property inspector and expand the Component Parameters section **C**.

3. To modify the text of the selected button instance, in the Label field enter a new name, such as **testComponent** **D**.

4. To confirm the text, press Enter, or click outside the active text field.

   With Flash's default settings, the new label text appears within the button-component instance. Be forewarned, if your text is wider than the button instance, Flash truncates the text to make it fit within the visible button area.

C When you select an instance of a component on the Stage, a set of modifiable parameters appear in the Component Parameters section of the Property inspector. Change an item in the Value column to modify the component instance.

D To rename a component, enter new text in the Label field, then press Enter to confirm the new label.

About Components

Flash CS6 offers two types of components: those that work with ActionScript versions 1.0 and 2.0, and those that work with version 3.0. Both types are stored in the *Components panel.* Components depend on ActionScript to carry out their intended behaviors, and the Components panel displays different items depending on which version of ActionScript is currently selected in the Publish Settings dialog. When you create a new Flash File (ActionScript 3.0) document, it is set up to work with the 3.0 components, so those are the only components that appear in the Components panel. (To learn about Publish Settings and switching ActionScript versions for your document, see Chapter 17.)

A component is a scripted movie-clip symbol. ActionScript 3.0's video components are a special type of movie clip called a *compiled clip,* but the 3.0 user-interface components are regular movie clips whose look you can easily modify. (See the sidebar "Modifying ActionScript 3.0 Component Skins.") You can modify the look of compiled clips, but that process is beyond the scope of this book. Flash lets you modify certain properties of a component—for example, the label of the button component—by changing them in the Component Parameters section of the Property inspector.

Advanced scripters can create their own components and share them with other Flash users. One source for new components is the Adobe Exchange portion of the Adobe website. Flash's Welcome screen contains a direct link to Adobe Exchange. (In the Extend section of the screen, click the Flash Exchange button.)

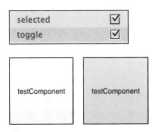

E Selecting the Toggle checkbox in the Component Parameters section of the Property inspector, sets the button to act as a toggle.

F For a button-component instance set to act as a toggle, use the Selected checkbox to determine the button's initial state. Deselect the checkbox to make the button look deselected initially (left); select the checkbox to make the button look selected initially (right). Here the button-component instances are viewed in Flash Player.

To set the button component to act as a toggle:

1. Select an instance of a button component on the Stage.

2. In the Component Parameters section of the Property inspector, select the Toggle checkbox **E**. The button now acts as a toggle; repeated clicks turn the button on and off.

3. To set the button's initial state at runtime, in the Component Parameters section of the Property inspector, select (or deselect) the Selected checkbox **F**.

Modifying ActionScript 3.0 Component Skins

You can edit ActionScript 3.0 User Interface components the way you would edit any movie-clip symbol. Let's look at the button component as an example.

When you drag an instance of the button component to the Stage, Flash adds the master button component and a Component Assets folder to the library of your document. A subfolder inside the assets folder contains the component's *skins*. The subfolder for the button component, named **ButtonSkins**, contains all the symbols that make up the button states.

You can modify these underlying symbols, as you would any symbol, to change the look of the component. To modify each skin symbol directly, double-click it in the library. Flash opens the symbol in symbol-editing mode. Alternatively, you can double-click a component instance on the Stage to gain access to all of that component's skins in symbol-editing mode. A word of warning when editing the skins: Many contain an element whose fill color has an Alpha value of 0 percent. As you examine different elements, you may pick up that setting for fill tools. When you apply a new color to an element that should be solid (or translucent) make sure that the fill color's Alpha value is greater than 0 percent.

The top layer of the component symbol's Timeline is labeled *assets*. Keyframe 2 of the asset layer contains a symbol that itself contains all the skins that make up the look of the component—in this case, the button states. Double-click any of the skins to edit it.

To change a button component's look yet retain a consistent, user-friendly button, you will probably need to modify every skin that relates to the button component. You may also need to modify other components if you plan to use them within the same application or website as your modified button component. The changes you make to the component's skins will affect every instance of the component in your movie.

Creating Movie-Clip Buttons

Flash's button symbols have just three states, and follow built-in rules about how to display them in response to the user's mouse pointer movements. You can, however, take control of that functionality and create a button that has more than three states by making a movie-clip button. In the following tasks, you assemble graphic elements in the frames of the movie clip to create a button with four states: Up, Over, Down, and Disabled. To give the movie-clip button even the first level of interactivity—the ability to respond to mouse movements by displaying different states—you must use ActionScript. (You learn to do that in Chapter 15.)

To create the button states:

1. Open a Flash document and choose Insert > New Symbol, or press Command-F8 (OS X) or Ctrl-F8 (Win).

2. In the Create New Symbol dialog that appears, in the Name field, enter a descriptive name, such as `MovieClipBtn`.

3. From the Type menu, choose Movie Clip Ⓐ.

4. Click OK. A new symbol appears in the Library panel, and Flash enters symbol-editing mode. The Timeline contains one layer, with a blank keyframe at Frame 1.

Ⓐ The first step in making a movie clip that acts like a button is creating a new symbol. Choose Insert > New Symbol, then set the symbol type to Movie Clip and enter a name in the Create New Symbol dialog.

Why Make Movie-Clip Buttons?

Flash's button symbols make it easy to create buttons quickly, but they limit you to just three states: Up, Over, and Down. In some situations, you'd like a button with more states. Here's an example: The best interface designs use elements consistently. That way, users know which options are available to them and where to find the interface elements for carrying out a task. Think of a typical slide show with a Next button. Ideally, the button is always present in the same location. When you view the last slide, the Next button should still be present, but it should be inactive (and look inactive). One way to handle that is to create a button that has four states: Up, Over, Down, and Disabled.

When you make your own movie-clip buttons, you can create as many states as you like.

B When you set up a movie-clip button, it's a good idea to create separate layers for the actions, text, and graphic elements. Use descriptive layer names that help you to remember which elements each layer contains.

C A movie-clip button needs a keyframe for each button state. Creating longer keyframe spans helps you organize the layers visually and makes room for frame labels.

5. Add two layers to the Timeline, for a total of three layers, and name them as follows **B**:

   ▸ Name the top layer Actions. It will contain ActionScript that tells the movie-clip button what to do.

   ▸ Name the second layer Labels. It will contain text identifying each keyframe that represents a button state.

   ▸ Name the bottom layer ButtonGraphics. It will contain the graphic elements that create the button's look for each state.

6. In the Timeline, in all three layers, insert blank keyframes at Frames 4, 7, and 10 **C**.

   Each layer needs enough keyframes to accommodate all four button states: Up, Over, Down, and Disabled. Spacing out the keyframes makes them easier to deal with and lets you view the frame labels that you create.

7. In the ButtonGraphics layer, select Keyframe 1. Using the oval tool, draw an oval centered over the registration mark on the Stage. Give the oval a red fill and a black stroke. Make the stroke fairly wide so the graphic looks more buttonlike. This graphic represents the button's Up state.

8. Select the oval, and choose Edit > Copy, or press Command-C (OS X) or Ctrl-C (Win).

Continues on next page

9. Select Keyframe 4 in the ButtonGraphics layer, and choose Edit > Paste in Place, or press Shift-Command-V (OS X) or Ctrl-Shift-V (Win). Change the fill color to green. This graphic represents the button's Over state.

10. Repeat Step 9 for Keyframes 7 and 10. In Keyframe 7, change the oval fill to blue, to represent the Down state. In Keyframe 10, change the fill to a light gray and the stroke to a dark gray, to represent the button in its Disabled state **D**.

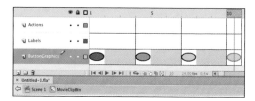

D With Preview selected as your frame-viewing mode, the Timeline displays all the button-state graphics you've placed in the keyframes of the movie-clip button symbol. Use shades of gray for the graphics in the frame that represents the Disabled state.

TIP For a movie-clip button that uses the same solid shape in each state, you needn't create a Hit-state keyframe. When you add the appropriate ActionScript (see Chapter 15), Flash defines the Hit area using the graphic element(s) in the frames of your movie clip that correspond to button states.

TIP For a movie-clip button with an irregular shape, such as a snowflake (or a movie-clip button that uses different shapes in different states), it's a good idea to add an "invisible" graphic element to define a good Hit area. For a snowflake button, for example, create a circular fill large enough to cover the snowflake, and give the fill an alpha value of 0. Place that circular fill on a layer at the bottom of the Timeline and add frames to the layer so that the circle "appears" in each button-state frame. The circle defines the Hit area and the mouse will trigger the Over state even in the cutout areas of the flake.

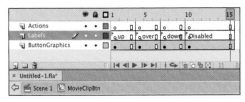

E Using the button state as the name for a selected keyframe reminds you what's in the frame, and you can use ActionScript to find a frame by label name. In the Label section of the Property inspector, enter the button-state description in the Name field. Choose Name from the Type menu.

F A red flag in a keyframe indicates that the frame has a label name. If enough in-between frames follow the keyframe, Flash displays the frame label as well as the flag. (Here, frames have been added at the end of the sequence to make the Disabled label visible.) The labeled keyframes in this movie-clip symbol indicate which button state the keyframe represents.

To assign frame labels to button-state keyframes:

1. Continuing with the file you created in the preceding task, in the Labels layer of the **MovieClipBtn** Timeline, select Keyframe 1.

2. In the Property inspector's Label section, in the Name field enter **_up**, and press Enter to confirm the name.

3. From the Type menu, choose Name (the default setting).

   The label type determines how Flash treats the text in the Name field. When Name is selected, Flash places a red-flag icon next to the label text in the keyframe span in the Timeline **E**. (Label names do not appear when you view frames in Preview or Preview in Context mode.)

4. Repeat Step 2 for Keyframes 4, 7, and 10, entering the names **_over**, **_down**, and **Disabled**, respectively **F**.

5. Return to document-editing mode.

6. Drag an instance of the **MovieClipBtn** symbol to the Stage. This movie clip is ready to be scripted to act like a button and carry out whatever tasks you set for it with ActionScript. You'll learn to complete the button's interactivity in Chapter 15.

7. To check out your button states, click the Play button in the symbol preview in the Library panel, or choose Control > Test Scene to play the symbol instance. Flash moves through the keyframes and displays each button state in turn.

8. Save this document for use in Chapter 15. Name it MyOwnBtn.fla.

TIP ActionScript recognizes the labels _up, _down, and _over as button states. Using these labels means you need do only minimal scripting to get the button to work (see Chapter 15). To make a more flexible button (for example, one that responds differently to different mouse movements), use other labels. You can use MyUp, MyOver, MyDown, MyDragOut, and so on.

TIP Another way to remind yourself what a keyframe does is to add a comment. To enter a frame comment, select the keyframe, and in the Name field in the Label section of the Property inspector, type two slashes (//) followed by your comment text **G**. Frame labels and frame comments are mutually exclusive. Each keyframe can have one or the other. To work around that limitation, add separate layers for comments and labels. Place keyframes in both layers, and then add comments to one layer and labels to the other, as needed.

TIP Instead of typing two slashes, you can just type the comment text. Then, from the Type pop-up menu, choose Comment. Flash adds the slashes for you.

G You can use the Name field in the Label section of the Property inspector to create comments for a selected keyframe. Enter two slashes in the field to begin comment text; or type the text of your comment, then choose Comment from the Type menu. Comments appear in the Timeline in the keyframe span; long comments are cut off by the next keyframe in the layer.

Frame-Labels: Best Practice

Why use labels? A label reminds you what's in the keyframe. More important, you can use ActionScript to find a frame by its label name and then display that frame. You'll use this technique to create a button's visual feedback in response to mouse movements (see Chapter 15).

Scripting Timeline interactions by targeting frame labels has another benefit: it helps preserve the correct interactivity of any assets you translate to JavaScript (for use with HTML5) using the Toolkit for CreateJS (see Chapter 17).

However, Flash is sensitive about names. Because frame-label names become part of target paths in ActionScripting, certain characters that have special meaning in scripting—slashes, equals signs, plus signs, and so on—are off-limits for labeling frames. To be safe, use only letters, numbers, and underscore characters in names. Don't even use spaces to separate words in frame labels. Instead, use capitalization and the underscore character.

15

Basic Interactivity

Adobe Flash CS6 Professional includes ActionScript (AS), a complete scripting language that you can use to create complex, interactive websites for e-learning, e-commerce, and other Internet applications. Teaching ActionScript and scripting in detail is beyond the scope of this book. However, it is possible to create scripts for a number of common tasks without much difficulty. Flash CS6 also comes with a panel of Code Snippets, which automate the creation of scripts for some common interactivities.

In this chapter you will use ActionScript 3.0 to add basic interactivity to your Flash content. To create scripts, you will enter code in segments. Each segment relates to an important AS task. Once you understand the meaning and purpose of each segment, you'll be able to reuse and combine them to create basic interactivity for your Flash content. Script figures, showing completed segments of code, accompany the tasks in this chapter.

In This Chapter

Touring the Actions Panel

The Actions panel **A** has three work areas: the Script pane, the Actions Toolbox, and the Script Navigator. To access the panel, choose Window > Actions or press Option-F9 (OS X) or F9 (Win).

The Script pane is a text window where you assemble scripts. You can enter actions into the pane manually (it acts like a text editor); and you can add actions from the Actions Toolbox or the Add pop-up menu. (To access the Add menu, click the plus sign ⬆ in the toolbar above the Script pane.) You can import scripts or pieces of script from an external file, such as one created with a stand-alone text editor.

The Actions Toolbox contains the words (actions) that make up the ActionScript language. These pieces of code appear in hierarchical lists. Click one of the category icons ⬀ to view its contents. Double-click an action to add it to the Script pane. You can also drag items from the Actions Toolbox to the Script pane. (The list of ActionScript actions also appears in the Add menu.)

The Script Navigator helps you locate and maneuver through the scripts in your movie. This feature is most useful when you've used a large number of frame scripts in keyframes throughout the Timeline.

ActionScript Versions

Flash CS6 contains two flavors of ActionScript—version 2.0 (which also incorporates 1.0) and version 3.0. This book focuses exclusively on version 3.0. To create scripts that use AS 3.0, you must set your Flash document's publish settings to AS 3.0 when you create the document initially, or in the Publish Settings dialog later. (You'll learn more about publishing in Chapter 17.)

About Scripting Tasks

In this book, you create scripts by entering segments of code. Some characters—such as opening and closing braces—act in combination to enclose code, so both characters must be present for the script to work. To help create accurate code, you will first enter such characters as a pair, and then insert the code between them. You will also revise and add to scripts as you go. The script figures accompanying the tasks show completed segments of code. For context, when a script figure illustrates specific steps in a task, the text that you enter for those steps is formatted in bold-face and red, while text that is already present from earlier steps appears in regular type. Full scripts are available from the book's companion website (www.peachpit.com/flashcs6vqs). For directions on how to access them, see the Introduction.

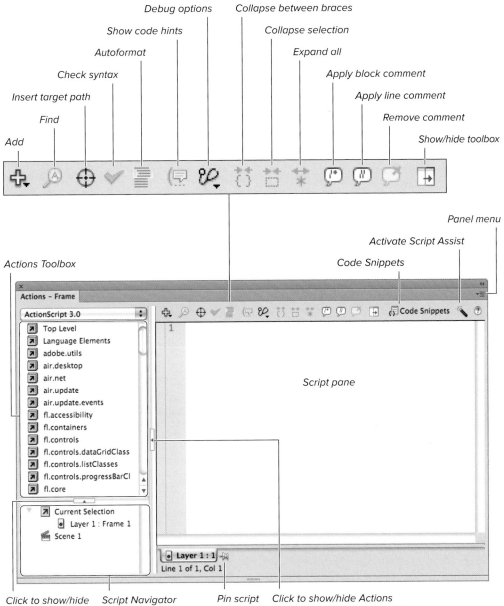

Add

Insert target path

Find

Check syntax

Autoformat

Show code hints

Debug options

Collapse between braces

Collapse selection

Expand all

Apply block comment

Apply line comment

Remove comment

Show/hide toolbox

Panel menu

Activate Script Assist

Code Snippets

Actions Toolbox

Script pane

Click to show/hide
Actions Toolbox

Script Navigator

Pin script

Click to show/hide Actions
Toolbox and Script Navigator

A The Actions panel has three main areas: the Actions Toolbox, where you can choose actions; the Script Navigator, where Flash displays the elements in your movie that have scripts attached; and the Script pane, where Flash assembles the ActionScript.

Organizing Frame Actions

A little letter *a* in the Timeline indicates a keyframe that has actions attached. Imagine the difficulty of searching through dozens—or hundreds—of layers and frames to find each little *a* when you need to modify or add to your code. To organize your code, put all frame actions in a single layer named Actions. Restricting frame actions to one layer avoids accidentally putting multiple frame actions at the same frame number in different layers, which can cause problems if you reorder the layers. Choose a consistent location for your Actions layer. For example, always put it near the top of the Timeline. It's also a good idea to lock the Actions layer, by clicking the bullet in the padlock column. You can't accidentally place or rearrange elements on the Stage for a locked layer, but you can still add actions to keyframes in a locked layer. (For detailed instructions on working with layers, see Chapter 6.)

How Scripting Works

ActionScript 3.0 lets you create *frame actions* by selecting a keyframe, then opening the Actions panel and entering the script. In the published movie, when the playhead reaches the keyframe that contains the script, Flash carries out the script's instructions. These instructions might be to control the Timeline directly (for example, pausing playback of the movie), to set up interactivity for buttons (for example, telling Flash what to do when someone clicks a particular button), or to change the properties of objects located in that keyframe (for example, to move a symbol instance across the Stage).

You can also create *custom classes,* which are similar to using symbols in the library. Creating or editing classes is beyond the scope of this book. Yet by doing the tasks in earlier chapters, you have already interacted with some of Flash's *built-in classes*, such as `SimpleButton` and `MovieClip`. Advanced scripters can create and edit custom classes using the ActionScript editor or an external text editor.

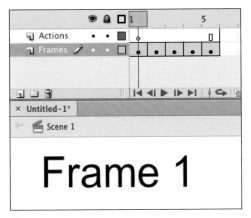

A To test frame actions—which instruct Flash to move to a specific frame or to start and stop playback—it's useful to have a document that identifies each frame. That way, you easily can see the results of your scripts.

What Is Interactivity?

Imagine a trivia quiz with a multiple-choice question. When the user selects the correct answer, a success message appears. When a wrong answer is chosen, the response is "Try Again!" A different type of quiz may require dragging elements in the correct order or entering text to answer questions.

To achieve this type of interactivity using ActionScript, you must create a script that directs the playback of your published Flash content.

Adding Frame Actions

Some of the most basic scripting tasks involve controlling movie playback: making your movie stop and start, and jump from place to place. By default, a movie begins running at playback; you can change that with frame actions.

To make your first script in Flash, set up a multiframe document that has identifying text in each frame. Then add a **stop** action to Keyframe 1, to make the movie pause on the first frame at playback. Save this file as a template for use in other scripting tasks.

To set up a document for testing frame actions:

1. Create a Flash document with two layers: Actions and Frames. By default, Flash creates a keyframe in the first frame of each layer.

2. In the Actions layer, add in-between frames in Frames 2–5.

3. In the Frames layer, create keyframes in Frames 2–5.

4. On the Stage, for each keyframe, add Classic text to identify the frame numbers (Frame 1, Frame 2, and so on).

   Your document should look like **A**. If you create the text as TLF, when you test your scripts, you may see warning dialogs and error messages related to publishing that could distract you from the scripting process.

To begin scripting by adding comments:

1. Continuing with the document you created in the preceding task, in the Actions layer, select Keyframe 1.

2. Access the Actions panel. If the panel isn't open, choose Window > Actions, or press Option-F9 (OS X) or F9 (Win). The name Actions-Frame appears in the title bar of the Actions panel.

3. To simplify working with code in the Script pane, in the upper-right corner of the Actions-Frame panel, open the panel menu 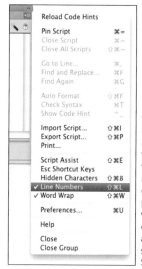, and make sure the following options are selected:

   ▸ **Line Numbers** help you to keep your place as you script.

   ▸ **Word Wrap** forces the lines of your script to break to fit within the Script pane.

4. In the toolbar above the Script pane of the Actions-Frame panel, make sure that Script Assist is inactive ✎ ◉. If necessary, click the Script Assist button ✎ to close the Script Assist window.

5. With the blinking I-beam cursor positioned in Line 1, type
   // Pause the movie on Frame 1 ◉.

   Your comment is added to the Script pane. With word wrap turned on, Flash wraps your text to fit in the Script pane; in the actual script, the comment is just one line.

> **TIP** With the Frame Property inspector active, to quickly access the Actions Panel click the ActionScript Panel ◉ button. The button is white when no actions are yet defined in the selected Keyframe; otherwise it is blue ◉.

B Open the panel menu in the Actions panel to make sure that line numbering and word wrap are active. (If not, select them to activate them.) Visible line numbers make it easier to keep your place while scripting; word wrap makes it easier to view scripts, as it forces them to stay within the visible Script pane area.

> **TIP** You can also create a comment by clicking the Apply Line Comment button ⬚ in the Actions Panel.

> **TIP** To toggle line numbers on/off in the Script pane, press Shift-Command-L (OS X) or Ctrl-Shift-L (Win). To toggle word wrap, press Shift-Command-W (OS X) or Ctrl-Shift-W (Win).

> **TIP** It's a good idea to write *comments* within your script to remind yourself what you intend it to do. Flash uses two comment types: *line comments* (single-line notes) and *block comments* (multiline notes). Pairs of special characters, called *opening and closing delimiters,* mark the beginning and end of each comment. When compiling a script for playback, Flash excludes everything between the opening and closing delimiters. A line comment begins with a double slash (//) and ends at the next paragraph return. A multiline comment begins with a slash followed by an asterisk (/*) and ends with an asterisk followed by a slash (*/).

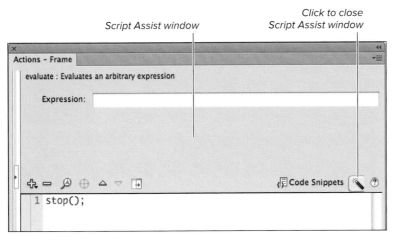

Script Assist window

Click to close
Script Assist window

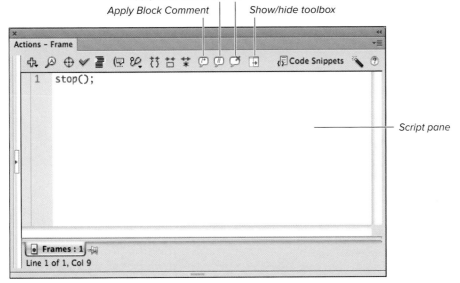

Apply Line Comment   Remove Comment
Apply Block Comment   Show/hide toolbox

Script pane

C The toolbar of the Actions panel contains a number of tools for working with scripts, including Script Assist. Deselect the Script Assist button to close the Script Assist window so that you can type directly in the Script pane.

D The two slashes indicate the beginning of a comment. When you add a comment using the Apply Line Comment button, Flash adds slashes to the script automatically.

To set the movie to pause at playback:

1. Continuing with the document you created in the preceding task, position the cursor at the end of Line 1 (your comment line) and press Enter. Flash creates Line 2 in the Script pane.

2. To add an action that pauses the Timeline, type **stop();**

   The new action appears in Line 2 in the Script pane; the word *stop* is highlighted in blue **E**.

3. Save the document as a template for future use; name it FrameActionsMaster. (For detailed instructions about saving documents as templates, see Chapter 1.)

4. Close the document.

TIP In the Preferences dialog, choose the ActionScript category to access settings for customizing the way Flash displays your scripts. Select the Automatic Close Brace checkbox to get help with creating the proper pairs of opening and closing braces in blocks of code you enter in the Actions panel.

```
1   // Pause the movie on Frame 1
2   stop();
```

E The **stop();** action in Line 2 sets the movie to be paused at runtime.

ActionScript Syntax Basics

ActionScript has its own rules, which are analogous to the rules of grammar and spelling in English. These rules, called *syntax,* govern such things as word order, capitalization, and punctuation of action statements. The following list briefly describes six crucial ActionScript punctuation marks that you'll use in writing scripts.

Dot (.) ActionScript uses *dot syntax,* meaning that periods act as links between objects and the *properties* (characteristics) and *methods* (behaviors) applied to them. In the statement

```
myClip.nextFrame();
```

the *dot* (the period) links the object (a movie-clip named **myClip**) with the method (**nextFrame**) that moves the playhead to the next frame in the Timeline. ActionScript also uses the dot in target paths. (See the sidebar "Scripting Nested Timelines" in this chapter.)

Semicolon (;) A semicolon indicates the end of a statement. The semicolon isn't required—Flash interprets the end of the line of statements correctly without it—but including it is good scripting practice. The semicolon also acts as a required separator in some action statements.

Colon (:) When you first set up a variable (a container for content that changes), a colon separates the text that is the name of the variable from the text that defines what type of variable it is.

```
var myName:String;
```

A colon also separates the name of a method from its type.

Braces ({}) Braces set off ActionScript statements that belong together. For example, a set of actions that are supposed to take place after **function greeting()** must be set off by braces. Note that the action statements within braces can require their own beginning and ending braces. The opening and closing braces must pair up evenly. Using Flash CS6's Automatic Close Brace feature helps ensure that you get the right number of opening and closing braces. Pay close attention to where you're adding statements and braces within the Script pane to make sure that you group the actions as intended.

Parentheses (()) Parentheses group the arguments that apply to a particular statement—defining the scene and frame in a **goto** action, for example. Parentheses also let you group operations, such as mathematical calculations, so that they take place in the right order.

Brackets ([]) Scripting frequently involves working with *arrays*, lists of similar elements. Placing a list inside brackets defines it as an array.

Programming Buttons with Frame Scripts

As you learned in the preceding chapter, Flash's button symbols and button components have certain actions built in. By default, when you move the mouse into the button area, Flash jumps to the Over frame. When you click the button, Flash takes you to the Down frame. To make the button carry out a task or to refine the way a button responds to a user's mouse movement, you attach ActionScript to a keyframe and target an instance of a button symbol or button component.

To add a button to be controlled by a frame script:

1. Using the FrameActionsMaster template you created earlier in this chapter, open a new document. (For details on opening new documents from templates, see Chapter 1.)

2. In the Timeline, add a new layer anywhere below the Actions layer, and name the new layer Buttons.

   Frame 1 of the new layer is a keyframe; Frames 2–5 are in-between frames. Any items you place on this layer will be visible throughout the five-frame movie **A**.

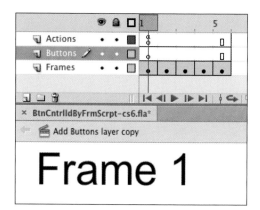

A To practice with button actions, create a movie with identifying text and separate layers for buttons and actions. Add in-between frames as needed so that all the layers are the same length.

B In-between frames extend the Buttons layer to match the length of the other layers; the button symbol in Keyframe 1 will be visible throughout the movie, although the identifying text from the Frames layer will change.

C Select the button symbol on the Stage, and enter a name in the Instance Name field in the Property inspector.

3. With the Buttons layer selected, place an instance of a button symbol on the Stage **B**.

   Follow the techniques in Chapter 14 to create a new button symbol, or use one from the Common Library of buttons. (To access this library, choose Window > Common Libraries > Buttons.) Drag a button-symbol instance from the library to the Stage.

4. To name the button instance, with the button selected on the Stage, access the Property inspector and type **enterBtn** in the Instance name field **C**. For ActionScript to control a symbol, the symbol must have a unique instance name.

5. Save your file.

TIP Scripting is a complex process, often involving trial and error. As you create scripts, you may wish you could go back to a point where you know everything works. Regularly using the Save As command makes that easier. Once you've set up your objects on the Stage and you're ready to add code, choose File > Save As. Each time you complete a segment of code that works the way you want, choose Save As again. Add a number, a letter, or an abbreviated description to the filename to make it easy to identify which version contains which completed work.

The Mechanics of Code Hints

How do code hints work? As you type text in the Script pane of the Actions panel, Flash tries to guess what you're about to script and help you out. Let's look at an example:

In Line 1 of your script, enter the following code:

```
var startLesson:SimpleButton;
```

As soon as you enter the colon, a code-hint window appears, listing available types 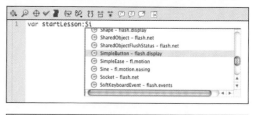. Continue to type, and the code-hint window follows along. As soon as you enter the letters **Si**, the code-hint window highlights **SimpleButton**. You can press Enter to accept the code hint and Flash adds it to your script, or you can keep typing to enter it manually.

When you accept the code hint, Flash automatically creates a new Line 1

```
import flash.display.SimpleButton;
```

and adds a blank Line 2. Line 1 instructs Flash to make the code for the **SimpleButton** class available in your script. The **import** statement is necessary for publishing, and it enables Flash to give you further code hints.

D When you enter a colon following a variable name, a code-hint window opens (top). As you continue typing characters, the code-hint window attempts to autocomplete your code (middle). When the matching code-hint highlights, press Enter to complete the script (bottom).

In subsequent lines of the script, whenever you type that instance name (**startLesson**) followed by a period (**.**), a similar code-hint window opens listing the actions and properties available for button symbols.

Continues on next page

The Mechanics of Code Hints *(continued)*

You have four options for dealing with a code-hint window:

- Use the Up Arrow and Down Arrow keys on your keyboard to navigate the list, select the item you want, and press Enter to add it to your script.

- Use the window's scroll bars to navigate the list, and then double-click the desired item to add it to your script.

- Continue typing to have Flash autocomplete your code: the code-hint window narrows in on an item according to the letters you type. When the item you want is highlighted, press Enter. Flash autocompletes that piece of code in your script.

- Override autocompleting by continuing to type manually in the Script pane. Keep in mind though that autocompleting helps you avoid typos and speeds the coding process.

If you close a code-hint window by accident, or you later want to change your selection, you can open the window by placing your cursor to the right of a period or an opening parenthesis and clicking the Code Hint button in the toolbar above the Script pane. You can also use the keyboard shortcut Control-Spacebar (OS X) or Ctrl-Spacebar (Win).

When you use code hints to automate entry of an action that requires a parameter, Flash automatically adds an opening parenthesis to your script and brings up another type of code hint, a *parameter hint* **E**. (If you override autocompleting, the parameter hint appears after you type an opening parenthesis in the Script pane.)

The parameter hint, which acts something like a tool tip, displays all possible parameters for the action you just entered. Parameter hints don't autocomplete code in the Script pane, but they can help you remember which parameters you need.

Sometimes, when Flash is able to guess the value of a parameter, it will display a code hint rather than a parameter hint. For example, for addEventListener, it will display a list of possible events you may want to use.

Code Hint button

```
1   import flash.display.SimpleButton;
2
3   // Pause the movie on Frame 1
4   stop();
5   // Declare Stage instances
6   var enterBtn:SimpleButton;
7   enterBtn.hasOwnProperty(
                            hasOwnProperty(V:*=null) : Boolean
```

E The parameter hint appears after you type an opening parenthesis (or after you use code hints to automate adding an action or property that takes a parameter).

To control a button using a frame script:

1. Continuing with the file that you created in the preceding task, make sure that the Actions panel is open and that code hints are enabled in the ActionScript category of Preferences (the default setting).

2. In the Actions layer, select Keyframe 1.

   The Script pane of the Actions panel displays the code you already created; Line 1 displays a comment; Line 2 displays the **stop();** action.

3. To declare a stage instance, do the following:

   ▸ To start a new line, place the cursor at the end of Line 2—after the **stop();** action—and press Enter. Flash adds Line 3 to the Script pane.

   ▸ In Lines 3 and 4, type

   // Declare Stage instances

   var enterBtn:SimpleButton;

   After you type the colon (**:**), code hints appear. When the code item you want highlights, press Enter to complete it, or keep typing to complete the code manually. If you use the code hint to enter **SimpleButton**, remember to type a semicolon (**;**) at the end of the line. Flash automatically creates an import statement in a new Line 1 **F**

   import flash.display.SimpleButton;

   and a blank Line 2, which pushes the text you just typed to Lines 5 and 6 **G**.

```
1  // Pause the movie on Frame 1
2  stop();
3  |
```

```
1  import flash.display.SimpleButton;
2
3  // Pause the movie on Frame 1
4  stop();
5  // Declare Stage instances
6  var enterBtn:SimpleButton;
```

F When you declare a Stage instance, Flash adds an **import** statement to the head of your script. If the script currently has no **import** statement, Flash adds it to Line 1 and adds a blank Line 2 to visually separate the **import** statements from the rest of the script. If the script already has **import** statements, Flash adds the new **import** statement in the line below the existing statements.

G Declaring a Stage instance.

```
1  import flash.display.SimpleButton;
2
3  // Pause the movie on Frame 1
4  stop();
5  // Declare Stage instances
6  var enterBtn:SimpleButton;
```

Defining the event handler.

```
1    import flash.display.SimpleButton;
2    import flash.events.MouseEvent;
3
4    // Pause the movie on Frame 1
5    stop();
6    // Declare Stage instances
7    var enterBtn:SimpleButton;
8    // Event handlers
9    function handleClick(pEvent:MouseEvent
     ):void
```

I Defining the body of the event-handler function.

```
9    function handleClick(pEvent:MouseEvent
     ):void
10   {
11
12   }
```

Wide Scripts—Narrow Columns

A single line of ActionScript can be quite long. You can resize the Script pane of Flash's Actions panel so that a lot of code fits on one line, but we can't resize the columns in this book; so for longer lines of code, the text has to wrap. In the Script figures, such as **H**, the line numbers make it clear where you should type a return to begin a new line. In the numbered steps of a task, when a column is too narrow, we'll use a small right arrow to indicate code that runs over to a new line simply because the column is too narrow. You would enter the following code, for example, as a single line of script, pressing the Enter key only after the word *void*.

```
function handleClick(
→ pEvent:MouseEvent):void
```

4. To create the event-handler function, with the cursor at the end of Line 6 press Enter, and in new Lines 7 and 8 type

```
// Event handlers
function handleClick(
→ pEvent:MouseEvent):void
```

After you type the colon (:), code hints appear again. The code inside the parentheses, called a *parameter,* provides information about where the event comes from (**pEvent**) and what kind of event it is (**MouseEvent**); a colon separates these two pieces of information. Once you complete typing **MouseEvent)**, Flash inserts a new Line 2:

```
import flash.events.MouseEvent;
```

This pushes the code you just entered to Lines 8 and 9 **H**.

5. To create the body of the event-handler function, with the cursor at the end of Line 9 press Enter, and in new Line 10 type

```
{
```

and then press Enter again.

Flash automatically creates paired braces spanning Lines 10–12 (see the sidebar "The Importance of Paired Braces") **I**.

Continues on next page

6. Do the following to make sure the event is triggered by **enterBtn**:

▸ With the cursor indented in Line 11, type

    if(pEvent.target == enterBtn)

▸ Press Enter.

▸ With the cursor indented in Line 12, type

    {

and press Enter to insert paired braces in Lines 12–14.

You have just created what's known as a *conditional statement*. (See the sidebar "How to Use the If Statement" in this chapter.) Flash executes the code within the braces only if the specified condition is met. In this case, you are checking whether the event's target matches the button instance you want to control with your script (**enterBtn**) ❶.

❶ Make sure the event was triggered by **enterBtn**.

```
9    function handleClick(pEvent:MouseEvent
     ):void
10   {
11       if(pEvent.target == enterBtn)
12       {
13
14       }
15   }
```

The Importance of Paired Braces

For scripts to run correctly, every opening brace must have a matching closing brace. When you've chosen the Automatic Close Brace option as an ActionScript Preference setting, Flash helps ensure that happens. To activate the feature, In the ActionScript category of the Preferences dialog, in the Editing section, select the Automatic Close Brace checkbox. When you type an opening brace (**{**) into the Script pane of the Actions panel and press Enter, Flash immediately cre-

```
9    function handleClick(pEvent:MouseEvent):void
10   {
11       |
12   }
```

❶ When Automatic Close Brace is selected in Preferences (as it is by default), each time you enter an opening brace, Flash adds the closing brace. The opening and closing braces appear on their own lines, and the cursor winds up on a blank line between the two, with the proper indent for the braces' current nesting level.

ates paired braces spanning three lines ❶. The opening-brace character appears in the line where you typed it (say, Line 10), then comes a blank line (11), and the closing brace appears in the following line (12). After entering the paired braces, Flash puts the cursor in the blank line (11) and creates tabbed indents appropriate to the nesting level of the braces. By isolating each brace on its own line and adding indents, Flash provides visual feedback about the code—reminding you that it is part of the function defined within the pair of braces. (To learn more about the construction of functions, see the sidebar "Functions Explained" in this chapter.)

L Here's the completed event handler.

```
9    function handleClick(pEvent:MouseEvent
     ):void
10   {
11       if(pEvent.target == enterBtn)
12       {
13           // Handle the event
14           nextFrame();
15       }
16   }
```

```
17   // Register events
18   enterBtn.ad
           ○  upState : DisplayObject - SimpleButton
           ○  useHandCursor : Boolean - SimpleButton
           ○  visible : Boolean - DisplayObject
           ○  width : Number - DisplayObject
           ○  x : Number - DisplayObject
           ○  y : Number - DisplayObject
           ○  z : Number - DisplayObject
           ○  addEventListener(type:String, listener:Function, useCapture:B◀ ▼
```

M As you enter code in the Script pane, the code-hint window suggests code items you might want. When the item you want appears highlighted, press Enter to add it to the Script pane.

Anatomy of a MouseEvent

Users have several ways to interact with a button in a Flash movie. They can move the mouse into and out of the active area of a button; they can click and release inside the active area; they can click inside the active area and, while still holding down the mouse button, roll outside the area; and so on. The code **MouseEvent.CLICK** describes one specific button event. The **MouseEvent** part tells Flash that the event to watch for is generated by an input device (like a mouse, graphics pen, touch screen, or touch tablet); the **CLICK** part tells Flash to notice when the user presses and then releases inside the active area of a button.

7. With the cursor indented in Line 13, type the code for Lines 13 and 14, as shown in **L**.

After you type the opening parenthesis, a code-hint window opens; just keep typing. Flash uses double indents in Lines 13 and 14 to visually remind you that this code is inside the braces and is part of the **if** statement.

The **nextFrame();** action will advance the playhead by one frame.

8. To start registering the event, place the cursor at the end of Line 16, press Enter, and in Lines 17 and 18 type

// Register events

enterBtn.addEventListener();

After you type the period, a code-hint window opens showing a list of action statements. As you type more characters, the statements in the list that start with those characters highlight. After you type the letters **ad**, the statement **addEventListener** followed by a list of parameters highlights **M**.

9. Press Enter (or double-click the statement) as soon as the desired statement highlights. Flash adds **addEventListener(** to the script and opens another code-hint window. Ignore the second window and type

);

to complete the statement.

Continues on next page

10. To finish registering the event, do the following:

- In Line 18, position the cursor within the parentheses.
- Then type

MouseEvent.CLICK, handleClick

After you type the period (**.**) the code-hint window appears. After you type the comma (**,**) a parameter-hint window opens; ignore this window and continue typing the rest of the code. The code **MouseEvent.CLICK** tells Flash which of the possible button events you want your event handler to listen for. (See the sidebar "Anatomy of a MouseEvent.")

The code **handleClick** points to the event-handler function you created in the preceding steps; it must match the text that follows the keyword **function** in Line 9.

You just programmed your first button event. The completed script should look like **N**. It's time to see your work in action.

11. Choose Control > Test Scene or press Option-Command-Return (OS X) or Ctrl-Alt-Enter (Win).

Flash publishes the movie and opens the SWF file in Flash Player. You see the text *Frame 1* and a button. Click the button, and the text *Frame 2* appears. Flash has moved the playhead to Frame 2 in response to your clicking the button, just as you requested via Action-Script. Each click of the button moves the playhead forward one frame until the playhead reaches Frame 5.

12. Save your document as a template for use throughout this chapter, and name it ButtonActionsMaster.

13. Close the document.

Ⓝ The completed frame script for controlling a button (this script becomes part of the ButtonActionsMaster template).

```
1    import flash.display.SimpleButton;
2    import flash.events.MouseEvent;
3
4    // Pause the movie on Frame 1
5    stop();
6    // Declare Stage instances
7    var enterBtn:SimpleButton;
8    // Event handlers
9    function handleClick(pEvent:MouseEvent
     ):void
10   {
11       if(pEvent.target == enterBtn)
12       {
13           // Handle the event
14           nextFrame();
15       }
16   }
17   // Register events
18   enterBtn.addEventListener(
     MouseEvent.CLICK, handleClick);
```

TIP If you don't get the expected result when you test the movie, try checking the syntax. (See the section "Previewing Actions at Work" in this chapter.)

TIP The code-hint window doesn't stop you from typing, but it ensures that the actions you enter are spelled correctly. When the code-hint window appears, you can continue entering text by hand.

TIP You just created a template with a script for programming buttons. You can use this script over and over again, modifying it to meet different situations as needed.

Instance Names: Best Practice

The name of an *instance* of an object on the Stage is an identifier that may wind up as part of a script. To prevent scripting problems, make sure instance names contain no spaces or characters that have special meaning in ActionScript. For example, you should avoid slashes or the equals sign. To be safe, use only letters, numbers, and underscore characters. Ideally, instance names should start with a lowercase letter.

When you name instances of button symbols, movie-clip symbols, and text fields, you can give Flash extra information about the object being named. Flash uses that information to assist you—giving you code hints as you type in the Actions panel.

To activate the code-hint feature for specific objects, you need to declare variables. That creates a connection between an *identifier*—a script element that describes the type of object—and the instance name you've created for that object on the Stage. To declare a variable that identifies an instance, type the keyword **var** followed by a space, then type the instance name you've created for the object, then a colon, and then enter the identifier for the type of object. For example, the lines

```
var startLesson:SimpleButton;
var circle:MovieClip;
var message:TextField;
```

identify a button instance named **startLesson**, a movie-clip instance named **circle**, and a text field named **message**.

Import Statements Explained

Classes are pieces of code that define the functionality of the elements you use in Flash. Action-Script 3.0's built-in elements rely on built-in classes. The built-in button and movie-clip symbols, for example, rely on the classes **SimpleButton** and **MovieClip.** (Advanced ActionScripters can also define new elements, for which they create custom classes.) A script that refers to a class—either built-in or custom—needs to include information about how to access the code that defines the class. In the section "Programming Buttons with Frame Scripts" in this chapter, you did that when you used code hints, which automatically add import statements at the head of the script.

ActionScript groups classes with related functionality together in packages. Let's look at the **import** statement for a button symbol:

```
import flash.display.SimpleButton;
```

The statement gives Flash the path to the required class code: **SimpleButton** is the name of the class, while **flash.display** describes the package. As a rule of thumb, all the classes built into the Flash Player are in the **flash** package; further divisions group similar classes, such as **.display** for interface elements and **.events** for events.

Event Handlers Explained

In ActionScript, as in English, the term *event* refers to something that happens, such as a user clicking a button. An *event handler* is a specific type of action statement, called a *function,* that describes what should happen in your Flash creation when a specific event occurs.

Events can be generated by humans or by the internal workings of your Flash creations. This chapter focuses on *user interactions,* events generated by people viewing and using your Flash content. (Some common user events are clicking a button, entering text, or swiping a finger across the screen.) Events not generated by users also affect the way a Flash movie runs, and you can write scripts that respond to such events. (Some common nonuser events are when a movie finishes loading onto the user's computer or when the playhead advances to the next frame.)

Scripting for Interactivity: Registering and Handling Events

To make your Flash creation respond to a specific user interaction (an event), you must create a script that does two things: *register to receive* the event created by that interaction, and *handle the event.* Handling an event means creating a routine for Flash to use only after the event takes place—the routine is known as an *event handler.* Registering an event means writing a script that connects the object that triggers the event (for example, a button) with the event handler.

Code for handling an event takes the following format:

```
function handleEvent(event)
{
    if(event.target == eventSource)
    {
        // Handle event...
    }
}
```

The event-handler function named **handleEvent** waits for an event to happen. If the event is triggered by the specified **eventSource**, the event handler will carry out its instructions. **handleEvent** represents the name you'll create for this specific situation. The **eventSource** might be a button instance, a button component, or a movie-clip instance. (For more technical details, see the sidebars "How to Use the If Statement" and "Functions Explained" in this chapter.)

Code for registering for an event takes the following format:

```
eventSource.addEventListener(eventName, handleEvent);
```

Here **eventSource** represents the object that will be the source of the event; **eventName** represents the event itself. The precise code depends on the source object—a **click** event, for example, can be generated by a button instance. (The code **eventName** represents actions for the objects you'll work with in this chapter and are built into ActionScript 3.0.) Finally, **handleEvent** represents the function you created for handling the event.

How to Use the If Statement

Often when you create Flash content, you want one thing to happen under certain conditions, and something else to happen if those conditions aren't met. Your script needs to take different paths depending on the state of affairs.

One way to accomplish this is by using the **if** *statement,* which takes this format:

```
if(condition)
{
    action();
}
```

Here's a real-world example:

```
if(numLives == 0)
{
    gotoAndStop("gameOver");
}
```

An **if** statement consists of the keyword **if**, followed by an opening parenthesis, then a condition that is either true or false, a closing parenthesis, and then a list of statements between braces. These statements execute only if the condition is true.

A condition could be a comparison. You might, for example, compare two items to see if they are equal or if the first is greater than the second. To script a comparison, you use an *operator* (a symbol or symbols) that describes the comparison. In ActionScript, the operator used to check for equality consists of two equals signs (**==**). ActionScript uses a single equals sign (**=**) to assign a value (for example, to say a rectangle's width is 1 inch), never to compare.

The most common, and important, comparison operators are as follows:

>   greater than

≥   greater than or equal to

<   less than

≤   less than or equal to

≠   not equal to

When you check for a condition, you may want to run one block of code when the condition is met, and a different block of code when it's not. You could write two separate **if** statements or use an **if-else** statement. **if-else** statements take the format

```
if(condition)
{
    // Code
}
else
{
    // Other code
}
```

Finally, it is also possible to link up multiple conditions in an **if-else-if-else** statement using the following format:

```
if(foodInFridge)
{
    // Eat at home
}
else if(haveMoney)
{
    // Go out
}
else
{
    // Call a friend
}
```

Functions Explained

A *function* groups a number of actions together under a single name. When the function name appears in a script, Flash executes that group of actions. The basic format looks like this:

```
function functionName():Type
{

    // Function code

}
```

The code block always starts with the *keyword* **function**. Next comes the function's name, represented here by **functionName**. (You get to create your function name, so make it descriptive.) Immediately following the function's name is a pair of parentheses.

Next comes a colon (**:**) that separates the function's name from its *type*. In this example, the code for type is represented by **Type.** The type defines what kind of result the function will have. To understand the purpose of type, imagine a restaurant-tip calculator; it needs to return numbers in the result (as opposed to letters, for example). A tip-calculator function would have **Number** as the type. The most common type for functions, however, is **void**, meaning, "there is no result." Actions that control Timeline playback, for example, have **void** as the type.

The braces (**{}**) enclose code that describes what the function actually does. Flash carries out the instructions within those braces only when certain conditions are met; in our example, this is when a user clicks the calculate-tip button.

Quite often, a function needs more information to operate; parameters convey that information. The tip-calculator function needs to know the cost of the meal. When you set up a function that requires parameters, the format changes slightly:

```
function functionName(param:Type, nextParam:Type):Type
{

    // Code

}
```

When a function has multiple parameters, the parameter names still go between the parentheses after the function name, but you must separate the names with commas.

Each parameter also has a type, just as the function has one.

```
1   import flash.display.SimpleButton;
2   import flash.events.MouseEvent;
```

A Click the Check Syntax button in the Actions panel to have Flash help you find syntax errors in your code.

Window	
Duplicate Window	⌥⌘K
Toolbars	▶
Timeline	⌥⌘T
Motion Editor	
✓ Tools	⌘F2
✓ Properties	⌘F3
Library	⌘L
Common Libraries	▶
Motion Presets	
Project	⇧F8
Actions	⌥F9
Code Snippets	
Behaviors	⇧F3
✓ Compiler Errors	⌥F2
Debug Panels	▶
	⌥F3

B In Document Editing mode, choose Window > Compiler Errors to open the Compiler Errors panel.

Previewing Actions at Work

To see your scripts in action, you need to view the movie in Flash Player. You can do this by publishing the movie (see Chapter 17) or by using one of the test modes. Test mode is an abbreviated form of publishing a movie while still working in the authoring environment. To preview and test your scripts safely, follow a three-step procedure: (1) save your work; (2) check the script's syntax; and (3) test the movie.

To check the script's syntax:

1. With the document containing your script open, select the keyframe with the script you want to check, and view it in the Script pane of the Actions panel.

2. In the toolbar above the Script pane, click the Check Syntax button ✔, or press Command-T (OS X) or Ctrl-T (Win) **A**.

   Flash runs its compiler (see the sidebar "What Is a Compiler?") to check the selected code for errors of syntax. (See the sidebar "ActionScript Syntax Basics" in this chapter.) The compiler beeps to indicate that the check is complete.

3. Access the Compiler Errors panel. If it's not open, choose Window > Compiler Errors, or press Option-F2 (OS X) or Alt-F2 (Win) **B**.

Continues on next page

4. Review the contents of the panel to see the results of the syntax check.

The number of syntax errors found appears in the lower-left corner of the panel. Within the main body of the panel, a separate entry describes each error 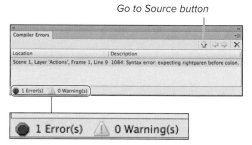.

5. If the selected code contains errors, do one of the following:

▸ Visually review the code in the Script pane and correct the errors you find.

▸ In the Compiler Errors panel, select the error and click the Go to Source button ⬆. Flash opens the Actions panel and highlights the line where the error occurred. Correct the error and repeat Step 2.

Flash generally refuses to run scripts with errors; you need to correct them all before you move on.

TIP Common scripting errors include missing, misplaced, or doubled commas, colons, parentheses, braces, and semicolons. Paired items, such as parentheses and braces, must have equal numbers of opening and closing elements, and they must be nested correctly. (See the sidebar "ActionScript Syntax Basics" in this chapter.) The ActionScript preference setting Automatic Close Brace helps you avoid this particular pitfall.

TIP A script that produces no errors doesn't necessarily do what you want it to do. The syntax check determines if your script follows the rules, but the compiler doesn't check the logic, and doesn't know what you intended the script to do.

Go to Source button

Total number of errors

C The Compiler Errors panel shows details about the errors in your script. When a syntax check finds no errors, the count of Total Errors is 0. Although the panel is resizable, the text within each column doesn't wrap; you may need to resize the columns to see the full error message. You can select the error in the panel and click the Go to Source button ⬆ to go directly to the error in the Script pane of the Actions panel.

What Is a Compiler?

ActionScript is a computer language that lets scripters write instructions for the Flash Player to execute. Although it takes time to learn the language, it is human-readable. A computer's CPU, however, works only with 0's and 1's; it can't read ActionScript directly. A *compiler* translates code written in a computer language into instructions that the processing unit can read. In the case of Flash, ActionScript is compiled into compact byte-code that Flash Player understands.

D To test the full animation and interactivity of ActionScript scripts, you must export your movie—for example, by choosing Control > Test Movie > In Flash Professional, or Control > Test Scene.

To test scripts:

- Choose Control > Test Movie > In Flash Professional (or Control > Test Scene), or press Option-Command-Return (OS X) or Ctrl-Alt-Enter (Win) **D**.

  Flash exports the movie (or scene) to a Flash Player file, adding the .swf extension (or the scene name plus the .swf extension) to the filename and using the current Publish settings. (For more information on Publish Settings, see Chapter 17.) During export, Flash displays the Exporting SWF Movie dialog.

  When it finishes exporting the movie, Flash opens the SWF file in Flash Player so you see the movie in action. The buttons and movie clips in the test window are all live, so you can see how they interact with the viewer's mouse actions. Any scripts you've created will run.

  When you finish testing, exit the Player by clicking the movie window's close button (OS X) or close box (Win). Flash returns you to the document-editing environment.

TIP Sometimes even when a script comes through the syntax check without errors, it has errors that show up when you test the movie. Flash opens the Output panel as soon as it encounters one of these *runtime errors*. These may occur, for example, when you try to target an object that doesn't exist, such as if you typed enerBtn as the instance name instead of enterBtn. The script still follows the syntax rules but fails to find the instance when it runs.

TIP To test the interactivity of a symbol—for example, a movie clip—choose Control > Test Scene while you are working on the symbol in Symbol Editing mode. Flash publishes just the symbol and the items nested within that symbol.

Modifying and Extending Button Scripts

When it comes to learning scripting, the first steps are often the most difficult, while subsequent steps expand on what you've already learned. Earlier, you set up a frame script that controlled a button on the Stage. In this section, that script becomes a stepping stone to creating different kinds of interactivity.

To create multiple actions in an event handler:

1. Using the ButtonActionsMaster template you created in the section "Programming Buttons with Frame Scripts," earlier in this chapter, open a new document.

   ButtonActionsMaster creates a five-frame document with identifying text for each frame, and one button instance. It also contains a **stop** action in Keyframe 1, and a script that activates the button for interactivity.

2. In the Timeline, in the Actions layer, select Keyframe 1 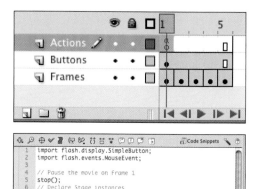.

3. To print a message in the Output window, place the cursor at the end of Line 14, press Enter, and type the code for Line 15 as shown in **B**.

   The block of code that makes up the event handler now contains two statements. The **nextFrame** statement moves the playhead to the next frame. The **trace** statement tells Flash to print a message to the Output window. (Here, Flash builds the message out of the words inside the quotes plus the number of the frame where the playhead is currently.)

A When you select a frame that contains actions, the script for that frame appears in the Actions panel.

B Adding the trace action to the event handler.

```
9    function handleClickm(pEvent:MouseEvent)
     :void
10   {
11       if(pEvent.target == enterBtn)
12       {
13           // Handle the event
14           nextFrame();
15           trace("Click! New frame: " +
             currentFrame);
16       }
17   }
```

Before clicking the button

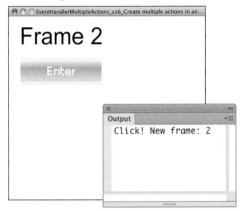

After clicking the button

C When you test a movie, the Output window displays your trace messages. For this movie, clicking the button creates a trace message.

D Sending the playhead to a frame number.

```
 9   function handleClick(pEvent:MouseEvent)
     :void
10   {
11      if(pEvent.target == enterBtn)
12      {
13         // Handle the event
14         gotoAndStop(5);
15         trace("Click! New frame: " +
           currentFrame);
16      }
17   }
```

4. Save the document as EventHandler-MultipleActions.fla.

5. Check the script's syntax and correct any errors.

6. Choose Control > Test Scene or press Option-Command-Return (OS X) or Ctrl-Alt-Enter (Win).

   Your movie opens in a Flash Player window. Each time you click the button, the words *Click! New frame:* appear in the Output panel, followed by the current frame number **C**. If the Output panel isn't visible, Flash opens it for you.

To send the playhead to a specific frame:

1. To use the script created in the preceding task as a building block, create a new copy of the document EventHandlerMultipleActions.fla (which you created earlier) by choosing File > Save As. Name the copy GoToFrame.fla.

2. In the Timeline, select Keyframe 1 of the Actions layer.

3. In the Script pane, in Line 14, select the code

   ```
   nextFrame();
   ```

   and replace it with

   ```
   gotoAndStop(5);
   ```

   Be sure to keep the code's original indentation. Instead of moving the playhead forward one frame at a time, the **gotoAndStop** action tells the playhead to jump to the frame number specified in parentheses.

4. Save the file, check the syntax (Line 14 of the script should match **D**) correct any errors, then test the movie. (See "Previewing Actions at Work.")

Continues on next page

Your movie opens in a Flash Player window. When you click the button, the movie jumps to Frame 5, and the message in the Output window confirms it.

To create a frame label:

1. Create a copy of the preceding task's document (GoToFrame.fla) and name it CreateFrameLabel.fla.

2. In the Timeline, create a new layer above the Actions layer, name it Labels, and lock it **E**.

   Having the Labels layer at the top helps you organize the Timeline. You can use labels to indicate the sections of your Movie.

3. Select Frame 3 of the Labels layer and insert a blank keyframe—for example, by choosing Insert > Timeline > Blank Keyframe.

4. With the new blank keyframe selected, access the Frame Property inspector; in the Label section, in the Name field, enter `myLabel` **F**.

5. To confirm the label, press Enter or click outside the field. In the Timeline a little red flag appears in Keyframe 3 of the Labels layer. Flash displays as much of your label as there's room for in the keyframe span **G**.

6. Position the playhead in Frame 5, but don't select a frame.

7. Insert a number of in-between frames (for example, by pressing F5) to make the span large enough to display the full label.

   Frame labels help you organize your Timeline. They are most effective when you can read them in the Timeline, rather than having to check the Property inspector.

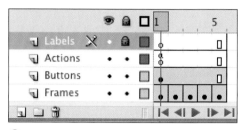

E A Labels layer lets you make notes in the Timeline about what's happening in different frames. To avoid accidentally placing graphic content on the Stage in the Labels layer, lock it. You can still add keyframes and labels to a locked layer.

Properties	Library	
	Frame	

▽ **LABEL**

Name: `myLabel`

Type: Name ▼

F Enter frame-label text in the Name field of the Frame Property inspector's Label section.

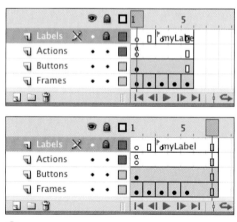

G Frame labels appear truncated if the keyframe span is too short to display the full text (top). To gain the full benefit of using frame labels as visual aids, expand the span by adding in-between frames (bottom).

H Sending the playhead to a frame label.

```
 9   function handleClick(pEvent:MouseEvent)
     :void
10   {
11       if(pEvent.target == enterBtn)
12       {
13           // Handle the event
14           gotoAndStop("myLabel");
15           trace("Click! New frame: " +
             currentFrame);
16       }
17   }
```

Why Target Frame Labels?

When using a **gotoAndStop** or **gotoAnd-Play** action, you can enter a frame number or a frame label. There's an advantage to using frame labels. If you ever add or remove frames from the type of movie-clip button you learned to create in Chapter 14, the frame numbers for the button states may change. If they do, you must go back into the script to update the frame numbers. If you target the frame by label, you never need to update the script to accommodate changes to frame numbers. In addition, targeting frame labels helps you preserve the correct interactivity of your Flash content should you decide to translate it to JavaScript using the Toolkit for CreateJS (see Chapter 17).

To send the playhead to a frame label:

1. Continuing with the file from the preceding task, select Keyframe 1 in the Actions layer, and access the Actions panel. Your script appears in the Script pane.

2. In the Script pane, in Line 14, select the code

    gotoAndStop(5);

    and replace it with

    gotoAndStop("myLabel");

    Be sure to keep the original indentation. With the **gotoAndstop** action, you can have the playhead go to a frame number or to a frame label.

3. Save the file, check the syntax (Line 14 of your script should match **H**), correct any errors, then test the movie.

    Your movie opens in a Flash Player window. When you click the button, the movie jumps to the frame that bears the label **myLabel** (in this case, Frame 3). The script also creates the **trace** message in the Output window.

TIP In the preceding task, you made the playhead move to a specific frame and stop playback. You can also make the playhead jump to a specific frame and resume playback from there. In Step 2, replace Line 14's gotoAndStop action with gotoAndPlay.

Working with Code Snippets

Flash CS6's Code Snippets panel lets you work with reusable pieces of ActionScript code. The panel's built-in snippets will be of special interest to anyone new to scripting. In addition to creating the necessary code for common tasks, each snippet creates comment code containing instructions on how to use and modify the snippet-created code to accomplish the results you want. You can also use the panel to build your own snippets.

There are 11 categories of built-in snippets. Actions snippets **A** create code for a variety of common interactivity tasks, from generating a random number to creating a custom mouse cursor. Timeline Navigation snippets **B** create code for controlling movie playback. Animation snippets **C** create code to animate objects programmatically instead of using the Timeline. Load and Unload snippets **D** create code for adding and removing assets from a movie at runtime. Audio and Video snippets **E** create code for controlling sounds and video clips. Event Handlers snippets **F** create code for responding to user input, such as clicking the mouse button.

Four of the Snippets categories will be of interest to anyone creating content for mobile devices. The Mobile Touch Events **G**, Mobile Gesture Events **H**, Mobile Actions **I**, and AIR for Mobile **J** snippets create code that enables your content to respond to events generated by touchscreens. Some of these snippets can also take data from accelerometers and display your geolocation. Snippets in the final category, AIR **K**, create code for common tasks in AIR desktop applications.

Continues on next page

Click to add code to current frame

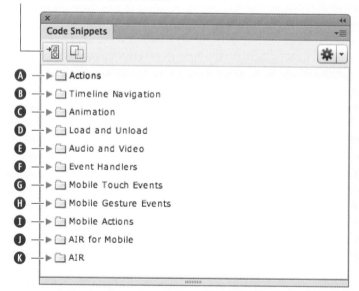

Working with Code Snippets *(continued)*

Here's a brief overview of how to use a predefined snippet.

- For code that works solely with the Timeline (for example, to pause the movie, or to respond to key-press events), select the frame where you want to add the code.

- For code that manipulates a movie-clip or button-symbol instance, select the instance on the Stage.

- Once you've selected a frame or symbol instance, access the Code Snippets panel, navigate to the snippet you want, and click its name. Two buttons appear next to the selected snippet ⬜ Stop a Movie Clip ⓘ {}. Click the Show Description button 🔲 to read a short description of the snippet.

- To create the code, you can double-click a snippet name (or select the name and click the Add to Current Frame button 🔲). If you've selected an unnamed instance on the Stage, the Set Instance Name dialog opens. For ActionScript to target a symbol instance, the instance must have a name. You can enter a new name in the dialog or use the default name that appears. Another option for creating the snippet code is to use the heads-up display (HUD). To open the HUD, click the Show Code button 🔲. The HUD lets you preview the snippet code and helps you assign instance names. Whether you double-click the snippet name to add the code or use the HUD, Flash places the code in a frame in an Actions layer in the Timeline (adding an Actions layer if the Timeline lacks one currently). The snippet code appears in the Script pane of the Actions panel.

- Access the Actions panel and review the comment lines in the snippet code ⓛ. They contain instructions on what the code does and, if necessary, how to modify the code to accomplish your particular task.

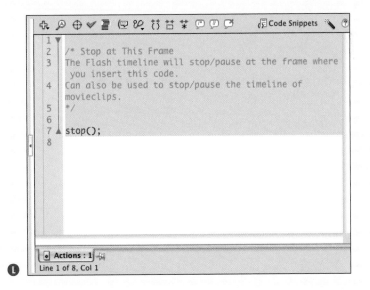

Choosing Events

As users interact with a button, their mouse movements trigger various events. Releasing the mouse button with a pointer still positioned over the button's active area triggers the **click** event. Rolling over and out of a button area triggers other events. To make a button react to these events, you must change your script to register for the desired event instead of **click**.

To handle an event when rolling over a button:

1. Open a new document using the ButtonActionsMaster template you created earlier in this chapter and save it as ButtonEvents.fla.

2. In the Actions layer, select Frame 1 and access the Actions panel. The template's script appears in the Script pane.

3. In Line 18, select the text

   `MouseEvent.CLICK`

   and replace it by typing

   `MouseEvent.ROLL_OVER`

4. Save the file, check the syntax (Lines 17 and 18 of your code should match Ⓐ), correct any errors, then test the movie.

   Your movie opens in a Flash Player window. Each time you roll over the button (move the pointer into the button's active area), the playhead moves one frame forward. Nothing happens when you click, other than the button showing the Down frame.

Ⓐ Switching from a **click** event to a **rollover** event.

```
17    // Register events
18    enterBtn.addEventListener(
      MouseEvent.ROLL_OVER, handleClick);
```

Registering for the **rollout** event.

```
17    // Register events
18    enterBtn.addEventListener(
      MouseEvent.ROLL_OUT, handleClick);
```

C Adding the second event handler.

```
14          nextFrame();
15      }
16  }
17  function handleRollOver(
    pEvent:MouseEvent):void
18  {
19      if(pEvent.target == enterBtn)
20      {
21          // Handle the event
22          gotoAndStop(2);
23      }
24  }
25  // Register events
```

TIP A faster way to replace the event is to delete the code **.CLICK** and retype the period to trigger the code-hint window. You can then select ROLL_OVER from the list and press Enter. You could also just delete **CLICK**, position the cursor after the period, and press the Code Hint button in the toolbar above the Script pane.

TIP In the preceding task, the event handler is still called **handleClick**. It would be more meaningful to rename it **handleRollOver**. Just make sure you change it in both Lines 9 and 18.

TIP If you want the script to react when rolling out of the button instead of over, in Line 18, select the text **MouseEvent.ROLL_OVER**, and replace it by typing **MouseEvent.ROLL_OUT** **B**.

To receive multiple events for a button:

1. Open a new document using the ButtonActionsMaster template you created earlier in this chapter and save it as ButtonMultiEvents.fla.

2. In the Timeline, in the Actions layer, select Keyframe 1 and access the Actions panel.

3. To define a second event handler, place the cursor at the end of Line 16 (after the closing brace) and press Enter to begin a new code block (the code that was originally on Lines 17 and 18 moves down).

   In Lines 17–24, type the code shown in **C**.

Continues on next page

4. To register for the **rollOver** event, place the cursor at the end of Line 26, press Enter, and in the new Line 27 type the code shown in **D**.

To receive multiple events from one button, you need to register for each event separately. You want the script to receive both events but react differently for each one. Defining a new event-handler function is a way to accomplish that.

5. Save the file, check the syntax (the complete script for the multi-event button should match **E**), correct any errors, then test the movie.

Your movie opens in a Flash Player window. Whenever you roll the pointer over the button, the playhead jumps to Frame 2, and when you click the button, the playhead moves to the next frame.

D Registering for the second event **(rollover)**.

```
25   // Register events
26   enterBtn.addEventListener(
     MouseEvent.CLICK, handleClick);
27   enterBtn.addEventListener(
     MouseEvent.ROLL_OVER, handleRollOver);
```

E The completed multi-event script.

```
1    import flash.display.SimpleButton;
2    import flash.events.MouseEvent;
3
4    // Pause the movie on Frame 1
5    stop();
6    // Declare Stage instances
7    var enterBtn:SimpleButton;
8    // Event handlers
9    function handleClick(pEvent:MouseEvent
     ):void
10   {
11       if(pEvent.target == enterBtn)
12       {
13           // Handle the event
14           nextFrame();
15       }
16   }
17   function handleRollOver(
     pEvent:MouseEvent):void
18   {
19       if(pEvent.target == enterBtn)
20       {
21           // Handle the event
22           gotoAndStop(2);
23       }
24   }
25   // Register events
26   enterBtn.addEventListener(
     MouseEvent.CLICK, handleClick);
27   enterBtn.addEventListener(
     MouseEvent.ROLL_OVER, handleRollOver);
```

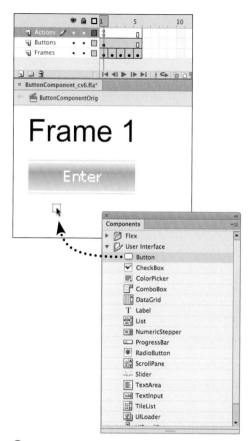

A Drag an instance of the button component from the Components panel to the Stage to add it to your movie.

B To target a component with ActionScript, you must give it an instance name. Note that the Object Type menu in the Property inspector reveals that the button component is actually a type of movie clip.

Button Components

Flash contains a selection of ready-made user interface (UI) elements. They can be found in the Components panel and include items such as RadioButton and ComboBox (for drop-down menus). Scripting the click-interactivity for button components and regular button symbols is similar.

To add a button component to your movie:

1. Open a new document using the ButtonActionsMaster template you created earlier in this chapter and save it as ButtonComponent.fla.

2. In the Timeline, in the Buttons layer, select Keyframe 1.

3. Access the Components panel and, from the User Interface category, choose Button. If the panel isn't visible, choose Window > Components, or press Command-F7 (OS X) or Ctrl-F7 (Win).

4. Drag an instance of the button component onto the Stage **A**.

5. Select the button-component instance on the Stage and access the Property inspector.

6. In the Instance Name field, enter **myComponent** **B**. You are now ready to create a script that makes the component carry out a task.

TIP You can modify a component's appearance by editing its skin.

To script a button component's interactivity:

1. Continuing with the file from the preceding task, select Keyframe 1 in the Actions layer and access the Actions panel. The template's script appears in the Script pane.

2. To enable code hints for the component instance, place the cursor at the end of Line 7, press Enter, and in new Line 8 type

    `var myComponent:Button;`

    A button component is more complex than a regular button, and enabling full code hints for components makes scripting them easier. Flash adds an **import** statement for the component in Line 3:

    `import fl.controls.Button;`

    This pushes the code you entered down to Line 9 **C**.

3. To create the event handler for the component, do the following:

    ▸ Place the cursor at the end of Line 18 (after the closing brace) and press Enter to begin a new code block.

    ▸ In Lines 19–26, type the code shown in **D**.

    Instead of moving the playhead to a new frame, this event handler hides the **enterBtn**.

C Declaring the variable for the button component.

```
1   import flash.display.SimpleButton;
2   import flash.events.MouseEvent;
3   import fl.controls.Button;
4
5   // Pause the movie on Frame 1
6   stop();
7   // Declare Stage instances
8   var enterBtn:SimpleButton;
9   var myComponent:Button;
10  // Event handlers
```

D The event handler for the button component.

```
16          nextFrame();
17      }
18  }
19  function handleComponent(
    pEvent:MouseEvent):void
20  {
21      if(pEvent.target == myComponent)
22      {
23          // Handle the event
24          enterBtn.visible = false;
25      }
26  }
```

E This code registers the **click** event handler of the button component.

```
27   // Register events
28   enterBtn.addEventListener(
     MouseEvent.CLICK, handleClick);
29   myComponent.addEventListener(
     MouseEvent.CLICK, handleComponent);
```

F Scripting a button component.

```
1    import flash.display.SimpleButton;
2    import flash.events.MouseEvent;
3    import fl.controls.Button;
4
5    // Pause the movie on Frame 1
6    stop();
7    // Declare Stage instances
8    var enterBtn:SimpleButton;
9    var myComponent:Button;
10   // Event handlers
11   function handleClick(
     pEvent:MouseEvent):void
12   {
13       if(pEvent.target == enterBtn )
14       {
15           // Handle the event
16           nextFrame();
17       }
18   }
19   function handleComponent(
     pEvent:MouseEvent):void
20   {
21       if(pEvent.target == myComponent)
22       {
23           // Handle the event
24           enterBtn.visible = false;
25       }
26   }
27   // Register events
28   enterBtn.addEventListener(
     MouseEvent.CLICK, handleClick);
29   myComponent.addEventListener(
     MouseEvent.CLICK, handleComponent);
```

4. Place the cursor at the end of Line 28 (after the semicolon), press Enter, and in new Line 29 type the code shown in **E**.

5. Save the file, check the syntax (the full script should match **F**), correct any errors, then test the movie.

Your movie opens in a Flash Player window. When you click the button component (named Label), Flash hides the button symbol (named Enter). When the button symbol is visible, clicking it still advances the Timeline as you originally scripted it to do.

Using One Event Handler for Multiple Events

Earlier in this chapter, you created individual event handlers for multiple events. Another way to deal with multiple events is to use one event handler with a parameter. With this technique, you create a script that examines the **pEvent** parameter that you've defined as part of the event-handler function to react differently for each button.

To add another button to be scripted:

1. Open a new document using the ButtonActionsMaster template you created earlier in this chapter. This document has one button instance—**enterBtn**—on the Stage. Save the document using the name MultiEventsOneHandler.fla.

2. Select the **enterBtn** instance and choose Edit > Duplicate—or press Command-D (OS X) or Ctrl-D (Win)—to create a new instance of the button. Position the duplicate so that it doesn't overlap the original button.

3. With the duplicate instance selected, access the Property inspector, and enter **prevBtn** in the Instance Name field 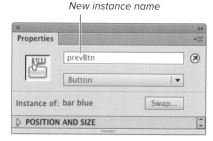.

   Now you have two buttons on the Stage that can be scripted to use the same event handler.

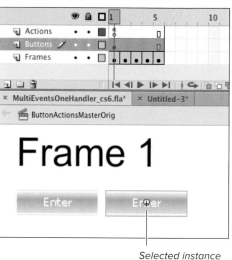

Selected instance

New instance name

Ⓐ To create an additional button quickly, duplicate the button instance, then modify the script. Be sure to give the duplicate a different instance name. You can later swap the symbol to change the graphics.

B Declaring the variable for the second button.

```
6    // Declare Stage instances
7    var enterBtn:SimpleButton;
8    var prevBtn:SimpleButton;
9    // Event handlers
```

C The interaction for the second button.

```
15            nextFrame();
16        }
17        else if(pEvent.target == prevBtn)
18        {
19            // Handle the prevBtn event
20            prevFrame();
21        }
22    }
```

D A single event handler for two buttons.

```
6    // Declare Stage instances
7    var enterBtn:SimpleButton;
8    var prevBtn:SimpleButton;
9    // Event handlers
10   function handleClick(pEvent:MouseEvent
     ):void
11   {
12       if(pEvent.target == enterBtn)
13       {
14           // Handle the event
15           nextFrame();
16       }
17       else if(pEvent.target == prevBtn)
18       {
19           // Handle the prevBtn event
20           prevFrame();
21       }
22   }
23   // Register events
24   enterBtn.addEventListener(
     MouseEvent.CLICK, handleClick);
25   prevBtn.addEventListener(
     MouseEvent.CLICK, handleClick);
```

To script the second button:

1. Continuing with the file from the preceding task, in the Timeline, in the Actions layer, select Keyframe 1 and access the Actions panel.

2. To create a variable for the second button (**prevBtn**), in the Action panel's Script pane, place the cursor at the end of Line 7, press Enter, and in new Line 8 type the code shown in **B**.

3. Place the cursor at the end of Line 16— after the closing brace (**}**)—and press Enter to create a new line.

   Be sure to place the cursor after the correct closing brace. The brace in Line 16 closes the **if** statement, while the brace in Line 17 closes the function.

4. To update the event handler for two buttons, in new Lines 17–21 type the code shown in **C**.

   This code extends the **if** statement to check for a second condition if the first condition is not met. The object of interest here is **prevBtn**. If **prevBtn** triggered the event, the script sends the playhead to the previous frame.

5. To register for the **click** event of the **prevBtn**, place the cursor at the end of Line 24, press Enter, and in new Line 25 type

   ```
   prevBtn.addEventListener(
    → MouseEvent.CLICK, handleClick);
   ```

6. Save the file, check the syntax (Lines 6–25 should match **D**), correct any errors, then test the movie.

   Clicking the **enterBtn** button advances the playhead one frame. Clicking the **prevBtn** sends the playhead back one frame.

Scripting Movie Clips to Act As Buttons

Flash's button symbols provide the most basic visual requirements for a button, giving you the options for different looks in the Up, Over, and Down states. Sometimes, however, you may need additional states. In a slide show, for example, the Next button should be disabled (and should look disabled) when you are viewing the final slide.

In Chapter 14, you set up a movie-clip symbol for use as a button that has a disabled state. In the following task, you learn to program that symbol to work as a button.

To enable button behavior for the movie-clip button:

1. Open the file named MyOwnBtn.fla that you created in Chapter 14, in the section "Creating Movie-Clip Buttons." This document contains a movie-clip symbol called `MovieClipBtn`.

2. On the Stage, double-click the instance of the `MovieClipBtn` symbol to enter symbol-editing mode.

   The symbol's Timeline has three layers—Actions, Labels, and ButtonGraphics. The symbol has keyframes labeled `_up`, `_over`, `_down`, and `Disabled`, and graphics that make each state obvious 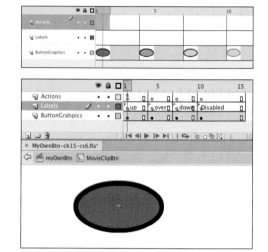.

3. In the symbol's Timeline, select Keyframe 1 in the Actions layer 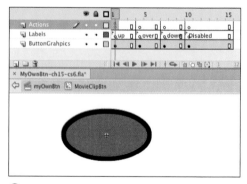.

A This movie-clip symbol has keyframes for four button states: the standard three—Up, Over, and Down—plus a fourth, Disabled. Each keyframe has an appropriate frame label. With the Preview selected in the Timeline's Frame View menu (top) you can see the graphic content of each button state. To see the frame labels, set the Timeline to one of the non-preview modes (bottom).

B To prevent the movie-clip button from displaying its frames as an animation, you need to add a stop action to the Timeline of the button itself. Add it to Frame 1 of the Actions layer.

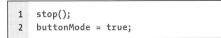 The code to activate button behavior.

```
1  stop();
2  buttonMode = true;
```

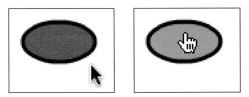

By labeling the frames of your movie-clip button **_up**, **_over**, and **_down**, you can take advantage of built-in ActionScript to give users feedback about the button. Adding the **buttonMode = true;** statement to the button's script tells Flash to change the pointer to the hand icon when it moves over the graphic content in a frame with one of those labels.

4. To pause the movie-clip button, in the Script pane of the Actions panel, in Line 1, type

   stop();

   By default, movie clips play at runtime. While that makes sense for animations, a button should stay in its Up state until the user interacts with it.

5. To activate button behavior for the movie clip, with the cursor at the end of Line 1 press Enter, and in new Line 2 type

   buttonMode = true;

   Until you do that, the movie clip doesn't know it's supposed to act like a button, despite the special frame labels you used.

6. Save your document, and check the syntax of your code (your script should match **C**).

7. Navigate back to the main Timeline— for example, by choosing Edit > Edit Document or pressing Command-E (OS X) or Ctrl-E (Win).

8. Choose Control > Test Scene, or press Option-Command-Return (OS X) or Ctrl-Alt-Enter (Win) .

   As the pointer rolls over the movie-clip button, it changes to a hand, and the playhead goes to the movie-clip's **_over** frame **D**. When you press the mouse button, the playhead goes to the **_down** frame—just as it does for a regular button.

   TIP If you want to try out your button without first returning to document-editing mode, choose **Control > Test Movie > In Flash Profes-sional. (Choosing Test Scene will not work.)**

To add a mouse event–handler that displays the disabled state:

1. Continuing with the file from the preceding task, select the **MovieClipBtn** instance on the Stage and access the Property inspector.

2. In the Instance Name field, enter **myBtn** 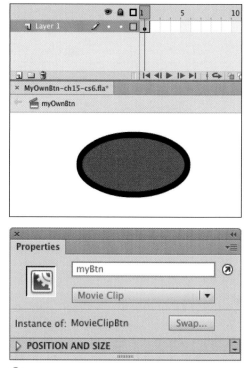.

3. In the Timeline of the document, create a new layer above the existing layer; name the new layer Actions. With multiple layers in the Timeline, it's a good idea to name them all. Name the layer containing the movie-clip button MC Button.

4. Select Keyframe 1 in the Actions layer, and access the Actions panel.

5. To document what you intend your script to do, in the Script pane, in Line 1, type

   `// Scripting a movie-clip button`

6. To pause the movie, with the cursor in Line 2, type **stop();** then press Enter to create a new line.

7. To create a variable for the symbol instance, in Lines 3 and 4 type

   `// Declare Stage instances`

   `var myBtn:MovieClip;`

   This activates code hints by telling Flash that the instance **myBtn** is a **MovieClip** object. Flash automatically creates an **import** statement in Line 1

   `import flash.display.MovieClip;`

   and the script you entered in this step moves down to Lines 5 and 6 **F**.

E To target the movie-clip button, you must name the instance in the Property inspector's Instance Name field.

F An import statement, a descriptive comment, pausing the Timeline, another descriptive comment, and declaring the Stage instance variable.

```
1   import flash.display.MovieClip;
2
3   // Scripting a movie-clip button
4   stop();
5   // Declare Stage instances
6   var myBtn:MovieClip;
```

G Adding the event handler.

```
1   import flash.display.MovieClip;
2   import flash.events.MouseEvent;
3
4   // Scripting a movie-clip button
5   stop();
6   // Declare Stage instances
7   var myBtn:MovieClip;
8   // Event handlers
9   function handleClick(pEvent:MouseEvent
    ):void
10  {
11     if(pEvent.target == myBtn)
12     {
13        myBtn.enabled = false;
14        myBtn.gotoAndStop("Disabled");
15     }
16  }
```

H The completed movie-clip button script.

```
1   import flash.display.MovieClip;
2   import flash.events.MouseEvent;
3
4   // Scripting a movie-clip button
5   stop();
6   // Declare Stage instances
7   var myBtn:MovieClip;
8   // Event handlers
9   function handleClick(pEvent:MouseEvent
    ):void
10  {
11     if(pEvent.target == myBtn)
12     {
13        myBtn.enabled = false;
14        myBtn.gotoAndStop("Disabled");
15     }
16  }
17  // Register events
18  myBtn.addEventListener(
    MouseEvent.CLICK, handleClick);
```

8. To define the event handler, with the cursor at the end of Line 6, press Enter to begin a new code block.

▸ Beginning in Line 7 type

```
// Event handlers

function handleClick(
    pEvent:MouseEvent):void

{

   if(pEvent.target == myBtn)

   {

      myBtn.enabled = false;

      myBtn.gotoAndStop("Disabled");

   }

}
```

After you enter **MouseEvent)** in Line 8, Flash automatically inserts an **import** statement in Line 2, followed by a blank line.

```
import flash.events.MouseEvent;
```

The code you just entered moves down. Line 9 defines the event handler. Line 11 makes sure the event was triggered by the button instance you intend, **myBtn**. Line 13 prevents the button from receiving any additional mouse events by setting the movie-clip instance's **enabled** property to **false**. Line 14 sends the playhead to the **Disabled** frame of the movie-clip (without the code in Line 13 the playhead would go back to the **_up** frame as soon as the user rolled out of the active movie-clip area) **G**.

9. To register for the click event, place the cursor at the end of Line 16, press Enter, and in new Lines 17 and 18 type the code shown in **H**.

Continues on next page

10. Save your document, check the syntax of your code, then choose Control > Test Scene, or press Option-Command-Return (OS X) or Ctrl-Alt-Enter (Win).

Your movie opens in a Flash Player window. The movie-clip button displays the **_up** frame. When you position the mouse pointer within the button, the button displays the **_over** frame. When you click the mouse button, the play-head moves to the **_down** frame. As soon as you release the mouse button, the playhead moves to the `Disabled` frame, and the movie-clip button no longer reacts to the mouse.

TIP The procedure for scripting interactive buttons and movie-clip buttons is identical. If you start a project using buttons, and later realize you need more functionality, you don't have to start over. You can replace the buttons with movie-clip buttons using the same instance names, and your code will still work. You can then add movie-clip–specific scripts to display additional states, as shown in the preceding task.

Using Buttons to Control Timelines

Most Flash creations employ a mixture of interface objects: button symbols, button components, and movie clips. You can script a button (or button component) to start and stop the playback of a movie clip, or make the playhead jump to a specific frame in a movie clip. The key is to specify the correct target path.

Scripting Nested Timelines

All Flash creations have a certain amount of structural complexity. Even a simple movie like the one created with ButtonActionsMaster has a hierarchy of nested objects. (The Timeline you see when you open a Flash document in the authoring environment is actually a movie-clip object, so any objects on this main Timeline are considered nested objects.)

But the structure gets really complex when you nest interactive objects inside other interactive objects—a button inside a movie clip, a movie clip inside a movie clip, a button inside a movie clip inside a movie clip, and so on.

A nested object is known as a *child object,* and the object containing that child is known as the *parent object.* As long as each parent and child has an instance name, it doesn't matter how complex the family relationship gets. You can create a script that manipulates any of the nested objects. The key is to identify the target object's place in the hierarchy of Timelines using a *target path.*

There are two types of target paths: *relative* and *absolute*. A relative target path starts with the target object and describes its relationship to other Timelines in the hierarchy—indicating, for example, that the target is me, or it's one level above me; or it's within me, one level down. An absolute target path starts with the highest-level Timeline and works its way down the hierarchy until it reaches the target object.

As if writing paths weren't already complicated, here's another detail to consider. ActionScript 3.0 has another type of interactive object, the *sprite*. A sprite is similar to a movie clip, but it has no Timeline and no frames. All of the animation and interactivity of a sprite happens because of scripting. Sprites can also be nested and have hierarchical relationships, and you use target paths to identify them. When you write target paths, you must distinguish between sprite objects and Timeline-based objects (movie clips) by using the code **Sprite()** or **MovieClip()**—as shown in the examples below. (In this book, we work only with Timeline-based objects.)

However, when you use the Actions panel's Insert Target Path button (see sidebar "Using Insert Target Path" in this chapter), Flash will insert the generic code **Object()** instead. This is technically correct and hides the differences between sprites and movie clips, but prevents you from getting code hints for actions like **gotoAndStop()**.

Continues on next page

Scripting Nested Timelines *(continued)*

To start a relative target path, simply type the instance name of the object you want to target, such as **animMc**.

A relative path isn't restricted to looking at objects contained within the current Timeline. You can also go one or more levels up or down. This is where the concept of parent and child comes into play.

Let's say you have a button with an instance name of **controlBtn** on the main Timeline where you've placed **animMc**. In the Timeline of **animMc**, you could type

```
MovieClip(parent).controlBtn
```

This path directs ActionScript to go one level up to the parent Timeline, the one containing **animMc** (in this example, it's the main Timeline) and access the instance named **controlBtn**. Whenever you use the code **parent** you must either distinguish between sprites and movie clips—by using **Sprite()** or **MovieClip()**—or hide the difference by using **Object()**.

To target child objects, use dot syntax (place a period between the parent object and its child). To direct ActionScript down a level, to access a movie-clip instance named **starMc** that's nested within **animMc**, the relative path would be **animMc.starMc**.

Optionally, you can start a relative target path with the code **this**. For example, **this.animMc.starMc** is the same as **animMc.starMc**.

An absolute path always starts at the main Timeline, which is also known as **root**. The format of an absolute target path for **starMC** looks like this:

```
MovieClip(root).animMc.starMc
```

Whenever you use the code **root** you must distinguish between sprites and movie clips—by using **Sprite()** or **MovieClip()**—or hide the difference by using **Object()**.

Using Insert Target Path

In the Actions panel, the toolbar above the Script pane displays an Insert Target Path button (⊕). This target-path tool is very helpful for creating both absolute and relative target paths. There is one caveat: the target-path tool creates incorrect relative paths when the Timeline panel has focus. As you prepare to insert a target path, make sure the Timeline doesn't have focus. Clicking a blank area of the Stage is an easy way to remove focus from the Timeline.

To add a target path to the Script pane, position the cursor at the location where you want to insert the code. Click the Insert Target Path button. The Insert Target Path dialog opens. As you click different objects in the dialog's representation of the Timeline hierarchy, the dialog's target-path field updates automatically. To determine which type of path to create, select the Absolute or Relative radio button at the bottom of the dialog. Once you have chosen the object you want to target and the type of path, click OK to add the path to the Script pane.

An example of an absolute path:

```
Object(root).oval
```

An example of a relative path:

```
Object(this.parent).oval
```

This format differs slightly from what you learned in the sidebar "Scripting Nested Timelines" in this chapter, using **Object()** instead of **MovieClip()**. Either code works; however, using **MovieClip()** gives you the added benefit of getting better code-hints when targeting **root** or **parent** directly.

To make a button that stops movie-clip playback:

1. Open a new ActionScript 3.0 Flash document. Add layers to create a three-layer document, and do the following:

   ▸ Name the top layer Actions.

   ▸ Name the second layer Buttons. In that layer, place a button-symbol instance at the upper-left corner of the Stage.

   ▸ Name the third layer MovieClips. In that layer, at the center of the Stage, place a movie-clip instance containing animation (for example, a simple classic tween or motion tween of a geometric shape that rotates and shrinks).

   ▸ Save the file and name it PauseClipControl.fla.

2. To prepare the instances for scripting, do the following:

   ▸ Access the Property inspector.

   ▸ Select the button, and in the Instance Name field, enter **controlBtn**.

   ▸ Select the movie clip, and in the Instance Name field, enter **animMc**.

3. In the Actions layer, select Frame 1 and access the Actions panel.

4. To comment your script and pause the main Timeline at startup, in the Script pane of the Actions panel, in Lines 1 and 2, type

   ```
   // Controlling a movie clip with
    a button
   stop();
   ```

Continues on next page

5. To enable code hints for the instances on the Stage, starting in Line 3 create the following variables:

// Declare Stage instances

var controlBtn:SimpleButton;

var animMc:MovieClip;

As you define the variables, Flash automatically inserts **import** statements in Lines 1 and 2 and adds a blank Line 3; the code you just entered moves down to Lines 6–8 **Ⓐ**.

6. To define an event handler that verifies the event source, starting in Line 9, type

// Event handler

function handleClick(
⇢ pEvent:MouseEvent):void

{

   if(pEvent.target == controlBtn)

   {

      // Handle event

   }

}

This defines an event handler that makes sure the event is triggered by **controlBtn**. After you enter **MouseEvent)**, Flash automatically creates an **import** statement in Line 3. The code you just entered moves down to Lines 10–17 **Ⓑ**.

Ⓐ This commented script pauses the Timeline and defines variables.

```
1   import flash.display.SimpleButton;
2   import flash.display.MovieClip;
3
4   // Controlling a movie clip with a
    button
5   stop();
6   // Declare Stage instances
7   var controlBtn:SimpleButton;
8   var animMc:MovieClip;
```

Ⓑ This script defines the event handler that checks for the event source.

```
2   import flash.display.MovieClip;
3   import flash.events.MouseEvent;
4
5   // Controlling a movie clip with a button
6   stop();
7   // Declare stage instances
8   var controlBtn:SimpleButton;
9   var animMc:MovieClip;
10  // Event handler
11  function handleClick(pEvent:MouseEvent
    ):void
12  {
13      if(pEvent.target == controlBtn)
14      {
15          // Handle event
16      }
17  }
```

C This code registers the **click** event of controlBtn.

```
18   // Register events
19   controlBtn.addEventListener(
     MouseEvent.CLICK, handleClick);
```

D The completed script pauses a clip when a button is clicked.

```
1    import flash.display.SimpleButton;
2    import flash.display.MovieClip;
3    import flash.events.MouseEvent;
4
5    // Controlling a movie clip with a button
6    stop();
7    // Declare Stage instances
8    var controlBtn:SimpleButton;
9    var animMc:MovieClip;
10   // Event handler
11   function handleClick(pEvent:MouseEvent
     ):void
12   {
13       if(pEvent.target == controlBtn)
14       {
15           // Handle event
16           animMc.stop();
17       }
18   }
19   // Register events
20   controlBtn.addEventListener(
     MouseEvent.CLICK, handleClick);
```

7. To register for the **controlBtn**'s **click** event, in Lines 18 and 19 type the code as in **C**.

   The main Timeline now receives the **click** event of the **controlBtn**, and you are ready to direct Flash to take control of the movie-clip instance **animMc**.

8. Place the cursor at the end of Line 15, press Enter, and in new Line 16 type

   animMc

   This is a relative target path: this script now aims from the main Timeline (where the script is located) to the **animMc** instance.

9. With the cursor at the end of Line 16, directly after the target path, type

   .stop();

   This **stop** action attached to the target path tells Flash to pause playback of the movie-clip instance named **animMc**.

10. Save the file, check the syntax (the code should match **D**), correct any errors, then test the movie.

    In the Flash Player window, the animation plays in a continuous loop. When you click the button, the animation pauses.

Linking to Other Web Pages

Flash gives you two ways to open new files by linking to URLs. You can select text on the Stage and turn it into a live link by entering a URL in the Link field in the Options section of the Text (Tool) Property inspector. Or you can use ActionScript to instruct Flash Player to open a URL. Both techniques let you open the new file in a different browser window or different frame of the current window.

To create a text link to a URL:

1. On the Stage, select the text that you want to be a link, and access the Property inspector.

   You can select individual letters or words using the text tool, or select an entire text field using the selection tool.

2. For TLF text, in the Advanced Character section, enter the desired URL in the Link field **A**.

A You can turn text into a live link for accessing web pages. Select the TLF text on the Stage (top). In the Advanced Character section of the Property inspector, type a URL in the Link field (middle). Flash creates a live link in the published Flash movie. Live-link text appears underlined in the authoring environment (bottom).

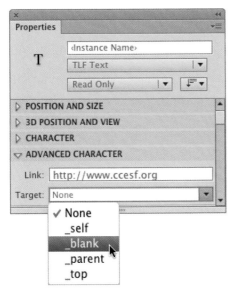

B The Target menu specifies how Flash should open the link's URL in a browser window.

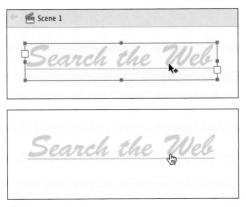

C The underlined TLF text (top) is a live link created in the Property inspector. In the published movie (bottom), the text is also underlined, and the hand pointer appears when you move the pointer into the text field.

3. To choose a method for displaying the specified URL in the browser window, from the Target pop-up menu B, choose one of the following:

None and **_blank** open the URL in a new browser window.

_self opens the URL in same frame of the browser window as that of the content being currently viewed.

_parent opens the URL in the parent of the current frame.

_top opens the URL in the top-level frame of the current browser window.

When you open the published HTML file from your hard drive and click the link to another website, you may get security errors. For links to work properly, you need to put the published files on a web server.

4. To try out your live link text, choose Control > Test Scene, or press Option-Command-Return (OS X) or Ctrl-Alt-Enter (Win).

When you move the pointer over the text, the hand pointer appears C; when you click the text, Flash opens the URL in the specified form of browser window.

TIP If you're creating your live link with Classic text, you'll find the Link field and Target menu in the Options section of the Text Property inspector.

To script a button that opens a web page:

1. Open a new document using the ButtonActionsMaster template you created earlier in this chapter, and save it as LinkBtn.fla.

   The Timeline has three layers: Actions, Buttons, and Frames.

2. To create the button that opens a new web page, do the following:

   ▸ In the Timeline, select Frame 5 of the Buttons layer, and insert a blank keyframe (for example, by choosing Insert > Timeline > Blank Keyframe).

   ▸ With Keyframe 5 of the Buttons layer selected, drag an instance of a button symbol to the Stage, and access the Property inspector.

   ▸ With the button instance selected on the Stage, in the Instance Name field, enter `linkBtn` 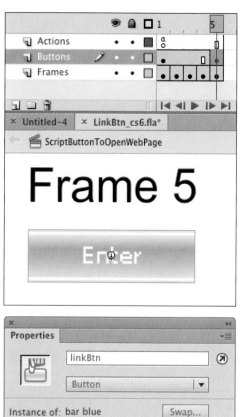.

3. In the Timeline, select Frame 5 of the Actions layer, insert a blank keyframe, and access the Actions panel.

   In preceding tasks you've always created scripts in Keyframe 1 that start working with objects in Frame 1. One way to create a script that relates to objects in a later frame is to add a blank keyframe in the Actions layer at that frame to hold the script ⓔ.

4. To create a variable that activates code hints, in the Script pane of the Actions panel, in Line 1 type

   `var linkBtn:SimpleButton;`

   Flash automatically adds an `import` statement in Line 1 and adds a blank Line 2.

ⓓ To target the button with ActionScript, the button must have an instance name. You create the instance name for the selected button in the Property inspector.

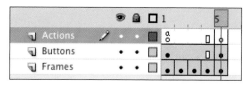

ⓔ You need not restrict yourself to creating scripts in Frame 1 of the Actions layer. When you want to script the actions of an object that appears in a keyframe at a later point in the movie, you can place the script in a keyframe at the same frame as the object. Here the button instance `linkBtn` is in Frame 5, so you would add a blank keyframe at Frame 5 of the Actions layer to hold the script.

Defining an event handler that checks for the event source.

```
1   import flash.display.SimpleButton;
2   import flash.events.MouseEvent;
3
4   var linkBtn:SimpleButton;
5   function handleLink(pEvent:MouseEvent
    ):void
6   {
7      if(pEvent.target == linkBtn)
8      {
9
10     }
11  }
```

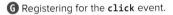 Registering for the **click** event.

```
10     }
11  }
12  linkBtn.addEventListener(
    MouseEvent.CLICK, handleLink);
```

5. To create the event handler that checks for the event source, place the cursor at the end of Line 3, press Enter, and in new Line 4 type

```
function handleLink(
→ pEvent:MouseEvent):void
{
   if(pEvent.target == linkBtn)
   {

   }
}
```

After you type **MouseEvent)** in Line 4, Flash automatically adds a second **import** statement in Line 2,

```
import flash.events.MouseEvent;
```

and pushes your code down to Lines 5–11. The code so far should match .

6. To register for the **click** event, press Enter at the end of Line 11 (after the closing brace), and in Line 12 type the code as in .

7. To create the network request, do the following:

▸ With the cursor indented in Line 9, type

```
var request:URLRequest =
→ new URLRequest("http://
→ www.peachpit.com");
```

Flash again adds an **import** statement in Line 3 as you enter this code, and pushes your code down to Line 10.

Replace the link to Peachpit with the URL you want to link to. In ActionScript 3.0, you need to create a **URLRequest** object with the URL to make any kind of external connection. Here the **URLRequest** is then stored in a custom variable called **request**.

Continues on next page

8. To create the code that tells Flash to execute the link, with the cursor at the end of Line 10 (after the semicolon), press Enter, and type

navigateToURL(request, "_blank");

The parameter **_blank** is the same type of method for opening a browser window that you chose from a menu in Step 3 of the first task in this section, "To create a text link to a URL." To use a different method, use the code **_self, _parent**, or **_top**; but be aware that you may need to create new security settings for those methods. (For more details, see the sidebar "A Note About Flash Player's Security Settings," in Chapter 17.)

9. Save the file, check the syntax (the code should match **H**), correct any errors, then test the movie.

The first button that appears is one that you scripted as part of the template document. Clicking this button advances the movie to the next frame. Click this button until you reach Frame 5. Clicking the button in Frame 5 makes the default browser open a new window or tab with the URL you specified.

TIP You don't always have to create scripts in a blank keyframe. Often the Actions layer's keyframe already exists with script for controlling another button instance. You can simply add the new script to the end of the existing script. In the preceding exercise, for example, try adding the web-page button to Keyframe 1. Create the script at the end of the script that was already in the ButtonActionsMaster document. The line numbers will be different, but the button should work just fine.

H Making a button link to another web page.

```
1   import flash.display.SimpleButton;
2   import flash.events.MouseEvent;
3   import flash.net.URLRequest;
4
5   var linkBtn:SimpleButton;
6   function handleLink(pEvent:MouseEvent
    ):void
7   {
8       if(pEvent.target == linkBtn)
9       {
10          var request:URLRequest =
            new URLRequest("http://
            www.peachpit.com");
11          navigateToURL(request,
            "_blank");
12      }
13  }
14  linkBtn.addEventListener(
    MouseEvent.CLICK, handleLink);
```

Adding Sound and Video

Adobe Flash Professional CS6 lets you incorporate sound and video in your projects to create a full multimedia experience. Sound in Flash can be an ongoing background element or a synchronized element that matches a particular piece of action. To add a sound, you import a sound-clip file to the library and then place an instance of the sound on the Stage. To add video, you import the video data and embed it into the Flash Timeline, or you add a component that displays external video files. Advanced scripters can use ActionScript to add and control sounds during playback or to display encoded video files as streaming video in their Flash creations. (Such scripting techniques, however, are beyond the scope of a *Visual QuickStart Guide*.) In all cases, the video data must be encoded in a format that's compatible with Flash; for embedded video, the file must be in FLV (Flash video) format. You can use Adobe Media Encoder CS6 (AME), which comes with Flash and is installed by default, to encode video files in an appropriate format.

In This Chapter

Importing Sounds

There are two commands for importing sounds: File > Import > Import to Stage, or File > Import > Import to Library. Both commands bring the sound file into the library for the current document. Neither actually places the sound, however. You must drag a copy of the sound from the Library panel to the Stage to make the sound available for assignment to a keyframe.

To import a sound file:

1. Open the file to which you want to add sounds.

2. Choose File > Import > Import to Stage, or press Command-R (OS X) or Ctrl-R (Win).

   or

   Choose File > Import > Import to Library.

   The first Import command of a work session requires some setup behind the scenes. A Preparing to Import progress bar appears before you see the File Import dialog.

Flashy Sounds

Flash CS6 comes with a common library of sound effects that you can use in your Flash movies. To access these sounds, choose Window > Common Libraries > Sounds. Flash opens a library containing 185 sounds. You use these sound assets just as you'd use sounds you imported to a document. Drag the sound asset from the Sounds common library to the Stage of your Flash document (see "Adding Sounds to Frames" in this chapter).

What Sound Formats Does Flash Import?

Flash deals only with *sampled sounds*—those that have been recorded digitally or converted to digital format. Flash imports files in AIFF format for OS X and in WAV format for Windows. For both platforms, Flash imports files in MP3 format and ASND format (a sound file format created by Adobe Soundbooth). In addition, with the combination of Flash CS6 and QuickTime 4 (or later versions), users on both platforms can import QuickTime movies containing just sounds (MOV, QT) and Sun AU files; Mac users can add import of WAV, Sound Designer II (SD2), and System 7 sounds (SND); and Windows users can add import of AIFF sounds. Any sounds you import or copy into a Flash document reside in the file's library.

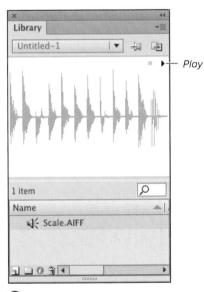

3. To view all sound files, in the Import dialog, from the Enable menu (OS X) or the Files of Type menu (Win), choose All Sound Formats **A**. To view sounds of only one format, choose a specific file format in the menu.

4. Navigate to the desired file, select it, and click Open. Flash imports the sound and places it in the library.

5. To preview the sound, select it in the library. The sound's waveform appears in the preview window **B**. Click the Play button in the preview window to listen to the selected sound.

A The Import dialog lets you bring sound files into Flash. To filter the files that appear in the dialog, choose a sound-file type that is appropriate for your platform from the menu of file types.

TIP Even when you choose Import to Stage (in Step 2), the sound winds up in the library. To use the sound, you must place it in a keyframe.

TIP Large sound files can take a long time to import. If you get tired of looking at the Importing progress bar, just click the Stop (OS X) or Cancel (Win) button to end the import process.

B Flash keeps sound files in the library. The waveform of a selected sound appears in the preview window. Click the Play button to hear the sound.

Adding Sounds to Frames

You can assign a sound to a keyframe the same way you place a symbol: by selecting the keyframe and then dragging a copy of the sound from an open Library panel (either that document's or another's) to the Stage. You can also assign any sound that resides in a document's library to a selected keyframe in that document by choosing the sound from the Name pop-up menu in the Sound section of the Frame Property inspector.

To assign a sound to a keyframe:

1. Using the PingPongRallyMaster template you created in Chapter 12, open a new document. The document—which contains a motion tween in which a ball connects with a paddle at four position keyframes—makes a good practice file for adding sound.

2. In the Timeline, add a new layer for the sounds in your document, and name it Sound. (For tips on working with layers containing sounds, see the sidebar "Organizing Sounds" in this chapter.)

3. Select the Sound layer and add keyframes at Frames 5, 10, 15, and 20. These keyframes match the position keyframes in which the ball connects with a paddle in the animation .

4. Import the sound you want to hear when the paddle connects with the ball.

5. In the Sound layer, select Keyframe 5, the first frame in which the ball and paddle connect.

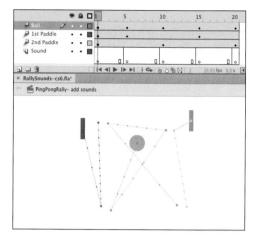

A Create a separate layer for the sounds in your movie. In that layer, add a keyframe at each place where you want a sound to occur. Here, the keyframes in the Sound layer correspond to the position keyframes in the tween spans where the ball makes contact with a paddle.

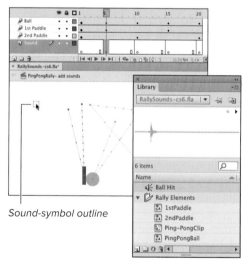

Sound-symbol outline

Waveform of the sound assigned to Keyframe 5

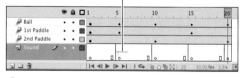

B After you've imported a sound, it appears in the Library panel. Select the sound, and drag it to a keyframe.

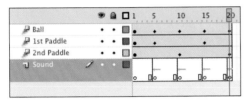

C In the Sound section of the Frame Property inspector, the Name pop-up menu lists all the sounds that are in the library of the current document. From this menu, you can choose a sound that you want to assign to the keyframe that's selected in the Timeline.

D For each spot in the movie where a sound should occur, add a sound to a keyframe in the Sound layer. A condensed image of the sound's waveform appears in the keyframe span. Within a single keyframe, you won't see much of the waveform; in Keyframe 20, for example, just part of the initial line is visible.

6. To assign the sound to the current key-frame, do one of the following:

   ▸ Access the Library panel and drag a copy of the desired sound to the Stage. A symbol outline appears as you drag. When you release the mouse button, the waveform displays throughout that keyframe span **B**.

   ▸ Access the Frame Property inspector's Sound section, and from the Name menu, choose the desired sound. The menu lists every sound in the document's library **C**. The selected sound's waveform appears in the current keyframe span.

7. Repeat Step 6 for Keyframes 10, 15, and 20.

   After adding the sound to the Sound layer's four keyframes **D**, play the movie to check out the sounds. As each paddle strikes the ball, the assigned sound plays, adding a level of realism to this simple Ping-Pong animation.

TIP If you don't have a sound file of your own to import, skip Step 4 in the task above. Instead, access the Flash CS6 common library named Sounds (see the sidebar "Flashy Sounds" in this chapter). In Step 6, drag a sound from the Sounds library to the Stage. To create a realistic effect, use the sound named Sports Ball Ping Pong Ball Hit Table Single 01.mp3. To create a humorous effect, you might add something unexpected, such as the common-library sound named Transportation Auto Avalanche Honk Horn Short 01.mp3.

Adding Sounds to Buttons

Auditory feedback helps people interact with buttons confidently. Adding a click sound to the Down frame can make a button feel more realistic. If you use fanciful buttons, or buttons disguised as part of the scenery, adding sound to the Over frame lets users know they've discovered a hot spot.

Organizing Sounds

Nothing prevents you from placing sounds in regular layers with other content, but your document will be easier to handle—and sounds will be easier to find for updating and editing—if you always put sounds in separate layers reserved for a soundtrack. You cannot place sounds in motion-tween spans or inverse kinematics (IK) pose spans. Here are some tips for working with layers for sounds.

- Name layers as a reminder of their content. For detailed instructions on working with layers, see Chapter 6.

- Place all the sound layers either at the bottom of the Timeline or at the top, so you can find them easily. The position of layers in the stacking order has no effect on the playback of sounds in the movie.

- Create a layer folder for sounds. When you work with multiple sounds playing simultaneously, you need lots of layers. Putting the sound layers inside a folder keeps all the sounds together, and gives you the ability to hide the layers when you're not working on sounds.

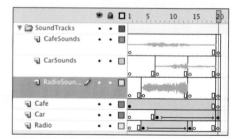

- Increase the height for sound layers to make it easier to see the waveform (a graphic image of the sound) for that layer. Select a layer, then choose Modify > Timeline > Layer Properties (or double-click the layer icon of the selected layer) to access the Layer Properties dialog. From the Layer Height pop-up menu, choose 200% or 300% to make the layer taller. Click OK.

- After you've placed sounds in a layer, lock the layer—to avoid accidentally adding graphics to it—by clicking the bullet in the Lock column.

- To avoid adding sounds to the wrong layer, Option-click (OS X) or Alt-click (Win) the bullet in the padlock column for the sound layer you want to work with. Flash locks all other layers.

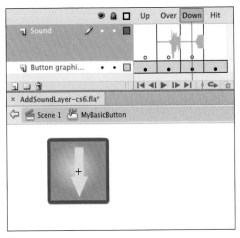

A Flash displays the waveform of the assigned sound in the keyframe. Here, the height of the Sound layer has been set to 300 percent so you can see a tiny bit of the sound's waveform.

To enhance buttons with auditory feedback:

1. Open a Flash document containing a button symbol, access the file's Library panel, and select the symbol you want to modify.

2. From the library's panel menu, choose Edit. Flash opens the button in symbol-editing mode.

3. In the button symbol's Timeline, add a new layer, increase its height, and name it Sound.

4. In the Sound layer, select the Over and Down frames, Control-click (OS X) or right-click (Win), and choose Convert to Blank Keyframes.

5. Assign one sound to the Over frame and a different sound to the Down frame.

   Flash displays as much of the waveform as possible in each frame **A**. In the Sound section of the Frame Property inspector, keep the default Sync setting (Event).

6. Return to document-editing mode. Every instance of the button symbol in the document now has sounds attached.

7. To hear the buttons in action, choose Control > Enable Simple Buttons. When you move the pointer over the button, the sound assigned to the Over frame plays. When you click the button, the sound assigned to the Down frame plays.

TIP The most common frames to use for button feedback are the Over and Down frames, but you can add sounds to any of the button symbol's frames. Sounds added to the Up frame play when the pointer rolls out of the active button area. Sounds added to the Hit frame play when you release the mouse button within the active button area.

Using Event Sounds

One of the parameters available in the Sound section of the Frame Property inspector is Sync. It determines the way Flash synchronizes the sounds in your movie. Sync has four settings: Event, Start, Stop, and Stream. The default is Event.

To make an assigned sound an event sound:

1. Open a new practice document using the SoundSyncMaster template (see the sidebar "Sounds to Play With").

2. In the Timeline, select Keyframe 5 of the Sound 1 layer **A** and assign a sound to it (this example uses a 15.8-second sound named Scale) **B**.

3. In the Frame Property inspector, in the Sound section, from the Sync pop-up menu, choose Event, the default **C**.

4. Move the playhead to Keyframe 1, and play your movie (choose Control > Play, or press Enter).

   In a movie with a standard frame rate of 24 frames per second (fps), the 15.8-second Scale sound continues to play after the playhead reaches the last frame of the movie.

TIP To understand better how Flash handles event sounds, choose Control > Loop Playback. Now play the movie again, and let it loop through a couple of times. Each time the playhead enters Keyframe 5, Flash starts another instance of the Scale sound, and you begin to hear not one set of notes going up the scale, but a cacophony of bad harmonies. When you stop the playback, each sound instance plays out until its end—an effect sort of like people singing a round.

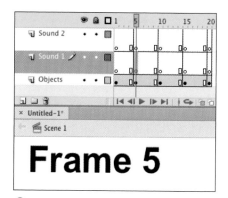

A Select the keyframe to which you want to assign a sound.

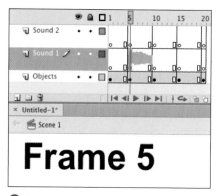

B Choosing a sound from the Name menu in the Sound section of the Property inspector assigns that sound to the current keyframe in the Timeline. The keyframe span displays the first part of the sound's waveform.

SOUND

Name: Scale.AIFF

Effect: None

Sync: Event
✓ Event
Start
Stop   Bit 15.7 s 345...
Stream

C From the Sync pop-up menu, choose Event to make the assigned sound start in the selected keyframe and play to the end of the sound, without synchronizing to any subsequent frames of the movie.

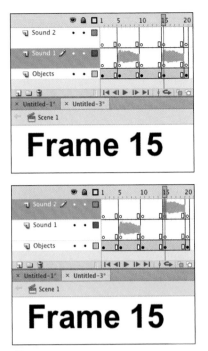

To play overlapping instances of the same sound:

1. Using the file you created in the preceding task, to assign a sound to a point later in the movie's Timeline, do one of the following:

   ▸ Select Keyframe 15 of the Sound 1 layer.

   ▸ Select Keyframe 15 of the Sound 2 layer.

   When you want two instances of the same sound to start playing at different times, you can add the second instance to the same layer as the first or to a different layer. Flash starts a new instance of an event sound even if that sound is already playing.

2. Assign Keyframe 15 the same sound that you assigned to Keyframe 5 (Scale) Ⓓ.

3. From the Sync pop-up menu, choose Event.

Continues on next page

Ⓓ You can add a second instance of your sound and make it play on top of the first. Event sounds play independently of the main Timeline, so you're free to add the second sound to the same layer as the first (top). Alternatively, you can add the second sound to its own layer (bottom).

Sounds to Play With

To understand synchronization, it's helpful to test different Sync styles in a file that has identifying text in keyframes. Create a document with three layers: Objects, Sound 1, and Sound 2. In all three layers, set up keyframes at Frames 5, 10, 15, and 20. In the Objects layer, place identifying text on the Stage for each keyframe. Import several sounds of different lengths into the file's library. The tasks in this book use Scale (a 15.8-second clip of a musical-scale passage, which you can download from the companion website for this book, www.peachpit.com/flashcs6vqs). In addition, the tasks use the following sounds from Flash's common library of sounds: Baby Talk (Cartoon Human Male Baby Talk 01.mp3), Bark (Animal Dog Bark 26.mp3), Drum Roll (Cartoon Drum Roll Tom 04.mp3), and Phone (Technology Electronic Phone Ring Multiple 01.mp3). To access these sounds, choose Window > Common Libraries > Sounds.

Save the document as a template for use throughout this chapter, and name it SoundSyncMaster. Be sure to close the template document after creating it. For detailed instructions on saving documents as templates, see Chapter 1.

4. Move the playhead to Keyframe 1, and play your movie one time.

When the playhead reaches Keyframe 5, the Scale sound starts. When the playhead reaches Keyframe 15, another instance of the Scale sound starts, and the two sounds play together (you hear two voices). When the first instance ends, you again hear only one voice. Within a single layer, each keyframe can contain only one sound. To make Flash begin playing different sounds at the same point in a movie, you must put the sounds in separate layers.

5. Save this file for use in a later task; name it OverlapSnds.fla.

TIP All the information required to play an event sound lives in the keyframe to which you assign that sound. When you play the movie, Flash pauses at that keyframe until all the information has downloaded. It's best to reserve event syncing for short sound clips; otherwise, your movie may be interrupted by long pauses for downloading sounds.

Independent Sounds vs. Synchronized Sounds

In Flash, unsynchronized sound clips are known as *event sounds*. They play independently of the Timeline. An event sound starts playing at a specific keyframe; but thereafter, the sound plays without relation to specific frames. On one viewer's computer, ten frames may appear before the sound finishes; on a slower setup, perhaps only five frames appear before the end of the sound.

An event sound continues to play until Flash reaches the end of the sound clip or encounters an instruction to stop playing that sound (or to stop playing all sounds). Long event sounds can continue to play after the playhead reaches the last frame in a movie. If the movie loops, every time the playhead passes a frame with an event sound, Flash starts playing another instance of that sound.

Flash can also synchronize sound clips with the Timeline. Flash breaks these *stream sounds* or *streaming sounds* into smaller pieces and attaches each piece to a specific frame. For streaming sounds, Flash forces the animation to keep up with the sounds. On slower setups, Flash skips drawing some frames to insure that important actions and sounds stay together.

Frame 5

E To simultaneously start playing two different sounds, you must put each sound in a different layer in a keyframe at the same spot in the Timeline (here, Keyframe 5).

To start different sounds simultaneously:

1. Open a new document using the SoundSyncMaster template (see the sidebar "Sounds to Play With").

2. In the Timeline, select Keyframe 5 of the Sound 1 layer and assign it the first sound, Scale.

3. From the Sync pop-up menu, choose Event.

4. In the Timeline, select Keyframe 5 of the Sound 2 layer and assign it the second sound, Drum Roll.

   The waveforms for the two sounds appear in their respective layers in the Timeline E.

5. In the Sound section of the Frame Property inspector, from the Sync pop-up menu, choose Event.

6. Move the playhead to Keyframe 1, and play your movie one time.

   When the playhead reaches Keyframe 5, Flash starts playing the Scale and Drum Roll sounds simultaneously.

Using Start Sounds

Start sounds behave just like event sounds, with one important difference: Flash does not play a new instance of a start sound if that sound is already playing.

To make an assigned sound a start sound:

1. Open OverlapSnds.fla, the file you created in "Using Event Sounds > To play overlapping instances of the same sound," earlier in this chapter.

   One instance of the Scale sound is in Keyframe 5; another is in Keyframe 15, in the Sound 1 or Sound 2 layer, depending on what you did in the earlier task.

2. In the Timeline, select the Keyframe 15 that contains the Scale sound **A**.

3. In the Sound section of the Frame Property inspector, from the Sync pop-up menu, choose Start **B**.

4. Move the playhead to Keyframe 1, and play your movie one time.

   When the playhead reaches Keyframe 5, the Scale sound starts. When the playhead reaches Keyframe 15, nothing changes; you continue to hear just one voice as the Scale sound continues playing. When a sound is playing and Flash encounters another instance of the same sound, the Sync setting determines whether Flash plays that sound. When Sync is set to Start, Flash does not play another instance of the sound.

TIP To avoid playing multiple instances of a sound when a movie loops, set the sound's Sync property to Start. If the sound is playing when the movie starts again, Flash adds no new sound. If the sound is done, Flash restarts the sound again when the playhead enters a keyframe containing the sound.

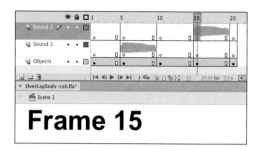

Frame 15

A To change a sound's Sync setting, first select the keyframe that contains the sound.

B To prevent Flash from playing another instance of a sound if that sound is already playing, choose Start from the Sync pop-up menu in the Sound section of the Frame Property inspector.

A To make Flash force a sound to synchronize with specific frames of your movie, choose Stream from the Sync pop-up menu in the Sound section of the Frame Property inspector.

About Streaming Sound

When you choose Stream as the Sync setting for a sound, Flash divides that sound clip into smaller subclips and embeds them in individual frames. The movie's frame rate determines the subclips' size. In a movie with a frame rate of 10 frames per second (fps), for example, Flash divides streaming sounds into subclips that are a tenth of a second long. For every ten frames, Flash plays one second of the sound.

Flash synchronizes the start of each subclip with a specific frame of the movie. If the sound plays back faster than the computer can draw frames, Flash skips drawing some frames of the animation so that sound and images match up as closely as possible. Setting a sound's Sync property to Stream ensures, for example, that you hear the door slam when you see it swing shut—not a few seconds before. If the discrepancy between sound-playback speed and frame-drawing speed is big enough, however, those dropped frames make the movie look jerky, just as if you had set a low frame rate to begin with.

Using Stream Sounds

Stream sounds are specifically geared for playback over the Internet. When Sync is set to Stream, Flash breaks the sound into smaller sound clips. Flash synchronizes these subclips with specific frames of the movie—as many frames as are required to play the sound. Flash stops streaming sounds when playback reaches either a new keyframe in the sound's layer or an instruction to stop playing that specific sound or all sounds.

Unlike event sounds, which must download fully before they can play, stream sounds can start playing after a few frames have downloaded. This situation makes streaming the best choice for long sounds, especially if your audience will be viewing your movie over the web or on mobile devices.

To make an assigned sound a stream sound:

1. Open a new document using the SoundSyncMaster template (see the sidebar "Sounds to Play With").

2. In the Timeline, in the Sound 1 layer, remove keyframe status from Keyframe 10. (Select it and choose Modify > Timeline > Clear Keyframe, or press Shift-F6.)

3. In the Timeline, in the Sound 1 layer, select Keyframe 5.

4. In the Sound section of the Frame Property inspector, from the Name pop-up menu, choose a long sound, such as Drum Roll.

5. From the Sync pop-up menu, choose Stream **A**.

Continues on next page

6. To see how the sound fits into the available time in your movie, in the Sound section of the Frame Property inspector, click the Edit Sound Envelope button ✎. The Edit Envelope dialog appears.

The Drum Roll sound is slightly more than three seconds long, too long to play completely in the frames between Keyframe 5 and Keyframe 15. When Sync is set to Stream, Flash plays only as much of the sound as can fit in the frames that are available to it—in this case, slightly less than a half second. In the Edit Envelope dialog, a vertical line in the graphs indicates where Flash truncates this instance of the sound **B**.

7. To close the Edit Envelope dialog, click OK or Cancel. The truncated waveform appears in the keyframe span **C**.

8. Move the playhead to Keyframe 1, and play your movie to hear the sound in action.

When the playhead reaches Keyframe 5, the Drum Roll sound starts. When the playhead reaches Keyframe 15, the keyframe span ends, and Flash stops playback of the Drum Roll sound.

9. Choose Control > Loop Playback, and then play the movie. Flash repeats the same snippet of sound, stopping it each time the playhead reaches Keyframe 15.

TIP You can hear streaming sounds play as you drag the playhead through the Timeline— a technique called *scrubbing*. As the playhead moves over the waveform, you can see how the images and sounds fit together. You can then add or delete frames to better synchronize the sounds with the images onscreen.

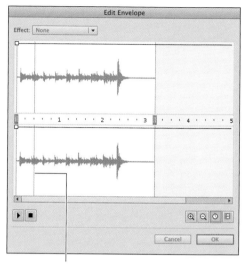

Sound will stop playing here

B When you set a sound's Sync to Stream, you can check how much of the sound will play, given the number of in-between frames there are for the sound to play in. The Edit Envelope dialog's sound-editing window graphs a sound's full waveform in relation to time or to frame numbers.

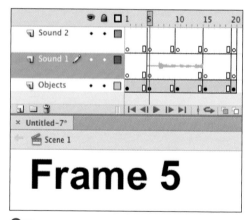

C The ten-frame keyframe span is long enough to play about 0.4 seconds of the Drum Roll sound. Just that much of the sound's waveform appears in the keyframe span in the Timeline.

The Baby Talk sound   The Phone sound

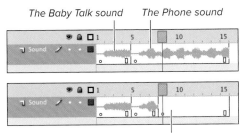

After adding blank keyframe

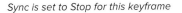

A Inserting a new keyframe cuts off your view of the preceding sound's waveform in the Timeline. If the truncated sound is an event sound, however, it continues playing even when the playhead moves past the keyframe.

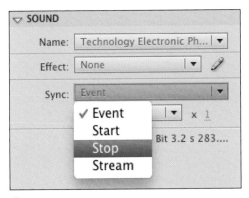

B To stop a sound's playback at a specific point in a movie, create a keyframe where the sound should stop. Then select that keyframe. In the Sound section of the Frame Property inspector, from the Name pop-up menu, choose the sound you want to stop. From the Sync pop-up menu, choose Stop. This Stop instruction refers to the Phone sound.

Sync is set to Stop for this keyframe

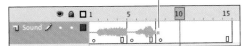

C In the Timeline, a small square in the middle of a keyframe indicates the presence of the stop-sound instruction.

Stopping Sounds

Although event sounds normally play to the end, you can force them to stop at a specific keyframe. To issue an instruction to stop a specific sound, set that sound's Sync property to Stop.

To stop playback of a sound:

1. Create a new single-layer 15-frame Flash document with two fairly long event sounds (at least two or three seconds each); place one sound in Keyframe 1 and the other in Keyframe 5. For example, use the Baby Talk sound for Keyframe 1 and the Phone sound for Keyframe 5. Make sure that Sync is set to Event for both sounds.

2. In the Timeline, at Frame 8, insert a new blank keyframe **A**. The blank keyframe cuts off the waveform in the Timeline, but on playback, both event sounds continue to play after the playhead reaches Keyframe 8.

3. Select Keyframe 8.

4. In the Frame Property inspector, in the Sound section, from the Name pop-up menu, choose the Phone sound.

5. From the Sync pop-up menu, choose Stop **B**.

    Flash uses this instruction to stop play-back of the Phone sound at Keyframe 8. A small square at Keyframe 8 in the Timeline indicates that the frame contains a stop-sound instruction **C**.

Continues on next page

6. Move the playhead to Keyframe 1, and play your movie to hear the sounds in action.

The Baby Talk sound starts immediately; the Phone sounds kicks in at Keyframe 5. When the playhead reaches Keyframe 8, The Phone sound cuts out, but the Baby Talk sound plays on even after the playhead reaches the end of the movie.

TIP The Stop setting and the sound that it stops can be in different layers. The Stop setting stops playback of all instances of the specified sound that are currently playing in any layer.

TIP To stop only one instance of a sound, set the Sync parameter of that instance to Stream. Then, in the layer containing that instance, put a blank keyframe at the frame where you want that instance of the sound to stop.

Using Buttons to Control Sounds

In this chapter, you use sounds two ways. You create user-friendly buttons with audio feedback by adding sounds to keyframes in button symbols; and you create soundtracks or sound effects for animation by adding and removing sound instances directly in the Timeline during authoring.

A third way to work with sound is to use ActionScript (AS) to control sounds during playback—loading, playing, and stopping sounds as needed at runtime.

Two of Flash's predefined Code Snippets create frame scripts that let end users accomplish common sound-related tasks by clicking a button: one script sets up a button that stops all the sounds currently playing; the other script sets up a button that toggles a sound loaded from an external file on and off.

Advanced scripters can also create their own sound-control objects, then add frame scripts that target those objects. When setting up buttons to control sounds, you must set the sound's Linkage properties. Scripting sounds is a complex task, beyond the scope of a *Visual QuickStart Guide*. To learn about creating basic frame scripts in Action-Script 3.0, see Chapter 15.

Editing Sounds

Flash lets you make limited changes in each instance of a sound in the Edit Envelope dialog. You can change the start point and end point of the sound (that is, cut a piece off the beginning or end of the waveform) and adjust the sound's volume.

To assign packaged volume effects:

1. Open a new document using the SoundSyncMaster template (see the sidebar "Sounds to Play With").

2. Select Keyframe 1 of the Sound 2 layer, and assign it the Bark sound. In this sound clip, a dog barks three times.

3. To enlarge the keyframe span to view more of the sound's waveform, select Frames 5–20 of the Sound 2 layer and choose Modify > Timeline > Clear Keyframe, or press Shift-F6.

4. In the Sound 2 layer, select any frame in the Keyframe 1 span.

5. In the Frame Property inspector, in the Sound section, click the Edit Sound Envelope button ✎.

6. In the Edit Envelope dialog that appears, click the Frames button ▦ **Ⓐ**.

   The sound-editing window shows the sound envelope (roughly equivalent to changes in volume over time) along with the sound's waveform in two windows, one for each sound channel. The horizontal axis graphs the length of the sound in seconds or frames. Clicking the Seconds button ◷ sets the units to seconds; clicking the Frames button ▦ sets the units to frames. The vertical axis graphs the percentage of available sound that will play at that point in the sound clip during playback.

Continues on next page

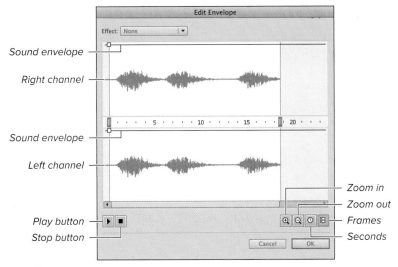

Ⓐ You can do simple sound editing—for length and volume—in the Edit Envelope dialog. The sound-editing window graphs the sound envelope and the waveform of the sound assigned to the keyframe currently selected in the Timeline; here, it's Keyframe 1. The vertical axis represents volume (the percentage of the full volume available). The horizontal axis represents time. To set the time units to frames, click the Frames button; to set the time units to seconds, click the Seconds button.

7. From the Effect pop-up menu, choose Fade In 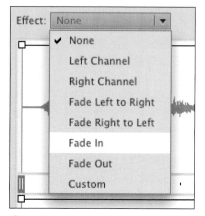.

Flash adjusts the sound envelope **C**. When the line is at the top of the graph, Flash plays 100 percent of the available sound. When the line is at the bottom of the graph, Flash plays 0 percent of the available sound.

8. Click the Play button to hear the sound with its fade-in effect. The change is subtle for this sound; the barking starts soft and grows slightly louder.

9. Click OK. Flash returns you to document-editing mode.

TIP If you don't need to see your sound's waveform, you can bypass the Edit Envelope dialog. Just choose an effect from the Effect pop-up menu in the Sound section of the Frame Property inspector.

B The Effect pop-up menu in the Edit Envelope dialog offers six templates for common sound effects that deal with volume. Choose Fade In to make the sound start soft and grow in volume.

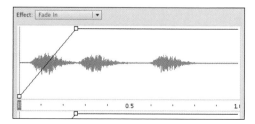

C The Fade In effect brings the sound's envelope down to 0 percent (the bottom of the sound-editing window) at the start of the sound and quickly raises it to 100 percent (the top of the sound-editing window).

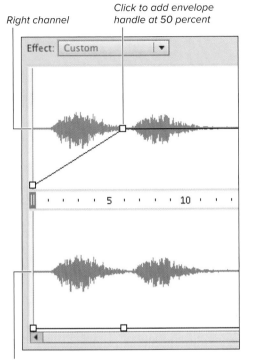

Right channel

Click to add envelope
handle at 50 percent

Effect: Custom ▼

5   10

Left channel

D To add a handle, click inside the waveform graph in either channel in the sound-editing window. The handle appears at the vertical level where you click. Drag the handle to adjust the sound envelope. You can make the sound envelope the same or different for both channels. For monaural sounds, both waveforms are identical.

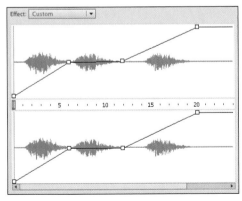

Effect: Custom ▼

5   10   15   20

E Adding three envelope handles enables you to divide the sound clip into three sections and set the volume level of each bark separately.

To customize volume effects:

1. Follow Steps 1–6 in the preceding task.

2. From the Effect pop-up menu in the Edit Envelope dialog, choose Custom.

3. In the sound-editing window, drag the square envelope handle that appears at the top left corner of each graph (100 percent) down to the bottom left corner (0 percent).

4. In the right channel (the top graph), at Frame 6, click in the middle of the waveform. A new envelope handle appears at the 50 percent level in the right channel and at 0 percent in the left channel **D**.

5. In the left channel, at Frame 6, drag the envelope handle to 50 percent.

6. Repeat Step 4 at Frame 12. New handles appear at the 50 percent level in both channels.

7. Repeat Steps 4 and 5 at Frame 20, this time dragging the envelope handles in both channels to the 100 percent level **E**.

8. Click the Play button to hear the sound with its fade-in effect. Flash fades in the dog's first bark, plays the second bark at half volume, and plays the last bark at full volume.

9. Click OK.

TIP To remove unwanted envelope handles, drag them out of the sound-editing window.

TIP You can use as many as eight handles to create a variety of volume changes within one sound.

TIP To avoid unintentionally adding a new handle when repositioning an existing one, click the existing handle and wait until it turns black before you start to drag.

To edit sounds for length:

1. Using the movie you created in the preceding task, select Keyframe 1 of the Sound 2 layer.

2. To access the Edit Envelope dialog, in the Frame Property inspector, in the Sound section, click the Edit Sound Envelope button.

3. In the sound-editing window, drag the Time-out control (on the right-hand side of the "Timeline" between the two channels) to the end of the sound where the waveform begins to go flat **F**. Flash shortens the sound in both channels.

4. Click OK to confirm your edits and return to document-editing mode. Now the waveform of the entire sound is visible in the keyframe span in the Timeline **G**.

> **TIP** If you don't see the Time-out control in the sound-editing window, scroll to the right to find the end of the waveform.

> **TIP** To remove dead air from the beginning of a sound, drag the Time-in control. Flash places a light-gray background behind the initial portion of the sound's waveform to indicate that it won't play.

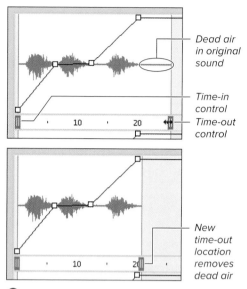

Dead air in original sound

Time-in control

Time-out control

New time-out location removes dead air

F Flash lets you trim the beginning and end of a sound in the Edit Envelope dialog's sound-editing window. Here, dragging the Time-out control clips off the end of the sound where the wave's amplitude is smaller, almost a flat line. (The small amplitude indicates a very soft sound or silence.)

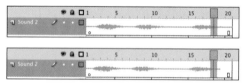

G After you reposition the Time-out control, the new, shorter waveform appears in the Edit Envelope dialog's sound-editing window (bottom).

About Encoding Video for Flash

Flash's Video Import Wizard can only handle files that have already been encoded in a Flash-compatible format (FLV and F4V are examples). When you choose to import for embedding, the wizard only allows files in FLV format. Flash includes a stand-alone video encoder—Adobe Media Encoder CS6—that lets you encode video data in the appropriate formats to work with Flash. AME lets you encode multiple files in batches. You create a list of files, then choose encoding options for video- and audio-compression, add filters, create cue points, and perform basic edits (cropping and resizing). Not sure if your video file is in a Flash-compatible format? Try importing it with the wizard. If the data is not encoded appropriately, the wizard notifies you. You can open up AME quickly by clicking the Launch Adobe Media Encoder button on the Select Video page of the wizard.

Adding Video to Flash

The process of adding video to Flash is similar to the process of adding sound. You start by choosing the Import Video command. This command accesses Flash's Video Import Wizard. The wizard asks you to locate an encoded video file and choose how you want to deliver the video. You can embed the video data to make it part of the FLA file during authoring. After you publish your movie for playback, the embedded video data becomes part of the SWF file (see Chapter 17).

Alternatively, you can create a link to an encoded video file and use a component to display the video data at runtime. The Video Import Wizard ensures that the video data you select is encoded correctly. The wizard then imports the data or makes the appropriate link to it. The precise steps vary somewhat depending on the delivery method you choose.

Importing Video for Streaming or Progressive Download

Flash can stream video over the web or deliver video as a progressive download. Both methods allow you to work with larger amounts of video data and avoid delays in playback while video data downloads to the end user's system. To deploy the video as streaming or progressive download, you must use a playback component to link to the video data in an external file. Flash Player displays the video inside the component at runtime.

About the Video Import Wizard

Flash CS6's Video Import Wizard guides you when importing video clips for use in Flash. The clips must already be encoded in a format that works with Flash, such as FLV (Flash video) or F4V. (F4V is a subset of the H.264 video-compression specification developed by the standards group known as the JVT [Joint Video Team]. Most video files encoded as MPEG-4—such as video podcasts in your Apple iTunes library—qualify as F4V.)

The biggest decision you have to make when using the wizard is how you want to deliver the video data to your viewers. You can embed the video data into the Flash document, or keep the data in an external file and display the video via a special Flash element—the FLVPlayback component.

Embedded video adds to the size of a published Flash movie, which may have a negative effect on your end users' experience as they wait for enough data to download to start playback. Video displayed using the FLVPlayback component doesn't add to the size of the published movie. How long users must wait to see the video depends on whether you use progressive or streaming video and on the particulars of each user's computer setup.

Flash can use progressive download for the video displayed with the FLVPlayback component. With this method, Flash downloads the entire video file from a web server. You can start watching data as it downloads, but if download speed is slow, you may catch up to the downloaded video and have to wait for more data to reach your system. You can't skip ahead to start downloading a later section of the video.

Flash can stream video displayed with the FLVPlayback component, either from an Adobe Flash Video Streaming Service or from your own server using Adobe Flash Media Server. For streaming, Flash divides the video data into small segments. The video can start playing as soon as a few segments have downloaded. The server continues to download video data while the end user watches. Users can skip around to different segments of the video easily. Streaming video is also more efficient for longer videos because when users watch only a portion of the video, they don't need to download the entire clip. And the video streams don't wind up in the user's cache.

To use streaming video, you must have access to a Flash Media Server, have a Flash Video Streaming Service account with your ISP, or use a dedicated streaming service, such as Limelight Networks.

In addition, Flash can deploy video for use with some mobile devices.

A The Import Video dialog offers options for displaying encoded video in your Flash movie. The first step is locating the video file you want to display.

Where is your video file?
⊙ On your computer:
   File path: [Browse...]

B To locate video on your computer for import, select the On Your Computer radio button; then click the Browse button, navigate to the file, and select it.

⊙ Already deployed to a web server, Flash Video Streaming Service, or Flash Media Server:
   URL: [   ]

   Examples: http://mydomain.com/directory/video.flv
              rtmp://mydomain.com/directory/video.xml

   Please enter the URL of your video file.

   The URL's scheme must be either rtmp or http. Relative URLs are assumed to be http.

C To import video that's on an external server, select the "Already deployed to a web server" radio button and enter the video file's URL.

To import video for display in a playback component:

1. In the Flash document where you want to add video, create a new layer and insert a blank keyframe at the frame where the video should start playing.

   It's best to create a separate layer for the video component that Flash will add at the end of this task. Keeping the component on a separate layer helps you organize the Timeline.

2. To begin the import process, with the desired keyframe selected, choose File > Import > Import Video. The Select Video page of the Import Video dialog appears **A**.

3. To use a file on your hard drive, select the On Your Computer radio button and click the Browse button in the File Path area **B**. When the Open dialog appears, navigate to your file, select it, and click the Open button. The Video Import Wizard returns you to the Select Video page and displays the file's path.

   or

   To use a file that is located on a web server, select the "Already deployed to a web server" radio button **C** and enter the file's address in the URL field.

   Continues on next page

4. Click Next. The Skinning page appears 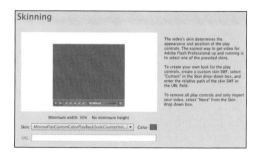.

5. To create playback controls for end users, from the Skin pop-up menu, choose one of the following:

▸ To create a controller bar that that uses space efficiently, choose a skin whose name starts with the word *Minima*.

▸ To create a controller bar that floats on top of the image in the video-display window, choose a skin whose name starts with the words *SkinOver* **E**.

▸ To create a controller bar that sits beneath the video-display window, choose a skin whose name starts with the words *SkinUnder*.

D In the Skinning page of the Import Video dialog, you can choose a skin that creates user-interface controls for the progressive or streaming video displayed in your Flash movie.

E Each skin in the pop-up menu uses a different set of elements to create the controller bar. Skins that contain the word *Minima* have small icons to save space; skins that contain the word *Over* are layered on top of the video image; skins that contain the word *Under* appear just below the video-display window.

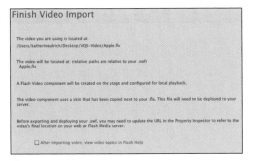

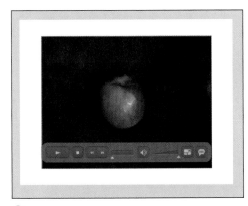

F The Finish Video Import page of the Import Video dialog provides information about how to work with the video files for publishing. To learn more, select the "After importing video, view video topics in Flash Help" checkbox.

G The imported video clip, along with any skin/controller you selected, appears on the Stage in the current keyframe.

6. Click Next. The Finish Video Import page appears **F**, describing the assets created by the wizard and giving a brief overview of how to use them (see the sidebar "Final Steps for Using FLVPlayback" in this chapter).

7. Click Finish. The Getting Metadata dialog with progress bar appears. When loading has finished, Flash places an instance of the FLVPlayback component on the Stage in the keyframe you selected. The properties of the instance are already set to point to the source video file and to use the skin you chose in Step 5 **G**.

TIP In Step 5 of the preceding task, to create a video clip with no controller bar, choose None from the Skin pop-up menu.

TIP You can select a color for any of the controller bar skins other than ones whose names start with *minimaSilver* or *MinimaUnder*. In the Video Import dialog's Skinning page, click the Color control and choose a new color from the pop-up swatch set.

TIP Best practice: Before importing the video, copy the encoded video file to the same folder as the FLA or SWF (or to a subfolder in the same folder). The URL Flash creates as the Source parameter (see the section "Working with the FLVPlayback Component" in this chapter) will be a relative path, ready to be put on a web server.

Importing Video for Embedding

When you choose to embed a video file, the video data becomes part of the FLA and SWF files. Embedded video must be in FLV format. When you import video for embedding, the Video Import Wizard has an extra page of settings.

To import and embed video:

1. Follow Steps 1–3 in the preceding task. You need to select a keyframe only if you want Flash to place the video in the Timeline for you.

2. Select the radio button labeled "Embed FLV in SWF and play in Timeline" **H**.

3. Click Next. The Embedding page of the Import Video dialog appears, with options for working with embedded video clips **I**.

4. From the Symbol Type pop-up menu **J**, choose one of the following:

   Embedded Video places the video frames directly into the main Timeline of your movie.

   Movie Clip places the video frames into the Timeline of a movie-clip symbol.

   Graphic places the video frames into the Timeline of an animated graphic symbol.

5. To have Flash automatically place video frames in the Timeline (if you chose Embedded Video in Step 4) or to place a symbol instance on the Stage (if you chose Movie Clip or Graphic in Step 4), select the "Place instance on Stage" checkbox.

   Upon completing the import process, Flash places the video or symbol instance in the currently selected keyframe.

Where is your video file?

⦿ On your computer:

File path: [Browse...]

/Users/katherineulrich/Desktop/VQS–Video/Apple.flv

◯ Load external video with playback component

⦿ Embed FLV in SWF and play in timeline

◯ Import as mobile device video bundled in SWF

WARNING: Embedded video is likely to cause audio synchronization issues. This method of importing video is ONLY recommended for short video clips with no audio track.

H When you choose embedding as the delivery method (top), Flash puts all of the video data into the published SWF file. This method has its pluses and minuses, as indicated in the warning text that appears in the dialog when you choose to embed (bottom).

Embedding

How would you like to embed the video?

Symbol type: [Embedded video ▾]

☑ Place instance on stage

☑ Expand timeline if needed

☑ Include audio

I You must choose settings for working with the embedded video. You can have Flash place an instance of the video clip on the Stage for you, expand the number of defined frames in the Timeline to display all the frames of the video, and include an audio track if the clip has one.

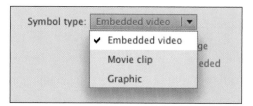

J The Symbol Type menu in the Embedding page of the Import Video dialog gives you the choice of turning the video clip into an animated graphic symbol or a movie-clip symbol, or placing the frames of the video directly into the main Timeline.

☑ Place instance on stage
☑ Expand timeline if needed
☑ Include audio

K With embedded video, you can include the soundtrack within the video itself or exclude it.

Finish Video Import

The video you are using is located at:
/Users/ku/Apple.flv

The video will be placed on the stage.

The timeline will be expanded to accommodate the playback length.

☐ After importing video, view video topics in Flash Help

L The Video Import Wizard summarizes the settings you chose for importing a video, telling you where the source video is. If you chose to have Flash place the video in your movie, or expand the Timeline to display the video, this window lets you know.

6. If you chose Embedded Video or Graphic in Step 4, to add frames to the selected keyframe span in the main Timeline to display all the video's frames, select the "Expand Timeline if needed" checkbox.

7. To include an audio track, select the Include Audio checkbox **K**.

8. Click Next. The Finish Video Import window appears **L**.

9. Click Finish. Flash completes the import process. For details, see Step 7 of the preceding task.

TIP When you import video for embedding, do not attempt to place it in a tween span or pose span. Flash doesn't allow embedded video in these types of spans. If you continue the import process with these types of spans selected, Flash disables the option to place an instance on the Stage. Flash places the video clip (and movie-clip or graphic symbol if you chose to create one) in the library of your document but places nothing on the Stage or in the Timeline.

CAUTION Don't change the frame rate of your document (FLA) after you've imported video, as that all but guarantees sync issues during playback. If you must change the frame rate, re-import the video afterward. It may also help to encode the video at the same frame rate as the FLA.

Working with Embedded Video

Depending on the settings you choose when you use the Video Import Wizard to create embedded video clips, Flash places an instance of the clip on the Stage or just places the embedded-video asset in the library. When automatically placing an instance on the Stage, Flash can create enough frames in the Timeline to show the full video, or allow the existing keyframe span to truncate the video. When you place an instance of an embedded clip into the Timeline yourself, you need to create a keyframe span that accommodates as much of the video as you want to show.

To place embedded video clips in the Timeline:

1. Open a Flash document and import the embedded video. For this task, deselect the "Place instance on Stage" checkbox in Step 5 of the preceding task.

2. In the Timeline, select the keyframe in which you want the embedded video to start playing. The keyframe must not be part of a motion tween's tween span or an IK pose span. Flash cannot use an embedded video clip as a tween target or an IK node.

3. From the Library panel, drag a copy of the embedded video clip to the Stage 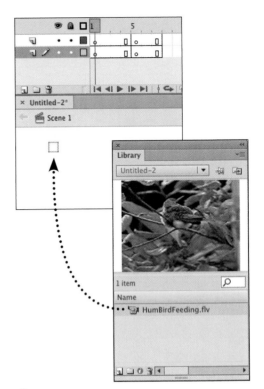.

A To place embedded video in a Flash movie, drag an instance of the embedded video clip from the library to the Stage.

Previewing Embedded Video Clips

In Flash's authoring environment, embedded video clips display their images within the keyframe span that contains the clip. You can simply play the movie (choose Control > Play) or move the playhead through the Timeline to view the changing video frames. When the embedded clip has an audio track, however, you must use one of the test modes to preview the sound. You must also use one of the test modes to see the embedded video in context with interactive elements, such as movie clips or scripted buttons.

B Flash alerts you when the selected keyframe span has fewer frames than the video.

Before adding embedded-video instance

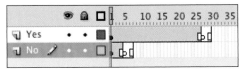

After adding embedded-video instance

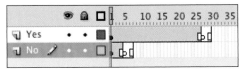

C The top layer in this Timeline shows the result of answering Yes in the dialog that warns that the current keyframe span is too short: Flash adds enough frames to display the full 27-frame clip. The bottom layer shows the result for answering No: the existing keyframe span truncates the video.

Unlike movie clips, which play in their own independent Timeline, embedded video clips need to fit their frames into the Timeline of the movie or movie clip containing them. Each time you drag an instance of an embedded video clip to the Stage, if the selected keyframe span contains fewer frames than the clip, a warning dialog asks whether you want to add enough frames to display the entire clip **B**.

4. To enlarge the keyframe span, click Yes. Flash adds enough frames to the span to reveal the entire video clip **C**.

   or

   To retain the current number of frames in the keyframe span, click No. Flash places the video clip on the Stage, but the keyframe span cuts off the end of the clip.

About Embedded Video

Embedded video clips bear similarities to some Flash symbols, yet embedded video is a unique type of element. Like animated graphic symbols, embedded video clips play within—and must synchronize with—frames in the main movie Timeline. Embedded video clips can contain audio—although if you import the audio as an integrated track, you won't see the sound's waveform in the Timeline.

As with any symbol, you place an instance of an embedded video clip by dragging a copy from the library window to the Stage. The Property inspector gives you information about selected instances of embedded video clips.

You can modify a selected instance of an embedded video clip in many of the ways that you modify other objects in Flash: you use the free-transform tool, for example, to resize, rotate, or skew the video image.

You can't use an embedded video clip as the tween target in a motion tween; you must put the embedded clip inside a Flash movie-clip symbol to tween the video. In addition, to give an embedded video clip an independent Timeline and to gain the same control over the clip's appearance that you have over movie clips (to be able to change the clip's brightness, tint, or alpha, for example), you must place the embedded video clip inside a Flash movie-clip symbol.

Working with the FLVPlayback Component

When you use Flash's Video Import Wizard to import video for use with a playback component, the wizard adds a component named FLVPlayback to the library and places an instance of it on the Stage. You can use the Property inspector to change the component's parameters, setting such things as the initial volume for the clip, the type of controller-bar skin and its color, and which video clip the component will display.

To choose source video for an FLVPlayback instance:

1. On the Stage, select the FLVPlayback-component instance.

2. To view the component's parameters, access the SWF Property inspector and expand the Component Parameters section **A**. The Source property displays the pathname of the video that appears in the selected FLVPlayback instance at runtime.

3. To choose a new source video, in the Source row, click the Content Path button ✐ or click the pathname directly. The Content Path dialog appears displaying a text field for the pathname of the current source.

4. To identify the source video file (it must be encoded in a Flash-compatible format, such as FLV or F4V), do one of the following:

   ▸ Enter a URL for the source video in the Content Path field **B**.

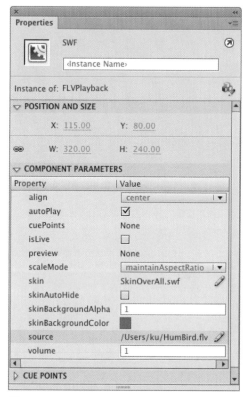

A The Component Parameters section of the SWF Property inspector panel contains settings for various modifiable properties of the selected FLVPlayback-component instance.

B The Content Path dialog lets you choose an external video file for the FLVPlayback-component instance to display for the end user.

| source | /Users/ku/Apple.flv | ✎ |

C The Source row of the Component Parameters section of the SWF Property inspector shows the pathname for the file that will play in the selected FLVPlayback-component instance in the finished movie.

TIP Instead of using the FLVPlayback component's prebuilt controller-bar skins, you can use other ActionScript 3.0 video components to create a user interface for controlling video that runs in the FLVPlayback window. Choose None as the skin for the FLVPlayback-component instance on the Stage. Access the Components panel and expand the Video folder. You'll see a number of user-interface components: PauseButton, PlayButton, VolumeBar, and so on. Drag an instance of each element you want to use to the Stage. You can position the elements anywhere and modify them as you did with the button component (see Chapter 14).

TIP You can change the size of an FLVPlay-back-component instance on the Stage using the free-transform tool, the Transform or Info panel, or the Position and Size section of the Property inspector. But if you've chosen a controller-bar skin for your video, be careful. The controller bar must be wide enough to hold all the user-interface elements that are part of the skin (the Play, Pause, and Mute buttons; the volume slider; and so on). If you narrow the component instance too much, the controller bar may stick out over the edges of the video-display window.

▸ To find the file you want, click the Browse button ■ to the right of the field. In the Browse for Source File dialog that appears, navigate to the file you want, and click Open. Flash enters the URL in the Content Path dialog.

5. To determine how Flash sizes the FLVPlayback-component instance, do one of the following:

▸ To resize the component to fit the source video, select the Match Source Dimensions checkbox.

▸ To resize the video to fit within the default FLVPlayback component (320 by 240 pixels), deselect the Match Source Dimensions checkbox.

6. Click OK. The Getting Metadata dialog with progress bar appears. Flash updates the Source parameter with the file name **C**. Depending on what you chose in Step 5, Flash also resizes the FLVPlayback-component instance on the Stage. The instance now points to the desired encoded video file.

TIP If the skin you've chosen for the FLVPlayback instance includes a volume-control slider, you can set its starting position at runtime. Enter a number in the Volume field: 1 sets the slider all the way to the right (full volume); values from 0.9 down to 0.1 set the slider farther to the left (lower volumes); a value of 0 sets the slider all the way to the left (no sound). You can enter values greater than 1, and those values create increasingly louder starting volumes, but the lever for the volume slider disappears. During playback, clicking anywhere in the slider brings the lever back, but end users may find this confusing.

About the FLVPlayback Component

Flash's Video Import Wizard imports encoded video files (such as FLV or F4V files) for use in your Flash movies. When you select the wizard's options to use the video with a playback component, the word *import* is a bit misleading. In fact, the data in the encoded file remains separate from your FLA and SWF files, but the wizard creates a link between your movie and the encoded video file via an element known as the *FLVPlayback component*. During the "import" process, the wizard places the FLVPlayback component in the library of your Flash document, places an instance of the component on the Stage, and sets the instance's source parameter to point to the file with the encoded video data. At runtime, the FLVPlayback component creates a video-display window within your Flash movie, and the video from the encoded source file appears in that window.

Components are a special type of Flash element. (You learned a bit about working with one component—the button component—in Chapter 14.) Components contain ActionScript that governs their behavior, but you can modify a component's behavior without actually doing any scripting; you simply change properties in the Component Parameters section of the Property inspector. ActionScript 3.0 user-interface components such as the button component are not fully compiled. You can modify the graphic elements that make up their appearance (their *skin*) the same way you'd modify any graphic element. The FLVPlayback component, however, is fully compiled; that is, you cannot directly access its skin to modify it. The FLVPlayback component comes with a variety of packaged skins that create a controller bar for the video-display window. You can choose a new controller-bar style by setting the skin property for an FLVPlayback-component instance. (Flash does allow you to create new skins for the FLVPlayback component, but that's beyond the scope of a *Visual QuickStart Guide*.)

Like other assets, the FLVPlayback component is reusable. To place another video-display window in your movie, drag a new instance of the FLVPlayback component to the Stage, then set the source property to point to the encoded video file you want to display. If you want, you can even bypass the Video Import Wizard. Access the Components panel (by choosing Window > Components, for example). Expand the panel's Video folder, then drag an instance of FLVPlayback to your document. The instance's source parameter is blank, but you can set it to point to an encoded video file as described in the task "To choose source video for an FLVPlayback instance" in this chapter.

D Use the Select Skin dialog to change the user controls for video playback.

E By default, the background of the controller bar is gray. To select a new background color for the bar, click the Color control in the Select Skin dialog to open a swatch set, and then choose the desired color. When you dismiss the dialog, the controller bar in the FLVPlayback instance on the Stage displays the new color (bottom).

To change controller-bar skins:

1. On the Stage, select the FLVPlayback-component instance, and access the SWF Property inspector.

2. To choose a controller-bar style, in the Component Parameters section, in the Skin row, click the Select Skin button ✐ or click the skin name directly.

   The Select Skin dialog appears, showing the same items as in the Skinning page of the Import Video Wizard **D**.

3. From the Skin pop-up menu, select a new skin.

4. If desired, use the Color control to select a new background color for the controller bar **E**. This option is not available for skins whose name starts with *MinimaSilver* or *MinimaUnder*.

5. Click OK. Flash updates the Skin property in the Component Parameters section of the SWF Property inspector and changes the controller bar in the FLVPlayback-component instance on the Stage.

> **TIP** When you choose a skin whose name starts with *skinOver*, *skinUnder,* or *MinimaFlatCustomColor*, you can change the controller bar's transparency. Select the FLVPlayback-component instance on the Stage and access the Component Parameters section of the SWF Property inspector. In the SkinBackgroundAlpha field, enter a value between 1 and 0 (1 equals opaque, 0.5 equals 50 percent transparent, and 0 equals fully transparent).

> **TIP** The style you choose for the FLVPlayback component's skin is persistent. Change the skin property, and the next time you place an FLVPlayback-component instance, it will be set to use that skin. The same is true for the skin's color and transparency settings.

Animating FLVPlayback Components

The FLVPlayback component has many similarities to a movie-clip symbol. The component is an asset that lives in the library, you can modify it using the free-transform tool, and you can mask its content using a mask layer. But there's an important difference: you can't use an FLVPlayback-component instance in a motion tween, a classic tween, or an IK armature. Flash lets you set up a tween using the FLVPlayback-component instance; but when you test the movie, it becomes clear that the tween doesn't work. The video-display window just sits in its original spot, and none of the changes you set up to animate occurs. The IK bone tool won't let you link FLVPlayback-component instances into an armature; if you try, a warning dialog appears.

When you want to animate the FLVPlayback component with motion or classic tweening, or use the component as part of an IK armature, first put the component instance inside a movie-clip symbol. You can then animate the movie-clip symbol instance to get the tween effects you want. (To review the process of creating movie-clip symbols, see Chapter 12; to review classic tweening, see Chapter 9; to review motion tweening, see Chapter 11; to review IK animation, see Chapter 13.)

Final Steps for Using FLVPlayback

When you finally publish a Flash movie for general distribution, you must place the resulting SWF file on the web server that hosts your creation. (You'll learn more about publishing in Chapter 17.) When you use the FLVPlayback component to deliver streaming video or progressive-download video, two other files must go onto the server: the file containing the encoded video (for example, an FLV file), and a SWF file containing the controller-bar skin (if you use one for your video). Whenever you issue a Publish command—by choosing Control > Test Scene, for example—Flash places the SWF file of your movie and the SWF file for the controller-bar skin in the folder with your FLA file. The encoded video file remains at its original location.

You may publish your movie many times as you test it during the authoring phase. During that phase, all the pathnames Flash uses to locate these required files let you test without problems. Before you publish your movie for final delivery to your audience, make sure that the Source property for each instance of the FLVPlayback component shows the correct URL for the final location of the source video file on the hosting server. (For details about setting the source parameter, see "To choose source video for an FLVPlayback instance" in this section.)

Delivering Movies to Your Audience

To make Adobe Flash Professional CS6 creations available to your audience, you must output your Flash content to a playback file format by publishing or exporting it.

To preserve all of the animation and interactivity of your FLA file, publish it to the Flash Player format (SWF). End users can view SWF files in a web browser that uses Flash Player to display Flash content. Viewers who have installed Flash Player can also open and run SWF files directly on their computer. Another option is to publish to a projector format to create a self-playing file.

You can export content—whole movies, individual frames, or the frames of a symbol—as bitmaps (JPEG, GIF, or PNG files). You can also export the frames of a symbol as a sprite sheet. You can export selected graphic elements in Adobe's graphics-exchange format (FXG) and use the Adobe Flash Professional Toolkit for CreateJS to translate certain types of content to JavaScript for display with HTML5.

Finally, you can print your entire movie, or individual frames of it, to hard copy for a variety of purposes, such as storyboarding.

In This Chapter

Examining Your Movie for Optimal Playback

When creating Flash movies for delivery via the web or for mobile devices, keeping file sizes small can be important. Elements that can increase a file's size include bitmaps (especially animated bitmaps), video clips (especially embedded video), sounds, multiple areas of simultaneous animation, embedded fonts, gradients, and separate graphic objects that are used instead of symbols and groups.

Flash's simulated streaming helps you find out where your movie is bogging down. The Size Report and Bandwidth Profiler reveal which frames may cause download hang-ups.

To use the Bandwidth Profiler:

1. Open your Flash document.

2. Choose Control > Test Scene, or press Option-Command-Return (OS X) or Ctrl-Alt-Enter (Win).

    or

    Choose Control > Test Movie > In Flash Professional.

    Flash publishes the movie and opens it in Flash Player.

About SWF History

Flash CS6's SWF History feature helps you track file size during authoring. When you publish a SWF file by certain methods—choosing File > Publish, Control > Test Movie > In Flash Professional, or Control > Test Movie > Test—Flash enters the SWF file's size, and the date and time of publishing, into the current document's SWF History log. (Choosing Control > Test Scene does not update the log.) The three most recent entries appear in the SWF History section of the Document Property inspector. (If the Property inspector is not visible, choose Window > Properties. To display Document properties, click a blank area of the Stage.) If there are more entries, clicking the SWF History section's Log button displays the full log in the Output panel. Flash warns you about large increases in file size by flagging increases greater than 50 percent with a warning triangle in the Property inspector. To clear the log, click the SWF History section's Clear button.

Name that appears in the menu

Speed to be simulated

Custom Download Settings		
Menu text:	**Bit rate:**	
14.4	1200	bytes/s
28.8	2400	bytes/s
56K	4800	bytes/s
DSL	33400	bytes/s
T1	134300	bytes/s
User Setting 6	2400	bytes/s
User Setting 7	2400	bytes/s
User Setting 8	2400	bytes/s

OK | Cancel | Reset

Ⓐ At its default setting, Flash offers choices for simulating five standard connection speeds. You can change the names and rates for these speeds in the Custom Download Settings dialog. You can also create your own settings.

Downloads within the set frame rate

Causes a delay in playback

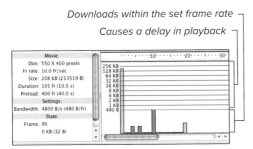

Ⓑ The Bandwidth Profiler graph at the top of the Flash Player window shows how much data each frame contains. Each bar in this version of the graph represents a frame of the movie.

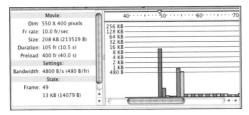

Ⓒ In Frame by Frame Graph mode, the height of each bar indicates how much data the frame holds. If a bar extends above the red line, the movie will pause at that frame while the data downloads.

3. From Flash Player's View menu, choose Download Settings, and select the download speed you want to test.

   The menu lists eight speeds, all of which are customizable. To change them, choose View > Download Settings > Customize. By default, Flash lists five common connection speeds—14.4 Kbps, 28.8 Kbps, 56 Kbps, DSL, and T1—with settings that simulate real-world data-transfer rates. You can see the settings in the Custom Download Settings dialog Ⓐ. To create a custom setting, enter new values, and then click OK.

4. From Flash Player's View menu, choose Bandwidth Profiler, or press Command-B (OS X) or Ctrl-B (Win).

   The profiler graphs the amount of data transmitted against the movie's Timeline Ⓑ. The red line represents the amount of data that will download fast enough to maintain the movie's assigned frame rate.

To view the contents of each frame separately:

1. With Bandwidth Profiler active, from the Flash Player's View menu, choose Frame by Frame Graph, or press Command-F (OS X) or Ctrl-F (Win).

   Each frame appears as a bar in the Bandwidth Profiler graph. The numbers along the top of the graph represent frames. The height of the bar represents the amount of data in that frame.

2. To view information about a specific frame in the profile window, click that frame's bar in the graph Ⓒ. The bar highlights in green.

To see how frames stream:

1. With Bandwidth Profiler active, from the Flash Player's View menu, choose Streaming Graph, or press Command-G (OS X) or Ctrl-G (Win).

    Flash displays the frames as alternating blocks of light and dark gray; the size of each block reflects the time that frame takes to download. Each number at the top of the streaming graph represents a unit of time based on the frame rate. (In a 10-fps movie, for example, each number represents 0.1 second.) Where frames contain little data, several blocks may appear in a single time unit. Frames with lots of data may stretch over several time units.

2. To view information about a specific frame in the profile window, click that frame's block in the graph **D**. The block highlights in reddish brown.

To display a download-progress bar:

- With Bandwidth Profiler active, from Flash Player's View menu, choose Simulate Download, or press Command-Return (OS X) or Ctrl-Enter (Win).

    As the animation plays in the test window, Flash highlights the numbers of the Timeline in green to show where you are in the download process **E**.

D In Streaming Graph mode, the width of each block indicates how long the frame takes to download at the given connection speed and frame rate. In this movie, Frame 49 (highlighted in reddish brown) contains 13 Kbytes of data and takes almost a third of a second to download at a frame rate of 10-fps over a 56-Kbps modem. The profile window to the left of the graph displays information about the movie.

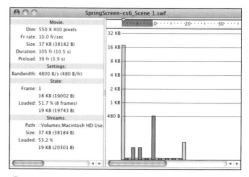

E When you choose View > Simulate Download, the playhead moves through the graph at the speed frames will appear on the end user's system. A green bar indicates how many frames of your movie have loaded so far. Precise details appear in the profile window.

To exit Bandwidth Profiler:

- From Flash Player's View menu, choose Bandwidth Profiler again to deselect it.

TIP **To view the amount of data in each frame in text form, in the Advanced section of the Flash tab of the Publish Settings dialog, choose Generate Size Report. During the publishing process, Flash creates a file enumerating the bytes of data in each movie frame. This information also appears in the Output panel in the authoring environment.**

A Note About Accessibility

Web designers use Flash not only to make media-rich websites, but also to convey information to a wide range of users, including those with disabilities. Remember that some of your users are unable to view or hear a site's content; and some may not use a mouse, but will navigate and explore your site by tabbing to each element in turn.

To help websites remain widely accessible, Flash lets you make content available to screen-reading software that uses Microsoft Active Accessibility (MSAA) technology. (At the time Flash CS6 was released, MSAA was available only for Windows.) Screen readers provide audio feedback about a variety of elements on a website—reading aloud the labels of buttons, for example, or reading the contents of text fields. Using Flash's accessibility features, you can create descriptions of objects for the screen reader; prevent the screen reader from attempting to describe certain objects (such as purely decorative movie clips); and assign keyboard commands that let users manipulate objects by pressing keys or tabbing through text fields.

In addition, Flash CS6 lets you create accessible video. Flash's FLVPlayback component (see Chapter 16) creates video controllers that respond to keyboard commands and screen readers. The FLVPlaybackCaptioning component allows you to create closed captions to provide a text version of audio content.

The considerations that go into making an effective, highly accessible site are too numerous and complex to cover in a *Visual QuickStart Guide*. You can examine the tools for defining accessible objects in the Accessibility panel. To open the panel, choose Window > Other Panels > Accessibility. The parameters for selected objects appear in the panel ❻. You can also learn about best practices for accessibility from Adobe's Accessibility Resource Center (www.adobe.com/accessibility/).

❻ The Accessibility panel contains settings for making selected objects in your movie available (or unavailable) to screen-reader software.

Publishing Movies

To make your Flash content available to the public, you must publish or export your movie. Flash's Publish command can prepare content for viewing in various formats. The default publishing options create files for viewing Flash content over the web, but you can also publish your content for delivery on mobile devices.

Publishing for the Web

By default, Flash's Publish command creates a Flash Player (SWF) file and an HTML file that includes JavaScript. The HTML and JavaScript work together, creating HTML code that displays the SWF file (running in Flash Player) in a browser window. The JavaScript can also perform version detection, ensuring that end users have the right version of Flash Player to view your content. Depending on the content of your FLA file, when you publish with the default settings, additional files may be created. When the FLA file contains TLF text, a SWZ file with instructions for handling the text is created; when the FLA file contains a component—such as the FLVPlayback component for displaying video clips—a SWF file may be created for the component skins.

To view publishing options:

- With a Flash document open, choose File > Publish Settings, or press Option-Shift-F12 (OS X) or Ctrl-Shift-F12 (Win). The Publish Settings dialog opens 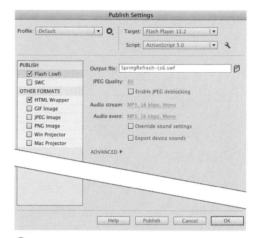 with all the options and settings available to you for the current Target and Script settings.

TIP To access the Publish Settings dialog when the Document Property inspector is open: in the Publish section's Profile area, click the Publish Settings button **B**.

A The formats list, on the left side of the Publish Settings dialog, displays the eight types of files that Flash can output during publishing. By default, Flash and HTML are selected. This combination outputs a SWF file and an HTML file containing the code needed to display the SWF file in a browser. The settings area, on the right side of the dialog, displays all the options for the selected format.

B The Document Property inspector's Publish section contains a Publish Settings button. Click it to open the Publish Settings dialog.

Other Publishing Options

The Publish command can create alternate file formats—GIF, JPEG, and PNG—and the HTML code needed to display them in the browser window. Alternate formats let you make some of the animation and interactivity of your site available even to end users who lack the Flash Player plug-in. The Publishing command can also create stand-alone projector files. The user simply double-clicks the projector icon to play the movie.

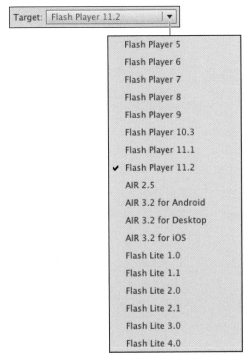

Target: Flash Player 11.2 ▼

Flash Player 5
Flash Player 6
Flash Player 7
Flash Player 8
Flash Player 9
Flash Player 10.3
Flash Player 11.1
✔ Flash Player 11.2
AIR 2.5
AIR 3.2 for Android
AIR 3.2 for Desktop
AIR 3.2 for iOS
Flash Lite 1.0
Flash Lite 1.1
Flash Lite 2.0
Flash Lite 2.1
Flash Lite 3.0
Flash Lite 4.0

C Choose which version of Flash Player the end user must have to view your content. Publishing to versions earlier than 11.2 makes some features of Flash CS6 unavailable, but ensures that a wider audience will have a compatible player. Note that Flash CS6 can't publish to the earliest versions of Flash Player, only versions 5 and later.

To choose a delivery platform:

■ To specify the platform you'll use to deliver your content, from the Target pop-up menu **C**, choose one of the following:

Flash Player is the standard platform for delivering Flash content to a web browser. Your choices are Flash Player 5, 6, 7, 8, 9, 10.3, 11.1, and 11.2. Publishing to early versions may make some Flash CS6 features unavailable, such as TLF text. A warning dialog appears when your content contains elements unavailable in your chosen Flash Player version.

AIR (which stands for Adobe Integrated Runtime) enables Flash content to run on a system or device without an Internet connection. Your choices are AIR 2.5 and 3.2 for desktop systems, and AIR 3.2 for Google Android devices and Apple iOS devices.

Flash Lite delivers Flash content to devices such as older mobile phones. Your choices are 1.0, 1.1, 2.0, 2.1, 3.0, and 4.0.

TIP When you choose Flash Player 6, 7, 8, 9, or 10, the Compress Movie checkbox becomes active. Compressing a file that has lots of text or ActionScript helps reduce the file size.

To choose an ActionScript version:

- From the Script pop-up menu, choose ActionScript version 1.0, 2.0, or 3.0 **D**.

  This setting tells Flash which version of the scripting language your document uses so that the compiler processes the code appropriately. The menu presents only the choices appropriate for the player version.

TIP Components, which rely on ActionScript to create their interactivity, are tied to a specific version of ActionScript. When ActionScript 3.0 is chosen in the Publish Settings dialog, the Components panel contains only ActionScript 3.0 components. Once you've placed a component in your FLA file, do not change the version of ActionScript in Publish Settings. If the FLA file contains components from one ActionScript version and you publish to another, the components will not work and the published movie may fail to carry out any ActionScript instructions.

TIP Before you start scripting with Action-Script, in the Flash section of the Publish Settings dialog, choose the earliest version of Flash Player you plan to support to deliver content. The Actions Toolbox in the Actions panel highlights actions that won't work in the player version currently chosen in the dialog.

Script: | ActionScript 3.0 | ▼ | ⚒

D ActionScript 1.0, 2.0, and 3.0 present different tasks for the compiler when Flash publishes a SWF file. Be sure to choose the version you used (or plan to use) for scripting. All of the tasks in this book use version 3.0.

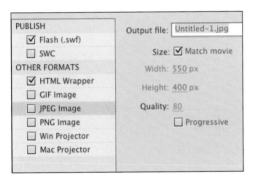

⑤ The left side of the Publish Settings dialog lists checkboxes for a variety of possible formats. The Publish command outputs files for each checkbox selected. Selecting a checkbox automatically highlights the format name, and settings for that format appear on right side of the dialog.

⑥ Click a format name in the list on the left side of the Publish Settings dialog to view settings for that format. The format's checkbox need not be selected. For example, to view JPEG options, click the name JPEG in the formats list. Settings pertaining to JPEG images appear on the right side of the dialog.

To choose a publishing format:

1. To determine which files Flash creates for this document during publishing, in the formats list, select one of the following checkboxes: Flash (.swf), SWC, HTML Wrapper, GIF Image, JPEG Image, PNG Image, Win Projector, and Mac Projector **⑤**.

2. To view the current settings for a specific format (whether or not its checkbox is currently selected), click its name **⑥**.

3. To confirm the current settings for all selected formats, and save them with the open FLA file. Return to the authoring environment, and OK.

   Flash uses these settings each time you choose the Publish or Publish Preview command for this document. Flash also uses a file's current publish settings when you enter test mode (for example, by choosing Control > Test Scene).

TIP When you select the SWC checkbox, the Publish command outputs the movie as a SWC file. Advanced Flash developers can use SWC files to archive the assets of the movie for incorporation into another Flash project. SWC files can also be incorporated into projects developed using Adobe Flex.

To publish a movie:

1. Open the Flash file you want to publish.

2. Choose File > Publish, or press Shift-Command-F12 (OS X) or Alt-Shift-F12 (Win). Flash uses the publish settings stored with your Flash document, creating a new file for each format selected in the Publish Settings dialog.

Advanced ActionScript Settings and TLF

When you select ActionScript 3.0 (or 2.0) as the target platform in the Publish Settings dialog, the ActionScript Settings button 🔧 to the right of the menu activates. Click the button to access the Advanced ActionScript 3.0 Settings dialog. Most of these settings come into play for movies that use advanced scripting techniques beyond the scope of this book. But a few settings relate to the publishing and playback of TLF text; these you may want to adjust ⓖ.

Runtime shared library settings

When you use default Publish Settings for a movie that contains TLF text, Flash Player must access the TLF SWZ file, which contains Action-Script code needed for displaying TLF text at runtime. With default settings, Flash creates the TLF SWZ file as a *runtime shared library* (RSL) in the same folder as the published SWF file.

(An RSL acts a bit like a public storage locker. It's a place to store assets and code outside your main movie SWF file. Flash Player caches RSLs the first time they're downloaded, which can help keep SWF files lean for faster download. RSLs can also make reusable assets available to multiple movies.)

Depending on how you plan to deploy your movie, you may relocate the folder containing your SWF file and the TLF SWZ file. If you do, you'll need to change the pathname. Default publishing also sets up links to Adobe's site as the primary location for accessing the TLF SWZ file. When you select the Library Path tab of the Advanced ActionScript Settings dialog, those links and pathnames appear in a scrolling window. Buttons above the window let you modify the settings, adding and removing items, and/or changing pathnames.

About the preloader

Unless the TLF SWZ file is already in the end user's Flash Player cache, default Publish Settings require downloading the entire TLF SWZ runtime shared library before playback can begin. That means with default settings a movie containing TLF text cannot stream, and users may need to wait for content to download. To ensure users have some feedback about what's happening, Flash links to a default preloader animation (found in the Configuration folder). However, you can use your own external preloader animation. In the Runtime Shared Library Settings section of the Advanced ActionScript 3.0 Settings dialog, from the Default Linkage menu, choose Runtime

ⓖ Use the Advanced ActionScript 3.0 Settings dialog to determine how Flash Player accesses the TLF SWZ file containing code needed to display TLF text at runtime. Using the default Publish settings (as shown), the TLF SWZ file works as a runtime shared library (RSL).

Continues on next page

H Click the Publish button at the bottom of the Publish Settings dialog to publish your Flash files using the current publishing settings.

I The File > Publish Preview submenu displays all the formats selected in the Publish Settings dialog. Flash publishes your movie in the selected format and opens it in your browser.

TIP You can also issue the Publish command from within the Publish Settings dialog by clicking the Publish button **H**.

TIP By default, Flash places each published file in the same location as the original Flash file. However, you can choose a new location for any or all of these files. In the Publish Settings dialog, select a format name, then in the settings area, click the Select Publish Destination button ⬚ to the right of the Output File text field. The Select Publish Destination dialog appears, allowing you to choose a new location for the file for that format.

TIP You can open your browser and preview a movie in one step. Choose File > Publish Preview. A submenu offers all the formats currently selected in the Publish Settings dialog **I**. When you choose a format, Flash uses the current settings to publish the file in that format, and then opens the movie in a browser window. Note that if you're using Publish Preview to test SWF files that reside on your local system, and your Flash movie links to a URL on the network, you can run into security issues. (See the sidebar "A Note About Flash Player's Security Settings" in this chapter.)

Advanced ActionScript Settings and TLF *(continued)*

Shared Library. From the Preloader Method menu, choose Preloader SWF and enter the URL for your SWF file in the Preloader SWF field. If you prefer to use ActionScript to monitor loading from within the SWF file and display an internal preloader animation, choose Custom Preloader Loop from the Preloader Method menu.

Embedding TLF SWZ code

You have the option to embed the TLF SWZ's code in your movie. One way is to embed the code of all shared runtime libraries. Select the Library Path button tab in the Advanced ActionScript 3.0 Settings dialog. In the Runtime Shared Library Settings section at the bottom of the dialog, from the Default Linkage menu, choose Merged into Code. You can also change the settings for individual libraries. Choose the library in the scrolling list (for the TLF SWZ file, you would choose the item named textLayout.swc), click the Set Linkage Option button ⓞ, then change settings in the Library Path Item Options dialog. (For example, deselect the "Use default shared library linkage" checkbox and choose Merged into Code from the Link Type pop-up menu.)

About Targeting Mobile Devices with AIR for Android and AIR for iOS

Technology is always changing and evolving. The desktop computer was once the dominant playback device, and Flash the dominant platform for delivering animated content over the web. Today mobile devices are everywhere, and not all of them allow Flash content to run directly in their operating systems. Flash developers can still target many of those devices by publishing to AIR for Android or AIR for iOS.

Creating content for mobile devices requires thought and planning. Some Flash features help you prepare content for mobile platforms. (Two examples are automatic scaling of graphics when you resize the Stage, and Mobile Gesture Events Code Snippets, which help you script UI elements that respond to gestures.) But considerations of design, user interface, and optimization for mobile-content delivery are beyond the scope of a *Visual QuickStart Guide*. Similarly, the specific requirements and settings for publishing for iOS or Android fall outside the scope of this book. The overall process of publishing to AIR is similar to that for publishing to Flash and HTML; but there are additional screens to fill out, and they are more hidden from view.

Accessing AIR Publishing Options

To access the AIR publishing formats for mobile devices, in the Publish Settings dialog, from the Target menu, choose AIR for Android or AIR for iOS. Click the Player Settings button 🔧 to the right of the target name to open the associated AIR Settings dialog . The dialog presents five categories of settings for Android ❶, four for iOS. To see the specific options in a category, click the category button.

Testing Touch Interfaces in Flash

When you choose AIR for Android or AIR for iOS as the target platform in the Publish Settings dialog, you have an option for testing touch-interface elements in the Flash authoring environment. Choose Control > Test Movie> in AIR Debug Launcher (Mobile). Your movie opens in Flash Player. In addition, the SimController application's Simulator panel opens ❷. This panel simulates three

❶ The AIR for Android Settings dialog contains five categories of settings. Click one of the category buttons to view the settings.

❷ The Simulator panel lets you use a mouse to interact with content designed for touch-screen devices.

Continues on next page

categories of input data. Accelerometer simulates tilt: you manipulate an *x-y-z* graph to change the simulated device's orientation in 3D space. Touch and Gesture simulates touch events: you use mouse actions, such as click and drag, to simulate touch actions, such as tap and swipe. Geolocation simulates GPS data: you use text fields to enter items such as latitude and longitude.

Testing on a Connected Android Device

When you choose AIR for Android as the target platform in the Publish Settings dialog, you have an option for testing on an Android device connected to your computer. Choose Control > Test Movie > On Device via USB. If you haven't yet chosen all of the required settings for publishing your app to an Android device, the AIR for Android Settings dialog opens, with the Deployment tab selected ❶. To use this testing option, you must fill in all of the settings required for publishing to your device, including providing certificate information. You'll also need to connect an Android device to your computer using a USB cable and enable the device's USB debugging feature.

❶ To test your content on an Android device connected to your computer, you must provide all the information required for publishing to that device.

Setting Flash Player Options

The stand-alone Flash Player is an application file that installs with Flash. The Player opens when you double-click the icon of a SWF file. (Within Flash Player, you can choose the File > Open command to open and play SWF files.) To prepare a Flash movie for playing in the stand-alone Player, you can choose either the Publish or Export command in the Flash editor.

To access settings for the Flash Player (SWF) file:

1. In the Publish Settings dialog, in the formats list, select the Flash (.swf) checkbox **Ⓐ**. The name highlights in dark gray, and the right side of the dialog displays settings relevant to creating the SWF file.

2. To select the folder where the SWF file is created, click the 🖉 button to the right of the Output file field. In the Select Publish Destination dialog, navigate to the desired folder and click OK. By default, Flash publishes the SWF file to the same folder as the original FLA file.

3. If you wish, type a new name in the Output file field.

To apply JPEG compression to bitmaps:

- In the Flash settings area, use the JPEG Quality hot-text control to enter a value between 0 and 100 **Ⓑ**. To get higher image quality in the published file, use a higher value.

Ⓐ In the Publish Settings dialog, selecting a checkbox in the formats list (on the left side of the dialog) displays corresponding options in the settings area (on the right side of the dialog). Here Flash is the selected format.

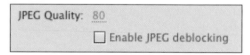

Ⓑ To set JPEG compression for any bitmaps in your movie, use the JPEG Quality hot-text control to enter a new value. A setting of 0 provides the most compression (resulting in the lowest quality, because that compression leads to loss of data); a setting of 100 provides the least compression (resulting in the highest quality).

TIP You can set compression for individual bitmaps in the library of your Flash document. Select the bitmap in the Library panel. From the panel menu, choose Properties to access the Bitmap Properties dialog. A Compression pop-up menu offers two choices: Photo (JPEG) and Lossless (PNG/GIF). The Photo option creates lossy compression.

TIP When you apply high levels of JPEG compression (low values in the JPEG Quality field), you can wind up with artifacts—areas that look blurry or blocky—in the published images. To smooth out blocky artifacts, select the Enable JPEG Deblocking checkbox just under the JPEG Quality slider.

Audio stream: MP3, 16 kbps, Mono

Audio event: MP3, 16 kbps, Mono

☐ Override sound settings

☐ Export device sounds

G You must set the sample rate and compression options for stream sounds and event sounds separately. Click the blue text to access the options for each type of sound.

Sound Settings

Compression: MP3 ▼   OK

☐ Use 8kHz sample rate   Cancel

Preprocessing: ☑ Convert stereo to mono

Bit rate: 16 kbps ▼

Quality: Fast ▼

Disable
ADPCM
✔ MP3
Raw
Speech

D Choose a compression method from the Compression pop-up menu. Options appropriate to the selected method appear. Choose Disable to turn off sound.

Compression: ADPCM ▼

Preprocessing: ☑ Convert stereo to mono   2 bit

Sample rate: 22kHz ▼   3 bit

ADPCM bits: 4 bit ▼   ✔ 4 bit

5 bit

E The ADPCM Bits pop-up menu lets you control the amount of compression applied to the sounds in your movie. Choose 2-Bit for the greatest degree of compression (resulting in the lowest-quality sound); choose 5-Bit for the least compression (resulting in the highest-quality sound).

To control compression and sample rate for all movie sounds:

1. In the Flash settings area, click the blue Audio Stream text (or Audio Event text) **G**.

   The Sound Settings dialog appears. Flash divides sounds into two types: stream and event (see Chapter 16). You must set the compression for each type separately, but the process and options are similar for both.

2. From the Compression pop-up menu **D**, choose one of the following options:

   Disable removes sound from the published file.

   ADPCM compression works best for movies containing mostly short event sounds, such as hand claps or button clicks. (Generally, you'll use this setting in the Audio Event section for sounds other than MP3s.) When you choose ADPCM, the dialog displays the ADPCM options. From the ADPCM Bits pop-up menu, choose one of the four bit rates to determine the degree of compression applied to the sounds **E**. With the ADPCM setting, you can also set a sample rate and convert stereo sound to mono.

   MP3 compression (the default setting) works best for movies containing mostly longer stream sounds. (Generally, you'll use this setting in the Audio Stream section.) When you choose MP3, the dialog displays MP3 options. From the

   Continues on next page

Bit Rate pop-up menu, choose one of 12 bit rates for the published sounds **F**. From the Quality pop-up menu, choose Fast when you are testing your movie; choose Medium or Best when you publish for your target audience, as these options provide better quality.

Raw performs no sound compression, but does let you control file size by choosing a sample rate and converting stereo sound to mono.

Speech sets compression for sounds consisting of spoken words. Choose a sample rate from the pop-up menu.

To compress the SWF file:

1. From the Target pop-up menu, choose Flash Player 6 (or later) or a version of AIR. Compression is not available for Flash Player 5 or any of the Flash Lite versions.

2. In the Flash settings area, access the Advanced section.

3. Select the Compress Movie checkbox, and from the compression algorithm pop-up menu **G**, choose one of the following:

   Deflate, the default, has the greatest effect on files that contain a lot of text, either on the Stage or in ActionScript.

   LZMA can compress vector images and text for Flash Player 11 and later.

   Neither form of compression has any effect on the JPEG-quality and audio-compression settings you chose in the preceding tasks.

To include XMP metadata:

- In the Flash settings area, in the Advanced section, select the Include XMP Metadata checkbox **H**.

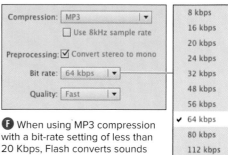

F When using MP3 compression with a bit-rate setting of less than 20 Kbps, Flash converts sounds from stereo to mono. At settings of 20 Kbps and above, you can publish stereo sounds or convert them to mono sounds.

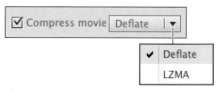

G When you've chosen to publish to Flash Player versions 6–11.2, you can also choose to compress the movie. Compression helps reduce the file size, especially for text-heavy movies or those with lots of ActionScript.

H When you select the Include XMP Metadata checkbox, the published SWF file includes metadata—such as titles, descriptions, and copyright notice—that you've entered into the XMP info document for the file.

Sample-Rate Rule of Thumb

Sample rates are measured in kHz (kilohertz). Flash works with 8-bit or 16-bit sounds at sample rates of 11 kHz, 22 kHz, or 44 kHz. Higher sampling rates produce higher-quality sound reproduction. Music CDs play at 44.1 kHz. For multimedia CD-ROMs, 22 kHz is a standard rate. For music clips in Flash movies played on the web, 11 kHz is often sufficient.

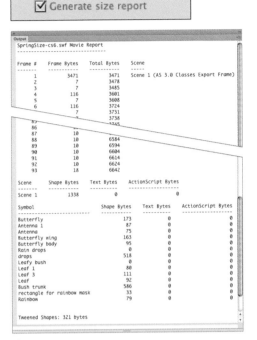

Frame #	Frame Bytes	Total Bytes	Scene
1	3471	3471	Scene 1 (AS 3.0 Classes Export Frame)
2	7	3478	
3	7	3485	
4	116	3601	
5	7	3608	
6	116	3724	
7	7	3731	
	7	3745	
86			
87	10		
88	10	6584	
89	10	6594	
90	10	6604	
91	10	6614	
92	10	6624	
93	18	6642	

Scene	Shape Bytes	Text Bytes	ActionScript Bytes
Scene 1	1338	0	0

Symbol	Shape Bytes	Text Bytes	ActionScript Bytes
Butterfly	173	0	0
Antenna 1	87	0	0
Antenna	75	0	0
Butterfly wing	163	0	0
Butterfly body	95	0	0
Rain drops	0	0	0
drops	518	0	0
Leafy bush	0	0	0
Leaf 1	80	0	0
Leaf 3	111	0	0
Leaf	92	0	0
Bush trunk	586	0	0
rectangle for rainbow mask	33	0	0
Rainbow	79	0	0

Tweened Shapes: 321 bytes

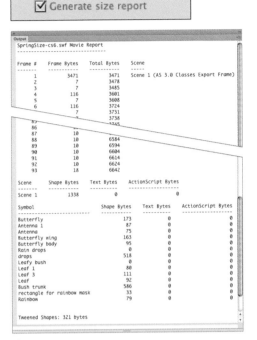 When you choose Generate Size Report (top), Flash uses the Output panel to list the amount of data in your movie (bottom).

To list the amount of data in each movie frame:

- In the Flash settings area, in the Advanced section, select the Generate Size Report checkbox ❶.

  In the Output panel, Flash lists the frames of the movie and how much data each frame contains. This data—known as the *Size Report*—helps you find frames that bog down the movie's playback. You can then optimize or eliminate some of the content in those frames.

TIP In addition to displaying the Size Report in the Output panel, Flash creates a text file containing the Size Report.

TIP The Size Report details how much data is in each symbol used in the movie. Symbols that aren't used appear in the report but contain 0 bytes of data. The Size Report also shows you the size of every exported sound, bitmap, and font.

TIP Depending on how you've sized the Output window, and the specific data generated by the Size Report, you may see only white space in the Output window. Resize the window or scroll up to view the Size Report data.

About XMP File Info

Flash CS6 lets you include XMP (Extensible Metadata Platform) information in your FLA file. Adding XMP data can be helpful when you work collaboratively, sharing the file with others and using multiple Adobe products to create content. You can also include XMP metadata as a part of a published SWF file, creating titles, descriptions, copyright notices, and so on. The XMP metadata included with a SWF file is available to Internet search engines for indexing.

To create XMP metadata during authoring, choose File > File Info. A tabbed document opens. Click the appropriate category tab for the type of information you'd like to include. For example, the Description tab has fields for entering a title, the author's name, a description, a star rating, keywords, a copyright notice, and so on. After you've entered information into all the desired categories, click OK. To add this information to the published SWF file, in the Publish Settings dialog, with the Flash (.swf) settings active, select the Include XMP Metadata checkbox. To access the XMP metadata document from the Publish Settings dialog, click the Modify button 🔲 to the right of the checkbox.

To protect your work:

1. In the Flash settings area, in the Advanced section, select the Protect from Import checkbox 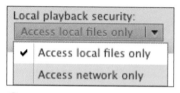. This setting prevents viewers from obtaining the SWF file and converting it back to a Flash (FLA) file.

2. To make the Protect from Import setting selective, enter a password in the Password field to limit those who can import the SWF file.

To control access to local and network files:

- To determine which types of files the SWF file can copy data from or write data to, in the Flash settings area, in the Advanced section, from the Local Playback Security pop-up menu **K**, choose one of the following options:

Access Local Files Only With local-only access, the SWF file can share information with files on the local system where the SWF file resides, but not with files located on the Internet. For example, local-only access prevents a SWF file from loading XML files from the Internet or posting data from an entry form to the Internet.

Access Network Only With network-only access, the SWF file can share information only with files located on the Internet, not with local files.

J Select the Protect from Import checkbox to prevent viewers from converting a SWF file back into a FLA file. Enter a password to allow selected individuals to import the SWF file. (Note that even those individuals won't be able to import the full capabilities of the original FLA file. The imported SWF file becomes a frame-by-frame animation after import. Third-party software is available that will decompile a SWF file and create a full FLA file.)

K Flash CS6 provides security by restricting SWF files from manipulating data on different systems. With Access Local Files Only as the setting, the published SWF file can copy or write data only to files on the local system. With Access Network Only, the SWF file can copy or write data only to files on the Internet and not on the local system.

(L) To allow your Flash content to access a high-end graphics card on the end user's system, choose one of the Hardware Acceleration options in the Flash settings area of the Publish Settings dialog.

To use hardware acceleration (if available):

- In the Flash settings area, in the Advanced section, from the Hardware Acceleration pop-up menu **(L)**, select one of the following:

  Level 1—Direct speeds playback by having Flash Player, instead of the browser, draw onscreen graphics.

  Level 2—GPU speeds video playback and playback of complex layered graphics if the end user's system has a high-end graphics card (a graphics processing unit).

TIP When you choose HTML Wrapper in the formats list, a Window Mode menu appears in the settings area. That menu also offers a Direct option. When you choose Level 1 or Level 2 for the Flash settings, that setting takes precedence over the Window Mode > Direct setting in HTML Wrapper settings.

TIP Selecting one of these acceleration modes adds code to the HTML wrapper, instructing the end user's system to use its graphics card to accelerate certain window-drawing tasks.

Advanced Sound Handling

Flash applies the sound-compression settings in the Publish Settings dialog to all sound assets that have no specific settings of their own. By assigning higher quality to some sounds, you can reduce file size and maintain high-quality sound where needed.

To set sound compression options individually, select a sound asset in the Library panel, and then click the Properties button at the bottom of the panel, or choose Properties from the panel menu. The Sound Properties dialog appears. Its Compression pop-up menu gives you access to the same sound-export settings you used in the task "To control compression and sample rate for all movie sounds" in this chapter.

When you apply individual sound-export settings to some sound assets, Flash uses those settings for those sounds when you publish the movie. For all other sounds in the movie, Flash uses the current sound settings in the Publish Settings dialog.

You can force Flash to ignore the individual sound settings and publish all sounds with the sound-export settings currently selected in the Publish Settings dialog. In the Publish Settings dialog, with the Flash (.swf) settings active, in the Audio section, select the Override Sound Settings checkbox. You might use this feature to make a lower-quality web version of a movie you created for DVD.

A Note About Flash Player's Security Settings

Flash CS6 and Flash Player versions later than 8 let you create content that uploads and/or downloads files at runtime. This capability has the potential to do harm. Downloaded files may be able to do something dangerous, such as copying information from your system and sending it to an outside location. Therefore, those versions of Flash Player use a security feature that ensures that SWF files can't perform malicious deeds on the systems of your target audience. Flash's default local-security settings prohibit SWF files running locally (on a single computer) from communicating with files being served on the Internet (and vice versa). To allow such communication, you must give Flash Player specific permissions.

When you choose Flash Player version 8 or later in Publish Settings, the security model comes into play. When you publish your Flash creation locally before deploying it to a server and you try out the movie in a browser, clicking a button or link in the movie that connects to the Internet may trigger a warning that Flash Player has stopped an operation that might be unsafe.

If the SWF file you're testing doesn't need to communicate with both the local system and the Internet, you can solve the problem by changing your Publish Settings. In the Publish Settings dialog, with the Flash (.swf) settings active, in the Advanced section, from the Local Playback Security pop-up menu, choose Access Network Only. Note that the security alert does not appear when you use one of the test modes (such as choosing Control > Test Scene). In a test mode, Flash automatically trusts all local files being accessed.

If you still get the warning after changing the Local Playback Security setting, you need to add your SWF file to a list of trusted locations. Flash Player always allows SWF files from trusted locations to communicate with the Internet, even if they're run locally. The warning dialog helps you start the process of adding trusted files. When the Adobe Flash Player Security dialog appears, click the Settings button .

 When a SWF file on a local computer attempts to access a file on the Internet, Flash Player versions 8 and later will prevent access, unless you use the proper security settings. A warning dialog alerts you to the fact that your settings prohibit this communication.

Continues on next page

A Note About Flash Player's Security Settings *(continued)*

In OS X, the Flash Player dialog opens. Select the Advanced tab, and then in the Developer Tools section, click the Trusted Location Settings button ⓝ. In the Trusted Location Settings window, click the Add button ⊞, and then navigate to the trusted file or folder to add it to the list.

In Windows, clicking the Settings button opens a browser window to a page of the Flash Player documentation on the Adobe site. This page gives you access to the Adobe Flash Player Settings Manager where you can create a list of trusted sites ⓞ. Select the manager's Global Security Settings tab ▦ to access tools for creating a list of trusted items.

If you'll be doing lots of this type of testing, it makes sense to set up a special Trusted folder where you keep only your own SWF files that you need to test. Don't allow Flash Player to trust folders on your system that might include SWF files downloaded from other sources.

ⓝ In the Advanced section of the Flash Player Settings dialog, click the Trusted Locations Setting button to create a list of your local folders and/or files that can communicate with the Internet.

ⓞ The Global Security Settings tab of the Adobe Flash Player Settings Manager lets you create a list of trusted files and/or folders for security in Flash Player versions 8 and later. Any SWF files in locations covered by this list can communicate with Internet files.

Publishing HTML for Flash Player Files

An HTML document is a master set of instructions that tells a browser how to display web content. The Publish function of Flash creates an HTML document that tells the browser how to display the published files for your document. (These files can be in SWF, GIF, JPEG, and/or PNG format—whichever you choose in the formats list in the Publish Settings dialog.) The Publish command creates the required HTML by filling in blanks in a template document. Flash comes with ten templates, and you can create your own.

To create HTML code for displaying a Flash file:

1. In an open Flash document, choose File > Publish Settings. The Publish Settings dialog appears.

2. In the formats list, select the HTML Wrapper checkbox. The Flash (.swf) checkbox is automatically selected as well. Options for displaying the SWF file in a browser window appear in the settings area **Ⓐ**.

3. From the Template pop-up menu **Ⓑ**, choose Flash Only.

   This template is the simplest. It uses HTML to display Flash content for viewers who are properly equipped with the Flash Player version currently selected as the Target in the Publish Settings dialog. When you publish the current file, Flash feeds your choices into the appropriate HTML tags and parameters in the template of your choice.

Ⓐ When you select HTML Wrapper in the formats list in the Publish Settings dialog, options for displaying your Flash movie in the browser window appear in the settings area.

Ⓑ Choose Flash Only as the template when you want to create HTML for displaying only a Flash movie with no options for alternate images.

C The Minor Revision (left) and Incremental Revision (right) hot-text controls enable you to specify the exact version of Flash Player you want your viewers to use.

D The HTML Template Info dialog contains a description of what the selected template does. To view it, click the Info button in the HTML Wrapper settings area of the Publish Settings dialog.

4. To allow viewers to install or upgrade their Flash Player, select the Detect Flash Version checkbox. The main Player version matches the current Target setting.

5. To specify a revision of that version, use the Minor Revision and/or Incremental Revision hot-text controls to enter the desired revision number **C**.

TIP The other nine choices in the Template pop-up menu create HTML that performs other tasks. The Image Map template, for example, creates HTML that displays alternate images or files when the viewer lacks the proper Flash Player plug-in.

TIP If you can't remember what one of the included HTML templates does, select it from the Template pop-up menu in the HTML Wrapper settings area of the Publish Settings dialog, and then click the Info button next to the menu. Flash displays a brief description, including instructions about choosing alternate formats, when necessary **D**.

Exporting Assets and Frames

Flash's File > Export commands translate Flash content directly into a single new format. For symbols that are selected on the Stage or in the Library panel, the contextual menu includes commands that export the symbol content. You can export one symbol's frames as a series of bitmaps (PNG files), or export one or more symbols' frames as a single PNG file known as a *sprite sheet.*

New to Flash CS6 is an extension called Toolkit for CreateJS, which lets you prepare Flash content for use with JavaScript and HTML5. The toolkit exports the symbols, sounds, and bitmaps from the library of your Flash document; translates the symbol and Timeline animation to JavaScript; and creates an HTML file that can preview the JavaScript in a browser. The full range of options and settings for exporting—especially for creating sprite sheets and JavaScript—are beyond the scope of this *Visual QuickStart Guide,* but the following tasks give you a quick look at how to use these tools.

Exporting to Single Formats

You can export the frames of an entire Flash document as a SWF movie; as a QuickTime movie; as an animated GIF; or as a sequence of JPEG, GIF, or PNG images. You can export a single frame as an image in the following formats: SWF, JPEG, GIF, PNG, or FXG (Adobe's graphics-exchange format). You can also select graphic objects on the Stage and export them as FXG files. Finally, you can export the frames of a symbol as a series of PNG files.

Exporting vs. Publishing

In general, the File > Export commands present you with the same settings and options for exporting to GIF, JPEG, and PNG, as the Publish Settings dialog does. The arrangement of options may differ, and in some cases, the options also differ. For example, the Publish Settings dialog lets you remove gradients from GIFs (to reduce the file size), whereas the Export GIF dialog lacks that option.

Another difference between publishing and exporting is that Flash stores the Publish Settings with the FLA file for reuse, but you must set export options each time you export a FLA file using the File > Export commands (even when you re-export the same FLA file to the same format).

When you export an entire movie, you have access to a delivery option that's unavailable when publishing: QuickTime. QuickTime export works by playing the SWF file in Flash Player, capturing each frame of the animation (including animation generated by ActionScript), and writing it to a frame in a QuickTime MOV file. As a result, you lose any interactivity features in your Flash movie.

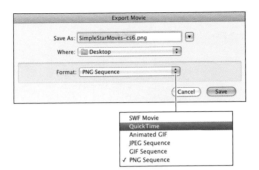

A The three File > Export commands let you choose an appropriate format and location for the exported file. The Export Movie option lets you save the frames of your movie in a QuickTime movie, a format that is not available in the Publish Settings dialog.

B When you use the contextual menu to export a symbol as a PNG sequence, you encounter two dialogs named Export PNG Sequence. The first is a standard Save As dialog, but its Format menu contains just one choice (top). Once you choose a location for the exported files and press Save, the second Export PNG Sequence dialog opens (lower left). In this dialog, you choose settings for the PNG files. In creating the export files, Flash adds a sequential number to each file name and outputs a series of images you can use to recreate the animation of the selected symbol (lower right).

To use the File > Export command:

1. In an open Flash document, choose File > Export.

2. From the submenu choose one of the following:

   Export Image exports the contents of the current keyframe.

   Export Selection exports items currently selected on the Stage.

   Export Movie exports all the frames of the Flash document.

3. In the Export dialog, choose a format and location for the exported file **A**.

4. Click Save. Flash exports the files and saves them to the specified location.

To export a symbol as a PNG sequence:

1. Open the Flash document containing the symbol you want to export and access the Library panel.

2. In the Library panel, Command-click (OS X) or right-click (Win) the name of the symbol.

   or

   On the Stage, Command-click (OS X) or right-click (Win) a symbol instance.

3. From the contextual menu, choose Export PNG Sequence. An Export PNG Sequence dialog appears.

4. Choose a location for the exported files. Note that PNG Sequence is the only file format option **B**.

5. Click Save. A different Export PNG Sequence dialog appears.

6. Choose your settings and click Export. Flash creates sequentially numbered PNG files for the movie.

Generating Sprite Sheets and XML

You can export the frames of a symbol as a series of static images that represent the animation. The images are compiled into a single PNG bitmap known as a *sprite sheet*. (See the sidebar "About Sprite Sheets.")

To export the frames of a symbol as sprites:

1. In the Library panel, or on the Stage, select each symbol that you want to include in the sprite sheet.

2. Control-click (OS X) or right-click (Win) one of the selected symbols, and from the contextual menu, choose Generate Sprite Sheet **C**.

   The Generate Sprite Sheet dialog appears **D**. The Symbol Information list displays all symbols that you have chosen to export as sprite sheets. By default each symbol's checkbox is selected.

3. To remove a symbol from the sheet, deselect it in the Symbol Information list.

4. In the Sprite Sheet Output section of the dialog, choose the data format for your target platform and set other options based on the specifics of your situation. (See the sidebar "Sprite Sheet Output Options" in this chapter.)

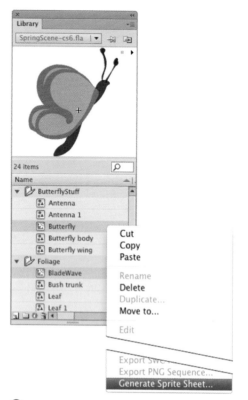

C Control-click (OS X) or right-click (Win) one or more selected symbol names in the library to access the command for generating a sprite sheet for those symbols.

D By default, the Generate Sprite Sheet dialog includes all of the symbols that were selected when you issued the command to generate the sprite sheet. Deselect a checkbox to exclude that symbol from the sprite sheet.

```
<?xml version="1.0" encoding="UTF-16"?>
<TextureAtlas imagePath="Spring-Butterfly.png">
  <!-- Created with Adobe Flash CS6 version 12.0.0.481 -->
  <!-- http://www.adobe.com/products/flash.html -->
  <SubTexture name="Butterfly0000" x="10" y="10" width="147" height="175" frameX="-67"
frameY="-19" frameWidth="214" frameHeight="194"/>
  <SubTexture name="Butterfly0001" x="10" y="10" width="147" height="175" frameX="-67"
frameY="-19" frameWidth="214" frameHeight="194"/>
  <SubTexture name="Butterfly0002" x="10" y="10" width="147" height="175" frameX="-67"
frameY="-19" frameWidth="214" frameHeight="194"/>
  <SubTexture name="Butterfly0003" x="10" y="10" width="147" height="175" frameX="-67"
frameY="-19" frameWidth="214" frameHeight="194"/>
  <SubTexture name="Butterfly0004" x="10" y="10" width="147" height="175" frameX="-67"
frameY="-19" frameWidth="214" frameHeight="194"/>
  <SubTexture name="Butterfly0005" x="157" y="10" width="175" height="192" frameX="0"
frameY="0" frameWidth="214" frameHeight="194"/>
  <SubTexture name="Butterfly0006" x="157" y="10" width="175" height="192" frameX="0"
frameY="0" frameWidth="214" frameHeight="194"/>
  <SubTexture name="Butterfly0007" x="157" y="10" width="175" height="192" frameX="0"
frameY="0" frameWidth="214" frameHeight="194"/>
  <SubTexture name="Butterfly0008" x="157" y="10" width="175" height="192" frameX="0"
frameY="0" frameWidth="214" frameHeight="194"/>
  <SubTexture name="Butterfly0009" x="332" y="10" width="148" height="174" frameX="0"
frameY="-2" frameWidth="214" frameHeight="194"/>
</TextureAtlas>
```

E The Generate Sprite Sheet command outputs two files: a PNG file with the full bitmap image and a data file that defines the bounding box of each sprite. The current selection in the Data Format menu determines the type of data file created. Here, for example, the data was output for easeljs, and the data is in an XML file.

5. To choose a location for the exported file, click the Browse button. In the Select Destination Folder dialog that appears, navigate to the desired location, and then click Save.

6. In the Sprite Sheet Filename field (located between the Browse and Export buttons), enter a name for your sprite sheet.

7. Click Export.

8. Flash creates a PNG file containing all the sprites and a data file that defines the location, width, and height of each sprite in the image **E**.

About Sprite Sheets

Flash does a wonderful job using vectors to create fluid animation, but during playback, all of those images must be rendered to the playback device. On devices with limited power, complex vector animations, even those enclosed in symbols, can slow things down and have a negative impact on the user experience. More and more, today's Flash developers are creating games and animated elements for mobile devices that lack the power of desktop computers.

Bitmap caching is one way to address the problem. For game developers, another solution is to create *sprites*. In this context, a sprite is a bitmap image of a reusable element. (In essence, to convert a selected Flash symbol to sprites, the Generate Sprite Sheet command captures a bitmap screen of each frame in the symbol's Timeline. An individual Flash sprite consists of all the graphic elements that appear in one frame.) A *sprite sheet* combines multiple sprites in a single bitmap. (Don't confuse the sprites of sprite sheets with ActionScript 3.0's sprite objects, which are more akin to movie-clip symbols.)

When you generate sprite sheets in Flash, an accompanying data file describes the coordinates of a bounding box that encloses each sprite. Game-development software can use the data in those two files to create animations by displaying subsets of the full bitmap—just enough to show the individual sprites—in sequence. By generating sprite sheets in Flash, you get to develop your characters and animation using all of Flash's options, including vector artwork, and then use a game development application to create efficient animation using bitmap sprites.

Sprite Sheet Output Options

Your goal in creating a sprite sheet is to reduce loading time during playback. To make the most efficient use of memory you want to fit as many graphics as possible into one bitmap. The settings in the Sprite Sheet Output section of the Generate Sprite Sheet dialog help you to do that.

Image Dimensions By default, Flash auto-sizes the sprite sheet, making it just large enough to accommodate all selected symbols. Choose a different size option from the menu, or use the Width and Height hot-text controls to create custom dimensions. If the dimensions you choose are too small to hold all of the sprites, a warning triangle appears.

Image Format Choose which type of bitmap to create: PNG 8-bit, 24-bit, or 32-bit; or JPEG.

Background Color By default, the sprites appear on a fully transparent background. Use the Background Color control Background color: ☐ to create an opaque or partially transparent background.

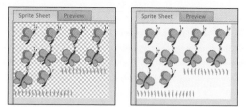

Transparent   Opaque

Algorithm There are two choices for arranging items within the rectangular sprite sheet image: Basic organizes sprites in rows, with equal space around each sprite's bounding box; MaxRects organizes the sprites for most efficient use of space.

Data Format Choose a format for the file that describes each sprite's location in the sprite-sheet image file. For example, easelJS creates a JavaScript file with coordinates for each sprite's bounding box.

Trim By default, the full area of a symbol's bounding box creates each sprite's tile in the sprite sheet. Select the Trim checkbox ☑ Trim to remove excess blank space.

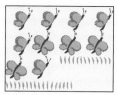 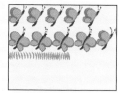

Untrimmed   Trimmed

Stack Frames By default, the sprite sheet includes an image for every frame of the symbol, including frames with identical content. Select the Stack Frames checkbox ☑ Stack frames to stack identical frames. In the final, flattened bitmap, they become a single sprite.

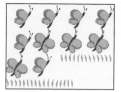 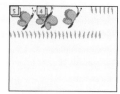

Unstacked frames   Stacked frames

Padding Increase the *Border Padding* value Border padding: 35 px to create extra space between the sprites and the edges of the sprite sheet. Increase the *Shape Padding* value Shape padding: 30 px to create extra space between sprites.

Without padding   With padding

F The Toolkit for CreateJS panel can translate the animation of your Flash movie to JavaScript, which you can then display using HTML5.

Getting the Toolkit into Flash

To work with the toolkit, you must install an extension from Adobe's website (www.adobe.com/go/createjs). Download the file Toolkit-for-CreateJS.zxp, double-click the file to open the Adobe Extension Manager, and then install the toolkit extension. You must close Flash to install the extension. The toolkit becomes available when you restart Flash. Note that although the toolkit is an extension, which you install with the Extension Manager, you'll find the toolkit under Other Panels in the Window menu (not under Extensions).

Generating JavaScript and HTML5

The Toolkit for CreateJS is an extension to Flash CS6. The toolkit translates much of the animation, interaction, and graphic content of your Flash movie into JavaScript code; exports the sounds and bitmaps from your movie's library; and creates an HTML document that works together with CreateJS libraries to play your movie in a browser using HTML5. The toolkit can't translate everything—it works only with classic text and classic tweens, for example—but it does warn you when the movie's content presents a problem. Think of the toolkit's results as a jumping off point from which to develop a more fully realized JavaScript-HTML5 project. The requirements of working with the toolkit to create such a project are beyond the scope of this book, but you can get started with a brief look at using the panel.

To publish the graphics, animation, and library assets of your movie for CreateJS:

1. To access the Toolkit for CreateJS panel, in an open Flash document, choose Window > Other Panels > Toolkit for CreateJS. The panel opens **F**.

2. To open the HTML document in your default browser after exporting, select the Preview checkbox.

3. To choose a location for the files created during export, click the Output Destination button 🔲, navigate to the desired location, then click Choose. The pathname to the location appears in the panel.

Continues on next page

4. To determine which assets the toolkit creates, select one or more of the following checkboxes:

Images contains the bitmaps in the movie's Library panel.

Sounds contains the sounds in the movie's Library panel.

JS Libraries contains the JavaScript libraries required to display your animation.

To change a folder's default name, double-click the blue text to highlight it in black. Then you can enter the new name **G**.

5. Select or deselect the checkboxes for the remaining options:

Include Hidden Layers exports the content of frames that are currently hidden in the Timeline. To omit this data, deselect the checkbox.

Compact Shapes creates compact instructions for drawing vector shapes. To view the code in a readable form, deselect the checkbox.

Publish HTML creates an HTML file for previewing your translated movie. If you just want to create the JavaScript file, deselect this checkbox.

Hosted Libs includes code in the HTML file to direct the end user's system to hosted servers on Adobe's website to get the CreateJS libraries. If you want to provide the CreateJS libraries yourself, deselect the checkbox.

6. Click the Publish button. The toolkit generates the files and folders in the specified location **H**.

TIP The blue text in the Toolkit for CreateJS panel is editable. Click the text to place the cursor, and drag to select individual characters; or double-click to select the entire text.

G To rename one of the output folders, select the blue text and type the name.

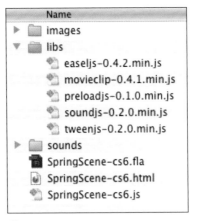

H By default, the toolkit's Publish operation creates the following items in the same location as your FLA file: a JS file containing code that re-creates supported types of graphics, animation, and symbols from your FLA file; an HTML document that automatically previews your exported content in your default browser; two folders containing assets exported from the library of your FLA file (one holds bitmap images, the other holds sounds); and a folder containing the CreateJS libraries needed to play the JavaScript-HTML5 combo in a browser.

A Note About Frame Numbers

Relying solely on frame numbers when scripting Timeline navigation in Flash may present a problem when you publish for CreateJS. Flash starts numbering frames at 1 (the first frame in the Timeline is Frame 1), while JavaScript starts numbering frames at 0. To avoid problems created by this mismatch, give your keyframes labels, and use those labels for Timeline navigation in your Action-Script code. Using this technique, Toolkit for CreateJS will create code that works correctly in HTML5. (To learn about creating frame labels for interactivity, see Chapters 14 and 15.)

Index

double slash (//), 330, 336
download-progress bar, 422
Down state, 314, 326, 327. See also button states
dragging
    bones, 311
    control points, 255
    frames, 176–178
    symbols, 198
    tween spans, 260
    tween targets, 251
drawing-objects
    adding strokes to, 53
    combining with primitives, 133
    converting other shape types to, 125
    converting TLF text to, 126
    converting to merge-shapes, 126
    grouping, 129
    selecting, 89, 90, 91–92
    tools for creating, 42
    undoing changes to, 100
    using one to remove part of another, 134
Drawing preferences, 43
drawing tools, 25, 26, 37
Duplicate Layers command, 266

E

easing, 292–295
    in classic tweens, 198, 292
    custom, 293, 294–295
    in motion tweens, 229, 243, 292, 295
    purpose of, 292
    in shape tweens, 292
ECMA-262 specification, xii
e-commerce applications, 331
Editable text, 57, 58, 59
Edit bar, 5
Edit Envelope dialog, 401–404
Edit Grid dialog, 20
Edit in Place command, 160
Edit Multiple Frames mode, 191–192, 277
Edit Scene menu, 153
Edit Selected command, 131
Edit Snapping dialog, 24

Edit Symbol menu, 160
e-learning applications, 331
embedded fonts, 75, 420
embedded video, 406, 410–413, 420
Enable Simple Buttons command, 322
End Angle field, 40
End Angle slider, 41
Envelope modifier, 102
equality operator, 351
Erase Normal setting, 129
eraser, 129
errors
    runtime, 355
    scripting, 354, 355
Essentials workspace, 13
event handler
    creating multiple actions in, 356–357
    defined, 350
    using one for multiple events, 368–369
Event Handler snippets, 360
events
    choosing, 362–364
    defined, 350
    examples of, 350
    handling, 350, 362–363
    receiving multiple, 363–364
    registering, 350
    using one event handler for multiple, 368–369
event sounds, 392–395
Export Image option, 443
exporting, 442–445
    frames, 444–445
    symbols, 443
    vs. publishing, 442
Exporting SWF Movie dialog, 291
Export Movie option, 443
Export Selection option, 443
Extension Manager, Adobe, 447
Eye icon, 139

F

F4V format, 405, 406
fade effects, 32
Family menu, 68

fields. See also text fields
    linked, 63–67
    point-text, 58, 59, 61, 80
    threaded, 63, 67
file backups, 3
file formats
    for exporting content, 419, 442
    Flash, xii, 4
    for images/graphics, 442
    for publishing content, 419, 424, 427
    for sound, 386
    for video, 405, 406
files. See also Flash documents
    backing up, 3
    creating, 4–5
    opening, 6
Fill Color control, 27, 33–34, 36, 86
fill paths, 112
fills
    adding strokes to, 52–53
    choosing colors for, 27, 34, 103, 105
    converting strokes to, 124
    creating geometric, 39
    defined, 34
    intersecting, 128
    locking, 51
    modifying, 105, 106–107, 109
    shape-tweening, 217
Fire Animation Brush pattern, 56
FLA files
    exporting to SWF files, 185
    including XMP metadata in, 435
    placing components in, 426
    pronunciation of, xii
    publishing to SWF files, 419
Flash
    authoring environment, xii, xiii, 1
    cross-platform issues, xiii
    documents (See Flash documents)
    extension, xi (See also CreateJS extension)
    file formats, xii, 4
    movie metaphor, xiii
    versions, xi

motion tweening, 223–264. *See also* motion tweens
  applying to multiple items, 225
  best practices, 224, 225
  creating bouncing ball with, 224–229
  and Distribute to Layers feature, 145
  orienting tween targets to curves in, 237
  swapping tween elements in, 238–241
  viewing information about, 242
  when to use, 194
  working with motion paths in, 230–236
Motion Tween Property inspector, 230, 231, 237, 241, 251, 252
motion tweens. *See also* motion tweening
  adding more motion to, 247–249
  autorotation in, 252
  controlling speed of, 262
  copying and pasting, 263
  drawing new paths for, 240
  duplicating keyframes in, 263
  multi-layer, 274–277
  recreating, 296–297
  reusing, 263
  reversing, 282–283, 284
  saving as presets, 229
  setting up, 224–225
  specifying length of, 224
  viewing property curves for, 242
  vs. other types, 223
motion-tween spans, 240, 243, 253, 263, 390. *See also* tween spans
mouse events, 347, 362
mouse-head graphic, 127
Move Guide dialog, 21
MOV files, 442
movie-clip buttons, 326–330
MovieClip class, 334
movie-clip symbols
  converting animations to, 285, 286

  display options for, 298
  placing instances of, 290
  scripting to act as buttons, 370–374
  Timeline for, 154
  using buttons to control playback of, 375–379
  viewing, 291
  vs. FLVPlayback components, 418
  vs. graphic symbols, 287
movies. *See also* animation; video
  accessing subfiles for, xii
  adding blank keyframe to, 167
  adding button components to, 365–367
  archiving assets for, 427
  compressing, 434
  controlling playback of, 335
  embedding TLF SWZ code in, 429
  examining for optimal playback, 420–423
  exporting, 442
  pausing, 338
  placing buttons in, 317
  placing symbol instances in, 156
  publishing, 353, 424–431
  scrubbing through, 183
moving
  anchor points, 115
  corner points, 113
  curve points, 114
  graphics, 98
  guides, 21
  layer folders, 141
  layers, 141, 146
MP3 compression, 433–434
MP3 format, 386
MPEG-4, 406
MSAA technology, 423
Multiline No Wrap option, 80
Multiline option, 80
multimedia projects, 385
multiple-choice questions, 335

N

naming/renaming
  bones in IK armatures, 305
  components, 324
  frames, 330
  instances, 349
  layer folders, 139
  layers, 139
nested Timelines, 375–376
New Document dialog, 4, 10
New Folder button, 151
New from Template dialog, 10
New Layer button, 137
New Symbol button, 152
New Workspace dialog, 12
Next button, 326
No Color button, 17, 37, 38
numeric values, 17

O

Object Drawing button, 42
Object Drawing mode
  and gradient fills, 51
  turning on, 42
  vs. other modes, 25, 42
objects
  combining, 133–134
  controlling stacking order of, 132
  grouping/ungrouping, 129–130
  preventing interaction between, 130
Object Spacing section, Edit Snapping, 24
onion skinning
  in classic tweening, 198
  in frame-by-frame animation, 189–190, 192
  in motion tweening, 277
  in shape tweening, 214, 216, 222
On Launch menu, 2
opening and closing delimiters, 336
open paths, 41, 47
OpenType fonts, 62, 84
operators, 351
Orient to Path checkbox, 204, 237

scripts. *See also* ActionScript; scripting

   for adding frame actions, 335–338

   basic syntax for, 339

   for button component interactivity, 366–367

   checking syntax in, 353–354

   common errors in, 354

   for controlling buttons, 340–348, 356–359

   enabling word wrap in, 336

   for handling events, 350

   how this book presents, 345

   for linking to web pages, 382–384

   for making comparisons, 351

   for making movie clips act as buttons, 370–374

   multi-event, 363–364

   numbering lines in, 336

   reusing, 348, 360–361

   for rolling over/out of buttons, 362–364

   saving, 341

   testing, 355

   for using buttons to control Timelines, 375–379

   using comments in, 336

   using **if** statements in, 351

SD2 files, 386

security settings, 436, 438–439

segmented lines, 128

Selectable text, 57, 58, 59, 61

selection methods, 88, 172, 174

selection pointer, 89, 109

selections

   adding elements to, 90

   deselecting, 93

   irregular, 92

   making, 89–93

   setting preferences for, 88

selection tools, 109–111

Select Publish Destination button, 429

semicolon (;), 339

Send Backward command, 132

Send to Back command, 132

shape hints, 219, 220–222

shape recognition, 43, 44

shapes. *See also* graphics

   adding perspective to, 102

   adding segments to, 45

   creating free-form, 43–50

   creating geometric, 37–42

   creating IK, 306–307

   modifying, 109–119

   shape-tweening multiple, 217–218

   transforming one to another, 215–216

shape tweening, 211–222

   applying, 213–214

   complex shapes, 219–222

   creating bouncing ball with, 212–214

   how it works, 211

   multi-layer, 278–279

   multiple shapes, 217–218

   preparing content for, 212

   transforming oval to rectangle with, 215–216

   when to use, 213

shape types, converting, 124–126

Shift Select checkbox, 88

Show Pen Preview checkbox, 43

Show Shape Hints command, 222

Show Solid Points checkbox, 43

Show Tooltips command, 255

sibling bones, 305

SimController, 430

SimpleButton class, 334

Simulator panel, 430–431

Single Line option, 80

Size Report, 435

Skew controls, 100–101, 253

skins, 325, 408, 415, 416, 417

slash asterisk (/*), 336

slashes (//), 330, 336, 337

Small Screen workspace, 13

Smooth Curves menu, 43

smoothing

   brush, 50

   curves, 43, 44

   frame-by-frame animation, 182

Smooth mode, 43, 44

smooth points, 255

snake animation, 289

Snap Accuracy setting, 23

snapping features

   Snap Align, 23, 24

   Snap to Grid, 19, 22

   Snap to Guides, 22

   Snap to Objects, 22

   Snap to Pixels, 23

SND format, 386

snippets. *See* code snippets

solid color, filling outline shape with, 54

Solid Color option, 27

Solid mode, 140

Soundbooth, Adobe, 386

sound formats, 386

sounds, 385–404

   adding to buttons, 390–391

   adding to frames, 388–389

   compression options, 433–434, 437

   editing, 401–404

   event, 392–395

   importing, 386–387

   independent *vs.* synchronized, 394

   organizing, 390

   removing dead air from, 404

   start, 396

   stopping, 399–400

   stream, 394, 397–398

   synchronizing, 392, 393

Sounds common library, 386, 389

Sound Settings dialog, 433

Space After control, 78

Space Before control, 78

span-based selection, 172, 174, 177

spans

   activating roving keyframes in, 262

   applying easing to, 292–293

   color-coding of, 166

   resizing, 177

   types of, 164

special characters, 75

Speech compression option, 434